Gary G. Forrest, EdD, PhD

Chemical Dependency and Antisocial Personality Disorder: Psychotherapy and Assessment Strategies

Pre-publication REVIEWS, COMMENTARIES, EVALUATIONS . . .

The Haworth Press, Inc.

Chemical Dependency and Antisocial Personality Disorder

Psychotherapy and Assessment Strategies

HAWORTH Addictions Treatment
F. Bruce Carruth, PhD
Senior Editor

New, Recent, and Forthcoming Titles:

Group Psychotherapy with Addicted Populations
by Philip J. Flores

Shame, Guilt and Alcoholism by Ronald T. Potter-Efron

Neuro-Linguistic Programming in Alcoholism Treatment
edited by Chelly M. Sterman

Cocaine Solutions: Help for Cocaine Abusers and Their Families
by Jennifer Rice-Licare and Katherine Delaney-McLoughlin

*Substance Abuse Strategies and Preschool Children: Prevention
and Intervention* by Pedro J. Lecca and Thomas D. Watts

*Addiction in Human Development: Developmental Perspectives
on Addiction and Recovery* by Jacqueline Wallen

*Chemical Dependency and Antisocial Personality Disorder:
Psychotherapy and Assessment Strategies* by Gary G. Forrest

Chemical Dependency and Antisocial Personality Disorder
Psychotherapy and Assessment Strategies

Gary G. Forrest, EdD, PhD

The Haworth Press
New York • London • Norwood (Australia)

The Haworth Press, Inc., 10 Alice Street, Binghamton, NY 13904-1580

Library of Congress Cataloging-in-Publication Data

Forrest, Gary G.
    Chemical dependency and antisocial personality disorder : psychotherapy and assessment strategies / Gary G. Forrest.
      p.   cm.
    Includes bibliographical references and index.
    ISBN 1-56024-308-2 (alk. paper).
    1. Substance abuse. 2. Antisocial personality disorders. I. Title.
RC564.F67   1992
616.86'0651–dc20   92-924
                                                                      CIP

ABOUT THE AUTHOR

Gary G. Forrest, EdD, PhD, is a licensed clinical psychologist in independent practice and Executive Director of Psychotherapy Associates, PC, and the Institute for Addictive Behavioral Change in Colorado Springs, Colorado. A nationally recognized speaker and educator, he has been involved in the treatment of alcoholics, substance abusers, and their families for over twenty-two years. Dr. Forrest is the author of many books and scholarly articles on alcoholism treatment, including *How To Live with a Problem Drinker and Survive*; *Alcoholism, Narcissism and Psychopathology*; *Intensive Psychotherapy of Alcoholism*; *Alcoholism and Substance Abuse: Strategies for Clinical Intervention*; and *Substance Abuse, Homicide, and Violent Behavior.* He is a member of the American Psychological Association, the National Register for Health Service Providers in Psychology, the American Counseling Association, and a diplomate in the Division of Psychotherapy of the International Academy of Behavioral Medicine, Counseling, and Psychotherapy.

CONTENTS

Foreword

Given the vast array of information available today in our society about psychiatric illness, it is quite remarkable that we have so little valid information about a population of people that consume such a disproportionate amount of human services resources. Antisocial personality disordered people represent no more than 2% of our total population but fill our criminal justice system and represent a significant minority of people in chemical dependency programs. The impacts of those affected by their disorder proportionately increase the toll of their behavior on society.

In the absence of valid information on the origins and treatment of the disorder, we tend to react more than plan, wasting resources on confronting symptoms rather than addressing the underlying problem. We also tend to judge the individuals harshly and moralize about their behavior, in effect, blaming the individual rather than the disorder. The result is that we end up frustrated and angry at the individual and do not get the outcomes we, and perhaps the individual we treat, would like to obtain.

We simply do not understand the dynamics of the Antisocial Personality Disorder. This text is a significant contribution to correcting that dilemma. Dr. Forrest not only explores the limited available research on the topic, but builds an understandable conceptual framework for the nature of the disorder. He then uses that framework to propose an effective paradigm for treatment. This work is long overdue and represents a significant contribution to the limited literature on the topic.

There are interesting similarities between how we regard and treat APD (and, indeed, all personality disordered people) today and how we regarded and treated alcoholic and other chemically dependent people in the 1960s. Thirty years ago there were "acceptable" chemically dependent clients, particularly white, middle-aged, middle class men who were motivated for treatment by environmental pressures, and there were "less acceptable" chemically dependent clients, for instance, heroin addicts, Native American alcoholics, and the elderly drug dependent. Basically, our degree of client acceptability was directly correlated with our knowledge about the disorder and our success in treatment.

Today, we have a hierarchy of "acceptable" personality disordered clients. And our acceptability of these people, as clients, is directly correlated with how much we know about the disorder and how successful they are with treatment. An examination of the available literature will show that we know the most about treating the abandonment-related disorders (obsessive, histrionic, dependent, passive-aggressive, avoidant and borderline), followed by the narcissistic conditions. We actually have much less information about treating the paranoid disorders (paranoid, schizoid and schizotypal), and we know least about treating antisocial personality disorder.

Our knowledge of treatment needs and successful treatment interventions seems directly related to how often a given group of clients presents in treatment. So we learn more, write more, and are more accepting of clients who present for care in our offices and institutions. People with antisocial and paranoid disorder may appear for treatment, for instance in chemical dependency treatment settings, but they don't tend to last in treatment very long. Our response is to react to their behavior in a judgmental manner, not understand the dynamics of their disorder, be relatively unsuccessful with treatment and blame the client for the treatment failure.

Today, we know that chemically dependent people can be successfully treated. But only if we understand the psychodynamics of addiction, accompany treatment with compassion and acceptance, and employ treatment methods that work for that illness. The same is true for personality disordered people. This book goes a long way in laying the groundwork for successful treatment with a group of people who are very difficult to treat.

F. Bruce Carruth, PhD
Senior Editor
Haworth Addictions Treatment

SECTION ONE: EPIDEMIOLOGY, ETIOLOGY, AND DIFFERENTIAL DIAGNOSIS

Chapter I

Introduction

The psychotherapy and treatment of chemical dependency involves all health service providers. It was only ten to 15 years ago that professional behavioral scientists and health service providers of virtually all disciplines generally refused to treat substance abusers. A few years ago, physicians, psychologists, and other therapists avoided working with chemically dependent persons. It was generally believed that this patient population was not capable of benefiting from psychotherapy or the various other standard treatment and rehabilitation modalities that were used to treat psychiatric patients.

As the medical, psychological, social work, rehabilitation, and counseling professions have become progressively more involved in chemical dependency treatment during the past 15 years, an emergent clinical consensus has developed relative to the treatability of these patients (Bratter and Forrest, 1985). Indeed, it is now widely recognized by all health professionals that many of these individuals can benefit significantly from a diversity of psychological-psychiatrically oriented treatments. This realization has contributed greatly to the growth and evolution of treatment and professional counseling services for chemically dependent clients.

The discovery that chemically dependent persons could be successfully rehabilitated concurrently led to the discovery that there were many more addicts in this country than was ever previously recognized. Moreover, a heightened public and professional awareness of the ever increasing problems of chemical dependency and substance abuse in this country has also contributed significantly to a social climate, or zeitgeist, for this particular clinical population. Shortly after the Vietnam War era, most Americans began to realize that we were indeed living in an "addictive society."

Another factor that has contributed to the development of more and better treatment alternatives for this clinical population involves our American health care system per se. Empty hospital beds, the creation of hundreds of nationwide HMOs, health insurance benefit plans that pay for chemical dependency and substance abuse treatments, big-business takeovers in the health industry, and the utilization of sophisticated and successful marketing techniques by the health care industry have also reinforced the "need" for a much larger nationwide chemical dependency treatment delivery system. Physicians and nurses are even beginning to enter the chemical dependency treatment field with long-term career goals! Indeed, the American health care industry has recently discovered that there is a great deal of money to be made in the area of chemical dependency treatment.

The American collective is much more "health conscious" than it was 20 or 30 years ago. More and more people exercise on a regular basis. Thousands have stopped smoking or are attempting to stop and we have become obsessed with weight control and personal appearance. Perhaps we have become an extremely narcissistic society. At any rate, these realities also effect social beliefs, attitudes, and perceptions related to chemical dependency and substance abuse (Forrest, 1987). It is not surprising that an increasing number of Americans are choosing to drink less. We are also becoming more "drug conscious."

All of these factors have simply created an emotional climate which makes people feel and believe that it is acceptable to seek help for chemical dependency or any other type of health problem. Unlike 30 to 40 years ago, it is now socially acceptable in America for a person to enter therapy or a residential treatment program as a result of alcoholism or some other form of chemical dependency. Recovering alcoholics and drug addicts are often very open and publicly disclosing about their diseases, behaviors, life-experiences, treatment, and recoveries. In recent years, the American public has watched and listened to celebrities, members of presidential families, and people from every walk of life share their devastating experiences with alcohol and drugs. Undoubtedly, these social changes have helped countless numbers of chemically dependent individuals enter treatment programs, and numerous positive gains have occurred as a result.

Similar global positive changes in the realms of public and professional interest, treatment and the development of more effective treatment interventions, and the American health care and institutional systems have not occurred relative to the antisocial personality. The American correctional system has not developed "new" or in any general way radically different and more effective treatments for this patient population. Psychologists, physicians, nurses, and counselors are not beginning to specialize in the treatment of antisocial personalities. Indeed, most health professionals continue to avoid working with these patients. Hundreds of private hospitals and psychiatric clinics across the United States are not opening "antisocial treatment centers" or programs that are marketed for "psychopaths." We do not find Congressmen or attorneys discussing their antisocial pasts and recoveries from sociopathy on national TV shows!

It is very reasonable to expect heightened professional, public, institutional, and health care interest in the treatment of severe personality disorders over the course of the next decade. This interest may in fact parallel the global changes that have occurred in the chemical dependency treatment field over the course of the past two decades.

The recent evolution of the chemical dependency treatment field has resulted in many positive gains for patients as well as clinicians and treatment personnel. As professionally trained and skilled behavioral scientists have devoted more of their time and research efforts to the chemical dependency treatment field, treatment techniques and programs have been developed that are believed to be more effective. Perhaps the most significant contribution to the chemical dependency field (Pattison, 1987; Emrick, 1986, 1991) during the past decade has been the realization that chemical dependent persons need and require a diversity of treatments. Indeed, matching individual patients with relatively specific treatments is a factor that frequently determines treatment outcome effectiveness.

Historically, the vast majority of chemically dependent persons were referred to Alcoholics Anonymous, Narcotics Anonymous, and similar self-help oriented programs for treatment. Self-help was essentially the only form of care available for chemically dependent persons prior to the 1960s. In essence, all patients received the same treatment regardless of individual patient characteristics and needs. While the Alcoholics Anonymous model of treatment continues to be widely used and is an integral component of most chemical dependency treatment programs, it is currently recognized and accepted that chemically dependent persons need to be involved in programs that provide individualized care and treatment. Matching patients and therapists constitutes another important aspect of the process of providing effective individualized health care for chemically dependent persons.

Chemically dependent patients manifest a broad spectrum of emotional problems. These individuals frequently manifest concurrent depressive symptoms, affective illness, organic brain syndrome, personality disorder, and even thought disturbance (Zimberg, 1982; Wilsnack and Beckman, 1984; Bratter and Forrest, 1985; Pattison, 1987; Forrest, 1989, 1991). Many chemically dependent patients present for treatment with significant depression and anxiety symptoms (Forrest, [1980] 1986). However, all chemically dependent patients do not manifest a clinically significant depression or anxiety disorder. It is quite apparent that only a very small percentage of alcoholics who enter treatment manifest an underlying thought disturbance (Gitlow and Peyser, 1980; Bean and Zimberg, 1981; Forrest, 1983, 1984). In sum, every chemically dependent person is relatively unique with regard to symptom structure, psychopathology, and adjustment style.

Clinicians have recognized for several decades that a very significant percent of chemically dependent persons who become involved in psychotherapy relationships and treatment programs manifest serious characterological defects and personality disorders. Unfortunately, there has been a generalized trend among clinicians and behavioral scientists over the past four decades to equate chemical dependency with psychopathy or antisocial personality disorder. The chemically dependent patient has frequently been diagnosed as an antisocial personality in an ipso facto manner. Most, if not all, chemically dependent patients were felt to be (Sutker, 1971) antisocial or passive-aggressive personalities, and early diagnostic models

(DSM II and other APA precursors to the DSM III-R) even listed alcoholism as a subtype of personality disorder.

It is widely recognized by chemical dependency counselors and behavioral scientists (Gottheil et al., 1983; Bratter, 1985; Brown, 1985; Selman, 1986; Forrest and Gordon, 1990; Nace, 1990) that a high percentage of people who receive treatment for chemical dependency manifest impulse control problems and passive-aggressive or antisocial personality features. Yet in a classic, diagnostic-clinical sense (Cleckley, [1941] 1976; Reid et al., 1986; Doren, 1987), the vast majority of these individuals may not be antisocial. Chemically dependent persons are generally impulsive, act-out, manifest low frustration tolerance, and behave in a manipulative, irresponsible, immature, egocentric manner (Forrest, 1983, 1984, 1989, 1991). However, many chemically dependent patients evidence several other affective, cognitive, and behavioral characteristics which may preclude a diagnosis of antisocial personality disorder. It is important to note that the terms sociopath, psychopath, and antisocial personality disorder tend to be used interchangeably by most clinicians.

The task of examining the clinical relationships between chemical dependency, substance use disorders, and antisocial personality is fundamentally a matter of differential diagnosis. The progress that has occurred within the chemical dependency treatment field during the past decade includes a growing awareness of the roles and importance of differential diagnosis in treatment. Moreover, there is an emergent interest in the differential diagnosis of the substance abuse disorders and antisocial personality disorder among chemically dependency treatment personnel. Psychiatrists, chemical dependency counselors, psychologists, social workers, and administrators who work in the chemical dependency treatment field are beginning to realize that (1) chemically dependent and substance abusing patients may or may not manifest concurrent antisocial personality disorder, (2) these patients manifest quantatively and qualitatively different gradients of antisocial and addictive behavior, (3) an accurate differential diagnosis is essential to the establishment of appropriate treatment interventions, goals, and planning with these clinical populations, (4) chemically dependent patients with concurrent antisocial personality disorders are generally more difficult to treat than other chemically dependent subtypes, (5) antisocial addicts are often disruptive within the context of residential as well as outpatient treatment programs, (6) these patients can in fact be dangerous and destructive, (7) relatively predictable and intense transference and countertransference problems develop in the treatment of chemically dependent patients who manifest concurrent antisocial personality disorder, and (8) chemically dependent patients who manifest concurrent antisocial personality disorder are recalcitrant and more resistant to treatment than other chemically dependent subtypes and therefore they tend to manifest a poor treatment outcome prognosis.

The remainder of Section One involves an examination of the first three of these clinical subject areas. Chapter II presents a brief discussion of the different historic clinical perspectives on addicts and psychopaths. The following chapters elucidate the epidemiology of substance use disorders and antisocial personality disorder, differential diagnosis of these syndromes, etiological models, and crucially important psychotherapy and treatment issues. Chapter V includes the DSM III-R (APA, 1987) diagnostic criteria as well as clinical interviewing and assessment guidelines for the differential diagnosis of substance use disorders and antisocial personality disorder. Case studies and therapy vignettes are utilized throughout Section One in order to provide the reader with actual clinical examples of the ideas and concepts that are presented. The content of Section Two is based upon the author's over 20 years of direct clinical experience in psychotherapy with several thousand chemically dependent and antisocial patients.

This book will provide valuable data, insight, and clinical information for all counselors and therapists who work with people who are chemically dependent. More specifically, Section One provides all clinicians in the chemical dependency treatment field with the essential information and clinical skills that are necessary for (1) assessing and evaluating the chemically dependent patient, (2) differentially diagnosing substance use disorders and antisocial personality disorder, and most importantly, (3) effectively treating *all* chemically dependent patients as well as chemically dependent patients who manifest concurrent antisocial personality disorder.

In an era of increased professional malpractice liability that is consistently associated with misdiagnosis, improper treatment and care, and a diversity of issues associated with the therapist-patient relationship, this text will be an invaluable resource for every psychotherapist who is involved in the treatment of chemically dependent patients and antisocial patients who manifest a concurrent addictive disease or substance use disorder.

Finally, this volume represents another step in the evolution of the chemical dependency treatment field. The identification of clinical subtypes among chemically dependent and antisocial patient populations and the development of relatively specific treatment strategies for these different clinical populations represents a significant contribution to the mental health and chemical dependency fields. Hopefully, many of the ideas and concepts that are discussed in this book will eventually be heuristic.

Chapter II

Historical Perspective: Chemical Dependency and Antisocial Personality Disorder

INTRODUCTION

Chemically dependent and antisocial persons (Cadoret, 1986) share several common clinical characteristics. These commonalities are discussed indepth throughout this text. Historically, chemically dependent and antisocial persons have been recognized in virtually every known society. The antisocial personality or psychopath has played a very destructive role (Doren, 1987) in the course of human development and evolution. These persons continue to exert a significantly destructive impact upon the lives of other human beings and the social systems and cultures in which they live. Alcoholics and chemically dependent persons have also been identified as individuals who consistently exert a diversity of destructive influences upon other human beings and social systems. Additionally, chemically dependent and antisocial persons tend to be very self-destructive.

This chapter discusses the history of chemical dependency and the antisocial personality in modern society, and provides basic definitions of chemical dependency or addiction, substance use disorder, and antisocial personality.

CHEMICAL DEPENDENCY

Alcoholics are depicted in the Bible as "drunkards." Alcohol abuse and alcohol dependence created rather widespread problems during the eras of Roman and Greek civilizations. Indeed, the misuse of ethanol is consistently reported throughout the written histories of virtually all societies and cultures. It is reasonable to hypothesize that at least 10 percent of the population constituting any culture or society is alcohol dependent. Such has been the case for hundreds if not thousands of years.

In most societies and cultures, the alcoholic has historically been perceived as a social outcast or deviant. Alcoholics were the first "chemical dependents" or "substance abusers" in the sense of being individuals who were perceived as deviating significantly from socially acceptable patterns of drug consumption. Throughout history these individuals have also been labeled and socially stigmatized as a result of their deviant or socially inappropriate alcohol use. However, the consistent misuse of alcohol upon the part of an individual may result in any number of negative social consequences. For example, such individuals may be socially avoided, physically assaulted, incarcerated, or even killed. Different cultures prescribe different consequences for their members who misuse ethanol.

Alcohol addiction and abuse have been widespread in Europe, Asia, China, the Americas, Africa, and every other part of the world. Other varieties of "chemical dependency" and "substance abuse" are generally very new. While marijuana addiction and opium or heroin addictions have been recognized for centuries, the development and abuse of psychedelic drugs, synthetic stimulants and depressants, psychotropics, "crack cocaine," and the so-called "designer drugs" are very recent social and health phenomena. It is also important to recognize that even the *widespread* use and abuse of such addictive drugs as marijuana and cocaine is also new. Furthermore, it is only in recent years that the general public has realized that marijuana and cocaine are highly addictive "drugs." In fact, medical researchers and behavioral scientists are only recently beginning to understand the addictive properties and chemical makeup of these substances (Bratter and Forrest, 1985; O'Connell, 1990). It is currently known that drugs such as marijuana, cocaine, tranquilizers, narcotics, and ethanol are highly addictive.

The ever increasing number of people who use, abuse, and become addicted to various drugs create myriad social, familial, legal, health, and personal problems. These people are referred to as "chemically dependent" or "substance abusers." They create and experience a diversity of problems within every country and culture in the modern world. Behavioral scientists throughout the world are beginning to understand the insidious and destructive causal relationships between drug abuse and chemical dependency and criminal behavior, child abuse, suicide, sexual dysfunction and deviation, physical and emotional illness or health, work, aging, and literally every other facet of life. Individuals in modern societies who become chemically dependent continue to be perceived as deviants. In spite of the fact that there are several million chemically dependent and substance abusing people in the United States alone, these individuals constitute a minority or subgroup within our society. As a minority group, chemically dependent persons and substance abusers have tended to be poorly understood, feared, abhorred, and avoided by the general public as well as health care providers.

Substance abuse and chemical dependency have created major health and social problems in the United States and throughout the world during the past three decades. At present, the United States is experiencing a drug epidemic or crisis as well as attempting to initiate a "war" against drug abuse and chemical dependency. Behavioral scientists are becoming more actively involved in the identification, assessment, and treatment of people who develop chemical dependency and abuse drugs. Indeed, there has been a recent proliferation of research and scientific literature in the Western world that is focused on these very issues. The American government and industrial complex has been spending millions and millions of dollars each year investigating all aspects of chemical dependency and substance abuse.

It is only during the past few decades that researchers and behavioral scientists have exerted a concerted effort to better understand addicts and provide effective treatments for these individuals. The brain chemistry of alcoholics (Wallace, 1985, 1991), psychodynamics of chemical dependency (Forrest, 1983b), cognitive-behavioral dimensions of chemical dependency and substance abuse (Yost and Mines, 1985), social-environmental aspects (Leigh, 1985), and affective dimensions of addictions (Wilsnack and Beckman, 1984) are focal areas of investigation within the chemical dependency field. It is apparent that all addictive diseases or disorders (Orford, 1985) are exceedingly complex and multifaceted processes. Chemical dependency is also a disorder that affects each person individually as well as totally. The chemically dependent person develops physical, psychological, social, and spiritual problems or symptoms. Indeed, chemical dependency is a disorder that can result in the destruction of the whole person.

In recent years, the assessment and treatment of a wide variety of substance use disorders has become "big business." The health care industry has realized that millions of people are in fact chemically dependent or substance abusers. Furthermore, treatment for these disorders generates millions and millions of dollars each year. Hospital-based chemical dependency treatment programs and outpatient programs have suddenly been developed throughout the United States. A plethora of health care issues have actively reinforced the need for professional treatments for chemically dependent persons. The care of these persons is now an accepted and legitimate undertaking for physicians, psychologists, nurses, counselors, and other health service providers.

The recent widespread media exposure that several prominent recovering chemically dependent persons have received seems to have lessened the social stigma associated with addictive illness. Indeed, many of the negative social perceptions surrounding chemical dependency have been modified by the personal disclosures of former First Lady Betty Ford and countless numbers of recovering professional athletes and other celebrities. Chemically dependent persons and substance abusers are entering treatment programs in ever increasing numbers. Most people are beginning to accept the reality that virtually anyone can develop a chemical dependency problem.

DEFINING CHEMICAL DEPENDENCY AND SUBSTANCE USE DISORDERS

In this section, the basic clinical and DSM III and DSM III-R (Diagnostic and Statistical Manual of Mental Disorders: American Psychiatric Association, 1980 and 1987, respectively) definitions of chemical dependency and substance use disorders are delineated.

An extensive clinical examination of the various signs and symptoms of these diagnostic categories is presented in Chapter V. The basic definitions of chemical dependency and substance use disorder(s) that are presented in this chapter are used throughout the remainder of the book.

Chemical dependency or addiction is a physical *and* psychological dependency upon a mood altering drug. Chemical dependency is evidenced by either physical tolerance to a drug or physical withdrawal from a drug. The DSM III refers to all forms of chemical dependency as "Substance Dependence." Tolerance is defined in the DSM III as meaning "that markedly increased amounts of the (addictive) substance is required to achieve the desired effect or there is a markedly diminished effect with regular use or the same dose" (p. 165). Withdrawal is defined in the DSM III as a "substance-specific syndrome that follows cessation of or reduction in intake of a substance that was previously regularly used by the individual to induce a physiological state of intoxication" (p. 165). Substance Dependence diagnostic categories are included in the DSM III and DSM III-R Substance Use Disorders classification rubric.

Chemical dependency and addiction are clinical terms that are used interchangeably throughout this book. Chemical dependency is almost always a more severe and pathological form of substance use disorder. Chemically dependent persons also experience myriad social, legal, familial, health, psychological, and vocation/job problems as a direct result of their chemical dependency. For example, alcoholic persons consistently experience significant marital discord, employment or job-related difficulties, and depression or affective symptoms (Forrest, [1980] 1986; Forrest 1989). Chemically dependent persons very often become socially dysfunctional as a result of their substance dependency and many of these individuals also develop very severe medical complications. Chemical dependency is a progressive and fatal illness when untreated.

The substance use disorder classification generally refers to (DSM III) "behavioral changes associated with more or less regular use of substances that affect the central nervous system. These behavioral changes in almost all subcultures would be viewed as extremely undesirable. Examples of such behavioral changes include impairment in social or occupational functioning as a consequence of substance use, inability to control use of or to stop taking the substance, and the development of serious withdrawal symptoms after cessation of or reduction in substance use. These conditions are conceptualized as mental disorders and therefore distinguished from nonpathological use for recreational or medical purposes" (p. 163).

Substance dependence is one major subcategory of the substance use disorders diagnostic class (DSM III; DSM III-R). Substance abuse is the second major subcategory of this classification. Substance abuse involves (1) a pattern of pathological use, (2) impairment in social or job functioning due to substance use, and (3) a minimum of one month of disturbed functioning as a result of substance use (DSM III).

The substance use disorders classification includes substance dependence and substance abuse categories for five classes of substances: alcohol, barbiturates, or similarly acting sedatives or hypnotics, opioids, amphetamines or similarly acting sympathomimetics, and cannabis. These classes of substances "are associated only with abuse because physiological dependence has not been demonstrated: cocaine, phencyclidine (PCP) or similarly acting arylcyclohexylamines, and hallucinogens" (p. 166). Tobacco is associated only with dependence. The substance use disorders (DSM III-R) are classified within the 303.9x through 305.9x categories.

In summary, the use of various addictive substances may result in eventual patterns of substance abuse or substance dependence. The different varieties and diagnostic characteristics of substance abuse and substance dependence are included in the DSM III-R substance use disorders classification category.

THE ANTISOCIAL PERSONALITY

The antisocial personality has also been recognized in virtually all societies and cultures for hundreds of years. However, the modern diagnostic classification of antisocial personality disorder (psychopathy) was established by the French psychiatrist Pinel during the early nineteenth century. Pinel diagnosed a man who "enraged at a woman who had used offensive language to him, he precipitated her into a well" as suffering with "manic sans delire." Pinel's description and clinical diagnosis of this patient's atypical and aggressive behavior eventually led to the concept of psychopathy. Another psychiatrist (Pritchard, 1835) expanded upon Pinel's work and coined the concept of "moral insanity" to describe patients in whom "the moral and active principles of the mind are strongly perverted or depraved; the power of self-government is lost or greatly impaired and the individual is found to be incapable, not of taking or reasoning upon any subject proposed to him, but of conducting himself with decency and propriety in the business of life" (p. 24).

The concept of moral insanity was widely utilized in medicine until the late 1800s. An Italian physician named Lombroso described the "born criminal" as a psychopath. According to Lombroso, the "born criminal" is a moral imbecile, guiltless, highly aggressive, boastful, impulsive, and sensitive to physical pain. It is interesting to note that President Garfield's assassin, Guiteau, was diagnosed as "morally insane" and it was determined that he should be executed because he "knew the difference between right and wrong." The issue of moral responsibility continues to perplex mental health workers as well as the legal system.

Due in large measure to legal and religious pressures, the term "moral insanity" was replaced by Koch in 1888. Koch (McCord and McCord, 1964) developed the label "psychopathic inferiority" which eventually led to the use of the terms "constitutional psychopathy" and "constitutional psychopathic inferiority." Koch implied that this disorder was caused by a constitutional predisposition.

By the end of World War I, psychiatrists generally agreed that psychopathy was a relatively well-defined disorder manifested in "strong vicious or criminal propensities on which punishment has had little or no deterrent effect" (McCord and McCord, 1964). Glueck (1918) was the first American psychiatrist to empirically investigate the psychopath. He reported that psychopaths had the highest rates of recidivism among criminals, the highest proportion of drunkenness and drug addiction, and the earliest onset of antisocial behavior. Glueck's pioneering research led to many subsequent studies of psychopathy in America and Europe during the late

1930s and 1940s. These investigations explored the symptoms, causes, and classification of psychopathy.

Kahn (1931) described psychopaths as "those personalities which are characterized by quantitative peculiarities in the impulse, temperament, or character strata" (p. 128). Karpman (1941) distinguished two types of psychopathy: "idiopathic" and "symptomatic." He felt that "symptomatic" cases were actually neurotics while "idiopathic" or "true" psychopathy never resulted from psychological causes. The symptomatic cases could be successfully treated. No treatment had been discovered for the cases of "true" psychopathy which were caused by an "unreasonable constitutional acquisitiveness and aggression."

Cleckley's classic book, *The Mask of Sanity* ([1941] 1976), included one of the most detailed clinical descriptions of psychopathy ever written. He delineated 16 descriptive characteristics of the psychopath. The following two decades produced a good deal of research and clinical data that focused upon the assessment and treatment of psychopathy (McCord and McCord, 1964).

Recently, behavioral scientists continue to be interested in the diagnosis and possible treatment of antisocial personality disorder or psychopathy (Yochelson and Samenow, 1977; Reid et al., 1986; Yochelson and Samenow, 1986; Doren, 1987; Nace, 1990). It is widely recognized that psychopaths continue to exert a multiplicity of destructive influences on every society and culture known to mankind. Although behavioral scientists have often inaccurately equated psychopathy with criminality, the fact remains that 25 to 50 percent of prison populations throughout the Western world are made up of psychopaths. It is important to note that all criminals are not psychopaths and all psychopaths are also not criminals! There continues to be limited optimism about the successful psychotherapeutic treatment (Cleckley, [1941] 1976; Forrest, 1983b; 1990; Yochelson and Samenow, 1986; Doren, 1987) of the antisocial personality.

There is a growing realization within the chemical dependency treatment field and correctional rehabilitation settings (Forrest, 1983b, 1984; Ross and Lightfoot, 1985; Reid et al., 1986; Doren, 1987; Yochelson and Samenow, 1986; Forrest and Gordon, 1990; Woolf-Reeve, 1990) that (1) chemically dependent patients generally manifest a number of antisocial personality, cognitive, behavioral, and life-style characteristics, and (2) criminals and antisocial personalities often abuse alcohol and other addictive substances. These issues are discussed at length in Chapter V. Suffice it to say in the present context that the antisocial chemical dependency "mix" exerts a more than doubly destructive combination of influences upon people and societies!

DEFINING PSYCHOPATHY AND ANTISOCIAL PERSONALITY DISORDER

In this section, the basic clinical and DSM III and DSM III-R (Diagnostic and Statistical Manual of Mental Disorders: APA, 1980 and 1987, respectively) definitions of antisocial personality disorder are delineated. As noted earlier in this chapter, an extensive clinical examination of the different signs and symptoms of these diagnostic categories is presented in Chapter V. The essential definitions of psychopathy or antisocial personality disorder that are delineated in this chapter are used interchangeably throughout the remainder of the book. These different clinical terms have been used to describe one general behavior syndrome or pattern of adjustment.

McCord and McCord (1964) state "the psychopath (antisocial personality) is an asocial, aggressive, highly impulsive person, who feels little or no guilt and is unable to form lasting bonds of affection with other human beings" (p. 3). These authors indicate that lovelessness and guiltlessness are the two essential features of psychopathy. Hare (1970) described the psychopath (antisocial personality) as "unable to show empathy or genuine concern for others. He manipulates and uses others to satisfy his own demands; yet, through a glib sophistication and superficial sincerity, he is often able to convince those he has used and harmed of his innocence or his motivation to change . . . Most clinical descriptions of the psychopath make some sort of reference to his egocentricity, lack of empathy, and inability to form warm, emotional relationships with others" (p. 5).

It is significant that McCord and McCord (1964) indicate that psychopathy, possibly more than other mental disorders, threatens the safety, serenity, and security of American life. They state "from the ranks of the psychopaths come political demagogues, the most violent of criminals, the riot leaders, sexual misfits, and drug addicts" (p. 2). Lindner (1948) believed that psychopathy represented the most expensive and most destructive of "all known forms of aberrant behavior."

The extensive and in-depth descriptive clinical characteristics of the psychopath which Cleckley ([1941] 1976) enumerated are discussed in Chapter V. Briefly, Cleckley indicated that psychopaths are unreliable, irresponsible, do not learn from experience, and do not manifest overt signs of neurosis or irrational thinking. He also stressed that these individuals fail to follow any life plan.

The Diagnostic and Statistical Manual of Mental Disorders (American Psychiatric Association: DSM III, 1980; DSM III-R, 1987) is the most recent professional resource that defines psychopathy. Psychopathy is referred to as "antisocial personality disorder" in the DSM III-R. The DSM III-R antisocial personality disorder classification is 301.70. According to the DSM III-R, the antisocial personality disorder is generally defined as "the essential feature is a Personality Disorder in which there are a history of continuous and chronic antisocial behaviors in which the rights of others are violated, persistence into adult life of a pattern of antisocial behavior that began before the age of 15, and failure to sustain good job performance over a period of several years . . . Lying, stealing, fighting, truancy, and resisting authority are typical childhood signs. In adolescence, unusually early or aggressive sexual behavior, excessive drinking, and use of illicit drugs are frequent. In adulthood, these kinds of behavior continue . . ." (pp. 317-318).

It is also important to note that the DSM III-R diagnosis of antisocial personality disorder emphasizes that these aberrant behaviors cannot be due to schizophrenia, severe mental retardation, or manic episodes. The antisocial personality manifests an impaired capacity to "sustain lasting, close, warm, and responsible relationships with family, friends, or sexual partners" (p. 318). Substance use disorders are frequently a complication of this classification.

In summary, the basic DSM III and DSM III-R clinical definition and description of antisocial personality disorder (classification category 301.70) is essentially congruous with the clinical definitions and descriptions of psychopathy provided by Cleckley ([1941] 1976), McCord and McCord (1964), Reid et al. (1986), Doren (1987), and Pattison (1987).

SUMMARY

Chemically dependent persons and the antisocial personality share common behavioral, characterological, personality, cognitive, and life-style characteristics. The alcoholic is the historical prototype of chemical dependency. Alcoholism and alcohol misuse have created myriad problems in every culture known to mankind for thousands of years.

During the past three decades, chemical dependency and substance abuse have created major health and social problems throughout the world. Ever increasing numbers of people are using, abusing, and becoming dependent upon an ever increasing number of readily available addictive, mind-altering drugs. Cocaine, marijuana, heroin, psychedelics, tranquilizers, and a variety of synthetic drugs are available to every segment of every society throughout the Western world.

In response to the rapidly growing numbers of people who are becoming physically and psychologically dependent upon these drugs, behavioral scientists in America and many other countries have initiated significant research and clinical investigations that examine every facet of substance abuse and chemical dependency. Indeed, the treatment of various substance use disorders has rapidly become a major "big-business" enterprise within the confines of modern medicine and the health care industry. Chemical dependency has become recognized and accepted as a bona fide disease that is *deserving* of bona fide medical and professional treatment in the United States.

Clinical as well as DSM III and DSM III-R descriptions and definitions of chemical dependency, substance use disorder, and psychopathy or antisocial personality disorder have been presented in this chapter. It is important to note that the terms psychopathy and antisocial personality disorder are used interchangeably throughout this book. An in-depth examination of the differential diagnosis of chemical dependency, substance use disorders, and antisocial personality disorder is elucidated in Chapter V.

Several researchers and clinicians have noted that chemically dependent patients and substance abusers tend to be rather antisocial (Cleckley, [1941] 1976; McCord and McCord, 1964; Sutker, 1971; Forrest, 1983b; Doren, 1987). McCord and McCord (1964) indicate "from the ranks of the psychopaths come political demagogues, the most violent criminals, the riot leaders, sexual misfits, and drug addicts." Indeed, there is a diversity of nefarious relationships between chemical dependency and antisocial personality disorder.

Chapter III

Epidemiology of Substance Use Disorders and Antisocial Personality Disorder

INTRODUCTION

As indicated in Chapter II, a significant segment of every society manifests alcoholism and other substance use disorders. Likewise, every society includes individuals with antisocial personality disorder. It is impossible to know the exact number or percentage of individuals in a specific society or population that manifest a particular substance use disorder or antisocial personality disorder. However, the data collection and analysis technologies that have been developed by the behavioral science professions during the past few decades make it possible to provide reasonably accurate epidemiological information pertaining to all facets of chemical dependency, antisocial personality disorder, and mental health.

This chapter examines the epidemiology of substance use disorders and antisocial personality disorder. Information and data pertaining to the prevalence, sex ratio, environmental and cultural aspects, and genetic-familial factors associated with the substance use disorders and antisocial personality disorder are presented. This data demonstrates the widespread and destructive consequences of chemical dependency and antisocial personality disorder upon individuals, families, communities, and cultures. The data that are presented in this chapter also reveal several interesting clinical relationships between the substance use disorders and antisocial personality disorder.

PREVALENCE OF SUBSTANCE USE DISORDERS

The DSM III (APA, 1980) reports that "most of the substance use disorders are common, especially those associated with alcohol and tobacco" (p. 168). Alcohol, marijuana, tobacco, and cocaine abuse or dependency disorders are quite prevalent in the United States and other Western countries. Substance use disorders such as narcotic or opioid abuse and solvent abuse are comparatively rare.

Alcohol is unquestionably the most widely used, abused, and dependency producing drug in the world (Forrest, 1987). Moreover, this fact has been a reality throughout the histories of every known culture or society. It is presently estimated that between 13 and 23 million adults in the United States are alcohol dependent (Mumey, 1986; Forrest, 1989). Furthermore, it is generally believed (Knauert, 1992) that one of every ten adults in the United States manifests some form of drinking disorder. Alcohol abusers and alcoholics are readily found within every age group and segment of society. Indeed, alcoholics and problem drinkers may be teens, middle aged, or elderly.

Over 3 million teenagers have received (Forrest, 1984; Burns, 1987) alcoholism treatment in the United States during recent years. Teen alcohol abuse is "epidemic" (Burns, 1987). Twenty-five percent of students in grades seven through 12 drink on a weekly basis. Young people typically begin to consume alcoholic beverages between the ages of 11 and 12 and approximately 6 percent of junior and senior high students report that they are daily drinkers (Forrest, 1984). Beer and wine consumption is higher among teens. Over 90 percent of high school seniors are drinkers and virtually all college students are drinkers.

Approximately 75 percent of adult Americans are drinkers. About 15 percent of these individuals are heavy drinkers. A heavy drinker (WHO, 1978) is defined as a person who consumes three or more alcoholic beverages per drinking occasion and drinks three or more times per week. The remaining 60 percent of adult drinkers in the United States manifest a diversity of drinking styles. It is reasonable to assume that most drinkers are "social drinkers." These individuals drink responsibly (Forrest, 1989). The DSM III reports that about 16 percent of the American public report "some problem associated with alcohol within the past three years, and about 4 percent report more than trivial problems" (p. 168). Simply stated, the prevalence of alcohol use as well as abuse or dependence is very high in the United States.

The prevalence of marijuana and cocaine substance use disorders is also high in the United States and throughout much of the world. Cocaine use is generally rising in the U.S. The use of such drugs as marijuana, LSD, and PCP is falling. In 1985, the number of cocaine users in the United States rose to 5.8 million. This number was up from 4.2 million in 1983. It is estimated that some 5,000 people try cocaine for the first time each day in the U.S. Ninety-five percent of all cocaine users "snort" the drug and a significant percentage of people have taken the drug intravenously. MacDonald (1986) reports that 44 percent of youth who have used cocaine have smoked freebase. Cocaine and "crack" dependence seems to be falling among some populations in the U.S. (Knauert, 1992).

Marijuana use has decreased in terms of numbers of users in the U.S. MacDonald (1986) indicates that 10 percent of the population used marijuana in 1985 as compared to 11 percent in 1982. However, about 6 million Americans use marijuana almost daily. Approximately one-half of high school seniors have "tried" marijuana and among young adults between the ages of 18 to 25, 39 percent of males and 24 percent of females have used marijuana 100 or more times (MacDonald, 1986). Recent research (Emrick, 1991) also suggests that marijuana use may be generally falling in the U.S.

The use of hallucinogens has generally decreased during the past decade. It is reasonable to estimate (Hofmann, 1983) that the prevalence of narcotic, stimulant, depressant, hallucinogenic, and prescription substance abuse has not changed radically in recent years. Cocaine use and dependence is an exception to this generalization. Less than 1 million Americans are heroin or opioid dependent. Orford (1985) reports that over 30 million prescriptions for minor tranquilizers were written by physicians in England during one recent year! The prevalence of glue and solvent "sniffing" has not increased significantly in recent years.

It is apparent that large numbers of people develop different substance use disorders. More people are using, abusing, and becoming dependent on these addictive substances and, in general, they are initiating patterns of substance abuse earlier in their lives. It is also true that significantly more people (Pattison, 1987) who enter chemical dependency treatment programs in the U.S. are "polydrug" abusers or addicts. These individuals develop substance use disorders that involve more than one addictive substance. For example, the chemically dependent patient may be an alcoholic who additionally smokes marijuana, takes tranquilizers or amphetamines, and also periodically uses cocaine. Such an individual can be psychologically and/or physically dependent upon several mood altering, addictive substances.

The prevalence of tobacco use and dependency is also high in the United States and throughout the world. The DSM III-R (APA, 1987) reports that the prevalence of clinically defined tobacco dependence in the U.S. is not known. However, it has been reported that nearly one-third of the adult population (Wallace, 1985) are smokers. While the percentage of adult smokers has declined significantly in recent years, more and more teens initiate smoking and tobacco use each day (Matuschka, 1989).

The DSM III-R reports data pertaining to the prevalence of several substance use disorders. According to the DSM III-R, approximately 13 percent of adults were alcohol abusers or alcohol dependent at some time in their lives. Approximately 2 percent of adults have abused amphetamines or a similarly acting sympathomimetic. It is also reported (DSM III-R) that "cannabis is the most widely used illicit psychoactive substance in the United States" (p. 177). Approximately 4 percent of adults have abused marijuana at some time in their lives. It is estimated that the prevalence of cocaine dependence is "far higher" than the rate of 0.2 percent reported in a 1981-83 study to gather data for the DSM III-R. No data pertaining to the prevalence of inhalant dependence or abuse is reported in the DSM III-R. Approximately 3 percent of adults have abused hallucinogens. The prevalence of opioid abuse or dependence is estimated to be 0.7 percent of the adult population. Finally, the prevalence of sedative, hypnotic, or anxiolytic abuse or dependence is approximately 1.1 percent of the adult population (DSM III-R).

SEX RATIO OF SUBSTANCE USE DISORDERS

It is presently estimated (Wilsnack and Beckman, 1984; Wilsnack, 1990) that the sex ratio between male and female alcoholics or symptomatic drinkers is 3:1. This ratio was reported to be 6:1

several years ago (Lindbeck, 1972). Wilsnack and Beckman (1984) state "epidemiological work going on in the late 1970's and early 1980's did not bear out claims that heavy drinking and alcohol abuse were increasing among women" (p. 18). These authors point out trend studies since the 1960s have demonstrated "little or no change" in women's drinking patterns over the last several decades. Rachal et al. (1975) indicated that 34 percent of boys and 23 percent of girls in a sample of junior and senior high school students in the U.S. were "problem drinkers."

Sutker and Archer (1984) indicate that it is estimated that 80 percent of narcotics addicts are male. Furthermore, 50 percent of narcotics addicts are predominantly black minorities and 62 percent are between the ages of 20 and 29. Slightly over 1 percent of high school seniors have used heroin and over 10 percent of these individuals have experimented with the opioid drugs.

Women are reported (Sadava, 1984) to be much heavier users of prescription and over-the-counter psychoactive drugs than men. Male-female drug use/abuse rate differences are concentrated in the stimulant, sedative-hypnotic, and minor tranquilizer drugs. Sadava (1984) states "women have been generally reported to be less prone to the abuse of alcohol, opiates, hallucinogens, and nonprescribed amphetamines, although evidence suggests that this picture is changing in the United States" (p. 643). It is also interesting to note that women tend to obtain drugs by prescription, while men tend to obtain drugs from illicit sources.

Marijuana and cocaine abuse are more prevalent among males as is polydrug use (Burns, 1987). The sex ratio for these substances is estimated to be between 1:3 and 1:4. Nearly one-half of male and female high school students have experimented with marijuana. Marijuana is invariably the first illicit drug to be tried by adolescents, and the use of cannabis often marks the "gateway" from alcohol use to polydrug abuse and chemical dependency. This is true for both adolescent males and females.

The DSM III-R indicates that substance use disorders "are diagnosed more commonly in men than in women" (p. 168). It is also noted in the DSM III-R that the use of barbiturates or similarly acting sedatives and hypnotics is more commonly found among females. Women tend to obtain these substances by prescription from a physician. The prevalence of tobacco use is greater among teenage and adult males than teenage and adult females (DSM III-R).

In general, men are significantly more prone than women to develop patterns of alcohol, opiate, and hallucinogen abuse. Women are more susceptible to prescription drug abuse and sedative-hypnotic dependency. Women are far more frequent abusers of the minor tranquilizers. A precise sex ratio for cocaine and marijuana abuse among adolescents and adults has not been established. However, it has been estimated that the sex ratio for these substances is between 1:3 and 1:4. The prevalence of cocaine and polydrug abuse has risen significantly during the past five years among both sexes and among most, if not all, age groups.

ENVIRONMENTAL AND CULTURAL ASPECTS OF SUBSTANCE USE DISORDERS

Environmental and cultural factors influence both individual and collective or societal patterns of substance use, abuse, and dependency. All substance use disorders involved (1) one or more addictive drugs (substances), (2) a person (the user), and (3) an environment which fosters, enables, or in various ways reinforces substance use. Availability of a drug is a fundamental prerequisite to the development of any substance use disorder in any environment or culture.

The environmental influence upon opiate abuse and dependence among Vietnam servicemen (Robins, Helzer, and Davis, 1975) is lucid and striking. Opiate addicted Vietnam veterans very frequently terminated their substance dependency after returning to the United States. Only 7 percent of addicted Vietnam vets relapsed during their initial 8-10 months after returning to the U.S., while some 70 percent of opiate addicts can be expected to relapse within the first six months of release from residential drug treatment programs to aftercare treatment programs. Sutker and Archer (1984) state "the type of addiction phenomenon peculiar to the Vietnam situation may have been generated by need or prompted by powerful environment forces among individuals in whom certain person needs or states were greatly frustrated. If this is true, the result of these follow-up studies lend strong support to a person-context model for explaining drug use and remission. It may be that for the highly illegal opiate drugs, both person and context factors must interact in such a manner that the effects of drug acquisition and self-administration are perceived as and remain largely pleasurable. However, if significant changes are made in person or environment systems, drug-taking behaviors may be expected to undergo dramatic changes" (p. 613).

It is apparent that several environmental factors are associated with the etiology of substance use disorders. The family environment plays a very significant role in the development of alcoholism and perhaps all other substance use disorders (Forrest, 1978). Geographical location, population density, socioeconomic class, climate, and familial structure are environmental variables that may affect patterns of drug use, drug availability, and frequency of abuse and/or dependency.

There are several environmental-sociologic theories of substance abuse and chemical dependency. In essence, these etiological models attempt to explain how various environmental factors cause or contribute to the development of individual and collective patterns of chemical dependency and/or substance abuse. For example, it has been theorized (Yochelson and Samenow, 1986) that (1) society creates addicts, (2) peer behavior is the "crucial determining factor" in adolescent drug use, (3) poverty causes drug use, (4) family living difficulties are causal factors in drug use, (5) deprivation causes drug use, (6) alienation, boredom, and lack of purpose among the affluent cause drug use, (7) the pressures of modern life cause drug use, (8) social anxiety, technology, and urbanization cause drug use, (9) the mass media and advertising contribute to drug use, (10) economic and national problems create a climate that reinforces drug use, and (11) "deep-seated" pathology in American society causes drug use.

The environmental and sociological theories of substance abuse do not adequately explain how or why individuals use and abuse addictive substances. A person's adjustment to a particular environment can be more important than the environmental press. Moreover, most people who grow up in a certain neighborhood or come from a broken home do not become substance abusers. Drug use cannot be explained by poverty alone. Choice is an important variable in substance use. It has even been argued (Friedman et al., 1980) that the drug use of adolescents causes family problems and that there is no familial basis per se for addiction. Over half of military drug users (Tennant et al., 1972) actually began using drugs prior to entering military service. A major weakness of all environmental as well as psychological theories of chemical dependency is that they do not adequately predict who will become a drug user or addict.

The DSM III-R does not elucidate environmental-sociological or specific cultural factors that cause or facilitate the development of substance use disorders. However, the DSM III-R does point out that one's adjustment to the work and family environments can be associated with various patterns of substance abuse.

Cultural variables influence patterns of substance use. When compared to American Caucasians, Black, Hispanic, and Native American ethnic groups (Zimberg, 1982; Wayne, 1984; Teboe, 1991; Jackson, 1991; Chavez, 1991) have very high rates of alcoholism and substance abuse. Irish Americans are also (Forrest, 1978) prone to heavy drinking. Catholics who live in the southeastern part of the United States tend to be heavier drinkers than Mormons who reside in Utah. Jews have a relatively low incidence of alcoholism. Thus, cultural factors such as ethnic origin, religious affiliation, and location influence individual and collective patterns of substance use. Age and peer group membership are potent variables that influence patterns of use as well as choice of substances used. In some cultures, it may be acceptable or normative to drink heavily but unacceptable to use cocaine or narcotics.

Culture shapes individual as well as collective beliefs, attitudes, roles, and expectations that pertain to substance use. When cultural attitudes about alcohol or other substance use (Orford, 1985) are highly permissive and/or ambivalent, it is rational to expect heavy use and frequent abuse. Many adolescent subcultures require drug use as a prerequisite for group membership (Forrest, 1984; Schwartz, 1986; Bell, 1991). The averred "macho" identity and mentality of many adolescent and young adult Hispanics (Chavez, 1991) is centered around the processes of heavy drinking and marijuana use.

Cultural and environmental realities operate in an interchange-able and multifaceted manner to synergize, reinforce, or impede substance use. Furthermore, this has been true with most cultures and environments throughout history. The "teenage drug crisis" of the late 1960s was replaced by another "teenage drug crisis" in the 1970s and again in the 1980s. In 1891, Crothers stated "this disease (opium use) is all about us and may invade our homes and firesides any time." Bender (1963) has reported that the United States expe-rienced a "wave of adolescent heroin addiction" between 1910 and 1920. In the 1990s we are being told repeatedly by behavioral scientists and the media that we are "waging all out war against drugs" and that America is an "addictive society." In reality, hu-man beings as well as the cultures and environments that they make up are addictive. The people and cultures of the world have abused addicting substances since 6400 B.C.!

GENETIC-FAMILIAL FACTORS ASSOCIATED WITH SUBSTANCE USE DISORDERS

It has been reported (Goodwin et al., 1974; Gottheil et al., 1983; Wallace, 1985, 1991) that alcoholism is a genetically determined and familially transmitted disease. Wallace (1985) states "there can be no doubt about it: alcoholism is a disease that runs in families" (p. 35). Alcoholism and alcohol abuse (Manchester, 1992) are sub-stance use disorders that have been investigated extensively from the perspectives of genetic-familial research.

The genetic-familial or biophysiological theories and explana-tions of substance use disorders purport that relatively specific physical factors cause or significantly contribute to the etiology of these disorders. The disease model of alcoholism and addictions is based upon the assumption that these disorders are inherited.

Goodwin et al. (1974) reported that the sons of Danish alcoholics are four times more likely to be alcoholic than the sons of nonalco-holics. Furthermore, these findings are not influenced by the envi-ronment. Sons raised by alcoholic parents and sons not raised by alcoholic parents were equally likely to develop alcoholism. How-ever, the adopted and nonadopted daughters of Danish alcoholics do not have a higher rate of alcoholism than adopted controls. Thus, research evidence strongly supports the contention that there is a genetic component in alcoholism among males, but the extent and influence of the genetic component within and between the sexes is poorly understood (Nathan and Hay, 1984).

Recent investigations (Cadoret, Cain, and Grove, 1980; Cloninger, 1983; Manchester, 1992) report consistent findings in support of the Goodwin et al. (1974) data. In fact, the Cloninger study found that if the biological father is an alcoholic the son has a *nine* times greater risk of developing alcoholism. The daughters of female alcoholics were three times more likely to develop alcoholism than the daughters of nonalcoholics in this study. According to Wallace (1985), Cloninger "estimated heritability at 90 percent in these men" (p. 36). This statistic applied to children manifesting "environmentally independent alcoholism."

It is apparent that most researchers agree that genetic factors play a major role in the family transmission of alcoholism. The genetic-familial viewpoint maintains that alcoholism is caused in families via the process of genetic transmission and not family dynamics (Brown, 1988) or parenting behaviors. Unfortunately, there are very little data and research evidence to support the notion of genetic-familial transmission of substance use disorders involving such drugs as cocaine, marijuana, heroin, minor tranquilizers, amphetamines, and hallucinogens. However, the research evidence in this realm (Sadava, 1984; Pattison, 1987) does consistently indicate that people who are alcohol dependent are prone to develop other drug dependencies. For example, it was found (Weller and Halikas, 1980) that 44 percent of a sample of marijuana abusers also experienced drinking problems. Cocaine abusers frequently abuse alcohol, marijuana, amphetamines, and other drugs (Pattison, 1987; Knauert, 1992).

One or perhaps several genetic-familial or biophysiological factors may operate to cause and facilitate the substance use disorders. Indeed, all substance use disorders and addictive diseases may someday be linked to brain chemistry abnormalities (Wallace, 1985, 1991). The brain produces beta-endorphin, met-enkephalin, and leu-enkephalin which are narcotic or morphine-like substances. It has been theorized that some people develop heroin addiction because they are born with or develop a deficiency in the brain's level of these morphine-like substances. The neurotransmitter Serotonin (Wallace, 1985, 1991) has been implicated in alcoholism research that reveals sharp reductions in brain levels of this chemical results in increased drinking and vice-versa. Neurochemistry abnormality may be the essential common denominator in all substance use disorders.

The DSM III-R does not delineate the roles of genetic-familial factors or biophysiological factors in the development and maintenance of the substance use disorders. It is noted in the DSM III that "alcohol abuse and dependence are more common among family members than in the general population. Evidence of a genetic factor is the increased prevalence of alcohol dependence in the early-adopted offspring of parents with the disorder" (p. 169). It is also noted in the DSM III that "cigarette smoking among family members of individuals with tobacco dependence is more common than in the general population. However, the evidence for a genetic factor is extremely weak" (p. 178).

It has been the author's clinical observation over the past 20 years of work with all types of addicts and substance abusers that between 30 and 60 percent of the offspring of alcoholics and other addicts eventually develop chemical dependency or a substance use disorder. The sons and daughters of alcoholics may develop a drinking disorder, an addiction to marijuana or some other addictive drug, or they may become polydrug abusers. Similar outcomes can be predicted for the children of heroin addicts, prescription drug abusers, and cocaine or marijuana addicts.

PREVALENCE OF ANTISOCIAL PERSONALITY DISORDER

Antisocial personality disorder or psychopathy is a rather well defined form of personality disorder. The antisocial personality is impulsive, aggressive, irresponsible, prone to alcohol and drug abuse, sexually promiscuous, and engages in criminal activities. However, the antisocial personality disorder is not a highly homogeneous (Cadoret, 1986) diagnostic subgroup.

Recent population studies (Regier et al., 1984) in several American cities examined the prevalence and distribution of antisocial personality disorder in society. These investigations defined antisocial personality disorder according to the DSM III-R (1987) classification criteria. It was found (Regier et al., 1984) that the overall lifetime prevalence of antisocial personality disorder is 2 to 3 percent of the population studied. Urban-rural comparisons revealed that the highest lifetime prevalence of antisocial personality disorder occurred in the central city: 5.7% of 983 core city inhabitants met the DSM III-R criteria for this diagnosis while only 3.1% of the 1,267 inner suburb and 2.4% of 740 rural inhabitants met the DSM criteria for the diagnosis of antisocial personality disorder.

It is also reported (Regier et al., 1984) that the incidence of antisocial personality disorder is lower among college graduates. McCord and McCord (1964) indicate that psychopaths tend to drop out of school prior to graduation. The incidence of antisocial personality disorder is not reliably associated with race.

Doren (1987) and the DSM III report that the incidence of antisocial personality disorder among Americans is estimated to be 4 percent. The DSM III states "the disorder is more common in lower class populations, partly because it is associated with impaired earning capacity and partly because fathers of those with the disorder frequently have the disorder themselves, and consequently their children often grow up in impoverished homes" (p. 319).

It should be noted that the actual classification of psychiatric patients includes a substantially higher percentage of antisocial personalities. For example, at one Illinois state prison 98 percent of the inmates were labeled "psychopathic" (McCord and McCord, 1964). Psychiatrists diagnosed only 5 percent of inmates at another mid-western prison as "psychopathic." Classification rates for psychiatric outpatients within the antisocial personality disorder rubric has been found (Brantley and Sutker, 1984) to range from 15 percent for males to 3 percent for females. These figures are significantly higher among opiate addicts and alcoholics.

The estimated prevalence of antisocial personality disorder and substance use disorders is based upon the numbers of people who are identified as manifesting these disorders vis à vis the process of entering some form of professional treatment. Thus, the true prevavalence of these disorders in society remains unknown. Most chemically dependent and antisocial persons do not enter treatment programs or enter psychotherapy relationships with professional therapists!

SEX RATIO OF ANTISOCIAL PERSONALITY DISORDER

McCord and McCord (1964) noted that psychopathy is most prevalent among men. A study of psychiatric outpatients (Woodruff, Guze, and Clayton, 1971) revealed that 15 percent of men and three percent of women manifested antisocial personality disorder. The antisocial personality disorder or psychopathy is the most frequent diagnosis given to criminals (Glueck, 1918; Cleckley, [1941] 1976; Guze, Goodwin, and Crane, 1970).

It is also reported (Robins, Helzer, and Davis, 1975) that the third most frequent diagnosis given to psychiatric emergency-room patients is antisocial personality disorder. Several investigators (Sutker, 1971; Caster and Parsons, 1977; Forrest, 1983b) have found that alcoholic and narcotic addicted treatment populations include many antisocial individuals.

A recent report (Cadoret, 1986) showed that the male to female ratio for antisocial personality disorder varies between 4:1 to 7.8:1. This finding was based upon the Regier et al. (1984) investigation of the prevalence and distribution of antisocial personality disorder as determined by applying DSM III criteria to population studies in several major American cities.

Doren (1987) indicates that the prevalence of psychopathy "seems to be about" 3 percent for American men and about 1 percent for American women. He also reports that the symptomatology usually becomes overt in males during early childhood while women usually manifest the signs of psychopathy during puberty.

The DSM III also reports "the disorder is much more common in males than in females" (p. 319). Furthermore, the DSM III states "estimates of the prevalence of antisocial personality disorder for American men are about 3 percent, and for American women, less than 1 percent" (p. 319). Thus, it is generally agreed upon that antisocial personality disorder occurs approximately three times more frequently among males than females.

ENVIRONMENTAL AND CULTURAL ASPECTS OF ANTISOCIAL PERSONALITY DISORDER

A plethora of environmental and familial factors have been etiologically associated with antisocial personality disorder as well as all other forms of aberrant behavior. Partridge (1928) is reported to be the first scientist to study the early environmental influence on psychopaths. He examined 12 psychopathic delinquents and found that all of these individuals hated their parents. Furthermore, all of the psychopaths in this early investigation were rejected by their parents as young children.

Environmental explanations and theories of antisocial personality disorder have generally been limited to the examination of rejected or isolated children, investigations of psychopaths' childhood experiences, and parental-familial studies. McCord and McCord (1964) review a number of investigations that elucidate these dimensions of psychopathy. The clinical and research investigations of antisocial personality disorder that were conducted during the 1930s through 1950s (McCord and McCord, 1964) generally conclude that (1) the parents and particularly the mothers of psychopaths are maladjusted, (2) the mothers of psychopaths reject their children, (3) psychopaths have been unloved by their parents, (4) the fathers of psychopaths are stern, rejecting, and often obsessional fathers, (5) psychopaths experienced brutal parental treatment, and (6) in study after study, it was reported that emotional deprivation precipitated the development of an antisocial personality structure.

More recent research (Buss, 1966; Hetherington, 1971; Olwens, 1978; Brantley and Sutker, 1984; Nace, 1990) suggests that antisocial behavior is most likely to occur among children whose parents are emotionally cold and inconsistent in reward and punishment practices. Parental attitudes and conflicted patterns of familial interaction and communication are also associated with adult psychopathy. Familial environments in which early childhood reinforcement patterns that reward active avoidance of punishment have been linked to the development of adult antisocial personality. As children, psychopaths experience continual inconsistent overindulgence or brutal punishment which results in the same behavioral consequences: they learn, believe, and feel that their reactions and behaviors have no predictable effect on others or the environment.

Parental antisocial attitudes and behaviors are predictive of psychopathy among offspring (Sutker, Archer, and Allain, 1978). Juvenile delinquents (Sarason, 1978) have not experienced constructive and healthy parental modeling. To the contrary, they have experienced antisocial parental modeling.

Doren (1987) has elucidated an integrative theory of psychopathy. In essence, this fascinating and complex theory of antisocial personality is based upon the premise that psychopathy is a persistent attempt to maintain environmental control.

The environmental aspects of antisocial personality disorder are summarized by Brantley and Sutker (1984): "Studies suggest that environmental factors peculiar to family situations, subcultural sets, and the societal whole are important in influencing the expression of sociopathy . . . Given our present state of knowledge, the most potent predictor of adult antisocial behavior seems to be the variety and types of childhood antisocial involvement. Family factors play a role in setting the stage for social deviance and its extent, and peer and subcultural influences are important in contributing to such behaviors" (p. 452).

The DSM III-R does not delineate specific environmental factors that are associated with antisocial personality disorder. However, the DSM III-R does indicate that both genetic and environmental influences are important in the etiology of this disorder. The DSM III-R also formally implicates the family environment in the development of antisocial personality disorder.

Cultural factors may also influence susceptibility to antisocial personality disorder. However, the effect of cultural variables upon the development of antisocial personality disorder are far less clearly understood than those pertaining to the substance use disorders. For example, it is not known if the prevalence of psychopathy is significantly higher among Native American, Black, Hispanic, or

Irish American ethnic groups. Cultural and ethnic beliefs, attitudes, customs and traditions, and values may reinforce or inhibit the expression of psychopathy.

McCord and McCord (1964) report that four social factors influence the development and incidence of psychopathy: (1) social crisis, (2) class structure, (3) technological-social complexity, and (4) cultural attitudes toward children. These authors explain how social crises such as war and economic depression can theoretically increase the incidence of psychopathy. They also present research evidence which suggests that socioeconomic class is associated with parenting style and parenting attitudes which in turn theoretically effect the incidence of antisocial personality disorder. Mothers from lower socioeconomic levels tend to have been rejected by their parents more often than mothers from upper-middle socioeconomic levels. Lower-class mothers are also emotionally "colder" toward their children, more overtly rejecting, and less demonstrative of their affection.

These authors (McCord and McCord, 1964) state "the trend of research tentatively suggests that the incidence of psychopathy remains low in the more stable, simple, and rigidly organized communities" (p. 90). Thus, it can be hypothesized that the prevalence of antisocial personality disorder will be greater in cultures or societies that are urban, technologically advanced, experiencing rapid growth, complex, and socially disorganized.

Cultural factors which reinforce or promote chemical dependency, violence and acting-out, sexual promiscuity, or criminal behaviors of any type can be expected to increase the prevalence of antisocial personality disorder in any society or cultural subgroup. It is significant that socialization within the family (McCord and McCord, 1964; Reid et al., 1986; Doren, 1987) continues to be the most widely investigated environmental-cultural facilitator of antisocial personality disorder.

The DSM III-R notes that extreme poverty, removal from the home, and growing up without parental figures "of both sexes" are predisposing factors to antisocial personality disorder. The DSM III-R also indicates that the development of substance abuse is often associated with antisocial behavior, but the specific roles of culture in the development of antisocial personality disorder are not explored in the DSM III.

GENETIC-FAMILIAL FACTORS ASSOCIATED WITH ANTISOCIAL PERSONALITY DISORDER

Early psychiatrists such as Pritchard, Pinel, and Kraepelin (McCord and McCord, 1964) hypothesized that psychopaths have an "inborn defect" or a hereditary lack of "moral sense" which caused their "moral insanity."

Researchers (Partridge, 1928; Gottlieb et al., 1946) who initially investigated the genealogy of psychopathy reported that approximately 50 percent of psychopaths had ancestral histories involving psychopathic traits, epilepsy, "maladjusted personality," or alcoholism. Newkirk (1957) declared that "psychopathic traits are inheritable." Kallman (1939) found that the children of psychopaths have a higher percentage of psychopathy than the siblings of psychopaths. He concluded that the incidence of psychopathy does not follow the closest lines of "blood kinship." The Gluecks (1956) found that juvenile delinquents were generally superior in gross body size, exhibited a homogenous body type, and developed rapidly after age 14. Sixty percent of delinquents were mesomorphs.

Rosenthal (1970) notes that evidence for genetic factors in psychiatric disorders comes from twin studies, adoptee studies, or "correlations of known genetic traits with behavioral pathology in linkage or association studies." Cadoret (1986) states "there are no studies relating criminality, delinquency or antisocial personality to *known* genetic traits, so only linkage or association data are available" (p. 31). Cadoret goes on to say "in the last decade a large amount of research has been done with adoptees in studying the inheritance of criminality, antisocial behavior, and antisocial personality. Although none of these studies addresses directly the inheritance of antisocial personality, the preponderance of evidence indicates a genetic factor in the etiology of antisocial behavior and antisocial personality" (p. 32).

Several studies (Schulsinger, 1977; Cadoret and Cain, 1981; Cadoret, 1985) of biologic and adoptive parents of adoptees with personality disorders report an increase in psychopathy in the biologic parents. Indeed, antisocial behavior in biologic parents is associated with antisocial behavior and/or conduct disorders in adolescents (Cadoret, 1986). Cadoret and Cain (1981) found that adolescent antisocial behaviors are increased in males with alcoholic biologic relatives and in females with antisocial biologic relatives. They also found that the experience of discontinuous mothering during the first year of life was associated with adolescent antisocial behavior. Bohman (1983) reported that criminality in women is related to criminality in a biologic parent. Furthermore, criminality rates are much higher in women's relatives than in men's relatives.

While it is possible that estimates of heritability of antisocial personality disorder may in part reflect the heritability of alcoholism or alcohol abuse, it has recently been found (Cadoret, 1985) that antisocial personality is found to have a "genetic background which is different from that of alcohol abuse, and that environmental factors are of additional importance" (p. 37). Adult criminality which is a basic manifestation of antisocial personality disorder has been shown to have genetic etiology. Thus, specificity of inheritance is suggested vis à vis studies that show independent and different biologic backgrounds for alcohol dependence and antisocial behaviors.

The DSM III states "antisocial personality disorder is particularly common in the fathers of both males and females with the disorder. Studies attempting to separate genetic from environmental influences within the family suggest that both are important, since there seems to be inheritance from biological fathers separated from their offspring early in life and a social influence from adoptive fathers. Because of a tendency toward assortative mating, the children of women with antisocial personality disorder who have the disorder themselves are likely to have both a mother and a father with the disorder" (p. 319).

It is clearly apparent that genetic-familial factors contribute to the development and maintenance of antisocial behaviors and antisocial personality disorder. Yet, it is important to recognize that antisocial personality disorder, substance use disorders, and all other varieties of psychopathology are multivariantly determined (Forrest, 1983, 1987, 1991).

PREVALENCE, SEX RATIO, ENVIRONMENTAL-CULTURAL, AND GENETIC-FAMILIAL FACTORS IN CONCURRENT SUBSTANCE USE DISORDERS AND ANTISOCIAL PERSONALITY DISORDER

Historically, data pertaining to the prevalence, sex ratio, environmental-cultural, and genetic-familial factors in *concurrently diagnosed* chemical dependency and antisocial personality disorder have been limited to anecdotal clinical reports and clinical case studies. A good deal of the information presented in this chapter and Chapter IV is based upon the observations of therapists and clinicians who have worked with chemically dependent as well as antisocial patients. As noted earlier, the generalized acting-out behavioral style of most chemically dependent persons has led to the historic clinical consensus that these individuals are concurrently antisocial. This viewpoint or position is not based upon extensive and consistent research evidence.

Recent research evidence (Nace, 1990) in the realm of prevalence of concurrent substance use disorder and antisocial personality disorder indicates significant concordance. Nace (1990) states: "A strong association between personality disorders and substance use disorders has been well documented in recent studies. The strongest relationship between substance use disorders is with antisocial personality disorder (ASPD)" (p. 185). Helzer and Pryzbeck (1988) report data in the co-occurrence of antisocial personality disorder with alcoholism. They report that 15 percent of alcoholic males manifested concurrent antisocial personality disorder. In this study, nonalcoholic males had a lifetime ASPD (antisocial personality disorder) prevalence of 4 percent. Ten percent of alcoholic women in the study manifested concurrent ASPD while less than 1 percent (0.81) of nonalcoholic women manifested ASPD.

Drake and Vaillant (1985) report that 37 percent of a sample of alcoholic males manifest a concurrent personality disorder and all of the subjects in this study with ASPD were also alcoholics. Koeningsberg's et al. (1985) investigation of some 2,400 psychiatric patients found that 36 percent also had personality disorders (46 percent of alcoholics and 61 percent of nonalcoholic drug abusers manifested a concurrent personality disorder). Hesselbrock, Meyer, and Kenner (1985) report ASPD as the most common concurrent diagnosis in a hospitalized sample of 200 male alcoholics. Rounsaville et al. (1983) diagnosed "primary" antisocial personality disorder in 27 percent of opiate addicts and "secondary" ASPD in another 27 percent of addicts. Khantzian and Treece (1985) found that 65 percent of a sample of 133 narcotic addicts met the DSM III AXIS II criteria for personality disorder and nearly one-half of the personality disorder diagnoses in this study were ASPD.

While borderline personality disorder is most likely the second most common personality disorder found in substance-abusing samples, Nace (1990) states "it would seem safe to assume from the clinical studies now available that within the substance-abusing population the prevalence of personality disorder is at least 50%" (p. 187).

Recent sex-ratio data pertaining to the concurrence of substance use disorder and antisocial personality disorder (Helzer and Pryzbeck, 1988) indicate that the male alcoholic is nearly four times more likely to manifest ASPD than the nonalcoholic female. Hesselbrock, Meyer, and Kenner (1985) found that 49 percent of a sample of 200 male alcoholics met the DSM III criteria for ASPD while 20 percent of female alcoholics in the study met the criteria for ASPD. As indicated in Chapters III and IV, several investigations of chemical dependency and substance abuse among male prison populations (Ross and Lightfoot, 1985; Forrest and Gordon, 1990) consistently indicate that between 50 and 80 percent of antisocial inmates manifest a concurrent substance use disorder.

The roles of environmental-cultural and genetic-familial factors in the etiology of concurrent chemical dependency and antisocial personality disorder remain unclear. These factors have not been investigated longitudinally. As elucidated in Chapter IV, chemically dependent and or drug abusing psychopaths show several common environmental-cultural and genetic-familial similarities: (1) narcissistic injury and early life deprivation, (2) severe and chronic family dysfunction, (3) family history of ASPD and alcohol and/or drug abuse (4) concurrent ASPD and chemical dependency, (5) severe physical abuse during early life, and (6) minority gang membership. Furthermore, childhood behavioral problems such as attention deficit disorder, hyperactivity, and conduct disorder are precursors to the development of both antisocial personality disorder and chemical dependency.

The current cocaine and "crack" epidemic among young black males in our inner cities is a clear example of the interactive effects of environment, culture, economics, family, and family genetics upon the prevalence of chemical dependency and crime specific to this population. Environmental, economic, and familial factors actively reinforce and synergize the incidence of minority group chemical dependency and antisocial behavior (Jackson, 1991). As we begin to investigate the concurrence of antisocial personality disorder and chemical dependency among Black, Hispanic, and Native American youth, it is reasonable to anticipate that between 20 and 25 percent of these populations will manifest both syndromes.

Hopefully, future research efforts will help us better understand the interactive roles of environment, culture, family, economics, and genetics in the etiology of concurrent antisocial personality disorder and chemical dependency.

SUMMARY

The epidemiology of substance use disorders and antisocial personality disorder was examined in this chapter. Data pertaining to the (1) prevalence, (2) sex ratio, (3) environmental and cultural aspects, and (4) genetic-familial factors associated with substance use disorders and antisocial personality disorder and concurrent substance use disorder and antisocial personality disorder were presented.

Several million Americans are alcohol dependent. It is estimated that between 20 and 35 million Americans abuse or are addicted to various mood altering substances. Indeed, the substance use disorders have been referred to as America's "number one health problem" (Forrest, 1987). Even the AIDS "epidemic" is associated with drug use! Chemical dependency is widespread throughout the world. More Americans are developing patterns of polydrug abuse.

It is presently estimated (Wilsnack and Beckman, 1984) that there are three alcoholic males for every alcoholic female in the

United States. Data pertaining to the sex ratio of several substance use disorders are discussed. The DSM III-R have been notes that substance use disorders in general are more commonly diagnosed among men.

The environmental and cultural factors which reinforce chemical dependency and substance abuse were outlined in this chapter. Briefly, it has been hypothesized that environmental and cultural variables shape individual as well as collective attitudes, beliefs, roles, and behaviors which pertain to the use and abuse of various addictive substances. Ethnic subgroups such as Blacks, Native Americans, Irish Americans, Hispanics, and Eskimos have been devastated by the effects of alcoholism and chemical dependency.

Alcoholism and other addictive disorders are believed to be (Wallace, 1985, 1989; Manchester, 1992) genetically determined. Addictions do "run in families." Research evidence supporting the genetic-familial model or theory of substance use disorders was touched upon in this chapter.

The incidence of antisocial personality disorder among Americans is estimated to be 4 percent (Doren, 1987). The male to female ratio for antisocial personality disorder varies between 4:1 to 7.8:1. Investigations of psychiatric populations reveal that many of these individuals manifest antisocial personality disorder or psychopathic traits.

A number of environmental and cultural factors appear to be related to the development of antisocial personality disorder and patterns of antisocial behavior. Most clinicians and researchers (McCord and McCord, 1964; Olwens, 1978; Brantley and Sutker, 1984) report that familial and parenting behaviors are etiologically associated with psychopathy. For example, Brantley and Sutker (1984) state "given our present state of knowledge, the most potent predictor of adult antisocial behavior seems to be the variety and types of childhood antisocial involvement" (p. 452). It is also important to point out that some clinicians (Yochelson and Samenow, 1977, 1986) do not believe that environmental or cultural variables are principally related to the development of antisocial personality disorder.

It has long been theorized that "psychopathic traits are inheritable" (Newkirk, 1957). Cadoret (1986) indicates "the preponderance of evidence indicates a genetic factor in the etiology of antisocial behavior and antisocial personality" (p. 32). Indeed, antisocial behavior in biologic parents is associated with antisocial behavior and/or conduct disorders in adolescents.

Data and information from the DSM III-R pertaining to the epidemiology of substance use disorders and antisocial personality disorder also have been included in this chapter.

The prevalence, sex ratio, environmental-cultural, and genetic-familial factors in *concurrent* substance use disorders and antisocial personality disorder were examined. Nace (1990) concludes: "A strong association between personality disorders and substance use disorders has been well established in recent studies. The strongest relationship between substance use disorders is with antisocial personality disorder (ASPD)" (p. 185).

Chapter IV

Etiology of Substance Use Disorders and Antisocial Personality Disorder

INTRODUCTION

It was pointed out in Chapter II that chemically dependent and antisocial persons have contributed to the general malaise of other individuals and societies throughout history. These individuals have also no doubt forever made themselves miserable and actively contributed to their own unhappiness! Indeed, in the end, chemically dependent and antisocial persons are always their own worst enemies. These individuals seem to be forever the victims of their own patterns of self-defeating behavior.

The behaviors and psychopathology of antisocial personality disorder and chemical dependency can range from confusing, baffling, humorous, and stimulating, to bizarre, self-destructive, dangerous, and extremely frightening. It is little wonder that behavioral scientists have long been interested and even fascinated with these individuals. Thus, as briefly touched upon in Chapter III, there are numerous theories that attempt to explain why people abuse drugs and develop chemical dependency as well as psychopathy. Behavioral scientists have formulated explanations and etiologic models that attempt to elucidate the causes and origins of substance abuse, chemical dependency, and antisocial behaviors or antisocial personality disorder.

As evidenced in the present chapter, the exact or precise etiology of the substance use disorders as well as antisocial personality disorder remain unknown. Most behavioral scientists (Forrest, 1978; Zimberg, 1982; Forrest, 1984; Wilsnack and Beckman, 1984; Blane and Leonard, 1987; Doren, 1987; Forrest and Gordon, 1990) agree that the substance use disorders and personality disorders are caused or determined by a multiplicity of factors. Several theories and etiological models of substance use disorders and antisocial personality disorder are examined in this chapter. These models attempt to explain why and how people develop chemical dependency, substance abuse problems, and antisocial personality disorder.

ETIOLOGICAL THEORIES
OF SUBSTANCE USE DISORDERS

Pre-scientific attempts to explain and understand chemical dependency and the substance use disorders were often religious in nature. Prior to the mid-1900s, alcoholics and other drug addicts or substance abusers were viewed as evil, "weak-willed," immoral, or simply lacking in "will-power" (Bean and Zimberg, 1981; Orford, 1985). Alcoholic persons are referred to as "drunkards" in the Bible and references to addicts and substance abusers are included in the literary histories of virtually all civilized societies.

With the advent of modern psychiatry, psychology, social work, and the other developing behavioral sciences came the first scientific attempts to elucidate the causes of alcohol dependence and other substance use disorders. During the past 50 years a number of psychological, sociological-environmental, and genetic-familial or biological theories of chemical dependency and substance use disorders have been developed. These different etiological models of substance use were generally developed via the use of scientific investigations and research or clinically-based methodology. The essential clinical and theoretical data pertaining to each of these etiological theories of substance use disorders are presented in the following section of this chapter.

PSYCHOLOGICAL THEORIES
OF SUBSTANCE USE DISORDERS

There are several psychological theories of chemical dependency and the substance use disorders. The major psychological theories of substance use, abuse, and chemical dependency are presented in this section of the chapter. These modern theories or explanations of addictive behavior have been developed during the past 50 years.

One of the earliest psychological theories of substance use (Jellinek, 1945; Cappell and Greeley, 1987) was based upon the tension reduction hypothesis. This general theory has been referred to as the "tension reduction theory," the "relief theory," or the "anxiety theory" of alcoholism (Milt, 1969). The tension reduction theory of alcohol abuse is behavioral and based upon simple learning principles. According to Cappell and Herman (1972), the ingestion of ethanol is not pathologic or unique but rather "one response among many in the (behavioral) repertoire of an organism: the existence of a tension state energized the response and the *relief* of tension provided by alcohol reinforced the drinking response" (pp. 33-34). Later versions of this theory distinguished between the hypothesis that alcohol use reduces tension and the hypothesis that people imbibe because of the tension-reducing properties of ethanol.

In essence, this theory of substance abuse and/or chemical dependency postulates that addictive behaviors are learned. The drug user learns that ingesting a psychoactive substance partially extinguishes feelings of tension, anxiety, or uncomfortableness. The use of alcohol or another drug thus provides "relief" or escape from an unpleasant feeling state. Since the drug-taking behavior "works" in the sense of extinguishing anxiety or pain and providing relief, the pattern of drug use is repeated, practiced, learned, and eventually over-learned and over-generalized. These aspects of learning theory explain how patterns of substance use can become increasingly maladaptive and pathologic and result in addiction.

Clearly, this model of substance abuse is based upon the principles of modern learning theory. However, it has been noted (Forrest, 1978, 1983a) that learning and conditioning-based models of chemical dependency eventually become physiologically determined when the person actually reaches that point in the addiction process of being chemically dependent or tissue dependent.

Social learning theories of alcoholism and substance use disorders (Bandura, 1969; Evans and Wellman, 1978; Abrams and Nianura, 1987) greatly expanded the earlier "relief theory" and posited that a diversity of social factors in combination with the basic principles of learning determine patterns of alcohol and drug use, abuse, and chemical dependence. The social learning theory (SLT) of substance use disorders integrates psychosocial, learning, cultural, and even biologic/genetic factors in its explanation of the origins and maintenance of addictive patterns of behavior. Applied social learning theory (Evans and Wellman, 1978) makes three primary assumptions regarding deviant (substance abuse or chemical dependency) behavior: "(1) all voluntary behavior is learned, (2) since behavior is learned, it can be "unlearned," or extinguished, and (3) the problem area is the maladaptive behavior" (p. 149).

According to social learning theory, abuse is likely to occur in situations where individuals feel overwhelmed, are unable to cope effectively, and perceive themselves as inadequate. Abrams and Nianura (1987) purport that substance use is a method of coping with the demands of daily living. Clinicians who treat chemically dependent persons and substance abusers in accord with the social learning theory utilize behavioral contracting (Forrest, 1985), relaxation training and biofeedback (Yost and Mines, 1985), multimodal interventions (Forrest and Gordon, 1990), assertive training and prosocial modeling (Evans and Wellman, 1978; Ross and Lightfoot, 1985), and other individualized treatment modalities (Klee, 1990).

Several personality theories of alcoholism and chemical dependency have been developed over the past 40 years (McCord and McCord, 1964; Blane, 1968; Blum and Blum, 1969; Forrest, 1983; Blane and Leonard, 1987; Cox, 1987). These historic personality theories of chemical dependency were univariant. While it is now widely recognized that there is no one "addictive personality type," it is known that personality traits and characteristics do play important roles in the etiology of substance use disorders (O'Connell, 1990).

The personality traits of the drug user have frequently been described as psychopathic, sociopathic, or neurotic (Yochelson and Samenow, 1986). These authors also note "for at least fifty years, psychiatric profiles of drug users have emphasized preponderantly their psychopathic features" (p. 34). Drug users are consistently reported to be irresponsible and immature (Forrest, 1978; Forrest [1980] 1986). Low self-esteem, hyper-narcissism or egocentricity, dependency, inadequacy and feelings of worthlessness, anxiety, low-frustration tolerance, manipulativeness, depression, guilt, and anger are also personality traits of alcoholics and substance abusers (Bratter and Forrest, 1985). Recent personality theories of alcoholism (McClelland et al., 1972; Wilsnack and Beckman, 1984) focus upon the power, gender, and sexual identity issues that are associated with alcoholism and pathological alcohol use.

Psychoanalytic personality theory emphasizes the regressive personality-character structure dimensions of chemically dependent persons and substance abusers. According to this model, the substance abuser attempts to resolve early life conflicts via alcohol and drug use. Fenichel (1945) viewed chemical dependency as an "impulse neurosis" and stressed the role of early life narcissistic injury, oral dependence, and latent homosexuality in the etiology of chemical dependency. The substance use disorders (Forrest, 1983a) also involve sadomasochistic personality features, self-system fragmentation or ego-deficit, and basic identity pathology. Freud (Yorke, 1970) emphasized in a letter to Fleiss the link between addiction and masturbation: "it has dawned upon me that masturbation is the one major habit, the "primal addiction" and that it was only as a substitute and replacement for it that the other addictions for alcohol, morphine, tobacco, etc., came into existence" (p. 142). Thus, masturbation is the prototype of chemical dependency. The personality make-up and character structure of the chemically dependent or substance abuser is reported to be the cause of these disorders according to Freudian and psychodynamic personality theorists.

Another psychological theory of chemical dependency and substance abuse hypothesizes that these disorders evolve as a result of attempts to block self-awareness and defend the self from painful emotions and/or cognitions (Hull, 1987). Chemical dependency and substance abuse are forms of self-medication whereby people pharmacologically attempt to modify their feelings, cognitions, and self-awareness. Drugs are used to cope with feelings of anxiety, frustration, and discomfort. Chemical dependency can serve as a defense (Forrest, 1984) against a diversity of other forms of psychopathology and thus may be viewed as paradoxically adaptive. Hull (1987) indicates that drinking to avoid negative self-evaluation is orthogonal with respect to other alcohol use motives. He also points out that alcohol (as well as other psychoactive drugs) decreases self-aware-ness, inhibits cognitive processes, decreases appropriate behaviors and self-evaluation based on past performance, and decreases nega-tive evaluation of the self following failure. These factors reinforce further substance use.

Related psychological theories of substance use disorders (Yost and Mines, 1985; Sher, 1987; O'Connell, 1990) focus upon the stress reducing effects of alcohol and drug use. In general, these models explain how alcohol or other drugs physiologically and/or psychologically reduce or "dampen" stress and therefore reinforce substance use behaviors in related stress inducing situations.

Recent cognitive or expectancy theories of substance use disor-ders (Goldman, Brown, and Christensen, 1987) stress the impor-tance of anticipation, systemic relationships, and nonpharmacologic factors in the etiology of addictive behaviors. For example, Berglas (1987) has related "self-handicapping" to alcohol abuse. The self-handicapping aspect of alcohol abuse enables the drinker to main-tain a sense of positive self-esteem or competence by controlling the attributions drawn from his or her behavior. Blane and Leonard (1987) note, "if failure occurs under the influence of alcohol, the individual's own competence is not assailed since poor perfor-mance is charged to alcohol; with success, the individual's image of competence is enhanced since he or she performed well under han-dicapped conditions" (p. 9).

A number of psychologists (Yochelson and Samenow, 1986) have emphasized that drug use and abuse is facilitated vis à vis attempts to (1) expand consciousness, (2) meet curiosity needs, (3) experience pleasure, (4) meet stimulation needs, or (5) enhance sensitivity and/or feelings of euphoria. Substance use is initiated and maintained for the "kick" or thrill, euphoria, or sense of eupho-ria and well-being caused by drug ingestion.

Recent psychological theories of chemical dependency and sub-stance abuse (Forrest, 1983a, 1984, 1985) are multivariate and stress the interrelationships between the person, substance, social environment, family, and genetics. For example, (Forrest, 1983a) explains in detail how early life narcissistic injury is associated with genetic, familial, character, personality, cognitive, and behavioral factors which etiologically relate to the initiation and maintenance of alcohol dependence. This model also elucidates the roles of adolescence, courtship, marriage, and procreation as these processes relate to the perpetuation of alcoholism and substance use disorders.

These basic psychological theories of substance use disorders have been applied to a plethora of patterns of substance abuse and chemical dependency. Most of these models were initially applied to alcoholism or patterns of alcohol abuse and then generalized to explain other addictive disorders. The DSM III (APA, 1980) and DSM III-R (APA, 1987) do not delineate psychological theories or models of the substance use disorders.

SOCIOLOGICAL-ENVIRONMENTAL THEORIES OF SUBSTANCE USE DISORDERS

Sociocultural and environmental factors influence patterns of drug use as well as all patterns of behavior. As touched upon briefly in Chapter III, sociologic-environmental theories of substance use disorders view the etiology of these behaviors to be the response of individuals to their environments. Brecher (1972) summarizes the sociological viewpoint on substance abuse: "society creates addicts and causes ex-addicts to relapse into addiction again. What these theories (sociological theories) have in common is the belief that the secret to addiction lies in the social context" (p. 67). This theme is germane to all of the sociological-environmental models of addictive behavior and chemical dependency.

It has long been recognized that alcoholism and addictive disorders tend to "run in families" (Zimberg, 1982; Gottheil et al., 1983; Mumey, 1984; Manchester, 1992). This observation has contributed to the development of a sociological-environmental theory of chemical dependency that focuses upon the role of family behaviors and dynamics in the etiology as well as maintenance of these disorders. According to this theory, pathologic patterns of family adjustment are viewed as causal factors in drug abuse. Several familial factors may contribute to the development of drug abuse and chemical dependency. A chemically dependent parent models a plethora of maladaptive behaviors within the family system (Forrest, 1978). Children in these families observe, learn, and are actively taught a wide range of addictive behaviors. Inadequate and weak or absent fathers and inconsistent, domineering, and seductive mothers (Yochelson and Samenow, 1986) may contribute to the development of substance use disorders in their children. Pathologic patterns of familial communication, interaction, emoting, and thinking (Forrest, 1978; Black, 1981; Wegscheider, 1981; Forrest, [1980] 1986; Brown, 1988; Forrest, 1991) contribute to the etiology of substance use disorders.

Poverty or deprivation has also been purported to be an antecedent or cause of chemical dependency. The environmental and psycho-social realities of ghetto or slum life contribute to the outcropping and reinforcement of drug use. It has been reported (Stimmel, 1972) that most drug addicts come from low socioeconomic groups. These environments also contribute to problems associated with selling or "dealing" drugs. Chemical dependency and substance abuse are escapes from the many stresses and frustrations that are associated with poverty and surviving within a slum environment.

Yochelson and Samenow (1986) indicate that "contagion" is one of the significant sociologic factors in the etiology of drug use. Addictive disorders and chemical dependency have been viewed as communicable diseases. Indeed, alcoholism (Forrest, 1978) has been characterized as a Reichian "emotional plague" phenomenon. Addicts and substance abusers in a community reinforce the use and abuse of drugs by other former non-using community members. Thus, addicts "spread" addictive diseases! According to the contagion theory of substance abuse, drug users and addicts "infect" other people with their "addictive diseases."

Peer group influence (Orford, 1985) has been viewed as a sociological factor that contributes to the development of substance use disorders. Adolescent drug abuse (Forrest, 1984; Orford, 1985; Rachman and Raubolt, 1985; Bell, 1991) is hypothesized to be caused by "peer group pressure" and social factors that are associated with peer group membership. Most people feel a need to be accepted by others and group membership is an expression of this need. Adolescents experience an intense need for group membership. Unfortunately, group membership may be based upon or centered around drug use. Teen peer groups may exclude individuals who do not use mood altering substances. The social groups and networks of many adults are also based upon the common denominator of substance use or even chemical dependency. Peer pressure is a social factor that contributes to the etiology of chemical dependency. The peer pressure model of substance use can also be linked to the "contagion" model. In particular, teens seem to be able to influence each other to experiment with drugs or even "spread" chemical dependency to peer group members.

Recently, counselors and behavioral scientists have started utilizing "positive peer pressure" as a strategy to curtail adolescent substance abuse. When peer group membership is contingent upon alcohol and drug abstinence, "peer pressure" is viewed as a positive or healthy social reality.

Kandel (1973) stated that "peer behavior is the crucial determining factor in adolescent drug use. When faced with conflict, adolescents are much more responsive to peers than to parents. Thus fifty-six percent of adolescents use marijuana when their best friends use marijuana, although their parents have never used psychoactive drugs" (p. 1069). It has been suggested that the best social predictor for drug use is the drug use history of an individual's close friends! Alcoholics (Forrest, 1983a) are invariably involved in an alcoholic interpersonal network (AIN) which actively supports, reinforces, and maintains the alcoholic behavioral repertoire of its membership. The AIN is an example par excellence of a "peer group" that causes or facilitates alcohol misuse upon the part of its members.

Chemical dependency has also been etiologically associated with social alienation, the "pressures of modern living," "high-tech" living, and social anxiety. The threat of nuclear holocaust, social institutions, laws, and even the mass media have been blamed for the "drug crisis" in America. Since the mid-1960s America has been viewed as a "sick society" by many sociologists and behavioral scientists. Social alienation and the mental health of a society or culture may be measured by rates of alcohol and drug consumption. Thus, the "something's rotten in America" belief system is supported by the various social and psychological realities that are associated with substance abuse.

Economic and political factors as well as the social climate of an environment shape or determine patterns of substance use. Drug availability in an environment also determines patterns of use and abuse. In spite of the fact that America is a society that has been under the influence of a diversity of drugs for over 30 years, social or environmental causation of substance abuse is complex.

Sociological explanations and theories of substance use disorders associate cultural factors with patterns of alcohol or drug abuse. For example, it has been found (Forrest, 1978) that first-generation Jewish Americans and Italian Americans have low rates of alcoholism. Yet, these individuals are from cultures where alcohol use is high and customarily takes place in religious and familial settings. To the contrary, Irish Americans have high rates of both abstinence and alcoholism. Irish Americans also tend to drink in barrooms and taverns. As different cultural groups become acculturated and assimilated into mainstream American culture, their rates of alcoholism, abstinence, and patterns of use become more similar. Cahalan (1978) reports that more second and third generation American Jews are diagnosed "alcoholic" than first-generation American Jews while the reverse is true of Irish Americans.

Alcohol abuse and addiction have created myriad problems among Black, Hispanic, Native American, and Eskimo ethnic groups (Teboe, 1991; Jackson, 1991). Bourne and Light (1979) state "alcohol abuse is the number one health problem among Black Americans–(alcohol) is both the cause and result of a plethora of other problems including unemployment, crime, broken marriages, and debilitating physical disease" (pp. 84-85).

Sociocultural factors may contribute to college student polydrug use and abuse, the use of amphetamines by middle-aged women and athletes, truck drivers, and medical students, and narcotic addiction or "crack" use in our inner cities. Chronic marijuana use is widespread and culturally acceptable in countries such as India, Jamaica, Egypt, and Morocco (Dornbush and Fink, 1977). Hallucinogenic drug use was largely a "counterculture" phenomena of the late 1960s and early 1970s. Cocaine abuse and dependence was largely limited to upper-middle class Americans prior to 1980. Sociocultural as well as economic and supply and demand factors have contributed to widespread cocaine and "crack" abuse among all classes of Americans in recent years (Forrest, 1989; Jackson, 1991).

Clearly, it is not known if racial or ethnic group membership causes heavy drinking and chemical dependency via sociocultural influence, genetic transmission, modeling, or psychological make-up. In spite of these unanswered questions, it is very apparent that sociocultural factors such as racial and ethnic group membership exert an influence on patterns of chemical dependency and substance use. Attitudes, feelings, values, and beliefs pertaining to alcohol and drug use are shaped and molded by sociocultural realities.

Recent sociological-environmental theories of substance abuse and chemical dependency (Yochelson and Samenow, 1986) are multivariate in nature. These models do not attempt to identify a single sociologic or environmental cause of drug abuse. Modern sociological theories of substance abuse explain chemical dependency and addictive behavior in terms of multiple causation. Clearly, the etiology of substance use disorders is not singularly rooted in poverty, childrearing practices, ethnic or cultural group membership, family dynamics, alienation, or the industrial/technological revolution. However, all of these social-cultural and environmental realities may interactively contribute to social causation of substance abuse problems and chemical dependency.

It is important to note that the sociological-cultural and environmental theories of substance use disorders are generally more theoretical and less empirically-oriented/based than the psychological models of substance abuse. The DSM III-R does not explore sociologic, cultural, or environmental theories or causes of substance use disorders and chemical dependency.

GENETIC-FAMILIAL AND BIOLOGICAL THEORIES OF SUBSTANCE USE DISORDERS

Genetic factors have long been associated with the etiology of substance use disorders. Crothers (1891) indicated "the children of both alcohol and opium inebriates display many forms of brain degeneration. The paranoiacs, criminals, prostitutes, paupers, and the army of defectives, all build upon a diathesis and favoring soil for the opium craze. Descendants from such parents will always be markedly defective" (p. 228). Sudduth (1896) also believed that narcotic addicts are victims of hereditary factors but as a physician he also stated "they are wholly given over to evil ways and the sooner they end their days the better for themselves and mankind at large" (p. 797).

These early behavioral scientists observed that alcoholism and chemical dependency tended to "run in families" and therefore concluded that substance use disorders were determined by genetic-hereditary or biophysiological factors.

The vast majority of research that examines genetic-familial and biophysiological factors in substance use disorders is limited to the specific area of alcohol addiction (Nathan and Hay, 1984). Biophysiological theories of the etiology of alcohol dependence purport that alcoholics and nonalcoholics metabolize ethanol differently. Korsten and Lieber (1979) report that alcoholics have two metabolic routes by which alcohol is metabolized while nonalcoholics have only one. The alcoholic's microsomal ethanol-oxidizing system enables these individuals to metabolize more ethanol than non-alcoholics. Alcoholics may also be able to metabolize ethanol faster than non-alcoholics who metabolize alcohol by the liver-metabolism route.

Although the findings of Korsten and Lieber (1979) have not been proven by extensive scientific research, it remains to be determined if the second metabolic route of alcoholics is a cause or effect of alcohol abuse and/or alcohol dependence. It is generally believed (Nathan and Hay, 1984) that the source of the alcoholic's microsomal ethanol-oxidizing system (MEOS) is genetic transmission.

Hopefully, further research pertaining to the MEOS hypothesis of alcoholism will not prove futile. Several earlier biophysiological theories of alcoholism did not adequately stand up to the test of empiricism and scientific investigation. For example, Smith (1950) proposed that alcoholism was caused by pituitary deficiency which resulted secondarily in adrenal-cortex exhaustion. The "allergy" theory of alcoholism (Haggard, 1944) maintained that a particular body chemistry results in addiction and/or loss of control of drinking. The nutritional theory of alcoholism (Forrest, 1978) asserts that a metabolic defect results in a cellular requirement for ethanol. These models or theories of alcohol dependence are not reviewed extensively in this chapter because they have all been scientifically disproven during the past 30 years.

Genetic-familial transmission is presently believed to be a key etiological factor in the development of alcoholism and drinking disorders (Zimberg, 1982; Gottheil et al., 1983; Forrest, 1983a; Brown, 1985; Manchester, 1992). Several years ago (Goodwin, Schulsinger, and Molster, 1974), it was found that the sons of Danish alcoholics were four times more likely to develop alcoholism than the sons of nonalcoholics. This finding occurred independently of the family or parenting environment. Thus, the sons of alcoholics were four times more likely to be alcoholic than the sons of nonalcoholics independently of whether they were raised by their alcoholic parents. A subsequent investigation (Goodwin et al., 1977) found that adopted and nonadopted daughters of Danish alcoholics did not have a higher rate of alcoholism than adopted controls.

Nathan and Hay (1984) indicate that these data were "the first to provide empirical confirmation of the widespread conviction that there is a genetic component to alcoholism" (p. 571). These authors also point out that the precise genetic influence between and within the sexes has not been established.

A recent investigation (Cadoret, Cain, and Grove, 1980) revealed findings that are congruent with those reported by Goodwin, Schulsinger, and Molster (1974). It was found in this study that male Iowa adoptees raised apart from alcoholic biologic parents were much more likely to develop alcohol dependence than adoptees of nonalcoholic biologic parents. In reviewing this study, Nathan and Hay (1984) state "no environmental factors–including psychiatric or alcohol problems in the adoptive family, the socioeconomic status of the adoptive family, or the stability of infant-adoptive mother relationship during the early months of life–predicting adoptee alcoholism" (p. 571).

A related study (Frances, Timm, and Bucky, 1980) found that alcoholics with at least one alcoholic family member manifested more severe alcohol dependence and psychopathology than alcoholics with no family history of alcoholism or drinking problems.

Family studies of alcoholism (Goodwin, 1983; Manchester, 1992) report that at least 25 percent of male relatives of alcoholics are themselves alcoholics or severe alcohol abusers. Goodwin

(1983) suggests that the concept of "familial alcoholism" is a useful diagnostic category. According to Goodwin, familial alcoholism includes the following features: (1) a family history of alcoholism, (2) early onset of alcoholism, and (3) severe symptoms that require treatment at an early age. It is important to bear in mind that familial is not synonymous with genetic. Goodwin (1983) summarized the results of twin studies of alcoholism as follows: "all point to genetic control of drinking behavior, but the evidence for a genetic determinant of alcoholism is inconsistent. Other twin studies indicate genetic control over the metabolism of alcohol, but varying rates of metabolism probably have no relevance to alcoholism" (p. 6).

Genetic research on alcoholism also reveals that 30 percent of the daughters raised by alcoholics are treated for depressive illness by the age of 32. Goodwin (1983) reports that the male children of alcoholics are specifically vulnerable to alcoholism and not at increased risk for other psychopathology. He also indicates that alcoholism is *not* on a continuum with heavy drinking or problem drinking. The daughters of alcoholics are far less prone to developing alcoholism than the sons of alcoholics, but the daughters who do drink heavily have an unusually higher chance of becoming alcohol dependent. Alcoholism often begins at a later age in women than in men.

Cloninger, Bohman, and Siguardsson (1981) have hypothesized that there are two distinct genetic types of male alcoholism. The "milieu-limited" type is characterized by mild alcohol abuse in parents, minimal criminality, and strong environmental-social influence upon style, frequency, and severity of alcoholism. The less common "male limited" type of alcoholism is transmitted from the father to son and is also associated with a parental history of severe criminal behavior. Environmental factors do not play an important role in the severity and frequency of alcohol use in this form of alcoholism.

Finally, it should be noted that animal studies (McGuffin and Reich, 1984; Wallace, 1989) demonstrate the presence of genetic influence in alcoholism. Laboratory strains of mice and rats can be bred to prefer alcohol solutions rather than water. Biochemical differences "have been demonstrated between alcohol-preferring and non-alcohol-preferring strains, with liver alcohol dehydrogenase activity accounting for about 10 percent of the variance in ethanol preference" (McGuffin and Reich, 1984, p. 69). It has also been found that crosses between inbred and selected lines fit the model of polygenic inheritance.

Sutker and Archer (1984) point out that surprisingly little research has been directed at the role of genetics in the etiology of opiate abuse and dependence. Unfortunately, the role of genetic factors in the etiology of all substance use disorders other than alcoholism has not been adequately studied. Genetic-familial and biophysiological aspects of marijuana, amphetamine, cocaine, minor/major tranquilizer, and hallucinogenic dependencies have not been investigated. A basic reason for this is simply that many of these substance use disorders did not exist or were not prevalent several years ago.

It has been found (Nichols and Hsiao, 1967) that selective breeding produces strains of rats that differ in susceptibility to morphine addiction. Hill, Cloninger, and Ayre (1977) report that alcoholism and opiate abuse tend to cluster in families. However, these findings are not clear indicators of genetic influence in the etiology of alcoholism or opiate abuse.

Gold and Pottash (1983) indicate that neurobiological theories of opiate addiction implicate premorbid neural factors in compulsive opiate use. The endogenous opioid peptides or endorphins are central to neurobiological theories of opiate addiction. It is generally believed (Gold and Pottash, 1983) that opiates modulate anxiety and panic states via an endorphin-locus coeruluns interaction. According to Gold and Pottash (1983), "the most obvious neurobiological theory for compulsive opiate use or self-administration is pre-existing endogenous opiate or endorphin deficiency. This theory suggests that addicts discover opiates more or less by chance and find it normalizes them in some or all ways presumably on the basis of a pre-existing endorphin deficiency" (p. 32). Opiates can decrease norepinephrine activity and turnover.

Bratter, Pennacchia, and Gauya (1985) report that the metabolic theory of heroin addiction is based upon the rationale that an altered response to narcotics is due to a metabolic change within the central nervous system. Moreover, this biophysiological theory of addiction purports that heroin addicts suffer from a metabolic disease or biochemical deficit which requires deficiency hypothesis of narcotic addiction.

Several authors (Orford, 1985; Brown, 1985; Gorski and Miller, 1986; Forrest and Gordon, 1990) indicate that there is a widespread belief among clinicians in the chemical dependency treatment field that the substance use disorders are diseases. Indeed, the disease model (Forrest, 1984; Orford, 1985) of alcoholism has been applied to virtually all patterns of substance abuse and addictive disorders. The disease model of alcoholism and chemical dependency is based upon the belief that these patterns of behavior are caused by genetic, physical, or biophysiological factors. Thus, the symptom structure, developmental course or "progression," cause and outcome of chemical dependency and substance use disorders are felt to be genetically determined by advocates of the disease model. Alcoholism has been recognized as a disease by the American Medical Association for nearly 30 years (Forrest, 1978).

It is important to note that there is virtually no research indicating that amphetamine, cannabis, cocaine, solvent, hallucinogenic, or sedative dependencies are genetically determined substance use disorders. However, the biologic children of parents who do develop these substance use disorders (Sadava, 1984) may be at a higher risk to develop some form of chemical dependency or pattern of substance abuse later in life. Furthermore, the heavy use of one drug almost invariably implies multiple or polydrug involvement. Weller and Halikas (1980) found that nearly 50 percent of a sample of marijuana abusers were also alcohol abusers. The genetic-familial factors associated with polydrug abuse or dependence and the susceptibility to polydrug abuse or dependence and the susceptibility to polydrug dependence (Pattison, 1987) have not been identified. It is rather common in general clinical practice to encounter patients who abuse various drugs and develop dependencies to virtually any or all addictive substances that they are exposed to.

The DSM III and the DSM III-R point out familial and genetic factors in the etiology of substance use disorders. For example, the DSM III states "alcohol abuse and dependence are more common among family members than in the general population. Evidence of a genetic factor is the increased prevalence of alcohol dependence in the early-adopted offspring of parents with the disorder" (p. 169).

Finally, it must be remembered that all human beings are biologically addictive. Virtually all people manifest the biologic capacity to develop a wide range of drug dependencies. A given individual will become drug dependent if he or she is exposed to sufficiently high doses of an addictive substance over sufficient time. Indeed, this fundamental reality is a paradoxical dimension of our biologic malleability and capacity for organismic adaptation.

ETIOLOGICAL THEORIES OF ANTISOCIAL PERSONALITY DISORDER

As touched upon in earlier chapters, psychopathy or antisocial personality disorder has been known to science for 150 years (McCord and McCord, 1964). Psychopaths have hurt, damaged, and destroyed countless numbers of human beings in every known society and culture. These individuals have been referred to as "morally insane," "moral imbeciles," evil, and depraved.

The causes of antisocial personality disorder have been clinically and empirically investigated for over 100 years. Psychological, sociological-environmental, and genetic or biological theories of antisocial personality disorder have been constructed. These etiological models of antisocial personality disorder are examined in the final section of this chapter.

PSYCHOLOGICAL THEORIES OF ANTISOCIAL PERSONALITY DISORDER

It is interesting and significant that a comprehensive univariate theory of antisocial personality disorder has never been developed. Unlike the early theories of alcoholism and other substance use disorder, antisocial personality disorder seems to have historically been viewed as a disorder with multiple etiological components.

Early emotional deprivation (McCord and McCord, 1964) has been associated with the development of antisocial personality disorder. A lack of parental love may be one major contributing factor in the etiology of psychopathy. Indeed, it was reported earlier in this text that a number of behavioral scientists (Partridge, 1928; Field, 1940; Lindner, 1944, 1948; Jenkins, 1960) have found psychological rejection and parental psychopathology to be causative factors in antisocial personality disorder. Field (1940) stated that 23 of 25 psychopathic children treated at a state psychiatric institute had been rejected by their parents. Furthermore, it was found that the mothers of these children were maladjusted and poorly integrated. The children in this study felt unloved by their parents. Clinicians have also reported that psychopaths have been rejected by their fathers but overindulged by their mothers. Parental approval (Szurek, 1942) of the child's destructive, deviant, and antisocial behaviors has also been cited as a causative factor in antisocial personality disorder. Szurek (1942) concluded that the unconscious encouragement of the mother caused "psychopathic" traits in the child.

Lindner (1944, 1948) believed that criminal psychopaths have experienced brutal parental treatment and also hypothesized that the psychopath has a deep hatred for his or her father. Deprived of healthy parental identification and an adequately developed superego, the psychopath projects his or her hatred and rage upon society.

A related psychological model of antisocial personality disorder (Jenkins, 1960) is based upon the clinical observation that psychopaths were not wanted by their violently abusive parents. Jenkins stated "the product of this background is a person of bottomless hostilities and endless bitterness, who feels cheated in life, views himself as the victim . . . and is grossly lacking in a guilt sense over his misconduct" (p. 326).

In spite of the redundant finding of several clinicians and researchers that emotional deprivation precipitates the antisocial personality structure, Hervey Cleckley (1959) states: "I have not regularly encountered any specific type of error in parent-child regulation in the early history of my cases . . . I am increasingly impressed with the difficulty in obtaining objective and reliable evidence of what was felt twenty or thirty years ago" (p. 584). It is important to note that Cleckley's ([1941] 1976) original treatise on psychopathy continues to be widely accepted within the behavioral science professions.

Bender (1947) reported that *all* the psychopathic children in her study had experienced emotional deprivation, neglect, or discontinuous parenting. Furthermore, it was her belief that emotional deprivation that occurs during the initial years of life leads to psychopathy. Any extended period of deprivation or parenting loss during the first five years was believed to cause psychopathy.

Recently (Yochelson and Samenow, 1976, 1977, 1986), it has been suggested that antisocial behavior is caused by faulty and irrational patterns of thinking rather than parental neglect, abuse, or early life deprivation. Indeed, Yochelson and Samenow (1976, 1977) provide an extensive clinical exploration of the faulty logic of the criminal mind and criminal modus operandi. These distorted thinking patterns cause, maintain, and reinforce the criminal's antisocial behavior style. These authors report that many, if not most, incarcerated psychopaths have responsible and relatively well adjusted parents. They provide convincing and exhaustive evidence which links criminal logic with antisocial behavior. Yochelson and Samenow (1986) reject traditional sociologic and psychologic "excuses" for criminality. They do note that all of the criminals in their study initiated a psychopathic lifestyle very early in life.

The antisocial personality (Kegan, 1986) has also been viewed as a "child" and developmental delay has been hypothesized to be the principal cause of this disorder. Antisocial personality disorder is a delay or developmental arrest at the level of latency. Research (Kegan, 1986) does suggest that psychopathy involves a disturbance in the ordinary progression of growth and development.

Doren (1987) has recently examined five comprehensive etiological models of antisocial personality disorder. However, these models are not explicit psychological theories of psychopathy. Each of these etiologic theories of antisocial personality disorder include sociological, genetic-familial, environmental, and psychological factors. Doren's (1987) integrative theory of psychopathy is clearly a multivariate model.

An interactive psychological-sociologic model (Gough, 1948) of psychopathy describes these individuals as manifesting a "deficiency in role-playing ability which is particularly liable to manifestation in social relationships" (p. 366). This deficit in role-playing is defined as "the capacity to look upon one's self as an object . . . or to identify with another's point of view" (p. 363). The psychopath (Gough, 1948) is unable to anticipate, understand, or internalize the roles of significant others or society in his or her life. Psychopaths can verbalize moral and social rules but they do not respond personally to these guidelines for behavior. Gough (1948) did not elucidate the origins of the psychopath's deficiency in role-playing ability. This theory of antisocial personality disorder has been well supported by two different avenues of research (Doren, 1987).

The Eysenck theory of psychopathy (Eysenck, 1964) is based upon a three-dimensional model of personality. Eysenck viewed the psychopath as a "genetically-predisposed" deficient learner. He also viewed psychopathy as "a half-way stage to psychosis." The conditionability deficiency theory of antisocial personality disorder describes psychopaths as "people located within a specific space within a multidimensional model of personality defined by high extraversion, high neuroticism, and high psychoticism" (Doren, 1987, p. 45). Research evidence with criminal populations utilizing the Eysenck psychometric instruments supports this theory. The psychological component of this theory explains antisocial behavior by elucidating why psychopaths do not condition with fear to aversive stimuli as do "normal" individuals. The general learning and conditioning components of this theory have also received substantial verification.

Another recent theory of antisocial personality disorder (Quay, 1965) purports that "an extreme of stimulation-seeking behavior" causes this disorder. Quay (1965) states "it is the impulsivity and the lack of even minimal tolerance for sameness which appear to be primary and distinctive features of the disorder . . . Psychopathic behavior (can be explained) in terms of the concepts of need for various sensory stimulation, adaption to sensory inputs, and the relationship of these to affect and motivation" (p. 180). In essence, there are two basic postulates to this theory of psychopathy: (1) psychopaths are characterized by a "primary abnormality in their physiological reaction to sensory input which causes a higher degree of optimal stimulation," and (2) "the psychopaths' assumed higher optimal level of stimulation leads to an extremely high degree of motivation to increase sensory stimulation so as to compensate for their underarousal due to physiological abnormality" (Doren, 1987, p. 49).

The Quay (1965) model of antisocial personality disorder theorizes that these individuals are born with a hyporeactive nervous system. A revision of this model (Quay, 1977) incorporates (1) the role of parental rejection, inconsistent discipline, and retreat in response to the psychopath's excessive stimulation-seeking during childhood, and (2) the psychopath's impaired ability to anticipate the painful and negative consequences of his or her physiologically determined stimulation-seeking behavior. Obviously, this etiological theory of antisocial personality disorder includes biological, familial, and psychological factors. It is also important to note that the sensation-seeking theory of antisocial personality disorder is well supported by empirical research (Doren, 1987).

A very recent theory of antisocial personality disorder (Doren, 1987) attempts to integrate the basic constructs, research evidence, and theoretical precepts from the Quay, Eysenck, Gough, and other models of this disorder. Doren's (1987) integrative or "control theory" of psychopathy is a complex and multidimensional psychological model of antisocial behavior. This model also includes biological-genetic factors and thus is not a "pure" psychological theory.

According to Doren (1987), antisocial personality disorder is caused by genetic-biologically determined lower levels of cortical arousal which also cause limbic system damage and a decreased capability to arrest or control behavior or general motor activity. Partial helplessness conditioning in combination with an inborn low level of cortical arousal are the "imperative factors for the development of psychopathy . . . these two factors together are necessary and sufficient, neither one being sufficient alone" (Doren, 1987, p. 83). Inconsistent discipline, parental punishment tactics, parental psychopathology, socialization, learned helplessness, and pathological control maneuvers are secondary factors which contribute to the etiology of antisocial personality disorder. Doren (1987) notes that "obtaining control over rewards by overcoming other people is what psychopaths' lives are all about" (p. 95). Indeed, the "control theory" of psychopathy illuminates the global and pathologic control tactics that constitute the basic pathology of the disorder. This etiologic model of psychopathy does include several major psychological components.

The DSM III and DSM III-R indicate that prepuberty conduct disorder and parental disciplinary style are predisposing psychological factors that contribute to the etiology of antisocial personality disorder. A psychological theory of antisocial personality disorder is not included in the DSM III or DSM III-R.

SOCIOLOGICAL-ENVIRONMENTAL THEORIES OF ANTISOCIAL PERSONALITY DISORDER

Sociologic and environmental theories of antisocial personality disorder generally view this form of behavior or adjustment style as a response of the individual to the conditions of his or her environment. Thus, societies and environments create psychopaths. This position is also central to sociologic and environmental theories of chemical dependency.

Poverty and deprivation (Yochelson and Samenow, 1986) have historically been viewed as primary causative factors in criminal behavior and psychopathy. It has been hypothesized that many people who grow up in ghettos and similar deprived environments develop criminal lifestyles in order to cope with the poverty, frustration, hopelessness, and anomie that can be caused by these environments.

It is interesting that most environmental examinations (McCord and McCord, 1964) of the origins and causes of psychopathy focus upon the early-life parenting and familial experiences of adult psychopaths. Unfortunately, these environmental and sociological models of antisocial personality disorder are also very psychological in nature. Thus, the roles of environmental, sociologic, and psychological factors in the etiology of antisocial personality disorder are interactive and not clearly defined. These theories are psychosocial in scope.

Parental antisocial behaviors and attitudes are associated with offspring psychopathy (Brantley and Sutker, 1984). Therefore, the family environment can contribute to the development of antisocial personality disorder. Psychopaths tend to have antisocial parents who model antisocial behaviors, attitudes, and cognitive styles. Moreover, these family environments do not include parents who model prosocial behaviors, attitudes, and beliefs. The psychological effects of ineffective or inadequate parenting upon personality development were discussed earlier in this chapter. These adverse realities may operate in combination with parental psychopathy to reinforce the development of antisocial personality disorder in offspring.

Peer group membership may also influence the development of antisocial personality disorder. Jessor and Jessor (1977) report that deviant or antisocial behaviors are interrelated. The peer social system is an environment which reinforces psychopathy when members of such a system engage in predominantly antisocial and nonconforming behaviors. Many adolescent peer groups (Orford, 1985) collectively engage in theft, school delinquency, sexual promiscuity, drinking, using other mood altering substances, and other antisocial behaviors. Adolescent rebellion involves varying degrees and types of antisocial acting-out.

Several other social and environmental factors have been associated with the etiology of antisocial personality disorder. Most of these explanations and models are very simplistic and cursory in scope. For example, the threat of nuclear holocaust, social alienation and anxiety, collective narcissism, social institutions, economic realities, permissive socialization, and "the American way of life" have all been cited as factors that cause or contribute to juvenile delinquency and antisocial behavior. Ultimately, social and environmental causation effects individual and collective patterns of adjustment in a very complex manner.

It should also be noted that anthropologists have investigated the cultural aspects of psychopathy and antisocial behavior. McCord and McCord (1964) indicate that social crisis, class structure, technological-social complexity, and cultural attitudes toward children influence the incidence of psychopathy within a culture. Cultural and anthropological studies of psychopathy were conducted during the 1930s and 1940s and generally involved the direct observation of social and familial behavior patterns among primitive cultures. DuBois (1944) observed a relationship between methods of socialization among the Alorese and psychopathic traits. The Alorese children were reared in an inconsistent, changing, and rejecting atmosphere. Alorese parents tease, ridicule, and deceive their children. According to DuBois (1944), this form of child training leads to a "typical" Alorese personality style which is psychopathic.

The DSM III-R indicates that "extreme poverty, removal from the home, and growing up without parental figures of both sexes" (p. 318) are predisposing factors in the etiology of antisocial personality disorder.

Sociologic and environmental theories of antisocial personality disorder are generally truncated and theoretical. These models are not empirically oriented and they are not based upon extensive research methodology. In sum, these models of antisocial personality disorder or psychopathy have contributed relatively little to our clinical understanding of the origins and evolution of this particular adjustment dynamism.

GENETIC-FAMILIAL AND BIOLOGICAL THEORIES OF ANTISOCIAL PERSONALITY DISORDER

Hereditary and genetic factors have long been associated with psychopathy. Pritchard, Pinel, Kraepelin, and the other "Victorian" psychiatrists postulated that an "inborn defect" caused "moral insanity." Thus, behavioral scientists have linked genetic factors with psychopathy for 150 years.

Partridge (1928) conducted one of the first comprehensive genealogical investigations of psychopathy and heredity. A meticulous examination of the lineage of 50 psychopaths revealed that 24 of the individuals had ancestors "in a direct line" who manifested psychopathic traits. Several similarly designed studies (Gottlieb, Ashley, and Knott, 1946) report that between 50 and 70 percent of psychopaths have ancestral disturbance. Newkirk (1957) stated "psychopathic traits are inheritable."

Kallman (1939) found that the children of psychopaths have a higher percentage of psychopathy than the siblings of psychopaths. Lange (1936) reported that 77 percent of identical twins and only 12 percent of fraternal twins had similar criminal histories. It is interesting that Glueck and Glueck (1956) report that delinquents are generally superior in gross body size, exhibit a more homogeneous build, and develop rapidly after the age of 14. These authors also report that over 60 percent of delinquents are mesomorphs. McCord and McCord (1964) conclude "the research on the constitutional or genetic basis of psychopathy is inconclusive and contradictory" (p. 60).

Recent investigations (Brantley and Sutker, 1984; Helzer and Pryzbeck, 1988) of the genetic transmission of antisocial behavior seem to generally indicate that genetic or congenital constitutional factors do play important roles in the transmission of psychopathy. These studies examine the twin offspring of psychopathic and/or criminal parents and the adopted children of criminals or psychopaths. Eysenck and Eysenck (1978) found that 55 percent of monozygous twins were concordant for criminal behavior as opposed to 13 percent of dizygous twins. Cloninger, Reich, and Guze (1978) reported concordance rates as high as 0.70 for monozygous twins and 0.28 for dizygous twins. This study provides a heritability estimate of 0.84. Schulsinger (1972) investigated adopted children and concluded that genetic factors are important in the etiology of psychopathy per se. In this study, it was found that psychopathy was more than five times as frequent among psychopathic probands' biologic fathers than adoptive fathers or the biologic fathers of control subjects.

Studies of prevalence of familial psychopathy and familial antisocial behavior (Cloninger, Reich, and Guze, 1978) report that hysteria and sociopathy occur more frequently among the relatives of psychopathic male, psychopathic female, and hysteric female probands than in the general population.

It is important to note that Cloninger, Reich, and Guze (1978) conclude that alcoholism and psychopathy may be genetically independent. Brantley and Sutker (1984) indicate "the literature indicates that the adult sons of Danish alcoholics adopted away in infancy showed an increased frequency of alcoholism but not of antisocial personality, while an increased proportion of psychopaths and criminals, but not alcoholics and drug dependents, was found among the adopted-away offspring of psychopathic parents" (p. 446). In a related study, Crowe (1974) found a higher incidence of antisocial personality among probands born to female felons than among the offspring of control subjects. The wives of convicted felons also came from disturbed family backgrounds and they manifest psychopathology that is similar to their husbands' first-degree relatives (Guze, Goodwin, and Crane, 1970).

Chromosomal aberrations have been found (Jacobs et al., 1965) among mentally subnormal male criminals who are also of tall stature and extremely aggressive or violent. This chromosomal aberration involves an extra Y chromosome and is referred to as the XYY genotype. The XYY genotype is associated with extreme episodic violence or aggression, low intelligence, behavioral pathology, and gonadal abnormalities. Many of these individuals are incarcerated in penal and psychiatric institutions. Recent research (Brantley and Sutker, 1984) suggests that the XYY genotype is not a potent predictor of antisocial or criminal behavior.

Several neurological or neurophysiological theories of antisocial personality disorder have been developed (McCord and McCord, 1964; Brantley and Sutker, 1984; Doren, 1987). Indeed, antisocial behavior has long been associated with brain damage and neurologic pathology. A few scientists (Thompson, 1953) have gone so far as to indicate that psychopathy is *always* related to cerebral injury. Aggressive and violent behavior is caused by damage to the area of the brain known as the hypothalamus. An extensive review of the clinical and research literature dealing with the neurologic aspects of psychopathy (McCord and McCord, 1964) reveals that (1) "psychopaths more often exhibit EEG abnormalities than do normal people, (2) compared with normal people, a greater proportion of psychopaths exhibit signs of neurological disorder (tremors, exaggerated reflexes, tics), (3) psychopaths are probably more physiologically responsive to physical changes in their environment, and (4) compared with normal people, a greater proportion of psychopaths have a history of early diseases which damage the brain" (p. 68). These findings have led some researchers to conclude that hypothalamus damage is frequently the cause of antisocial personality disorder. Hypothalamus damage may be caused by hereditary or genetic factors as well as intrauterine or post-birth head trauma.

Childhood hyperactivity (Satterfield, 1978; Morrison, 1980; Nace, 1990) has been theorized to be a precursor of antisocial personality disorder. Thus, excessive motor behaviors, high distractibility, short attention span, impulsivity, learning deficits, and low frustration tolerance may be precursors to juvenile delinquency and subsequent adult antisocial personality disorder.

Eysenck's theory of psychopathy (1964) purports that the psychopath has a sympathetic nervous system and limbic system which are excessively reactive to external stimuli. According to this model, the psychopath is described as a genetically-predisposed deficient learner who is cortically underaroused. Eysenck (1964) also demonstrated that psychopaths manifest a diminished capacity to learn when confronted with punishing stimuli as well as suppressed emotional reactivity to stimuli.

Quay (1965) described psychopathy as "an extreme of stimulation-seeking behavior" (p. 180). This biologically-based model of antisocial personality disorder is based upon two primary postulates: "psychopaths are characterized by a primary abnormality in their physiological reaction to sensory input which causes a high degree of optimal stimulation," and "the psychopaths' assumed higher optimal level of stimulation leads to an extremely high degree of motivation to increase sensory stimulation so as to compensate for their underarousal due to their physiological abnormality" (Doren, 1987, pp. 48-49). The psychopath begins life with an "inborn" hyporeactive nervous system. It should be noted that the sensation-seeking theory of antisocial personality disorder is strongly supported by empirical data.

Perhaps Hare's (1970) theory of antisocial personality disorder is the most in-depth biologic model presently available. This theory is based upon extensive research pertaining to the psychopath's physiology. According to Hare (1970), the psychopath manifests lesions (i.e., contusions) in the limbic system of the brain. These lesions affect the psychopath's ability to inhibit ongoing behavior and also impede behaviors or acts that are known to result in punishment. Thus, the antisocial person will engage in perseverative behavior regardless of the consequences that are associated with these acts. Hare points out that between 49 and 80 percent of psychopaths manifest abnormal EEGs with widespread slow-wave activity. Hare did not indicate if the brain lesions of psychopaths are genetically determined or caused by such factors as head trauma or faulty brain chemistry.

The most recent theories or models of antisocial personality disorder (Brantley and Sutker, 1984; Yochelson and Samenow, 1986; Reid et al., 1986; Doren, 1987; Nace, 1990) are multivariate in scope. These models do not purport that psychopathy is univariately caused by a genetic or biophysiological factor. For example, Doren (1987) states that "two factors are necessary and sufficient for the development of psychopathy: low cortical arousal and partial helplessness conditioning" (p. 132). While Doren theorizes that the psychopath has an "inborn" low level of cortical arousal, he also notes that psychopathy is facilitated vis à vis a diversity of familial, psychological, and social factors. Even the advocates of a neurochemical etiology of antisocial personality disorder (Porges, 1976; Mawson and Mawson, 1977) indicate that other factors contribute to the development of this disorder.

As touched upon earlier, antisocial behavior, delinquency, criminality, alcoholism, and chemical dependency have always been associated with families (Stanton, 1985; Cadoret, 1986). Lewis, Robins, and Rice (1985) found that over 57 percent of antisocial black males were also alcoholic. Only 15.4 percent of the nonantisocial males in this study were alcoholic. In this study alcohol abuse in probands seemed to be more related to familial alcohol problems while antisocial personality disorder was more related to familial antisocial behavior. Similarly, Cadoret and Cain (1981) found that adolescent antisocial behavior is increased in males who have alcoholic biologic parents (relatives) and in females who have antisocial biologic relatives.

Cadoret (1986) emphasizes the importance of a combination of genetic, familial, and environmental factors in the etiology of antisocial behavior. Crime and psychopathy are both related to alcohol abuse and dependency. Cadoret (1986) summarizes the research findings of Bohman and coworkers: "they found that criminality alone in the biologic parents tended to increase the risk of criminality in adopted-away sons but not to increase their alcohol abuse. On the other hand, alcohol abuse alone in the biologic parents increased the risk of alcohol abuse, but not criminality, in those sons. Parents manifesting both criminality and alcohol abuse seemed heterogeneous, in that sons showed an increased risk for alcohol abuse but not for both alcohol abuse and criminality. These investigations concluded that different genetic and environmental antecedents influenced the development of criminality" (pp. 35-36). It is also reported that criminality related to alcohol abuse is usually more violent, repetitive, and damaging to other people (Forrest and Gordon, 1990).

Criminality in women is related to criminality in a biologic parent (Bohman, 1983) and criminality rates are much higher in women's relatives than men's relatives. Cadoret (1986) indicates that alcohol abuse is "one of the more common behaviors of those with antisocial personality" (p. 36). He also suggests that estimates of heritability of antisocial personality may reflect the heritability of alcoholism or alcohol abuse. However, Cadoret (1985) found that "alcohol problems in biologic parents predicted increased alcohol abuse in the adopted-away children but not antisocial personality" (p. 37). According to these authors, this study demonstrates that "even when alcohol abuse and its genetic inheritance are controlled in a statistical model, antisocial personality is found to have a genetic background which is different from that of alcohol abuse, and that environmental factors are of additional importance" (p. 37). Indeed, family studies (Vaillant, 1983) and adoption studies show independent and different biological backgrounds for antisocial behavior and alcoholism. This research evidence suggests that there is a genetic and possibly environmental specificity of inheritance in these disorders.

The DSM III and DSM III-R indicate that biologic and familial factors contribute to the etiology of antisocial personality disorder. For example, the DSM III-R states "antisocial personality disorder is five times more common among first-degree biologic relatives of males with the disorder than among the general population. The risk to the first-degree biologic relatives of females with the disorder is nearly ten times that of the general population. Within a family that has a member with antisocial personality disorder, males more often have antisocial personality disorder and psychoactive substance use disorders, whereas females more often have somatization disorder. Adoption studies show that both genetic and environmental factors contribute to the risk of this group of disorders" (pp. 343-344). The DSM III-R clearly indicates that antisocial personality disorder and alcohol dependence or another substance use disorder are frequently co-existing diagnoses.

ETIOLOGICAL THEORIES
OF CONCURRENT *ANTISOCIAL PERSONALITY*
DISORDER AND SUBSTANCE USE DISORDER

At present, there are no systematic or comprehensive etiological theories of concurrent antisocial personality disorder and substance use disorder. Various psychological, sociological-environmental, and genetic-familial or biologic observations and clinical similarities pertaining to the etiology of concurrent antisocial personality and chemical dependency or substance abuse have been reported by clinicians and behavioral scientists (McCord and McCord, 1964; Cloninger, Reich, and Guzel, 1978; Forrest, 1983, 1990; Helzer and Pryzbeck, 1988; Nace, 1990). However, this data has not been synthesized into an integrated etiological theory or model of concurrent antisocial personality disorder and substance use disorder.

Psychological, environmental, and genetic-familial or biologic factors operate independently and interactively to shape or determine personality and adjustment style. Thus, these factors also interactively effect or facilitate the development of concurrent antisocial personality and chemical dependency or substance abuse. The DSM III-R recognizes three clusters of personality disorders. Cluster B personality disorders are characterized by erratic, emotional, or dramatic behavior and include the antisocial, narcissistic, borderline, and histrionic personality disorders. This cluster of personality disorders "has the strongest association with substance use disorders" (Nace, 1990). Cluster C personality disorders (passive-aggressive, obsessive-compulsive, dependent, and avoidant) also commonly include concurrent substance use disorders. Substance use disorders are less commonly reported among the Cluster A personality disorders (paranoid, schizoid, and schizotypal).

As reported earlier in this chapter, the commonality rate of substance use disorder and personality disorder is high. Antisocial personality disorder is the most commonly reported type of personality disorder in substance abusing patients (Nace, 1990). Researchers and clinicians have not yet reported the roles of specific etiological factors in this finding.

Essential psychological factors in the etiology of concurrent antisocial personality disorder and substance abuse disorder include childhood behavioral problems, hyperactivity, attention-deficit disorder, impulse control problems, conduct disorder, and affect intolerance (McCord and McCord, 1964; Doren, 1987). Early-life narcissistic injury and the development of an avoidance defense system (Forrest, 1983, 1984, 1991) are additional psychological precursors to the development of concurrent antisocial personality disorder and chemical dependency.

Family dysfunction (Black, 1981; Lawson and Lawson, 1992) is also central to the development of concurrent antisocial personality disorder and substance use disorder. The chemically dependent psychopath (Brantley and Sutker, 1984) evolves from a complicated and dysfunctional family system. The parents or surrogate parents of the adult antisocial and chemically dependent person tend to be physically abusive, cold, critical, brutal, and passive-aggressive or antisocial (Forrest, 1990). These parents also frequently have a learning disorder and/or are chemically dependent or substance abusers.

Environmental deprivation is a common characteristic of antisocial substance abusers. Perhaps the roles of environmental deprivation and family dysfunction in the etiology of concurrent ASPD and chemical dependency are most commonly seen among young blacks and other inner city minority groups. The inner city "crack" addict generally comes from a broken or fatherless home, manifests an extended history of physical and psychological abuse, drops out of school, and is socially, psychologically, and economically impoverished. These individuals are also hyperactive, angry and enraged, poorly controlled, and experience chronic difficulties with authority figures.

Genetic and biologic factors (Cloninger, Reich, and Gize, 1978; Wallace, 1985, 1992; Manchester, 1992) are clearly causative variables in the etiology of ASPD, alcoholism, and substance use disorders. The specific influence of genetic and biologic factors in the etiology of concurrent ASPD and substance use disorders remains unclear. Some researchers and clinicians (Cloninger, Reich, and Guze, 1978) conclude that alcoholism and antisocial personality disorder seem to be genetically independent. Brantley and Sutker (1984) report that identical twin research involving alcoholic and antisocial populations supports this position. However, Lewis, Robins, and Rice (1985) found that over 57 percent of antisocial black males were alcoholics. Only 15.4 percent of the nonantisocial males in this study were alcoholic. As noted earlier, studies by Hesselbrock, Meyer, and Kenner (1985), Rounsaville et al. (1983), and Hesselbrock and Pryzbeck (1988) report a high concordance of ASPD and alcoholism or substance use disorder. Cadoret (1986) stresses the importance of a combination of genetic, familial, and environmental factors in the etiology of antisocial behavior. Yet, as noted earlier in this chapter, Cadoret concluded "antisocial personality is found to have a genetic background which is different from that of alcohol abuse, and environmental factors are of additional importance."

Finally, it must be noted that chemical dependency is a precursor to the development of antisocial personality disorder and/or other personality disorders and vice versa. Personality disorder can also be considered a predisposing factor in substance use disorder! Substance use and chemical dependency facilitate acting-out, poor impulse control, self-centeredness, anger and aggressiveness, manipulativeness, brain dysfunction, and the various other cognitive-behavioral-affective-social parameters of ASPD. Likewise, the "set" of symptoms which the personality disordered child or adolescent manifest simply increases the probability of developing a substance use disorder during late adolescence or adulthood.

Nace (1990) astutely notes that substance abuse may produce a syndrome that is diagnostically compatible with the personality disorders. He states "etiologically, intoxicating substances produce a combination of toxic-organic effects on brain function and reinforcement of regressive behavior. This combination may result in a "generic" personality disorder which is secondary, not primary, to alcoholism and drug dependence" (p. 188). Thus, a personality disorder increases an individual's vulnerability to substance use disorder while substance abuse also leads to the development of ASPD or a clinically similar personality disorder.

The following brief case study illustrates several etiologic factors in the development of concurrent antisocial personality disorder and chemical dependency.

Tanya C. was a 19-year-old single college student. She was referred for therapy by her parents shortly after making a suicide attempt and following a subsequent psychiatric hospitalization while in college.

The client was initially seen in two family therapy sessions. At this point, the client refused to participate in further family treatment and was seen within the context of individual therapy sessions. During the course of limited treatment engagement, the client revealed to the therapist that she began drinking on weekends at age 11, smoked marijuana several times each day for three years, and episodically abused "speed" and cocaine. She experienced her first alcohol-induced "blackout" at age 13. She began "cutting classes" in the eighth grade, experienced chronic academic and peer difficulties, and ran away from home for short intervals of time on several occasions while in high school. The client became sexually active at age 14. She engaged in group sex a number of times during her freshmen year of college and eventually became pregnant and had an abortion while in college.

Tanya was described by her parents as "out of control." Mr. C. was a high school administrator and his wife was an elementary school teacher. Both parents had completed graduate degrees and were quite successful in their careers. However, Mr. C. described himself as a "former alcoholic." He had been totally alcohol abstinent for some 17 years at the time of treatment engagement. His father had committed suicide and was described as a "heavy drinker." Mr. and Mrs. C. were quite concerned and perplexed about Tanya's acting-out. While Mr. and Mrs. C. were on vacation Tanya had "parties" in the family home. Some of the parties involved as many as 50-100 other teens and resulted in hundreds of dollars of damage to the C's home. Needless to say, alcohol, drugs, fights, and sexual acting-out were central to these "parties." Tanya was actually physically assaulted at one party and one of her "friends" stole her father's checkbook and forged several hundred dollars of checks at a local grocery store! The C's were equally concerned about Tanya's chronic inability to tell the truth, lying, manipulativeness, and irresponsibility. Tanya seemed to live life according to her own truths and demands and always expected others to do what she wanted.

A few weeks after Tanya unilaterally terminated therapy sessions, the therapist received a "crisis" call from her parents. Tanya had stolen one of the family cars, two credit cards, and several hundred dollars and left the state. Her parents were understandably distraught and anxious about reporting these events to the police. Mr. C. stated to the therapist "I've known she was an alcoholic or druggie for years, but it's hard to accept that your own kid is a psychopath . . . or just no good." Nearly two years after the last contact with the client's parents, the therapist read in a local newspaper that she had been arrested for manufacturing, selling, and distributing illicit drugs. Eventually, Tanya was sent to the state penitentiary.

This case study involved several of the psychological, social, and genetic-familial factors that were discussed earlier in the chapter: early onset substance use disorder, familial alcoholism and/or mental illness, school problems, sexual promiscuity, impulsiveness, and conduct disorder. These processes interactively shape and determine the course of concurrent antisocial personality disorder and chemical dependency or substance use disorder.

SUMMARY

This chapter examined the etiology of substance use disorders, antisocial personality disorder, and concurrent antisocial personality disorder and substance use disorder. The major psychological, sociological-environmental, and genetic-familial-biologic theories or etiological models of substance use disorders, antisocial personality disorder, and concurrent ASPD and substance use disorder were elucidated.

The tension reduction or "relief" theory of alcoholism was reviewed. Social learning models, personality theory, psychoanalytic theory, and recent expectancy, cognitive, and multivariate theories of alcoholism and substance abuse were also reviewed. The roles of family, environment, culture, poverty, peer group influence, economy, politics, deprivation, and minority group membership in the etiology of alcoholism and substance use disorders were explored in this chapter.

Genetic and biophysical factors in the etiology of substance use disorders were discussed. Most of these models (Wallace, 1989; Manchester, 1992) are based upon familial, longitudinal, or biologic investigations of alcoholics and their offspring. Goodwin et al. (1977) report that the sons of alcoholics are four times more likely to be alcoholic than the sons of nonalcoholics independently of whether they are raised by their alcoholic parents. Furthermore, there may be genetic subtypes of alcoholism. The "disease" model of addictions and DSM III-R genetic-familial information were briefly discussed. It is generally believed (Forrest and Gordon, 1990) that all substance use disorders are multivariantly determined.

Unlike the early theories of alcoholism and other substance use disorders, antisocial personality disorder seems to have historically been viewed as a disorder with multiple etiologic causality. Thus, parental rejection, emotional deprivation, parental psychopathology, and physical abuse by parents have been hypothesized to be key etiologic factors in antisocial personality disorder. The recent psychological theories of ASPD (Gough, 1948; Eysenck, 1964; Quay, 1965; Yochelson and Samenow, 1986; Doren, 1987) were discussed in this chapter.

Several sociological and environmental theories of antisocial personality disorder were also examined in this chapter. Poverty and deprivation, parental psychopathy, peer influence, and cultural factors have been theorized to cause or influence the development of antisocial personality disorder.

Psychiatrists and behavioral scientists of the mid- and late 1800s speculated than an "inborn defect" caused "moral insanity." Early investigations of genetic and familial factors in psychopathy (Gottlieb, Ashley, and Knott, 1946) found that well over half of psychopaths have ancestral histories that include psychopaths, epileptics, and schizophrenics. Newkirk (1957) indicated that psychopathic traits are "inheritable." Recently, Eysenck and Eysenck (1978) found that 55 percent of monozygous twins were concordant for criminal behavior as opposed to 13 percent of dizygous twins. Several other researchers and clinicians (Schulsinger, 1972; Cloninger, Reich, and Guze, 1978; Brantley and Sutker, 1984) conclude that genetic and familial factors contribute significantly to the etiology of antisocial personality disorder.

The Eysenck (1964), Jacobs et al. (1965), Quay (1965), Hare (1970), Yochelson and Samenow (1976, 1977, 1986), Cadoret (1986), and Doren (1987) theories of antisocial personality disorder were examined in this chapter. DSM-III and DSM III-R information pertaining to genetic and familial factors in antisocial personality disorder were also included.

The genetic-familial and biological interrelationships between antisocial behavior, delinquency, criminality, alcoholism, and substance use disorders were discussed. Homicide and a diversity of violent behaviors are closely associated with alcoholism and drug abuse (Forrest and Gordon, 1990). Substance use disorder can be a precursor to the development of ASPD and ASPD is often a precursor to the onset of chemical dependency (Nace, 1990).

It is clearly apparent that multiple causality associated with assortative mating, genetics, learning and conditioning, familial dynamics, environment, culture, and brain chemistry (Wallace, 1985, 1989) causes and maintains both ASPD and substance use disorders. Univariate models of antisocial personality disorder and substance use disorders do not adequately explain the causes and persistence of these patterns of adjustment.

Chapter V

Differential Diagnosis
of Substance Use Disorders,
Antisocial Personality Disorder,
and Related Personality Disorders

INTRODUCTION

The differential diagnosis and assessment of psychological disorders is always germane to the processes of providing effective and appropriate treatments for such disorders. For example, a psychiatrist or psychologist must first determine that a given patient is in fact clinically depressed prior to treating the patient for a depressive disorder. It would be clinically inappropriate and highly unethical to prescribe antidepressant medication and provide various other treatments for depression to people who are not depressed.

Unfortunately, an accurate differential diagnosis of psychological disorders and psychiatric "diseases" is not always easily accomplished. Furthermore, behavioral scientists manifest a diversity of opinions and beliefs about the usefulness and therapeutic efficacy of "diagnosing" people who manifest psychological problems. Many behavioral scientists (Rogers, 1952; Glasser, 1965; Szasz, 1976) reject the concept of "psychiatric disease" and thus do not diagnose the psychological illnesses or pathology of their clients. According to Szasz (1961, 1974, 1976), it is highly irrational for psychiatrists or other behavioral scientists to (1) "diagnose" diseases that are, in fact, not diseases, and (2) attempt to provide treatments, based upon the diagnosis of diseases that are not diseases, that will "cure" these non-existent diseases! Szasz (1961) refers to these realities in his book, *The Myth of Mental Illness.* He also indicates that many, if not most, people who are diagnosed as manifesting some form of mental illness or disease do not really want to be "treated" for their malaise. Thus, psychiatric diagnoses became labels that stigmatize, dehumanize, and alienate people. This viewpoint of the diagnostic process further suggests that diagnostic labels can be iatrogenic rather than therapeutic and beneficial to the well-being of the patient.

In spite of the many controversial issues that are associated with the roles and relevance of differential diagnosis in the mental health and chemical dependency treatment fields, most behavioral scientists agree that effective treatment interventions are directly related to appropriate differential assessment or diagnosis (Forrest, 1984; Yalisove, 1989). Indeed, increasing numbers of mental health clinicians are being sued for malpractice associated with improper or misdiagnosis that results in the use of inadequate or inappropriate treatment interventions. There is also a growing awareness among mental health and chemical dependency treatment personnel (Pattison, 1987; Emrick, 1991) that maximally effective psychotherapy or psychological care is contingent upon matching patients with therapists and appropriate treatments. These processes are obviously related to an accurate differential diagnosis or assessment of the client as well as other therapist skills!

This chapter examines the (1) diagnostic process and treatment oriented sources of gain that are associated with the process of differential diagnosis, (2) clinical diagnosis of substance use disorders, (3) DSM III-R (APA, 1987) diagnosis of substance use disorders, (4) clinical diagnosis of antisocial personality disorder, (5) DSM III-R diagnosis of antisocial personality disorder, (6) differential diagnosis of substance use disorders and antisocial personality disorder, and (7) differential diagnosis of related personality disorders.

THE DIAGNOSTIC PROCESS

It is important to realize that the clinician determines a client's diagnosis vis-à-vis the diagnostic process. Diagnosis is process oriented and the diagnostic process begins when the "patient enters the therapist's office and begins to communicate and interact with the secretary or other office personnel" (Forrest, 1984, p. 29). For example, some chemically dependent clients are angry and even verbally abusive toward the therapist's receptionist. Transactions such as these may give the therapist clues about the patient's behavior style and personality structure.

The therapist formulates an initial diagnostic impression of the patient as he or she begins to interact with the patient within the context of the initial clinical interview. The diagnostic process continues to develop as the therapist and patient interact throughout the course of subsequent diagnostic assessment sessions or perhaps via the therapeutic relationship. During the initial process of diagnostic interviewing, the clinician actively explores the patient's substance use history, family history, legal history, medical history, social history, educational history, and vocational-career status. Psychological testing, medical evaluation, and consultation with the patient's spouse, children, parents, employer, or significant others can add depth and clinical validity to the initial diagnostic impression.

An initial diagnosis or diagnostic impression is not absolute or final. Indeed, the experienced and astute clinician views an initial diagnostic impression as tentative and subject to change. This is especially true in situations where the patient enters intensive psychotherapy (Fromm-Reichmann, 1949; Kernberg, 1984; Forrest, 1984, 1991; Yalisove, 1989). The psychotherapist continues to expand and refine his or her initial diagnostic impression of the patient based upon the depth and intense learning that occurs within the context of the therapeutic relationship. As the therapeutic alliance intensifies and develops, the patient progressively reveals more and more in-depth information and experiential data about himself or herself. The therapeutic process helps the therapist continually build upon or modify his or her initial assessment of the patient.

The psychotherapeutic process always reveals and uncovers diagnostic information that was not known to the therapist during the initial contacts with the patient. For example, the patient who appears to manifest a passive-aggressive personality disorder may begin to lie to the therapist, miss scheduled appointments, fail to pay for treatment or begin to write "bad checks" for treatment, or physically threaten the therapist. This pattern of behavior may not be overtly apparent during the initial three or four contacts with a patient. However, the evolution of this pattern of behavior within the context of the therapeutic relationship and in combination with other acting-out conflicts upon the part of the patient should result in the therapist's consideration of a diagnosis of antisocial personality disorder. The evolution and unmasking of the real self within the context of the therapeutic relationship can result in a different diagnosis of the patient at different points in the treatment process.

Effective psychotherapeutic treatment always modifies the patient's initial diagnosis. Thus, a patient who is successfully treated for anxiety neurosis is no longer diagnosed as manifesting an anxiety disorder! Recovering substance abusers or chemically dependent patients are classified "in remission" (DSM III-R).

The diagnostic status of a patient (Forrest, 1991) may change radically at any point in the psychotherapeutic process. A moderately depressed patient might become psychotically depressive or even manic while in treatment. In all of these situations, the clinician needs to remember that (1) the patient's initial diagnosis will not always be final, (2) all diagnoses are process oriented rather than static in nature, and (3) a patient's diagnosis may change radically over a period of hours, days, or months. Furthermore, as elucidated later in this chapter, many patients are appropriately diagnosed as manifesting two or more concurrent disorders.

When the therapist has formulated his or her initial diagnostic impression of the patient, I have suggested (Forrest, 1978, 1984, 1985, 1991) that this formulation be openly and honestly shared with the patient. This general clinical-diagnostic stance is particularly appropriate in psychotherapeutic work with the chemically dependent patient. It is also appropriate for the clinician to openly tell the patient that he or she (1) has not been able to formulate a precise diagnosis of the patient's substance use and/or psychological disorder, (2) has changed the patient's diagnosis, or (3) has diagnosed the patient as manifesting multiple or "dual" diagnoses.

The practice of openly discussing the patient's diagnosis facilitates several sources of therapeutic gain. This technique is based upon the clinician's willingness to be open, honest, and straightforward with the patient. It does not encompass therapeutic distortion, manipulation, deception, or denial. The basic reality of the patient's symptom structure is shared with the patient in a supportive and non-threatening manner. This procedure lets the patient know exactly how the therapist perceives his or her symptom structure, helps to minimize therapist involvement in "patsy" roles, and provides for further patient-to-therapist exploration of the patient's problems. This therapeutic strategy is helpful in assessing the patient's readiness for therapy and motivation or commitment to treatment.

The diagnostic process facilitates the development of a working and productive therapeutic alliance. Indeed, the diagnostic process is a precursor to the therapeutic process. It can be extremely therapeutic for the patient to simply hear and learn that another human being understands his or her difficulties. The diagnostic process also helps to instill in the patient a sense of hope. Diagnosis literally means "knowing through." The therapeutic technique of openly and actively sharing the patient's diagnosis incorporates the magic of words (May, 1973) and is tantamount to the therapist saying "I understand your conflicts and their cause—we can work together to effect constructive and positive changes in your life."

Finally, the technique of openly discussing diagnostic information with the patient helps to establish (1) the need or lack of need for psychotherapy, (2) appropriate treatment modalities, (3) treatment goals and what can be expected to change as a function of treatment, and (4) areas of psychotherapy or treatment outcome assessment. It is important for the therapist to explain to the patient why he or she needs to enter treatment as well as what the patient can realistically expect to gain from the experience of psychotherapy. These issues need to be addressed prior to the actual initiation of treatment. This technique is confrontation oriented (Forrest, 1982) and represents the therapist's first systematic attempt to resolve the chemically dependent patient's avoidance defense system (Forrest, 1983). Diagnostic sharing can be an integral component in therapeutic relationship building.

All of the factors discussed in this section of the chapter help to clarify the usefulness and therapeutic relevance of diagnosis in the mental health and addictions field. When utilized appropriately, the diagnostic process facilitates patient engagement with the therapist and enhances therapeutic outcome. These sources of gain are antithetical to patient alienation, labeling, and the alleged stigmas that have been purported to occur as a function of the diagnostic process (Szasz, 1961, 1976). Indeed, the diagnostic process can serve to motivate the patient for treatment and facilitate movement toward and with the therapist as well as significant others. All chemical dependency counselors and mental health therapists can improve their therapeutic efficiency by utilizing the diagnostic model that was developed in this section of the chapter.

CLINICAL DIAGNOSIS
OF SUBSTANCE USE DISORDERS

In a basic and simple sense, substance abusers are individuals who (1) excessively ingest any mood altering substance, (2) develop an obsessive-compulsive and thus uncontrollable style or pattern of ingesting an addictive, mood altering substance, (3) experience interpersonal problems as a result of substance use, (4) develop medical, legal, social, psychological, or other significant living problems as a result of substance use, and (5) usually are unable to stop or radically modify their pattern of substance abuse for a protracted period of time without treatment or some form of external intervention.

In accord with the clinical diagnostic parameters of this simplistic definition of "substance abuser," substance abuse can be distinguished from substance use and chemical dependency. Substance use is *not* the excessive ingestion of an addictive, mood altering substance. Thus, the social drinker or responsible drinker (Forrest, 1989) engages in substance use (drinking involves the ingestion of an addictive, mood altering chemical) but not substance abuse or chemical dependency. Substance abuse *is* the excessive ingestion of an addictive, mood altering substance. However, substance abuse is not clinically the same as substance dependence. The chemically dependent person, unlike the substance abuser, manifests an obsessive-compulsive and uncontrollable pattern of ingesting an addictive, mood altering substance. These individuals are also physiologically dependent and addicted.

People who develop patterns of substance abuse and chemical dependency may experience interpersonal, medical, legal, psychological, and various other living problems as a direct result of their abusive or addictive use of any mood altering drug. It is also clinically important to note that many substance abusers as well as chemically dependent persons do not manifest *overt* medical, social, legal, or other living problems as a result of their use of addictive substances. Yet, these problems almost invariably become overt at some point in the chemically dependent person's career of substance use. Virtually all alcoholics experience global deterioration during the later stages (Forrest, 1978) of the addiction process.

Substance use can always potentially lead to the development of a substance use disorder or substance dependence. The user of a mood altering, addictive substance can develop a pattern of substance abuse or chemical dependency. In most cases of substance use disorder, the progression from substance use to abuse and eventually dependence occurs over a protracted period of time. For example, alcoholism or minor tranquilizer dependence is usually diagnosed (Zimberg, 1982; Forrest, 1984) after years of use and abuse and addiction may occur (Helfrisch, 1986; Knauert, 1992) in a matter of weeks or months.

Historically, the clinical diagnosis of alcoholism and other substance use disorders (Wallace, 1985, 1991; Bratter and Forrest, 1985) has been closely associated with the medical and "disease" models of health care. Alcoholics Anonymous, Narcotics Anonymous, and several other self-help treatment programs are based upon the disease model of alcoholism or drug addiction. According to the disease model (Wallace, 1985, 1989), alcoholism and other addictive "diseases" (1) are progressive, (2) have diagnosable symptoms, (3) run in families, (4) are treatable, and (5) are often fatal when left untreated. Wallace (1985) states "there is little doubt that alcoholism is a disease." He provides extensive brain chemistry and family history-genetic data to support the disease model of alcoholism. Thus, a clinical diagnosis of substance dependence or chemical dependency is made when the patient has *progressed* in his or her use/abuse of an addictive, mood altering substance to the point of being physically and psychologically dependent. The patient has also developed an increased tolerance to the physical and psychological effects of an addictive, mood altering substance when a clinical diagnosis of chemical dependency is made. Furthermore, the patient will experience a varying degree of physical and psychological withdrawal when he or she terminates the use of the addictive substance.

The disease model of substance abuse and chemical dependency provides rather gross diagnostic parameters that are based upon the patient's history and course of substance use. Medical or physiological symptoms may help to facilitate the diagnosis of alcohol dependence. Cirrhosis of the liver, cardiomyopathy, neurological symptoms, gastrointestinal complications, elevated blood pressure, and malnutrition are but a few of the clinical signs and symptoms that are frequently associated with a diagnosis of chronic alcoholism. These medical symptoms may develop as an explicit result of chronic, heavy ethanol use and they tend to become progressively worse as the patient continues to drink. Several thousand alcoholics die each year as a result of these complications.

Various psychological, social and familial, and other symptoms have been associated with the disease-oriented clinical diagnostic model of substance use disorders. Thus, loss of control, personality deterioration or changes, "black-outs," divorce and family dysfunction, sexual dysfunction or deviation, and "craving" are but a few of the psychosocial diagnostic indices of the substance use disorders. According to the disease model, the substance user who has an addictive disease progressively experiences loss of control, "uncontrollable craving" for alcohol or another drug, personality and behavioral deterioration, and myriad other psychosocial symptoms as he or she progresses from substance use to abuse and eventually chemical dependency. The disease model of chemical dependency has both helped and hindered the treatment of hundreds of thousands of people over the past 50 years. It is only in recent years that advocates of the disease model have begun to focus upon the treatment of familial, psychosocial, and intrapsychic pathology that is caused or associated with the disease of chemical dependency.

The clinical diagnosis and differential assessment of substance use disorders (Knauert, 1979; Forrest, 1984; Gorski and Miller, 1986) has encompassed a reliance upon the disease model for over 40 years. This model is univariant and has been criticized (Blane and Leonard, 1987) for its failure to take into account the multivariant as well as individualized aspects of all addictive disorders. Clinicians who rely heavily upon the disease model of substance use have assumed a priori that all substance abusers progress through a series of developmental stages that eventually result in chemical dependency. Such is not the case. Chemically dependent persons and substance abusers manifest a diversity of personality traits, substance use/abuse/dependency styles, and cognitive-affective adjustments. Indeed, it has been noted (Forrest, 1989) that the essential common denominator among all alcoholics is simply the inability to drink responsibly or with control! Many substance users do not progress to the stage of abuse and many abusers do not become floridly dependent.

Jellinek (1960) was one of the first behavioral scientists to empirically describe and define different diagnostic patterns of substance abuse and chemical dependency. He described five primary subtypes of alcoholism: alpha, beta, gamma, delta, and epsilon. Jellinek defined alcoholism as "any use of alcoholic beverages that causes any damage to the individual or society or both." Alpha alcoholism was described as a dependence on the effects of alcohol to relieve emotional and/or physical pain. According to Jellinek (1960), alpha alcoholics have not lost the ability to control their drinking and they do not experience acute withdrawal symptoms when they stop drinking. These individuals do not experience a progression of the disease process. Beta alcoholism does not involve physical or physiological dependence upon ethanol. However, gamma alcoholism was defined as an addiction to alcohol with progressive loss of control over drinking. This form of alcoholism is felt to be very prevalent in the United States (Jellinek, 1960) and is closely associated with the disease model of alcoholism. Delta alcoholism is similar to gamma alcoholism. However, Delta alcoholics may be able to stop drinking for short periods of time. Epsilon alcoholism is closely associated with episodic or "binge" drinking.

The clinical diagnosis of all substance use disorders and "addictive diseases" has generally followed the guidelines established by Jellinek (1960) and the disease concept that was originally developed by Alcoholics Anonymous (1939). Thus, most clinicians and behavioral scientists rely heavily upon the disease model in order to assess and treat people who manifest a diversity of substance use disorders. The disease model became widely recognized and utilized as a diagnostic tool within the confines of alcohol and drug treatment centers throughout the United States during the 1970s and 1980s.

In accord with this clinical model, the marijuana or cocaine abuser is an individual who is unable to control his or her drug use. As touched upon earlier, all chemically dependent persons experience a compulsion to engage in drug taking behavior and these individuals are generally unable to remain drug abstinent for extended periods of time. Chemical dependency frequently results in the outcropping of family, marital, legal, vocational, psychological, and spiritual problems. Many substance abusers progress in their drug taking behaviors and careers to the stage of addiction or chemical dependency. At this point, the chemically dependent person is physically and psychologically drug dependent. Most chemically dependent persons manifest drug related problems that affect every aspect of their lives.

The disease-oriented model of assessment can be applied to all forms of substance use, abuse, and dependency. This model can also be utilized to diagnose and evaluate various other forms of addictive or compulsive behavior. The disease model has been used to assess eating disorders (Valette, 1990), gambling (Hunter, 1988), and compulsive sexual behavior (Vraa, 1988; Eisenstadt, 1989, 1992).

Knight (1937) developed a clinical diagnostic model of alcoholism that has recently been applied to other substance use disorders (Forrest, 1984; Forrest and Gordon, 1990). This model originally (Knight, 1937; Knauert, 1979) described three subtypes of alcoholism. Primary alcoholism occurs "(1) in the absence of a co-existing psychiatric disorder, or (2) when the psychiatric disorder develops after the onset of alcoholism. Secondary alcoholism develops after the onset of a major psychiatric disorder and reactive alcoholism occurs in response to a major traumatic life event" (Forrest, 1984, pp. 33-34).

The primary alcoholic or primary chemically dependent person does not manifest a major underlying psychiatric/psychological disorder. These individuals also have not experienced a specific life event that has triggered their excessive alcohol consumption or other chemical dependency. Primary alcoholics and primary chemically dependent individuals manifest an intense relationship with alcohol or other addictive substances, and this relationship seems to be present as soon as they discover the effects of substance use. These patients develop a physical and psychological dependence upon alcohol and/or other mood altering chemicals. Their dependency relationship with ethanol is denied. However, this relationship is so intense that it emotionally parallels a love relationship. Narcissistic injury (Forrest, 1983, 1985) is a basic component of primary chemical dependency. Parental and family drug abuse, alcoholism, and chemical dependency are frequently associated with this diagnostic category. Hyperactivity, anxiety, depression, acting-out, and a lengthy history of substance use are essential characteristics of primary alcoholics and other substance abusers. A final diagnostic feature of primary substance use disorder involves the rather fast return to a relatively normal cognitive, interpersonal, and affective adjustment that occurs when these individuals establish and maintain drug abstinence.

Secondary alcoholism and chemical dependency develops in people who use alcohol and other mood altering chemicals for purposes of self-medication. These individuals abuse and/or become addicted to various substances in order to cope with a major, underlying psychiatric disorder. Secondary substance abusers or secondary alcoholics may manifest a thought disturbance, manic-depressive illness, borderline personality disorder, organic brain syndrome, or severe psychoneurotic disturbance. Many of these individuals remain at the stage of substance abuse and do not become chemically dependent or physiologically addicted. The onset of serious psychological/psychiatric disturbance preempts the development of alcohol/substance abuse and/or chemical dependency in secondary substance dependence. Secondary substance abusers often experience an acute exacerbation of their psychological problems following detoxification or an extended period of drug abstinence. An accurate diagnosis of secondary alcoholism or secondary substance use disorder can be made after the patient has been totally drug-free for a few weeks. Gross psychiatric symptomatology in the absence of alcohol/drug use is essential to this diagnosis. Appropriate treatment of the underlying psychiatric disorder may result in the amelioration of the patient's secondary substance use disorder.

Reactive substance dependence is triggered by a traumatic or situational life event. Thus, an object loss, serious accident or illness, or job loss may precipitate a pattern of substance abuse or even substance dependence. Reactive alcoholism (Zimberg, 1982) may develop in response to a divorce, death of a spouse or child, or other major trauma. Reactive substance abuse or chemical dependency can be viewed as an attempt to deny, repress, and cope with very ego-threatening feelings that are associated with object loss via intoxication. Drug abstinence and therapeutic resolution of the patient's affects and pathologic cognitions that are associated with object loss are central ingredients in the successful treatment of reactive alcoholics and reactive substance abusers. Most of these patients have an excellent treatment prognosis.

There are several psychological tests and medical tests that can be used to diagnose the substance use disorders. The Minnesota Multiphasic Personality Inventory (Dahlstrom and Welsh, 1960) is useful in the assessment of substance use disorders. A few specific MMPI profile configurations (Forrest, 1984; Forrest and Gordon, 1990) are consistently associated with alcoholism and substance abuse. The MacAndrew Alcoholism Scale (MacAndrew, 1965), Alcohol Use Inventory (Horn, Wanberg, and Foster, 1974), Michigan Alcoholism Screening Test (Selzer, 1971), and the Self-Administered Alcoholism Screening Test (Morse and Swenson, 1975) are psychological tests that are widely used in the diagnosis and assessment of drinking disorders. Most of these instruments are designed to assess drinking patterns and behaviors. Psychological tests are being developed to specifically assess other substance use disorders. Unfortunately, most of the instruments that are presently available to diagnose substance use disorders other than alcoholism/alcohol abuse do not meet acceptable validity and reliability standards (Emrick, 1991).

Medical and physical examinations can aid in the diagnosis of substance use disorders. Basic urinanalysis testing (Sauls, 1988) can detect the use of substances such as cocaine, marijuana, tranquilizers, narcotics, alcohol, amphetamines, barbiturates, phenothiazines or major tranquilizers, caffeine, nicotine, and anti-depressants. One test of abnormal liver function (Seram gamma-glutamy transterase or GGT) appears to be useful in the diagnosis of alcoholism (Schuckit, 1981). The amino acid metabolism test, and computer analysis of the SMA-12, SMA-22, and CBC tests can also be useful in the diagnosis of drinking disorders.

The following two brief case studies are presented as clinical examples of substance use disorders. These cases include the various diagnostic features that are associated with the clinical assessment of substance use disorders as discussed in this section of the chapter.

Case 1. Larry S., a 41-year-old self-employed barber, entered outpatient psychotherapy with the author some six years ago. The patient stated in the initial interview "I'm just drinking too damned much and I think that I need some help to stop." The patient was seen within the context of 11 individual psychotherapy sessions over a period of three and one-half months. At present, the patient has been totally alcohol and drug abstinent for over six years.

At the point of treatment engagement, Larry was anxious and experiencing acute relationship conflicts with his common law wife. In essence, she had recently given him an ultimatum: "Get sober, or get out!" This relationship had lasted over six years. Larry had been married once previously and he indicated that he did not want his present common law marital relationship to end as a result of his drinking. The patient reported that he had been consuming between a pint and a fifth of bourbon every night for approximately ten years prior to entering treatment. He had not seen a physician or completed any type of physical examination in over 15 years!

The patient completed the Minnesota Multiphasic Personality Inventory (MMPI) and the Alcohol Use Inventory (AUI) following the initial psychotherapy session. His overall MMPI profile (4-2-7) was suggestive of impulse control problems, low frustration tolerance, depression, obsessive-compulsive traits, and heavy drinking. All of the MMPI t-scores were below 80. The patient's AUI results indicated that he was an obsessive-compulsive drinker, a sustained drinker, experiencing loss of control when drinking, experiencing post-drinking worry, guilt, and fear, and his drinking was provoking marital conflict. His general alcoholism scale was at the 84th percentile. In sum, the psychological test results were indicative of alcohol dependence. Clinically, the patient was anxious and mildly depressive. There was no indication of thought disturbance, brain impairment, major affective illness, or severe personality disorder. The patient's clinical diagnosis was primary alcoholism.

Larry's father had died from alcoholic liver disease at age 52. His mother's father was also an alcoholic. The patient's parents divorced when Larry was a child. Larry began drinking and driving at age 14 and was arrested for drinking and driving at age 19. He regretted that his first wife repeatedly referred to him as a "drunk." The patient's pattern of drinking had been a major factor in his previous divorce. The patient indicated "I knew I had a drinking problem when I was 18, but I wouldn't admit it–I sure as hell didn't want to see a shrink." He also verbalized "I've always drank a lot because I like the way it makes me feel–I drink for the effects, . . . it feels like magic, and I don't know if I want to stop . . . maybe I can't stop and that means I'm a real alkie." The patient had attempted to stop drinking without professional treatment several times but failed. He had also experienced mild alcohol withdrawal symptoms in the past and indicated that he "craved" alcohol daily.

This patient was referred for medical evaluation and was subsequently detoxified on an inpatient basis for five days. He was then seen 11 times in outpatient psychotherapy. The patient refused to attend Alcoholics Anonymous and did not take Antabuse. His therapy was essentially supportive in nature and involved a limited amount of genetic reconstruction work. Treatment was highly effective in this case. Larry has been abstinent for over six years and the "marital" relationship is reportedly radically improved. The patient's anxiety and depression remitted shortly after detoxification was completed. The patient continues to call the author by phone once a year to remind him that "it's been another year without drinking."

Case 2. A 33-year-old female attorney entered psychotherapy as a result of chronic depression and marijuana dependence. The patient had also completed doctoral studies in
Counseling Psychology. She was divorced and living with
another male attorney at the point of treatment engagement.
The patient had a seven-year-old son from her first marriage.
She decided to enter psychotherapy after sporadically attending Alcoholics Anonymous and Narcotics Anonymous for
five years. To date, she has been drug abstinent for three years.

This patient had "experimented" with a plethora of mood
altering drugs. However, she reported that her "drugs of
choice" were cocaine and marijuana. The patient had never
been an alcohol abuser and she had stopped using cocaine some
15 months before entering therapy. She stated that she stopped
using cocaine "because its so wonderful–so addicting, and I am
so afraid of it." She had smoked several marijuana "joints"
daily for a period of 14 years prior to entering therapy.

The patient completed the Minnesota Multiphasic Inventory
(MMPI) following the initial therapy session. Her basic MMPI
profile configurations (2-4) indicated that she was both clinically depressed and passive-aggressive. The test results were
not suggestive of thought disturbance or other severe psychopathology. Clinically, Laura manifested flat affect and verbalized that she felt "depressed" and "hopeless." She wept
openly during the initial therapy session and indicated that
both of her siblings were "addicts." She described her older
brother as a "psychopath." He was incarcerated for selling
drugs and had a long history of criminal behavior. The patient's diagnosis was marijuana dependence with concurrent
depressive disorder.

Laura indicated in therapy she had "always" been a rather
"nervous and hyperactive" person. Marijuana had initially
helped her feel less anxious and apparently was therapeutically relaxing. However, she also suspected that her marijuana
dependence had contributed to her feelings of depression for
several months if not longer. She realized that she had developed a psychological dependence on the drug and stated "it
seems like I can't do anything without smoking pot first–I

smoke a "number" before I go to the office in the morning, I smoke at lunch–I smoke to get to sleep at night . . . it really is a compulsion and I'm obsessed about it all the time."

This patient continues to be seen in weekly group psychotherapy. She was initially seen in weekly individual psychotherapy for eight sessions and then placed in group treatment due to financial considerations. The patient did begin to actively attend AA and NA two to three times each week after initiating psychotherapy. Following some three months of treatment and total marijuana abstinence, Laura's depressive disorder began to improve. Her mood and affect began to elevate, she began to be much more productive in her career, she no longer felt hopeless, and her personal appearance radically improved. The relationship with a "live-in" boyfriend remained conflicted as his continued use of marijuana was particularly conflictual for the patient.

Case 1 is a lucid diagnostic example of primary alcoholism. The patient's drinking history, family history, test profile, psychological relationship with alcohol, marital relationship dynamics, response to treatment, and even referral dynamics are clearly indicative of alcohol dependence. Case 2 involves a diagnosis of marijuana dependence with concurrent depressive neurosis or dysthymic disorder. While heavy marijuana use can facilitate or contribute to a depressive reaction, it was the author's opinion that the patient manifested a depressive disorder prior to her initiation of drug abuse and dependence.

In summary, the clinical diagnosis of substance use disorder is based upon an examination of the patient's (1) history and style or pattern of substance abuse, use, or dependence, (2) behavioral consequences of substance use, (3) social-familial aspects of substance use, (4) psychological, affective, and cognitive consequences of substance use, (5) medical or biophysiological aspects of substance use, and (6) legal history associated with substance use. The medical, psychological, and disease models that are used in the clinical diagnosis of substance use disorders were examined in this section of the chapter. It should be noted that the patient's legal history can be a very important component of the clinical diagnostic process.

The simple use of any illegal substance constitutes legally defined substance abuse! Individuals who have been arrested for drunken driving (DUI or DWAI) more than three times in a lifetime have a high clinical-statistical probability of being alcoholic (Timkin, 1987). The clinician must astutely assess all of these factors in the process of formulating a specific substance use disorder diagnosis.

DSM III-R DIAGNOSIS OF SUBSTANCE USE DISORDERS

The DSM III-R is a revision of the third edition of the American Psychiatric Association's Diagnostic and Statistical Manual of Mental Disorders. The first edition (DSM I) of this APA manual was published in 1952. A DSM II was subsequently published in 1968 and then the DSM III was published in 1980.

Unlike the DSM I and DSM II, the DSM III and DSM III-R include specific diagnostic criteria and guidelines that help the clinician render an appropriate diagnosis. However, the clinician must exercise clinical prudence in categorizing a patient according to the diagnostic criteria that are associated with each DSM III-R diagnostic category. The diagnostic criteria in the DSM III-R form an index of clinical symptoms of which a certain number, but no single symptom, is required to make each diagnosis. It is felt that this polythetic diagnostic format will enhance diagnostic reliability and interjudge diagnostic reliability.

The diagnostic categories in the DSM III are hierarchically organized. In DSM III-R, these diagnostic hierarchies are governed by two principles: "(1) When an Organic Mental Disorder can account for the symptoms, it preempts the diagnosis of any other disorder that could produce the same symptoms (i.e., Organic Anxiety Disorder preempts Panic Disorder), and (2) When a more pervasive disorder such as Schizophrenia, commonly has associated symptoms that are the defining symptoms of a less pervasive disorder such as Dysthymia, only the more pervasive disorder is diagnosed if both its defining symptoms and associated symptoms are present" (pp. XXIV-XXV). Thus, the DSM III-R hierarchical diagnostic model prevents giving a patient multiple diagnoses when different syndromes occur together.

The DSM III-R provides a classification schema or model of

"mental disorders." However, it is noted in the DSM III-R that "no definition adequately specifies precise boundaries for the concept mental disorders" (p. XXII). Each "mental disorder" in the volume is "conceptualized as a clinically significant behavioral or psychological syndrome or pattern that occurs in a person and that is associated with present distress (a painful symptom) or disability (impairment in one or more important areas of functioning) or with a significantly increased risk of suffering, death, pain, disability, or an important loss of freedom" (p. XXII). The DSM III-R also points out that there is no assumption that each mental disorder is a "discrete entity with sharp boundaries (discontinuity) between it and other mental disorders, or between it and no mental disorder." This is a classification system for various disorders that people have.

It is noted in the DSM III-R that the precise etiology of mental disorders is unknown. The approach taken in the DSM III-R is generally theoretical with regard to etiology. This classification system is "descriptive." Thus, the definitions of mental disorders in this model are generally limited to descriptions of the basic clinical features of the disorders. The basic clinical features of each disorder are described in easily identifiable behavioral signs and symptoms.

The DSM III-R diagnostic model is multiaxial. The five axes encompass: mental disorders (I and II), physical disorders and conditions (III), severity of psychosocial stressors (IV), and global assessment of functioning (V). This model provides a biopsychosocial approach to diagnosis and assessment. Each disorder is described in terms of essential features, associated features, age at onset, course, impairment, complications, predisposing factors, prevalence, sex ratio, familial pattern, and differential diagnosis.

It is noted in the Psychiatric Substance Use Disorders section of the DSM III-R that the use of mood altering substances is regarded as "normal and appropriate" in many social situations. Responsible ethanol use (Forrest, 1989), the use of caffeine in coffee or soft drinks, and the use of various medically prescribed psychoactive substances are appropriate and normal forms of drug use in American society. However, the Psychoactive Substance Use Disorders diagnostic class "deals with symptoms and maladaptive behavioral changes associated with more or less regular use of psychoactive substances that affect the central nervous system. These behavioral changes would be viewed as extremely undesirable in almost all cultures" (p. 165). These conditions are viewed as "mental disorders" and they can be distinguished from nonpathological psychoactive substance use. Disorders that are included in the Psychoactive Substance Use Disorders class are distinguished from disorders in the Psychoactive Substance Induced Organic Mental Disorders. The disorders that are included in the latter classification "describe the direct, acute or chronic effects of such substances on the central nervous system" (p. 165).

All substance use disorders are broadly classified within the Psychoactive Substance Dependence or Psychoactive Substance Abuse categories in the DSM III-R.

PSYCHOACTIVE SUBSTANCE DEPENDENCE

This classification of substance use disorder is applied to individuals who have developed a physical addiction to any psychoactive substance. The essential feature of this disorder (DSM III-R) is "a cluster of cognitive, behavioral, and physiological symptoms that indicate that the person has impaired control of psychoactive substance use and continues use of the substance despite adverse consequences" (p. 166). Symptoms associated with tolerance and withdrawal are essential characteristics of substance dependence. There are nine symptoms or characteristics of substance dependence. These nine symptoms of substance dependence are delineated in the DSM III-R. The diagnosis of psychoactive substance dependence requires that three or more of these symptoms are manifest. Furthermore, the diagnosis of substance dependence requires that some of these symptoms have persisted for one month or longer and/or occurred repeatedly over an extended period of time. It is also important to note that DSM III-R does provide diagnostic guidelines for assessing the severity of dependence as well as partial or full remission of dependence.

The diagnostic features of psychoactive substance dependence (DSM III-R) include at least three of the following:

(1) substance often taken in large amounts or over a longer period than the person intended, (2) persistent desire or one or

more unsuccessful efforts to cut down or control substance use, (3) a great deal of time spent in activities necessary to get the substance (e.g., theft, taking the substance, chain smoking, or recovering from its effects), (4) frequent intoxication or withdrawal symptoms when expected to fulfill major role obligations at work, school, or home (e.g., does not go to work because hung over, goes to school or work "high," intoxicated while taking care of his or her children), or when substance use is physically hazardous (e.g., drives when intoxicated), (5) important social, occupational, or recreational activities given up or reduced because of substance use, (6) continued substance use despite knowledge of having a persistent or recurrent social, psychological, or physical problem that is caused or exacerbated by the use of the substance (e.g., keeps using heroin despite family arguments about it, cocaine induced depression, or having an ulcer made worse by drinking), (7) marked tolerance: need for markedly increased amounts of the substance (i.e., at least 50% increase) in order to achieve intoxication or desired effect, or markedly diminished effect with continued use of same amount (NOTE: The following items may not apply to cannabis, hallucinogens, or phencyclidine [PCP]), (8) characteristic withdrawal symptoms (see specific withdrawal syndromes under Psychoactive Substance Induced Organic Metal Disorders), and (9) substance often taken to relieve or avoid withdrawal symptoms. Some symptoms of the disturbance have persisted for at least one month, or have occurred repeatedly over a longer period of time. (pp. 167-168)

The criteria for severity of Psychoactive Substance Dependence are also delineated in the DSM III-R. These criteria are defined as follows: "*MILD*–Few, if any, symptoms in excess of those required to make the diagnosis, and the symptoms result in no more than mild impairment in occupational functioning or in usual social activities or relationships with others; *MODERATE*–Symptoms or functional impairment between "mild" and "severe"; *SEVERE*–Many symptoms in excess of those required to make the diagnosis, and the symptoms markedly interfere with occupational functioning or with usual social activities or relationships with others; In Partial Remission–During the past six months, some use of the substance and some symptoms of dependence; In Full Remission–During the past six months, either no use of the substance, or use of the substance and no symptoms of dependence" (p. 168).

The Psychoactive Substance Dependence diagnostic category incorporates the essential clinical features of primary chemical dependency as well as the addictive disease model of substance use. Thus, chemically dependent patients experience loss of control, obsessive-compulsive behaviors and ideation, psychological and physical withdrawal, family problems, relationship conflicts, and possible medical and/or legal problems associated with substance use. Most chemically dependent persons are unable to terminate their chemical dependency and remain abstinent without treatment or intervention. The essential clinical diagnostic features of this classification is physical addiction or tissue dependence (Forrest, 1984) as well as psychological dependence.

PSYCHOACTIVE SUBSTANCE ABUSE

This class of substance use disorders includes various maladaptive patterns of substance use. According to the DSM III-R, substance abuse involves "(1) continued use of the psychoactive substance despite knowledge of having a persistent or recurrent social, occupational, psychological, or physical problem that is caused or exacerbated by use of the substance or (2) recurrent use of the substance is situations when use is physically hazardous (e.g., driving while intoxicated). The diagnosis is made only if some symptoms of the disturbance have persisted for at least one month or have occurred repeatedly over a longer period of time" (p. 169).

A diagnosis of psychoactive substance abuse is made when the pattern of substance use does not involve physiologic addiction, tolerance, or withdrawal. Episodic alcohol intoxication or "weekend" marijuana use are examples of substance abuse.

Diagnostic criteria for Psychoactive Substance Abuse (DSM III-R) include: "A. A maladaptive pattern of psychoactive substance use indicated by at least one of the following: (1) continued use despite knowledge of having a persistent or recurrent social, occupational, psychological, or physical problem that is caused or exacerbated by use of the psychoactive substance, or (2) recurrent use in situations in which use is physically hazardous (e.g., driving while intoxicated); B. Some symptoms of the disturbance have persisted for at least one month, or have occurred repeatedly over a longer period of time; C. Were not the criteria for Psychoactive Substance Dependence for this substance" (p. 169).

Thus, the DSM III-R distinguishes between two diagnostic categories of psychoactive substance use: psychoactive substance dependence and psychoactive substance abuse. The differential diagnosis of these categories is principally determined by physical dependence. The substance dependent person is physiologically dependent and drug addicted. Psychoactive substance abuse is diagnosed when the person has been ingesting a psychoactive substance for a shorter duration of time. Furthermore, the symptoms that are associated with this diagnostic category are not primarily physiologic in nature. Psychoactive substance dependence involves both physiologic and psychologic dependence or addiction. Psychoactive substance abuse involves psychological dependence or addiction.

DESCRIPTIVE INFORMATION AND DSM III-R CODINGS

The DSM III-R lists nine types of psychoactive substances that are frequently abused or cause dependence. These addictive substances include: alcohol; amphetamines and similar sympathomimetics; marijuana; cocaine; hallucinogens; opioids; PCP and similar acting arylcyclohexylamines; and sedatives, hynotics, and anxiolytics. Multiple substance abuse and dependencies are discussed in the DSM III-R as well as route of administration, duration of effects, associated features, age at onset, complications, impairments, course, predisposing factors, and sex ratio.

Descriptions for each of the nine classes of psychoactive substance dependence or psychoactive substance abuse are also included in the DSM III-R. These clinical descriptions include information pertaining to patterns of use, associated features, course, prevalence, and familial pattern for each class of psychoactive dependence or abuse. The familial pattern data are limited to the alcohol use classification.

The diagnostic codes and descriptions for each substance use disorder in the DSM III-R are: alcohol dependence (303.90) and alcohol abuse (305.00); amphetamine or similar acting sympathomimetic dependence (304.40) and amphetamine or similarly acting sympathomimetic abuse (305.70); cannabis dependence (304.30) and cannabis abuse (305.20); cocaine dependence (304.20); cocaine abuse (305.60); hallucinogen dependence (304.50) and hallucinogen abuse (305.30); inhalant dependence (304.60) and inhalant abuse (305.90); nicotine dependence (305.10); opioid dependence (304.00) and opioid abuse (305.50); phencyclidine (PCP) or similarly acting arylcyclohexylamine dependence (304.50) and phencyclidine (PCP) or similar acting arylcyclohexylamine abuse (305.90); sedative, hypnotic, or anxiolytic abuse (305.40); polysubstance dependence (304.90); psychoactive substance dependence not otherwise specified (304.90); and psychoactive substance abuse not otherwise specified (305.90).

The polysubstance dependence classification is used when the person has been dependent upon three or more psychoactive substances for a period of at least six months. The final two diagnostic classes are used when an individual is dependent upon or abusing a psychoactive substance that "cannot be classified according to any of the previous categories, or for use as an initial diagnosis in cases of dependence (or abuse) in which the specific substance is not yet known" (p. 185).

It is important to note that the DSM III-R descriptive information pertaining to each class of psychoactive substance dependence and abuse is diagnostically-oriented. For example, within the alcohol dependence-alcohol abuse classifications it is noted that "most adults" in the United States are light drinkers. About 35% abstain, 55% drink fewer than three alcoholic drinks a week, and only 11% consume an average of one ounce or more of alcohol a day. Drinking patterns vary by age and sex. "For both males and females, the prevalence of drinking is highest and abstention is lowest in the 21-34 year age range. At all ages, two to five times more males than females are 'heavy' drinkers; 10% of drinkers consume 50% of the total amount of alcohol consumed" (p. 173). Furthermore, it is pointed out in the patterns of use section of this classification model that "there are three main patterns of chronic alcohol abuse or dependence. The first consists of regular daily intake of large amounts; the second, of regular heavy drinking limited to weekends; the third, of long periods of sobriety interspersed with binges of daily heavy drinking lasting for weeks or months. It is a mistake to associate one of these particular patterns exclusively with 'alcoholism' " (p. 173).

The data and information included in the patterns of use, associated features, course, and prevalence sections of each diagnostic classification of psychoactive substance use disorder explains how these disorders develop. The information in these sections is geared to help the clinician better understand the scope of each substance use disorder as well as accurately diagnose these conditions. Indeed, research findings in combination with clinical descriptive data pertaining to each substance use disorder are presented in a manner which enables the clinician to readily assess any pattern of substance use.

The following case study is presented as an example of a DSM III-R based diagnostic case of psychoactive substance use disorder. The patient's DSM III-R diagnostic classification and the DSM III-R diagnostic features that led to his diagnosis are included in the case presentation.

Rich C. was a 34-year-old corporate employee. He entered psychotherapy as a result of marital discord. However, the client revealed in the initial clinical interview that he also had "a real problem with cocaine" and that he had been "addicted" to various drugs since his undergraduate college days. He proceeded to give the therapist a detailed history of his chemical dependency: As an undergraduate student at a major university he smoked marijuana several times each week, "shot-up" speed hundreds of times, "dropped" acid weekly, took prescription tranquilizers regularly, and experimented with a diversity of other mood altering drugs. Furthermore, the client had been a campus "drug dealer" for over two years. He estimated his weekly drug selling income to be over $1,000!

The client's first two marriages had ended in divorce and he indicated to the therapist that drug abuse was a major causative factor in his prior marital failures. His present marriage was severely conflictual and his wife had threatened to leave if he did not seek help for his chemical dependency. Moreover, he reported that his family had recently "given up on me" as a result of his chemical dependency, chronic lying, and irresponsible behavior. He had stolen several thousand dollars from his employer over a period of four years. The client had not been caught in this matter. According to the client, the money that he took from his employer had been spent "supporting my habit."

A few years before entering psychotherapy, the patient was able to stop drinking completely for over two years. However, he did continue to smoke "pot" daily during this time. Approximately a year before entering therapy, the patient began to "experiment" with cocaine. Within a matter of months the patient indicated that he became cocaine dependent. He would spend $300-$1000 a week doing "coke runs." The client would inject and/or "snort" cocaine for hours at a time. He borrowed money from his parents, used charge cards, sold valuable family artifacts, and stole to maintain his cocaine dependency. Additionally, the client drank heavily and took minor tranquilizers in order to "come down" from his "coke binges."

The client indicated to the therapist that he was "hooked" and described himself as "obsessed" with drugs: "I'll do anything to get high, I sure as hell can't stop taking drugs, and it seems like I always need more–I've always been an addict from the moment I began using them." The client consciously related his marital, familial, health, financial, and legal problems with his pattern of previously uncontrollable polydrug dependence. His DSM III-R diagnosis was 304.90 (Polysubstance dependence).

Identity and sexual conflicts were also associated with the client's drug use. He reported that he was rarely interested in sex and that his father and mother viewed him as a "complete failure." The client's father was a retired military general. Both parents were perceived as "heavy drinkers" by the client. They were also described as "aloof and emotionally cold." After the patient had entered a residential drug treatment center, he was told by his mother "you sure don't have any damned disease, you're just weak and there aren't any other weak men on your father's side of the family or on mine."

This patient was referred to a 30-day residential chemical dependency treatment center. Following completion of residential treatment, the patient was seen in weekly individual and weekly con-joint therapy for three years. He also attended CA, NA, and AA several times each week. At present, he has been totally abstinent from all mood and addictive substances for four and one-half years.

This client was diagnosed as manifesting polysubstance dependence (DSM III-R category 304.90). He repeatedly used several categories of psychoactive substances, and had actually been addicted to different drugs at different points in his history of drug use. The client was cocaine dependent (DSM III-R category 304.30) at the point of treatment engagement. Physical and psychological dependence, tolerance, withdrawal, occupational, personal, familial, and marital symptoms of dependence were clearly apparent in this case study.

CLINICAL DIAGNOSIS OF ANTISOCIAL PERSONALITY DISORDER

A clinical diagnosis of psychopathy or antisocial personality disorder is applied to individuals who are impulsive, manipulative, chronic liars, guiltless, aggressive, and unable to love or form lasting human attachments (Doren, 1987). Cadoret (1986) indicates that antisocial personality disorder is "one of the better defined personality disorders." The concept of ASPD encompasses a potpourri of behaviors that range from early indulgence in sex, drugs, and alcohol to social irresponsibility.

Perhaps Cleckley ([1941] 1976) developed the most widely recognized descriptive assessment model of psychopathy or antisocial personality disorder. The "Cleckley Psychopath" manifested 16 basic characteristics: (1) superficial charm and good intelligence,

(2) absence of delusions and other signs of irrational thinking, (3) absence of "nervousness" or psychoneurotic manifestations, (4) unreliability, (5) untruthfulness and insincerity, (6) lack of remorse or shame (7) inadequately motivated antisocial behavior, (8) poor judgement and failure to learn from experience, (9) pathologic egocentricity and incapacity to love, (10) general poverty in major affective reactions, (11) specific loss of insight, (12) unresponsiveness in general interpersonal relations, (13) fantastic and uninviting behavior with drink and sometimes without, (14) suicide rarely carried out, (15) sex life impersonal, trivial and poorly integrated, and (16) failure to follow any life plan.

Hare (1970) indicates that most clinicians consider "the core" of psychopathy to be: "an inability to develop warm, genuine relationships with others, a lack of empathy, and a callous disregard for the rights and feelings of others" (p. 16). Indeed, McCord and McCord (1964) define the psychopath as "an asocial, aggressive, highly impulsive person, who feels little or no guilt and is unable to form lasting bonds of affection with other human beings" (p. 3). McCord and McCord (1964) delineate seven diagnostic features or characteristics of psychopathy: (1) the psychopath is asocial, (2) the psychopath is driven by uncontrolled desires, (3) the psychopath is highly impulsive, (4) the psychopath is aggressive, (5) the psychopath feels little guilt, (6) the psychopath has a warped capacity for love, and (7) the psychopathic syndrome. The final diagnostic feature of antisocial personality disorder or psychopathy is referred to as "the psychopathic syndrome" because it includes all of the forgoing traits together.

According to McCord and McCord (1964), unless an individual exhibits "the two critical psychopathic traits–guiltlessness and lovelessness," he should not be categorized as a psychopath. They characterize the psychopath in the following manner: "The psychopath is asocial. His conduct often brings him into conflict with society. The psychopath is driven by primitive desires and an exaggerated craving for excitement. In his self-centered search for pleasure, he ignores restrictions of his culture. The psychopath is highly impulsive. He is a man for whom the moment is a segment of time detached from all others. His actions are unplanned and guided by his whims. The psychopath is aggressive. He has learned few socialized ways of coping with frustrations. The psychopath feels little, if any, guilt. He can commit the most appalling acts, yet view them without remorse. The psychopath has a warped capacity for love. His emotional relationships, when they exist, are meager, fleeting and designed to satisfy his own desires. These last two traits, guiltlessness and lovelessness, conspicuously mark the psychopath as different from other men" (pp. 16-17).

Although some behavioral scientists purport that terms such as antisocial personality and psychopathy represent "wastebasket" diagnostic categories, there is a remarkable agreement among clinicians relative to the behavioral, affective, and psychological traits or characteristics of people who are so labeled. These traits include (Brantley and Sutker, 1984) inability to learn from experience, early onset, irresponsibility, lack of impulse control, inability to form meaningful relationships, and lack of guilt and feelings.

Chemical dependency and substance abuse are consistently associated with ASPD (Brantley and Sutker, 1984). These authors state "regardless of the criteria used for classification, the literature suggests considerable overlap among the groups described in terms of dyssocial reaction, alcoholism, and sociopathy" (p. 422). It is also indicated that "most commonly, sociopathy has been conceptualized as a psychiatric symptom cluster of genetic and/or learned origins that has become maladaptive in nature by virtue of its inflexibility and inappropriateness and that leads to unfortunate consequences" (Brantley and Sutker, 1984, p. 440). Thus, the clinical assessment of antisocial personality disorder is based upon the observation that an individual repeatedly engages in a set of negative, destructive, blatantly antisocial behaviors.

The following clinical case study of psychopathy or antisocial personality disorder involves an account of the Nazi, Hermann Goering, chief of the Luftwaffe. This account of Goering is taken from the McCords' (1964) book *The Psychopath: An Essay on the Criminal Mind.*

G.M. Gilbert, chief psychologist at the Nuremberg trials, described Hermann Goering as an "amiable psychopath." Gilbert pointed to Goering's brutal, loveless childhood as typical of the psychopath's background. Gilbert (1948) states "Goering's father was a stern Prussian official who valued military discipline above all else. Goering's earliest memory was of lashing his mother in the face with both fists when she came to embrace him after a prolonged absence."

As a child, Goering loved excitement, the glaring splash of military uniforms, and eagerly exhibited his taste for sadistic brutality. Uncontrolled behavior and vicious attacks on his sisters led his parents to shift Goering from school to school. His mother predicted "Hermann will either be a great man or a great criminal!"

In his youth, Goering's drive for glory, his brutality, his emotional impulsiveness, and his aggressiveness found its most desirable expression in the military prerogatives of his culture. Goering's recklessness earned him the distinction of being one of Germany's top air aces in WWI, but his uncontrolled greed brought him into illegal wartime adventures. He took illicit leaves, accepted bribes, and established a clandestine army supply company.

After the war, he married a rich Swedish countess. Despite his early found wealth, Goering missed the excitement of war. Attracted by Hitler's military, Goering was swept into the Nazi party. He moved from honor to honor as president of the Reichstag, head of Nazi industry, and chief of the Luftwaffe. His objective was expressed in a Reichstag speech: "I am not here to exercise justice, but to wipe out and exterminate!"

Goering's spectacular rise to power provided him with the means to satisfy his craving for pleasure. He turned to drug addiction, mistresses, and "Roman" orgies. As Germany collapsed, Goering pranced through his palace, Karinhall, dressed in a toga, with painted fingernails and lips.

With the fall of Germany, Goering, along with the other Nazi leaders, went on trial for his part in the war crimes. Gilbert, who came to know Goering during the trial, noticed a singular lack of guilt. After seeing a documentary film of mutilated bodies from a concentration camp, for example, Goering commented only: "It was such a good afternoon, too, until they showed that film–they were reading my telephone conversations on the Austrian matter and everybody was

laughing with me–and then they showed that awful film, and it
just spoiled everything."

Before ending his life with poison, Goering left this mes-
sage for the West: "You Americans are making a stupid mistake with your talk of democracy and morality . . . Don't think
that Germans have become more Christian and less nationalis-
tic all of a sudden . . . you can take your morality and your
repentance and your democracy and stick it up!" (pp. 35-36)

This case study clearly demonstrates the clinical symptoms and
features of antisocial personality disorder. Hermann Goering was
impulsive, guiltless, violent, unable to love, and asocial. Indeed, he
manifested virtually all of the clinical diagnostic features of antisocial personality disorder as delineated earlier in this chapter.

The clinical assessment of antisocial personality disorder has
been facilitated vis à vis the use of psychological testing. Brantley
and Sutker (1984) state: "Probably the most widely used index of
sociopathy is derived from the classification rules applied to MMPI
(Minnesota Multiphasic Personality Inventory) protocol data.
Scales 4 (Pd) and 9 (Ma) are typically considered indicators of
sociopathy, and Welsh's Anxiety (A) scale and the clinical scale 7
(Pt) may be used to distinguish between the primary and the secondary types" (p. 467). The classic MMPI 4-9 and 4 profiles (Gilberstadt and Duker, 1965) include the following cardinal features:
irresponsibility, immaturity, self-centeredness, impulsiveness, suicide attempts, sexual acting-out, aggressiveness, alcoholism, low
frustration tolerance, outgoingness, and poor socialization of morals and standards.

Research data (Sutker, 1971; Hedlund, 1977; Sutker and Allain,
1983) consistently indicate that the behavioral correlates of MMPI
4 and 4-9 types are hostility, angry outbursts, assaultive or homicidal thoughts, arrests, and marital fighting. It is significant that the
MMPI 4-9, 9-4, and 4 patterns have been described as "protypical
profile types" for groups of male and female drug addicts (Brantley
and Sutker, 1984).

It should also be noted that several other psychological tests have
been developed to assess ASPD. Indeed, the assessment of antisocial
personality disorder or psychopathy is multidimensional and can

include (1) sensation seeking, (2) delay of gratification, (3) learning and performance, (4) interpersonal factors, (5) various measures of physiologic arousal, and (6) personality-behavioral assessment. Personality and behavioral assessment of antisocial personality disorder may be accomplished by using interview ratings, symptoms checklists, objective tests such as the MMPI or CPI, and projective tests such as the Rorschach.

In summary, a clinical diagnosis of antisocial personality disorder or psychopathy is applied to individuals who manifest a *chronic* personality and behavioral adjustment style that is characterized by: impulsiveness; aggressiveness; lack of guilt or conscience; asocial nature; inability to love and maintain meaningful, indepth human relationships; extreme self-centeredness; global irresponsibility; and manipulativeness. The chronic affective style of the psychopath is impoverished. A diagnosis of antisocial personality disorder is applied to individuals who are emotionally cold, unable to experience and express emotions or affect, and highly impersonal or detached in all human relations. The chronic cognitive style of the psychopath (Yochelson and Samenow, 1986) is structured around being important and powerful, avoiding feelings and thoughts of inadequacy or a "zero-state," and "conning" or "getting over" on other people as well as social systems.

It is important to note that the cognitive, behavioral, personality, affective, and social style of the psychopath does not include the fundamental clinical diagnostic features that are associated with various neurotic and psychotic adjustment styles. Finally, it must be emphasized that antisocial personality disorder is a chronic personality or character disorder and not a situational or short-term adjustment style.

THE FUNCTIONAL PSYCHOPATH

Clinicians have long recognized (McCord and McCord, 1964; Doren, 1987; Forrest, 1989b) that some psychopaths are able to remain socially functional. These individuals are manipulative, self-centered, irresponsible, impulsive, poorly controlled, prone to substance abuse, promiscuous, immature, and angry. Nonetheless, they are not incarcerated or socially dysfunctional in an overt sense. The functional psychopath may be bright, socially skilled, and "slick" enough to avoid major conflicts with the police, employers, or other authority figures. Functional psychopaths seem to function well in sales and people-oriented occupations. Used car salesmen, police officers, lawyers, realtors, clergymen, and even psychiatrists (Christie and Geis, 1976) have been described as manipulative, exploitive, and machiavellian. Military personnel may also include a disproportionate number of antisocial personalities.

The pathologic adjustment style of the functional psychopath may eventually become socially overt. The Rev. Jim Bakker appears to be an excellent example of a decompensated functional psychopath. The sexual escapades, extravagant spending, deceit, incongruent life-style, and manipulativeness of Reverend Bakker essentially led to his demise. The overt behaviors and actions of the Bakkers' were grossly incongruous with their conflicted and sociopathic personal lives. The movie character Elmer Gantry is another example of a functional psychopath. In many respects, President Saddam Hussein of Iraq also appears to manifest a functional ASPD.

It is the observation of the author that functional psychopaths tend to become less psychopathic during their 50s and 60s. Indeed, the global psychopathic adjustment style of these individuals seem to consistently diminish with the aging process.

Functional psychopaths can exert a very malignant influence upon the individuals and systems with which they become involved. Antisocial physicians and health service providers are consistently involved in insurance fraud, unethical practice, and litigation. Yet, it may take years to legally convict these persons and remove them from their careers. Psychopathic government personnel, military leaders, and corporate heads impact our society and the world in a diversity of very destructive ways.

The functional psychopath is usually a poor candidate for psychotherapy. These persons will enter a treatment relationship or treatment program for very self-serving reasons. They seem to be recalcitrant to change. Functional psychopaths are usually drinkers and substance abusers but like the classic psychopath or antisocial personality, they infrequently become chemically dependent. They are incredibly adroit at using, manipulating, and "conning" significant others. The functional psychopath thrives on "getting over," "pulling a slick deal," and "selling" others. These persons are also grandiose, narcissistic, and preoccupied with attractiveness and physical appearance. They are narcissistically absorbed with self and establish only superficial attachments with others. Their verbal transactions with others are exceedingly "I-oriented."

Needless to say, antisocial counselors and therapists exert a multiplicity of destructive influences upon their clients. These individuals also negatively impact the mental health professions and organizational systems with which they become involved.

DSM III-R DIAGNOSIS
OF ANTISOCIAL PERSONALITY DISORDER

The DSM III-R delineates several specific diagnostic criteria for psychopathy or antisocial personality disorder. According to the DSM III-R, the "essential feature of this disorder (antisocial personality) is a pattern of irresponsible and antisocial behavior beginning in childhood or early adolescence and continuing into adulthood" (p. 342). A diagnosis of antisocial personality disorder also requires that an individual be at least 18 years of age and manifest a history of conduct disorder prior to age 14.

Several general personality and behavior characteristics of the person with antisocial personality disorder are discussed in the DSM III-R. For example, the "typical childhood signs" of adult antisocial personality disorder include lying, stealing, truancy, vandalism, initiating fights, running away from home, and physical cruelty. Behaviors and traits that are associated with the adult antisocial personality disorder may include (DSM III-R) *failure* "to honor financial obligations, to function as a responsible parent or to plan ahead, and an inability to sustain consistent work behavior. These people fail to conform to social norms and repeatedly perform antisocial acts that are grounds for arrest, such as destroying property, harassing others, stealing, and having an illegal occupation" (p. 342).

The DSM III-R also notes that people with antisocial personality disorder are impulsive, aggressive, frequently drive while intoxicated, and repeatedly become involved in physical fights and assaults. These people show little regard for the personal safety of themselves or others. They are promiscuous (defined in the DSM III-R as never having sustained a monogamous relationship for more than a year) and "generally have no remorse about the effects of their behavior on others; they may even feel justified in having hurt or mistreated others" (p. 342). It is also noted in the DSM III-R that the flagrant antisocial behaviors of these individuals may diminish after age 30.

It is important to point out that psychopaths tend to abuse alcohol, drugs, and engage in voluntary sexual intercourse earlier in adolescence than their peers. According to the DSM III-R, psychoactive substance use disorders are commonly associated with antisocial personality disorder or psychopathy. These individuals also tend to complain of tension, depression, and chronic interpersonal conflicts. The DSM III-R reports "almost invariably there is a markedly impaired capacity to sustain lasting, close, warm, and responsible relationships with family, friends, or sexual partners" (p. 343). Thus, severe and chronic interpersonal dysfunction is a diagnostic sine qua non of ASPD.

The DSM III-R reports that antisocial personality disorder is often "incapacitating" and has an early onset. Premature violent death is associated with this disorder. As discussed in Chapter IV, ASPD tends to run in families. According to the DSM III-R, "antisocial personality disorder is five times more common among first-degree biologic relatives of males with the disorder than among the general population. The risk to the first-degree biologic relatives of females with the disorder in nearly ten times that of the general population . . . Within a family that has a member with Antisocial Personality Disorder, males more often have Antisocial Personality Disorder and Psychoactive Substance Use Disorders, whereas females more often have Somatization Disorder; but there is an increase in all of these disorders in both males and females compared with the general population" (pp. 343-344). Based upon this information, it can be diagnostically helpful for the clinician to evaluate the history of ASPD in a patient's family of origin.

The following *specific* diagnostic criteria for Antisocial Personality Disorder (code 301.70) are delineated in the DSM III-R :

A. Current Age at least 18.
B. Evidence of Conduct Disorder with onset before age 15, as indicated by a history of *three* or more of the following:
   (1) was often truant
   (2) ran away from home overnight at least twice while living in parental or parental surrogate home (or once without returning)
   (3) often initiated physical fights
   (4) used a weapon in more than one fight
   (5) forced someone into sexual activity with him or her
   (6) was physically cruel to animals
   (7) was physically cruel to people
   (8) deliberately destroyed others' property (other than by fire-setting)
   (9) deliberately engaged in fire-setting
  (10) often lied (other than to avoid physical or sexual abuse)
  (11) has stolen without confrontation of a victim on more than one occasion (including forgery)
  (12) has stolen with confrontation of a victim (e.g., mugging, purse-snatching, extortion, armed robbery)
C. A pattern of irresponsible and antisocial behavior since the age of 15, as indicated by at least *four* of the following:
   (1) is unable to sustain consistent work behavior, as indicated by any of the following (including similar behavior in academic settings if the person is a student):
     (a) significant unemployment for six months or more within five years when expected to and work was available
     (b) repeated absences from work unexplained by illness in self or family
     (c) abandonment of several jobs without realistic plans for others
   (2) fails to conform to social norms with respect to lawful behavior as indicated by repeatedly performing antisocial acts that are grounds for arrest (whether arrested or not), e.g., destroying property, harassing others, stealing, pursuing an illegal occupation

(3) is irritable and aggressive, as indicated by repeated physical fights or assaults (not required by one's job or to defend someone or oneself), including spouse- or child-beating

(4) repeatedly fails to honor financial obligations, as indicated by defaulting on debts or failing to provide child support or support for other dependents on a regular basis

(5) fails to plan ahead, or is impulsive as indicated by one or both of the following:

    (a) traveling from place to place without a prearranged job or clear goal for the period of travel or clear idea about when the travel will terminate

    (b) lack of fixed address for a month or more

(6) has no regard for the truth, as indicated by repeated lying, use of aliases, or "conning" others for personal profit or pleasure

(7) is reckless regarding his or her own or others' personal safety, as indicated by driving while intoxicated, or recurrent speeding

(8) if a parent or guardian, lacks ability to function as a responsible parent, as indicated by one or more of the following:

    (a) malnutrition of child

    (b) child's illness resulting from lack of minimal hygiene

    (c) failure to obtain medical care for a seriously ill child

    (d) child's dependence on neighbors or nonresident relatives for food or shelter

    (e) failure to arrange for a caretaker for a young child when the parent is away from home

    (f) repeated squandering, on personal items, of money required for household necessities

(9) has never sustained a totally monogamous relationship for more than one year

(10) lacks remorse (feels justified in having hurt, mistreated, or stolen from another)

D. Occurrence of antisocial behavior not exclusively during the course of Schizophrenia or Manic Episodes. (pp. 344-346)

In sum, the DSM III-R provides several specific diagnostic criteria for Antisocial Personality Disorder. These diagnostic characteristics are more specific and better defined than the general traits of psychopathy that were discussed in the earlier section of this chapter. However, the clinical diagnostic features and DSM III-R (1987) diagnostic criteria for antisocial personality disorder or psychopathy are essentially congruent.

DIFFERENTIAL AND CONCURRENT DIAGNOSIS OF SUBSTANCE USE DISORDER AND ANTISOCIAL PERSONALITY DISORDER

This section of the text is extremely important for a number of reasons. Foremost in this regard are the issues of providing appropriate and efficacious treatments for these patient populations. Most counselors and clinicians who work with chemically dependent patients and substance abusers are not familiar with the psychopath. Furthermore, these health professionals do not generally have the academic and clinical training or clinical experience that is necessary to differentially diagnose these specific clinical populations. Treatment interventions that "work" and are efficacious with substance abusers are ineffective and can even be very inappropriate when utilized with antisocial persons.

These same clinical dilemmas may apply to the few behavioral scientists and counselors who work primarily with antisocial persons. These clinicians are not experienced and well trained in the realm of substance abuse and chemical dependency. Counselors and behavior scientists who work within the corrections field are cognizant of the fact that many of their clients "abuse" alcohol and other addictive substances, but they are generally unable to differentially diagnose (1) the client or offender who manifests concurrent antisocial personality disorder, (2) the client or offender who is chemically dependent but not antisocial, (3) the client or offender who is a substance abuser but not antisocial, (4) the client or offender who is either chemically dependent or a substance abuser in addition to being antisocial. Obviously, a basic failure to understand these various clinical realities can be tantamount to an inability to provide effective treatments for these clinical subpopulations.

The various clinical, professional, ethical, and legal ramifications that are associated with these realities are complex. At best, all therapists and treatment systems are simply ineffective. At worst, change agents and treatment systems that fail to accurately diagnose or assess individuals also fail to provide appropriate treatments for these people. They also reinforce pathology rather than facilitate constructive behavioral change and recovery. Counselor ineffectiveness, systemic treatment inadequacies, and program ineffectiveness are predictably related to inappropriate treatment interventions that are based upon misdiagnosis.

An accurate clinical differential diagnosis of the substance use disorders and antisocial personality disorder is made by focusing upon each patient's (1) pattern of substance use, (2) interpersonal adjustment style, (3) cognitive style, and (4) affective make-up. The clinician must closely assess each of these facets of the patient's historic and current adjustment style in order to arrive at an accurate differential diagnosis and plan subsequent appropriate treatment interventions.

The antisocial personality tends not to be chemically dependent. Indeed, it has been my observation during the course of over 20 years of clinical practice with alcoholics, substance abusers, and psychopaths that less than 20 percent of psychopaths manifest a history of protracted tissue dependence (Forrest, 1983a). Antisocial patients rarely report consuming a fifth of vodka or a case of beer daily for a period of 5-20 years. However, the vast majority of antisocial persons are *consistent abusers* of alcohol and other psychoactive substances. Thus, approximately 90 percent of antisocial personalities periodically *abuse* alcohol and other drugs rather than developing a physical dependence upon these substances. These individuals may get drunk two or three times a week, once a month, or ten times a year, but they are not maintenance drinkers or addicts. The antisocial personality is psychologically dependent upon mood altering substances. Antisocial persons infrequently develop psychological *and* physical drug dependence.

In view of these factors, it is not surprising that the antisocial patient rather easily refrains from alcohol and other drug use for short or even extended periods of time. Unlike chemically dependent patients and substance abusers, the antisocial personality does not find it particularly difficult or psychologically stressful to stop drinking or using other drugs. These individuals often confuse treatment personnel and patients alike in residential treatment settings. They may actively reinforce the substance use of other patients during the course of weekend passes while completely abstaining themselves or drinking/using in relative moderation. Thus, primary alcoholics and substance abusers ingest mood altering substances in an obsessive-compulsive and out-of-control manner (Forrest, 1983a, 1984; Forrest and Gordon, 1990) while psychopaths ingest these same substances in a far less obsessive-compulsive fashion. The antisocial patient may use drugs without control and with compulsion for a day or several days, but not on a daily basis for several years.

Somewhat paradoxically, antisocial patients are rarely able to remain totally drug abstinent for a period of five to ten or more years. Antisocial persons also rarely commit themselves to psychotherapy, Alcoholics Anonymous, or the various other self-help treatment alternatives, long-term outpatient treatment, or even highly structured religious programs for a period of several years in the absence of being incarcerated. Thus, the differential diagnosis of ASPD and substance use disorder can in part be accomplished from a retrospective perspective. Patients who are unable to maintain abstinence, relapse repeatedly, fail to make a commitment to various treatment modalities, and persist in a pattern of grossly irresponsible acting-out *after* being treated in a residential or out-patient chemical dependency treatment program often manifest antisocial personality disorder.

Antisocial personalities tend to be self-identified "alcoholics" and "drug addicts" when arrested, confronted by a judge or jury, while incarcerated, or when going before a parole board. These persons can be very active in Alcoholics Anonymous or chemical dependency programs that are offered "behind the walls." Unfortunately, the antisocial patient attempts to placate the judicial and correctional systems and "cons" others vis-à-vis the process of chemical dependency self-labeling within an institutional setting. It has been estimated (Ross and Lightfoot, 1985) that less than 5 percent of these individuals remain totally drug abstinent and actively committed to AA, NA, or other treatment regimens after leaving a correctional facility. These realities partially explain the recidivistic nature of both substance abuse and criminal activities among antisocial personalities. Persons who manifest chemical dependency with concurrent ASPD are unable to terminate their acting-out vis-à-vis substance abuse for protracted periods of time.

The interpersonal adjustment style of primary addicts and substance abusers is substantially different from that of the antisocial personality disorder. As noted in earlier sections of this book, antisocial personalities are impulsive, aggressive, violent, and unable to sustain human relationships. The psychopath tends to move *against* significant others in a plethora of violent, aggressive, and destructive ways. To the contrary, primary alcoholics and substance abusers tend to neurotically attempt to move *toward* people and/or *away from* significant others via substance dependence. Thus, the "alcoholic is not asocial. The sociopath is asocial and without values . . . The alcoholic acts out against himself or herself. Sociopaths channel violence and acting out directly against all others" (Forrest, 1983, p. 192).

The interpersonal style of the antisocial personality disorder does not involve long-term or lasting relationships. The interpersonal world of the antisocial personality is limited to brief, superficial, nonemotional attachments to *non*-significant others. Antisocial personalities are unable to establish and maintain meaningful long-term human attachments. The psychopath uses and manipulates other people. Human beings are perceived by the psychopath as objects that are to be used, disposed of, and replaced. The interpersonal adjustment style of chemically dependent persons is qualitatively and quantitively different from that of the antisocial personality. Most alcoholics are able to establish and maintain long-term interpersonal relationships. Although these relationships are chronically conflicted, chemically dependent persons need human relationships and they tend to develop overly dependent human attachments. The chemically dependent person or substance abuser is far less destructive and malicious in his or her manipulative and "conning" transactions with other human beings.

Chemically dependent patients are usually involved in an interpersonal support system. This support system is used to maintain the addict's substance dependence (I have referred to this support system as the AIN–Alcoholic Interpersonal Network: Forrest, 1983) and these relationships may persist for years. Antisocial personalities make good first impressions but they are unable to sustain relationships with virtually all other human beings over an extended period of time–even other psychopaths!

Substance abusers and chemically dependent people are also interpersonally anxious. Interpersonal anxiety and social uncomfortableness are essential diagnostic features of the alcoholic. However, the antisocial personality is rarely, if ever, interpersonally anxious. Interpersonal closeness and human intimacy creates intense anxiety in the alcoholic (Forrest, 1984) while the sociopath responds to these aspects of human encounters with ease and self-confidence. Indeed, antisocial personalities tend to be socially adroit and facile–the antithesis of the alcoholic or addict.

The cognitive style of the antisocial personality is extremely narcissistic and self-oriented. These individuals are unable to focus upon the needs and sensitivities of other people. Yochelson and Samenow (1976, 1986) indicate that the cognitive style and intrapersonal modus operandi of the criminal centers around avoiding a "zero state." Criminal personalities utilize a diversity of cognitive techniques in order to avoid feeling inadequate, stupid, weak, worthless, or akin to a "zero." The core problem in psychopathy is "criminal thinking patterns" (Yochelson and Samenow, 1986). Furthermore, the cognitive style of the antisocial personality is pathologically obsessed with (1) gaining a sense of personal power, (2) eliminating any sense of conscience, (3) finding and expressing excitement, (4) justifying irresponsible behaviors, thoughts and impulses, (5) lying and deceiving ("conning") others, (6) gratifying sexual impulses and fantasies, (7) avoiding work, (8) repressing fear, (9) maintaining a basic sense of self-esteem and rejecting the notion of self as a criminal or antisocial person, and (10) finding excuses or rationalizing antisocial acts. The global cognitive style of the antisocial personality is perpetually directed at meeting these ten self-serving goals. Getting-over, scheming, using others, being important and powerful, justifying one's actions, and maintaining a sense of "Mr. Big" are but a few of the obsessively narcissistic cognitive features of the antisocial personality.

Chemically dependent patients and substance abusers have a

cognitive style that involves profound self-beliefs and dialogue that center around issues of inadequacy, low self-esteem, and worthlessness. The narcissism of chemically dependent persons vacillates between grandiosity or omnipotence and several gradients of worthlessness. Chemically dependent patients are also cognitively obsessed with obtaining and ingesting various mood altering drugs. They are equally obsessed with the effects of drug use. Substance abusers are cognitively unable to cut off or repress cognitions that involve fear, anxiety, personal responsibility or culpability, conscience, and low self-esteem. The cognitive style or thought process of the primary chemically dependent patient becomes essentially normal following drug abstinence and involvement in psychotherapy or an extended program of recovery.

Chemically dependent patients and substance abusers are resentful, angry, and enraged. However, they do not obsessively ruminate about acts of murder, violence, and destruction. Antisocial personalities and criminals (Yochelson and Samenow, 1986; Reid et al., 1986) often ruminate about committing violent and destructive acts.

The cognitive style of the antisocial personality does not include a basic sense of right and wrong. Antisocial personalities do not have a conscience, and thus, they are unable to distinguish between right and wrong or moral and immoral acts in an integrated cognitive fashion. The psychopath thinks only in terms of "me" or self. To the contrary, chemically dependent patients do manifest a conscience and are at least able to inconsistently differentiate between right and wrong or moral and immoral behaviors. Chemically dependent patients and substance abusers are able to intermittently anesthetize their super-ego or consciences via intoxication and subsequently act-out "as if" they were antisocial personalities. The overly primitive and harsh super-ego structure of the alcoholic becomes operational with abstinence. Such a change in cognitive style is rarely, if ever, seen in antisocial patients who stop drinking or enter some form of rehabilitation program.

The affective make-up of the antisocial personality differs quantatively and qualitatively from that of chemically dependent and substance abusing individuals. Foremost, chemically dependent persons are chronically anxious. Alcoholics are intrapersonally and interpersonally anxious. These individuals manifest intense and chronic fears associated with "going crazy" and death (Forrest, 1983). The chemically dependent person also experiences fear, depression, guilt, and remorse. Affect disturbance is basic to the substance use disorders (Zimberg, 1982; Wilsnack and Beckman, 1984). Antisocial persons may experience depressive feelings, anxiety, fear, or even guilt for a few minutes or hours. The antisocial personality is not chronically perplexed and conflicted by guilt feelings or depression. As I have indicated earlier (Forrest, 1983), "the sociopath lacks the ability to internalize conflict and respond appropriately in an affective sense. Sociopaths lack the capacity to experience genuine affect. The sociopath experiences no empathy or affective attachment for those who fall victim to his or her vicious and mercenary manipulations. The psychopath also experiences no guilt, depression, or remorse over his or her damaging use and abuse of others" (pp. 192-193).

Chemically dependent persons experience chronic emotional disturbance as a result of acting in or internalized affective pathology. Antisocial personalities lack the capacity to act-in. They can only act-out! Many substance abusers become progressively more affectively disturbed as they move into the middle and later stages of the addiction process (Forrest, 1978). Chemically dependent patients and substance abusers are affectively human: they feel, fear, love, hate, become depressed and anxious, and experience guilt and remorse. Chemically dependent persons are neurotic managers of their affects and their affective lives while antisocial persons essentially have no affects or affective lives.

Table I summarizes the essential clinical differential diagnostic characteristics of substance use disorders and antisocial personality disorder. This table can be utilized to differentially diagnose (1) antisocial personality disorder, (2) chemically dependent patients or substance abusers without concurrent ASPD, (3) chemically dependent patients or substance abusers with concurrent antisocial personality disorder.

Obviously, the DSM III-R is an excellent additional resource for differentially assessing substance use disorders and ASPD. In order to determine an accurate differential diagnosis involving combinations of substance use disorder and antisocial personality disorder, the clinician simply needs to be familiar with the DSM III-R diag-

Table I: Differential Diagnosis of Substance Use Disorders and Antisocial Personality Disorder

	Chemically Dependent/ Substance Abuser	Antisocial Personality
Pattern of Substance Use	Obsessive-compulsive use of mood-altering drugs; physical and/or psychological dependence; has capacity to establish and maintain long-term drug-free lifestyle; will make commitment to alcohol/drug therapy; may be chemically dependent or substance abuser.	Episodic use and abuse of any/all mood-altering drugs; physical dependence uncommon; finds it easy to stop using drugs for short periods of time but very difficult to remain drug abstinence for long periods of time; will not commit to treatment.
Inter-personal Style	Interpersonally anxious (chronic); neurotic attempt to move toward and with significant others; has ability to maintain long-term relationships; dependency conflicts manifest in interpersonal realm.	Lack of interpersonal anxiety; easily establishes superficial relationships; manipulatively exploits others; does not maintain long-term relationships; lacks capacity to establish intimate human relationships; "gets over" and moves against others.

Cognitive Style	Self-dialogue and self-system permeated with self-doubt, low self-esteem, fear, and inadequacy; vacillating narcissism; cognitive obsession and compulsion with drugs and effects of drug use; resentful and harbors angry thoughts; has "superego" or overly strict conscience; cognitive style "normalizes" with abstinence/treatment.	Avoids "zero-state" thinking; obsessed with being "Mr. Big" or omnipotent; narcissistic and total self-orientation; "cuts off" all sense of responsibility associated with irresponsible behavior, etc.; harbors violent/murderous thoughts; no change in cognitive style following abstinence or treatment.
Affective Makeup	Chronic interpersonal and intrapersonal anxiety; fearful; concurrent depressive symptoms; guilty; remorseful; has capacity to love; affectively neurotic; empathic.	Globally affectless; pathologic inability to experience feelings of anxiety, fear, depression, guilt, remorse, love, empathy.

nostic criteria that were delineated earlier in this chapter. The assessment of chemically dependent patients with concurrent antisocial personality disorder is discussed at length in Chapter VIII of Section Two.

It is important for therapists and clinicians to remember that all adjustment typologies exist on a continuum. Therefore, ASPD and substance use disorders are not univariant or absolute entities. There are various gradients of antisocial personality disorder and substance abuse. The information in Table I and this section of the chapter will help clinicians discern these gradients of antisocial personality disorder and substance use. For example, an individual who meets the specific DSM III-R criteria and clinical criteria of substance *dependence* and antisocial personality disorder or substance *abuse* with antisocial personality is dually diagnosed as such.

As indicated earlier in this chapter, substance abuse and chemical dependency generally reinforce acting-out and the outcropping of antisocial behavior. Alcoholics are notorious as "con artists," liars, and manipulators. Chemically dependent patients display many antisocial symptoms. For these reasons, it is essential that the process of differential diagnosis with substance using clients and antisocial clients be extended to include a period of protracted complete drug abstinence. Antisocial personalities continue to act-out after establishing abstinence (Wallace, 1985; Forrest, 1990; Forrest and Gordon, 1990; Nace, 1990). Many chemically dependent patients and substance abusers become pathologically rigid, controlled, armored, and defensive shortly after terminating their chemical dependency.

In sum, chemically dependent persons and substance abusers are chronically anxious, dependent, depressive, guilt-ridden, manifest feelings of inadequacy and worthlessness, and experience self-system fragmentation. These individuals are capable of establishing and maintaining functional but neurotic interpersonal relationships. They also love in a neurotic or conflicted fashion. The super-ego structure and cognitive style of the substance abuser is often self-punitive in nature. Antisocial personalities do not experience intense or chronic interpersonal anxiety. The antisocial person rarely develops tissue dependence but is almost always a substance abuser. These individuals do not experience guilt, depression, or remorse and they are unable to love and maintain long-term functional human relationships. The antisocial personality is narcissistically fixated and rarely feels inadequate or worthless. Psychopaths can be very dangerous. They are malicious manipulators and their superego structure is extremely underdeveloped. Tragically, a small percentage of persons manifest the essential clinical diagnostic features of antisocial personality disorder in combination with substance *dependence*. It has been estimated (Forrest, 1990) that 90 percent of antisocial personalities manifest concurrent patterns of substance abuse. The treatment of individuals who manifest chemical dependency or substance abuse with concurrent ASPD is more difficult, complex, and less successful.

DIFFERENTIAL DIAGNOSIS
OF RELATED PERSONALITY DISORDERS

There are several different classifications or types of personality disorder. For example, the DSM III-R lists 11 primary personality disorders: paranoid personality disorder, schizoid personality disorder, schiztypal personality disorder, antisocial personality disorder, borderline personality disorder, histrionic personality disorder, narcissistic personality disorder, avoidant personality disorder, dependent personality disorder, obsessive-compulsive personality disorder, and passive-aggressive personality disorder. Kernberg (1984) delineates additional forms of personality disorder.

It is important for clinicians to conceptually understand the basic meaning of the "personality disorder" concept. According to the DSM III-R, personality *traits* are "enduring patterns of perceiving, relating to, and thinking about the environment and oneself, and are exhibited in a wide range of important social and personal contexts. It is only when personality *traits* are inflexible and maladaptive and cause either significant functional impairment or subjective distress that they constitute *personality disorders*" (p. 335). It is also noted in the DSM III-R that the symptoms of personality disorders are often manifest by the era of adolescence and these symptoms continue throughout adult life. The DSM III-R states "the diagnostic criteria for the Personality Disorders refers to behaviors or traits that are characteristic of the person's recent (past year) and long-term functioning since early adulthood. The constellation of behaviors or traits causes either significant impairment in social or occupational functioning or subjective distress. The diagnosis of a Personality Disorder should be made only when the characteristic features are typical of the person's long-term functioning and are not limited to discrete episodes of illness" (p. 335).

Chemically dependent persons and substance abusers frequently manifest a concurrent personality disorder. In fact, it has been the author's observation (Forrest, 1983, 1984) that the majority of primary alcoholics who are treated within the context of outpatient psychotherapy manifest concurrent passive-aggressive, dependent, obsessive-compulsive, or borderline personality *features.* Clinicians and therapists need to be able to provide the proper dual-diagnosis (O'Connell, 1990) for these individuals. DSM III-R provides an extensive diagnostic framework for differentially diagnosing individuals who manifest a substance use disorder in combination with one or more Personality Disorders. The reader is encouraged to be familiar with the extensive diagnostic data that are provided for the various personality disorders in the DSM III-R.

The following delineation of the essential features for each major Personality Disorder (DSM III-R) will provide counselors and clinicians with a basic frame of reference relative to the differential and concurrent diagnosis of substance use disorders and Personality Disorders.

> *Paranoid Personality Disorder (301.00):* The essential feature of this disorder is a pervasive and unwarranted tendency, beginning by early adulthood and present in a variety of contexts, to interpret the actions of people as deliberately demeaning or threatening. (p. 337)

> *Schizoid Personality Disorder (301.20):* The essential feature of this disorder is a pervasive pattern of indifference to social relationships and a restricted range of emotional experience and expression, beginning by early adulthood and present in a variety of contexts. (p. 339)

> *Schizopal Personality Disorder (301.22):* The essential feature of this disorder is a pervasive pattern of peculiarities of

ideation, appearance, and behavior and deficits in interpersonal relatedness, beginning by early adulthood and present in a variety of contexts, that are not severe enough to meet the criteria for Schizophrenia. (p. 340)

Antisocial Personality Disorder (301.70): Refer to earlier sections of this chapter and book.

Borderline Personality Disorder (301.83): The essential feature of this disorder is a pervasive pattern of instability of self-image, interpersonal relationships, and mood, beginning by early adulthood and present in a variety of contexts. (p. 346)

Histrionic Personality Disorder (301.50): The essential feature of this disorder is a pervasive pattern of excessive emotionality and attention-seeking, beginning by early adulthood and present in a variety of contexts. (p. 348)

Narcissistic Personality Disorder (301.81): The essential feature of this disorder is a pervasive pattern of grandiosity (in fantasy or behavior), hypersensitivity to the evaluation of others, and lack of empathy that begins by early adulthood and is present in a variety of contexts. (p. 349)

Avoidant Personality Disorder (301.82): The essential feature of this disorder is a pervasive pattern of social discomfort, fear of negative evaluation, and timidity, beginning by early adulthood and present in a variety of contexts. (p. 351)

Dependent Personality Disorder (301.60): The essential feature of this disorder is a pervasive pattern of dependent and submissive behavior beginning by early adulthood and present in a variety of contexts. (p. 354)

Obsessive-Compulsive Personality Disorder (301.40): The essential feature of this disorder is a pervasive pattern of perfectionism and inflexibility, beginning by early adulthood and present in a variety of contexts. (p. 354)

Passive-Aggressive Personality Disorder (301.84): The essential feature of this disorder is a pervasive pattern of passive resistance to demands for adequate social and occupational performance, beginning by early adulthood and present in a variety of contexts. The resistance is expressed indirectly rather than directly, and results in pervasive and persistent social and occupational ineffectiveness even when more self-assertive and effective behavior is possible. (p. 356)

The associated features, impairments, complications, predisposing factors, prevalence, sex ratio, familial patterns, differential diagnoses, and specific diagnostic criteria for each of the above personality disorder classifications are included in the DSM III-R.

As indicated earlier, substance abusers and chemically dependent individuals manifest various concurrent personality disorders. Likewise, antisocial persons manifest various patterns of substance use and dependence. The following case study demonstrates the difficulties and complexities that can be associated with differentially diagnosing substance use disorders and personality disorders.

Jerry R., a 45-year-old, married, Caucasian male and alleged business executive, scheduled a conjoint therapy session (with his wife) with the author. The patient indicated to the author in a pre-therapy phone conversation that he was a "recovering alcoholic." The patient also verbalized that he had been experiencing marital problems due to his wife's rejection of Al-Anon and her inability to "work a program."

The R's were seen in five subsequent conjoint therapy sessions, over a period of two months. After the initial conjoint therapy session, Mr. R. sent the therapist a letter indicating that both he and his wife had lied extensively to the therapist during the first treatment session. When this issue was openly discussed by the therapist with Mr. and Mrs. R. in the second conjoint therapy session, Mrs. R. indicated that (1) Mr. R. lied to her and "everyone else, all the time–I never know if he's telling the truth," (2) she had no idea about what Mr. R. did for a job or career, (3) she knew nothing about their finances or the sources of their income, and (4) she had never in five years of marriage seen Mr. R. intoxicated. Furthermore, Mrs. R. revealed that she had never seen her husband consume more than "one or two drinks" and indicated that he drank only one or two times per month and that he never used other drugs. The R's had been separated for three months prior to initiating conjoint therapy.

During the third therapy session, Mrs. R. revealed that she was extremely anxious about the fact that they had not filed their Federal Income Tax returns to the IRS in five years. She also expressed considerable guilt and wept openly about an episode that had occurred two years earlier. This situation allegedly involved Mr. R's having "swindled" $25,000 from their neighbors and friends. Mrs. R. also revealed to the therapist that Mr. R. had been incarcerated in another state several years ago and that she "knew" he had been married to other women, but she suspected that he had been married several times. She was confused about Mr. R.'s involvement in AA and did not perceive him to be alcoholic. Mr. R. did attend church on a regular basis (the couple actually met at a church function!) and he dressed in expensive three-piece suits, wore expensive shoes, and maintained several offices in the most expensive office areas in their city.

Mr. R. appeared to be bright, emotionally controlled, affectively "cool," and pleasant throughout the brief course of therapy. He explained to the therapist and Mrs. R. that he intended to take care of his "tax problem," and that he felt no guilt about his past problems. He also stressed that Alcoholics Anonymous is a "selfish program." The police came to Mrs. R.'s residence looking for Mr. R. for "questioning" and "bad checks" on several occasions while they were in treatment.

At the end of the fourth conjoint therapy session, Mr. R. indicated that treatment was "a waste of time" and that his wife was not changing. However, he did want to continue having sex with Mrs. R. on a regular basis. He verbalized that his business activities were none of her business and expressed anger at her concerns about the IRS and police.

Mrs. R. decided to file for divorce several weeks after the final conjoint therapy session. She also indicated to the therapist that Mr. R. had left the state and that she had not heard from him again. She was told by a friend that Mr. R. had taken a young woman with him to Arizona.

Unfortunately, no follow-up data are available on the R.'s. A few months after their divorce, Mrs. R. left the state and moved in with her parents. Mrs. R. did pay for her therapy sessions (both Mr. and Mrs. R. decided to "split" the cost of therapy at the time of the first session). Mr. R. paid for his share of the first therapy session but left town owing the therapist for all other sessions.

The R.'s had experienced chronic and severe marital discord prior to entering conjoint therapy. Therapy was not efficacious in this case. It was apparent to the author that Mr. R. was a very manipulative, passive-aggressive, and self-centered man. His prior history of acting-out and antisocial behavior remained unknown to his wife and these issues were not openly explored in treatment. It was the author's opinion that Mr. R. was clearly not alcohol dependent. He was able to gain a great deal of support via his AA involvement and it was suspected that he was also able to financially and psychologically exploit and use other AA members. He was given a diagnosis of passive-aggressive personality disorder. However, the patient could have also been diagnosed as an antisocial personality disorder with concurrent alcohol abuse.

This case clearly demonstrates the complexities of differential diagnostic work with individuals who manifest personality disorders and/or substance use disorders. Mr. R. may also have been a "functional psychopath." These individuals tend to be better socialized, less aggressive, brighter, more controlled, and generally "slicker" than the vast majority of psychopaths. In fact, many functional psychopaths are able to achieve considerable success as lawyers, politicians, businessmen, and health professionals. Passive-aggressive personalities and functional psychopaths may be over-represented among the ranks of chemical dependency counselors and mental health professionals.

SUMMARY

This chapter provided an in-depth examination of the (1) treatment oriented gains that are associated with differential diagnosis, (2) clinical diagnosis of substance use disorders, (3) DSM III-R diagnosis of substance use disorders, (4) clinical diagnosis of antisocial personality disorder, (5) DSM III-R diagnosis of antisocial personality disorder, (6) differential and concurrent diagnosis of substance use disorders and antisocial personality disorder, and (7) differential diagnosis of related personality disorders.

The diagnostic process occurs within the context of the therapist-patient relationship. The practice of openly discussing the patient's diagnosis (with the patient) facilitates several sources of therapeutic gain. This technique often "fosters" alacrity and the development of a working and productive therapeutic alliance.

The clinical assessment of substance use disorders involves an examination of patterns of substance use, interpersonal and psychological factors, medical, legal, and social aspects of substance use, and self-regulation issues. Substance use was distinguished from substance abuse and substance dependence in this chapter. The disease model of substance abuse was also explored. Primary, secondary, and reactive forms of alcoholism or chemical dependency were outlined. A number of medical and psychological tests that are used to diagnose substance use disorders were discussed.

DSM III-R criteria for the diagnosis of psychoactive substance dependence and psychoactive substance abuse were included in this chapter.

A clinical diagnosis of antisocial personality disorder is applied to individuals who are impulsive, manipulative, guiltless, aggressive, and unable to love or form lasting human relationships. The 16 basic characteristics of the "Cleckley Psychopath" ([1941] 1976) were elucidated in this chapter. An in-depth clinical examination of the Nazi Luftwaffe Chief, Hermann Goering, was also presented.

DSM III-R criteria for the diagnosis of antisocial personality disorder was included in the chapter.

The section that discusses the differential and concurrent diagnosis of substance use disorders and antisocial personality disorder is very important. It is emphasized that antisocial persons are rarely substance dependent. However, the vast majority of psychopaths are substance abusers. Substance abuse (Forrest and Gordon, 1990; Forrest, 1990) is associated with most forms of criminal behavior. Qualitative and quantative factors associated with total drug abstinence can be essential to the differential diagnosis of antisocial personality disorder and substance use disorders. It is estimated that less than 20 percent of chemically dependent individuals manifest a concurrent antisocial personality disorder. Table I outlined the pattern of substance use, interpersonal style, cognitive style, and affective make-up that differentiates ASPD's and primary substance abusers. It is emphasized in this section of the chapter that all adjustment typologies exist on continuum and that virtually all forms of substance abuse reinforce the outcropping of antisocial behaviors and patterns of adjustment.

The essential diagnostic features of 11 (DSM III-R) additional personality disorders were included in this chapter. Personality disorder is also defined in the final section. Substance abusers and substance dependent persons may manifest one or more concurrent personality disorders. Alcoholics are notoriously "passive-aggressive" in their interactions with significant others. A number of case studies were presented. These case studies demonstrate the various caveats that are associated with differentially assessing the substance use disorders, antisocial personality disorder, and related personality disorders.

Chapter VI

Conclusion to Section One

As indicated in Chapter I of this section, antisocial persons and chemically dependent persons have created myriad social problems throughout the course of human history. Behavioral scientists have historically tended to view alcoholics and chemically dependent persons as "psychopaths." Indeed, it has long been apparent that chemically dependent and antisocial persons generally share a number of common cognitive, behavioral, interpersonal, and affective characteristics. Yet, antisocial and chemically dependent persons are often radically different in some or many areas of functioning.

Saddam Hussein, the international terrorist and President of Iraq, is a frightening example of antisocial personality disorder. Adolph Hitler and Saddam Hussein are perhaps the "best" or worst examples of antisocial personality disorder in modern history. Hitler eventually became chemically dependent as the Third Reich began to crumble. We know very little about the substance use history of Saddam Hussein. Perhaps Hussein will also become chemically dependent.

Chapters II through V examined the major facets of antisocial personality disorder and chemical dependency: prevalence, sex ratio, environmental and cultural factors, genetic and family factors, etiology and etiological theories, diagnosis, differential and concurrent diagnosis, and case studies. The data pertaining to each of these areas of investigation are related to antisocial personality disorder and the substance use disorders.

It is the author's opinion that virtually all chemically dependent persons manifest one or more concurrent personality disorders. Chemically dependent persons are by definition "dependent" and thus manifest concurrent dependent personality disorder. Chemically dependent patients and substance abusers are notoriously passive-aggressive. Perhaps 80 percent of chemically dependent patients have concurrent passive-aggressive personality disorder. Relatively few (less than 20 percent) chemically dependent persons manifest bona fide concurrent antisocial personality disorder.

An accurate diagnosis and differential diagnosis of chemical dependence and concurrent antisocial personality disorder is essential to the effective treatment of these clinical populations. The information and data presented in this section will contribute greatly to the practicing clinician's ability to properly diagnose and treat chemically dependent/substance abusing clients as well as antisocial clients who manifest a concurrent substance use disorder. Antisocial persons who manifest concurrent chemical dependency and/or substance abuse are doubly or perhaps triply difficult to treat! Techniques and methods for treating chemically dependent antisocial persons are presented in Section Two.

Antisocial behavior as well as addictive behavior exists on a continuum. These particular adjustment styles also seem to be interactively dependent and reinforcing. Substance abuse and chemical dependency facilitate acting-out and antisocial behavior (Forrest and Gordon, 1990). Antisocial persons are usually under the influence of alcohol and/or other mood altering drugs when they act-out (Hansen, 1991). Drug use upon the part of any antisocial person generally escalates the risk of dangerousness or potential for violent acting-out upon the part of such a person.

Chemical dependency counselors have only recently begun to understand the various interactive complexities that are associated with the problem of "dual diagnosis." Therapists in the chemical dependency field have struggled in their treatment relationships with chemically dependent or substance abusing antisocial personalities. Corrections counselors and therapists who work with antisocial persons on a regular basis understand the pathology and dynamics of antisocial personality disorder all too well. Unfortunately, these clinicians tend to be poorly trained in the areas of chemical dependency assessment and treatment. This section provides extensive diagnostic and treatment information for all mental health workers who are involved with antisocial, chemically dependent, or concurrently antisocial and chemically dependent patients.

As noted earlier, it is the author's opinion that a fundamental understanding of the information presented in this section is prerequisite to the task of attempting to treat personality disordered substance abusers and chemically dependent persons. The treatment of the chemically dependent or substance abusing antisocial patient is addressed throughout Section Two of this book.

SECTION TWO:
PSYCHOTHERAPY
AND REHABILITATION

Chapter VII

Treatment Implications:
Introduction and Overview

Section One examined the diagnostic parameters of the substance use disorders and antisocial personality disorder. It was emphasized in Section One that an accurate differential diagnosis of the substance use disorders and ASPD is essential to the effective treatment and clinical management of these patient subgroups.

Section Two includes an in-depth exploration of effective strategies of psychotherapy and treatment for substance abusers and chemically dependent persons who manifest a concurrent antisocial personality disorder. Clinicians agree (Bratter, 1980; Zimberg, 1982; Forrest, 1983, 1984; Wallace, 1985, 1989; Forrest and Gordon, 1990; Nace, 1990) that alcoholics and substance abusers can be very difficult to treat. Indeed, these patients may be poor candidates for traditional dynamically oriented psychotherapies and treatments (Forrest, 1978). It is also widely accepted (Cleckley, [1941] 1976; Reid et al., 1986; Doren, 1987; Forrest, 1991) that antisocial patients are very difficult to treat. The psychotherapy outcome prognosis of the ASPD (McCord and McCord, 1964; Yochelson and Samenow, 1977, 1986) has traditionally been reported to be very poor.

In view of these realities, it is not surprising that therapists and clinicians have historically been less than enthusiastic and optimistic about working with chemically dependent and antisocial persons. No doubt therapist negative treatment outcome expectancy can play an important role in fostering actual negative therapeutic outcomes! Several other major factors have contributed to our unsuccessful attempts to treat chemically dependent and antisocial persons. First of all, it is important to simply realize that these particular clinical subpopulations *are* difficult to treat. Therapists have tried to work with these patients for several decades. A diversity of behavioral scientists has consistently reported that their efforts with antisocial and substance abusing patients have not been successful. If these patients were easy to treat and had an excellent therapeutic prognosis, large numbers of clinicians would have been reporting these findings for several years! Such has not been the case.

One factor that has clearly impeded our efforts to successfully treat these individuals is the historic lack of creative or innovative treatment models within the mental health and chemical dependency fields. Prior to the 1960s, virtually all psychopaths and substance abusers received the same "brand" or type of treatment. In essence, psychoanalytic and psychodynamic treatment approaches were redundantly utilized to treat these individuals. It is now widely recognized (Zimberg, 1982; Brown, 1985, 1988; Bratter and Forrest, 1985; Pattison, 1987; O'Connell, 1990) that these treatments systematically do not work when they are applied to chemically dependent and/or antisocial populations. Furthermore, the systems of psychotherapy and models of treatment that were innovatively developed during the 1950s through the early 1970s have not proven particularly effective in the treatment of these disorders (Rogers, 1952; Ellis and Harper, 1961; Glasser, 1965; Harris, 1969; Truax and Carkhuff, 1967; Bowen, 1978).

Thus, it is not particularly surprising that most behavioral scientists who attempted to work with antisocial and/or chemically dependent patients during earlier decades reached the same basic conclusion: psychotherapy or psychological treatment does very little to benefit these individuals. In a corollary fashion, as increasing numbers of therapists utilized essentially the same treatments with these patients and consistently failed in their therapeutic efforts, fewer and fewer therapists chose to work with these difficult populations.

A number of practical factors has also contributed to the problematic nature of treating antisocial and chemically dependent patients. These patients are manipulative, angry, demanding and self-centered, and impulsive. They frequently miss treatment sessions, refuse to pay bills, lie to the therapist, and may actually physically threaten the therapist. These individuals are also prone to violent acting-out against spouses, children, and other family members.

They also experience alcohol/drug relapses while in treatment (Gorski, 1989, 1991), and their motivation for entering and remaining in treatment is extrinsically determined. Therapists who work with these individuals find themselves enmeshed with other family members, the police, employers, probation or parole officers, lawyers, and the court system. In sum, it is very easy to understand why most therapists and behavioral scientists have historically avoided working with substance abusers and antisocial persons!

This global sense of pessimism about the treatment of chemical dependency began to change in the United States in the early 1970s. Indeed, the Vietnam War era ushered in a new sense of awareness and optimism about the treatment of chemical dependency. The treatment of chemical dependency also became a political as well as a psychosocial issue at that time. Large numbers of behavioral scientists were "drafted" into military alcohol and drug rehabilitation programs between 1965 and 1975. For the first time in modern behavioral science history, clinicians began to report large numbers of successfully treated cases of chemical dependency. Hundreds of chemical dependency rehabilitation programs were mandatorily established in every branch of the military service throughout the United States and abroad.

The development of military alcohol and drug rehabilitation programs facilitated the involvement of thousands of professional and paraprofessional behavioral scientists in the chemical dependency treatment field. This process synergized the development and practical application of different or innovative treatment strategies within the field of chemical dependency. Bona fide careers for physicians, psychologists, counselors, social workers, nurses, and other health professionals emerged within the chemical dependency field.

The American collective began to develop an awareness of a pervasive "drug abuse crisis" during the early 1970s. This awareness was fostered by many factors. Certainly the return of thousands of young alcohol and drug abusing soldiers from Vietnam made Americans more aware of the growing "drug problem" in our society. The establishment of a diversity of rehabilitation programs in the military also fostered this growing collective awareness and concern about drug abuse. In short, an overabundant and multifaceted "supply" of chemical dependency related "problems" in Ameri-

ca eventually led to a collective *demand* for treatment or professional rehabilitation services for substance abusers. Chemically dependent persons began to be perceived as "sick" individuals who required and deserved professional health care, as well as self-help.
Moreover, by the mid-1970s, many health service providers, as well
as health corporations, realized that the demand and need for chemical dependency rehabilitation services would annually generate bil-
lions of dollars for treatment services. Research monies, educational
grants, training stipends, and funding for treatment programs became available for individuals and agencies who were involved in
chemical dependency. In short, alcohol and drug education, prevention, and rehabilitation became "big business" in the United States.
It is clear that the "drug crisis" of the late 1960s and 1970s has not
abated or been resolved. Unfortunately, the problems that are
associated with chemical dependency became increasingly more
pervasive, complex, and recalcitrant during the decade of the 1980s,
and continue in the 1990s.

Many of these realities parallel the history and development of
treatment strategies for antisocial persons. As noted in earlier chapters, behavioral scientists have generally avoided treating "psychopaths." The treatment prognosis for antisocial personality disorder
has long been negative. These individuals are notoriously manipulative, self-centered, impulsive, aggressive, and insensitive to the social and moral values that govern human behavior. Many of these
individuals are also substance abusers. Some are extremely dangerous, and protracted clinical interaction with these individuals may
prove to be psychonoxious for the therapist! Needless to say, antisocial persons resist treatment and are not motivated to remain in
programs that utilize intensive or long-term rehabilitation models.

These problematic treatment issues are made even more difficult
by the reality of the large number of antisocial persons within our
society. The fact is that American jails, prisons, correctional facilities, and detention centers are filled with antisocial persons! There is
a continuously increasing social and political demand for the treatment of antisocial persons in the United States and throughout much
of the modern world. It is reasonable to expect that comprehensive
treatment programs for antisocial persons will become "big business" within the mental health field during the next two decades.

These programs for antisocial personality disordered persons will grow and flourish like the programs that were developed for alcoholics and substance abusers during the 1970s and 1980s. Indeed, the private business sector may very soon become the biggest single provider of clinical services for antisocial persons. The federal government and state governments are financially unable to "warehouse" the vast number of antisocial persons in basic institutional facilities, let alone finance the treatment and rehabilitation of these individuals.

As behavioral scientists develop more effective and innovative treatments for antisocial persons (Reid et al., 1986; Doren, 1987; Forrest, 1990), it is only reasonable to expect that the treatment of these individuals will assume a more accepted, prestigious, and widespread position within the field of mental health. The ability to consistently demonstrate that a particular patient population can be successfully treated synergizes (1) the development of widespread interest in this population; (2) the creation of relatively different and innovative treatments specific to the population; (3) financial and manpower expenditures for treatment, prevention, research, training, and education specific to the population; and (4) widespread economic, political, and collective attitudinal and perceptual changes relative to the population. All of these processes are at least obsequiously operational within the purview of mental health.

This section summarizes and expands upon the progress that has been made within the chemical dependency and mental health fields during the past 20 years. A great deal of the content in these chapters is based upon the direct clinical experience of the author with chemically dependent or abusing patients and antisocial patients with concurrent substance use disorders. This clinical experience encompasses over 20 years of private practice and agency work with these specific patient populations.

In essence, this section addresses the psychotherapy and treatment of very difficult patient populations. The treatment of substance abusers with concurrent antisocial personality disorder may be as difficult as the treatment of chronic schizophrenics. Yet, a segment of this clinical population is amenable to treatment. Structure is an important practical, as well as dynamic, component of the psychotherapy and rehabilitation of patients with impulse control problems. A plethora of relationship issues impacts the process of psychotherapy with substance abusers and antisocial persons. Many, if not all, antisocial patients can be considered dangerous. Thus, the process of psychotherapy with these individuals is always fraught with pitfalls and dangers. Most substance abusers and alcoholics (Emrick, 1991; Miller, 1988; Gorski, 1991) evidence positive gains as a function of involvement in various psychological treatments. The prognosis for chemically dependent antisocial patients seems to be very poor (Nace, 1990).

The content of this section is new. These issues have not been examined in depth by other psychotherapists and clinicians in the chemical dependency treatment field. The reader will find that an appreciation and understanding of the many sensitive treatment issues discussed in this section will greatly enhance his or her treatment effectiveness with substance abusers in general, as well as with chemically dependent patients who manifest concurrent ASPD.

Chapter VIII

Dual Diagnosis Dilemmas: Treatment of Chemically Dependent Patients with Concurrent Antisocial Personality Disorder

INTRODUCTION

As noted in Section One, substance abusers and chemically dependent patients have historically tended to be diagnosed as "psychopaths," acting-out neurotics, and passive-aggressive personalities. Substance abusers have generally been perceived as a unidimensional clinical population by behavioral scientists and diagnosticians. These individuals have also historically received unidimensional treatment. Indeed, chemically dependent and substance abusing patients have been perceived as: (1) basically "all the same" with regard to cognitive, affective, behavioral, interpersonal, and psychodynamic makeup; (2) unsuitable for involvement in traditional psychological/psychiatric treatment models; and (3) appropriate candidates for essentially one form of treatment: self-help treatment, such as Alcoholics Anonymous, Narcotics Anonymous, and Cocaine Anonymous.

These beliefs and perceptions have changed significantly during the past 15 years. Modern behavioral scientists and clinicians (Forrest, 1978; Lawson, Ellis, and Rivers, 1984; Bratter and Forrest, 1985; Pattison, 1987; Emrick, 1991) realize that substance abusers manifest various personality, behavioral, affective, cognitive, and interpersonal characteristics. The one essential common denominator of substance abuse and chemical dependency is simply the inability of the addict or abuser to stop and/or control his or her ingestion of an addictive substance (Forrest, 1984). Thus, it is now recognized by behavioral scientists that "all drug addicts and substance abusers are *not* the same."

Therapists are also beginning to discover that modified traditional treatment modalities can be successfully utilized to treat large numbers of substance abusers. It is now widely recognized that there are hundreds of thousands of recovering alcoholics and substance abusers in the United States. Behavioral scientists, as well as the general public, are also beginning to realize that there are several effective treatments currently available for chemical dependency and substance abuse. Alcoholics Anonymous (McFadden, 1991) is not the only effective treatment for alcohol dependence, and researchers are finding (Ogborne and Glaser, 1985; Emrick, 1990, 1991) that self-help, such as AA, actually fosters psychonoxious treatment outcomes for select individuals.

There is a growing realization on the part of behavioral scientists in the chemical dependency treatment field (Zimberg, 1982; Forrest, 1984; Forrest and Gordon, 1990) that many substance abusers manifest a concurrent antisocial personality disorder. It has been estimated (Forrest, 1983b) that roughly 10 percent of chemically dependent individuals entering alcohol and drug rehabilitation programs manifest concurrent ASPD. Approximately 90 percent of antisocial personalities are *substance abusers* (Forrest, 1983b; Forrest and Gordon, 1990). Although most antisocial personalities are frequent or episodic substance abusers, it is clinically significant that these individuals are perhaps no more likely to develop chemical dependency than individuals randomly selected from the general population.

The treatment of substance abusers and chemically dependent persons with concurrent antisocial personality disorder is always difficult (Nace, 1990). This chapter examines various facets of the treatment of substance abusers with concurrent antisocial personality disorder. These dual diagnosis dilemmas contribute to the nefarious treatment complications that therapists routinely experience in their work with chemically dependent and substance abusing antisocial patients. In essence, the present chapter will help clinicians: (1) recognize when they are dealing with chemically dependent or substance abusing clients who manifest concurrent ASPD; and (2) utilize more efficacious and individualized treatment interventions or strategies in their clinical work with these individuals.

It should also be noted that the treatment of substance abusers with concurrent antisocial personality disorder represents only one of the major "dual diagnosis dilemmas" confronting therapists in the chemical dependency treatment field. Substance abusers and chemically dependent patients can manifest a plethora of dual diagnosis dilemmas associated with concurrent depression or affective disorder, thought disturbance, brain syndrome, sexual disturbance, other personality disorders, and virtually every other form of psychopathology known to mankind!

DIFFERENTIAL ASSESSMENT

As indicated in Chapter V (Section One), substance abusers with concurrent antisocial personality disorder are individuals who manifest the essential clinical and/or DSM III-R (APA, 1987) diagnostic characteristics of *both* classifications of adjustment and behavior. In general, a diagnosis of substance *abuse* with concurrent antisocial personality disorder is applied to individuals who: (1) use and abuse but are not physically addicted to one or more mood-altering, psychoactive substances; and (2) also manifest a long-term adjustment style that is characterized by irresponsible and antisocial behavior. Individuals who are diagnosed as substance *dependent* with concurrent antisocial personality disorder are physically and psychologically addicted to one or more mood-altering substances. These people also manifest a long-term adjustment style that is characterized by irresponsible and antisocial behavior. Physical addiction or tissue dependence (Forrest, 1983a, 1984, 1991) is the essential differentiating clinical feature that determines a diagnosis of substance *dependence* with concurrent antisocial personality disorder in contrast to substance *abuse* with concurrent antisocial personality disorder.

Aside from the important clinical distinctions between substance abuse and substance dependence, individuals who manifest any form of substance use disorder in combination with antisocial personality disorder are globally irresponsible, impulsive, self-centered, immature, aggressive, promiscuous, unable to love or sustain lasting, close, warm, empathetic relationships with others, and lack the capacity to experience guilt. These individuals abuse or sometimes become addicted to alcohol and various other mood-altering drugs. Lying, stealing, driving while intoxicated, fighting, truancy, arrests and incarceration, and severe narcissism are also characteristics of the substance abuser or chemically dependent patient with concurrent antisocial personality disorder.

The following case study is an example of alcohol dependence and polydrug abuse with concurrent antisocial personality disorder.

> Lester C. was a 41-year-old Vietnam veteran. The patient entered psychotherapy shortly after assaulting a man in a barroom. Lester reported in the initial therapy session that he had been drinking "two to three six-packs of beer, plus at least a pint of vodka, every day for over ten years." He also stated, "I've never been able to control my temper–I'm a bad son of a bitch, drunk or sober." The patient had been court-ordered to enter therapy as an alternative to incarceration. He was seen within the context of 18 individual psychotherapy sessions.
>
> As a young child and adolescent, the patient had been physically and verbally abused by his alcoholic father. His mother was described as a passive-dependent and inadequate woman who was continually abused by Lester's brutal father. Lester's mother "disappeared" when he was 16 years old and was never seen again. The patient began to physically fight with his father around the age of 14 and reported that he could "beat the shit out of the old man by the time I was 16." Lester was continually in fights in school. He was expelled several times between the seventh and tenth grades and finally dropped out of school in the eleventh grade. Lester described his one younger sister as "a saint in comparison with me." He also revealed in therapy that his father had sexually abused his sister.
>
> The patient joined the Army a few months after quitting high school and subsequently served two tours of duty in Vietnam. He was awarded several medals, including one Purple Heart, for acts of gallantry and heroism while in Vietnam.

Although Lester indicated that he began drinking alcohol at age 11 and repeatedly drank to the point of intoxication between the ages of 11 and 17, he did not become a maintenance drinker or alcohol dependent until several months after his discharge from the Army.

After leaving the service, Lester was unable to hold a job. He was repeatedly arrested for assaults, public intoxication, driving while intoxicated, writing bad checks, and various other antisocial behaviors. He smoked marijuana and regularly used cocaine and "speed" for several years. He became a "collections man" for "the syndicate" and actively sold and distributed narcotics and other drugs for ten years. Lester was also hospitalized and "dried out" in three different Veterans' Administration medical centers between 1973 and 1977.

The patient was married for three years during the early 1970s. He indicated that this relationship was very conflicted and that he periodically abused his wife after coming home drunk. She divorced the patient in 1973, and he had no further contact with her or his son. Lester took great pride in not having paid "one red cent in alimony or support to that bitch." He had dated and lived with a long series of women after the marital relationship ended.

It is important to point out that Lester was referred for medical evaluation and subsequent hospitalization following his initial therapy session. The patient was medically detoxified for a period of eight days and then seen in weekly outpatient psychotherapy for over three months. He refused to attend AA meetings, missed scheduled therapy sessions, drank and used other drugs while in treatment, failed to complete his payments for therapy, and unilaterally terminated treatment via leaving the state while on probation. He did not perceive himself as an "alcoholic" but did indicate to the therapist that he "sometimes felt bad" about an elderly couple whom he had killed in an automobile accident some five years before entering therapy. This patient had been arrested for DUI 18 times in the state of Colorado between 1977 and 1981.

This case study clearly demonstrates alcohol dependence and concurrent antisocial personality disorder. The patient manifested a long history of antisocial behavior in combination with a protracted history of alcohol addiction. An accurate clinical assessment of substance abuse or substance dependence in combination with antisocial personality disorder constitutes one major dual diagnosis dilemma that impacts the treatment process and outcome with these patients.

When therapists fail to accurately diagnose substance abuse or chemical dependency with concurrent ASPD, their treatment interventions are consistently inappropriate or strategically ineffectual. Thus, therapists are confronted with the dilemma of first knowing what malady or aberration for which a patient requires therapy before they are able to utilize treatments which can reliably be expected to modify the patient's symptom structure.

PATIENT MOTIVATION
TO ENTER AND REMAIN COMMITTED
TO THE TREATMENT PROCESS

Chemically dependent and antisocial persons are notoriously difficult to treat (Forrest, 1978, 1985; Anderson, 1989; Matuschka, 1988; Nace, 1990). Furthermore, these clinical populations are also consistently reluctant to enter and remain in psychotherapy and other psychologically oriented treatments. In view of the fact that the vast majority of chemically dependent and antisocial persons do not experience a "spontaneous remission" of their pathologic symptoms (Zimberg, 1982; Wallace, 1985; Knauert, 1992; Forrest, 1990), it is imperative that therapists make every effort to somehow motivate these individuals to persist in treatment. The globally destructive characteristics of these individuals were discussed in Section One. It is logical to expect that these patients will not "recover" or radically modify their adjustment styles in the absence of an active, extended, and committed involvement to some form of effective treatment regimen.

In view of these difficult realities and caveats, another major dual diagnosis dilemma with which the therapist is faced in working with these patients is simply finding and utilizing therapeutic strategies which motivate the patient to both enter and remain committed to the treatment process. This task is even more difficult and complicated in working with substance abusers or chemically dependent persons who are concurrently antisocial. Chemically dependent patients deny that they have a "drinking" or "drug" problem, and they actively avoid involvement in most forms of treatment. The chemically dependent or substance abusing patient who is also antisocial will sometimes go to any lengths to avoid therapy or being involved in a treatment program. These persons can be extremely manipulative, ruthless, and cunning in their efforts to avoid treatment. Needless to say, it can be even more difficult to keep them in treatment once they enter therapy or some other form of treatment program.

Chemically dependent patients and substance abusers with concurrent antisocial personalities are not *internally* motivated to enter and remain committed to the treatment process. However, many of these individuals become externally motivated to enter treatment vis à vis the courts or legal system. Their alcohol and drug facilitated acting-out behaviors eventually result in arrests and involvement with the court system. It is clinically appropriate and efficacious for counselors who work with these clients to utilize the legal system per se to motivate the client to enter and remain committed to a treatment program. Therapy, self-help involvement, psychotropic medication, and other treatments can be mandated components of a penal institution or probation program. Therapists need to be wise, creative, and firm in their efforts to utilize the legal system to motivate these patients to remain in treatment. Indeed, the therapist's armamentarium must encompass techniques, structures, and leverage that are not limited to the patient-therapist relationship.

Antisocial personalities with concurrent substance use disorder simply do not enter psychotherapy or some other form of treatment on a self-motivated basis and then remain committed to the treatment process for several months or years. Indeed, it is generally correct to assume that these individuals only enter treatment when they are externally forced or "nudged" into treatment. It is imperative that counselors and treatment systems "lock in" on the client and make every effort to provide appropriate, effective, and timely treatments.

The psychotherapist can begin to focus upon issues that pertain to fostering the patient's intrinsic motivation to remain in treatment after the patient becomes engaged in any system that forces him or her into treatment. A diversity of therapeutic techniques and strategies (Lazarus, 1981; Bratter and Forrest, 1985; Yochelson and Samenow, 1986; Doren, 1987; Forrest and Gordon, 1990) can be utilized to motivate these clients to remain in treatment after they become engaged in treatment. Furthermore, these treatment modalities can be effective.

Thus, a major dilemma and deterrent to the treatment of substance abusers with concurrent ASPD is basically the inability to motivate these individuals to enter treatment programs and remain committed to the treatment process. It is generally much easier to motivate chemically dependent patients and substance abusers who are not antisocial to enter therapy and remain in treatment. The antisocial substance abuser views others, the "system," and the world as the source of his or her problems. He or she is not at fault. He or she is not in need of treatment. The dilemma that counselors and treatment programs face in working with these extremely resistive clients is modifying and overcoming the client's resistance.

THE ABSTINENCE DILEMMA

Clinicians who work with chemically dependent patients and substance abusers generally agree that primary addicts or individuals who have protracted histories of tissue dependence (Forrest, 1983b) need to be involved in treatment programs that advocate total drug abstinence. There is less agreement among behavioral scientists about the need for total abstinence for *abusers* (Miller, 1988; Forrest, 1989). Researchers (Miller, 1988; Emrick, 1990, 1991) have consistently reported that some alcohol abusers and possibly even alcoholics can return to social or "controlled" drinking. The issue of controlled use of marijuana, cocaine, narcotics, prescription drugs, and other addictive substances is even more confusing and conflictual. Is it appropriate for therapists and treatment programs to advocate complete abstinence from substances like cocaine and marijuana if a patient has never been addicted to these particular drugs?

Substance *dependent* persons who manifest a concurrent antisocial personality disorder clearly need to be involved in therapies and treatment programs that actively and consistently advocate total abstinence. But what about substance *abusers* who manifest a concurrent antisocial personality disorder? Do these patients need to be committed to total abstinence for life? These questions appear to be even more difficult to answer when we take into account the fact that the vast majority of antisocial personalities are substance abusers and not chemically dependent.

It is the author's opinion that the dilemma of total drug abstinence for substance abusers with concurrent ASPD is really not a dilemma! These individuals, like substance dependent antisocial persons, need to be involved in therapies and treatment programs that actively and consistently advocate total abstinence from the use of any/all mood-altering substances. The antisocial behaviors, cognitions, and adjustment styles of all antisocial substance abusers are reinforced, become less controlled, and become more pathologic as a result of any use of mood-altering drugs.

Substance abusers with antisocial personality disorder are far more likely to act out against significant others, society, and themselves when they are under the influence of alcohol or other addictive substances (Forrest and Gordon, 1990). These individuals continue to act out in potentially dangerous and pathologic ways when they are ingesting drugs. If they are drunk or under the influence of drugs daily, once a week, once a month, or only once a year, this reality does not change. Any and all drug use upon the part of these patients synergizes their criminal and antisocial trends. Thus, the patient needs to remain drug free.

It has been stressed throughout this text that antisocial persons with concurrent substance use disorder are extremely difficult to treat. It is virtually impossible to treat these individuals when they are intoxicated or continuing to use mood-altering substances while in therapy. Indeed, a basic precursor to the initiation of any type of psychotherapy with this patient population is drug abstinence. It is just as difficult and impossible to treat substance abusing antisocial patients who continue to ingest drugs while in treatment as it is to treat substance dependent antisocial patients who continue to use mood-altering drugs while in treatment!

In view of these realities, perhaps the major dilemma with which counselors and therapists are faced in working with these patients is that of maintaining patient drug abstinence throughout the course of treatment. Drug and alcohol relapses or "massive regressions" (Forrest, 1978; Gorski and Miller, 1986; Gorski, 1989; Forrest, 1991) are rather predictable components of effective as well as ineffective treatment of the substance use disorders. While it is impossible for the therapist or treatment program to keep the patient sober or drug abstinent, it is important for these agents of change to actively foster the patient's commitment to a drug-free lifestyle. It is clinically appropriate for the therapist to utilize random urine testing, the "breathalizer" test, Antabuse maintenance, narcotic blockers, AA and other self-help adjuncts, and various other therapeutic modalities in his or her efforts to facilitate abstinence and the recovery process.

Effective treatment of these individuals occurs when the patient has developed an internalized and self-sustained capacity to remain committed to total drug abstinence during and after completion of the treatment process. Counselors need to be flexible, creative, persistent, and focused in their efforts to help antisocial patients with concurrent substance use disorder accept the commitment to total drug abstinence.

THE TREATABILITY DILEMMA

Are substance abusing and chemically dependent antisocial patients treatable? Is it reasonable to expect that some or many of these individuals can be successfully treated? Are there certain treatment modalities that have proven therapeutically efficacious for these persons?

Unfortunately, questions such as these are very difficult to answer. The historic behavioral science perspective on antisocial and substance abusing patients is that they are very difficult to treat. Furthermore, a diversity of treatments (Yalisove, 1989) has been applied to these individuals with limited success. Nonetheless, hundreds of thousands of antisocial substance abusers and chemically dependent persons receive a diversity of treatments each day throughout the United States and elsewhere in the world. These individuals have received treatment in private clinics, psychiatric hospitals, prisons, correctional facilities, alcohol and drug programs, halfway houses, social service agencies, and mental health centers for several decades. Furthermore, antisocial persons and substance abusers will continue to be seen for treatment in these settings for several decades to come.

From a pragmatic perspective, it matters very little if these individuals are truly treatable. They have been and will continue to be treated by behavioral scientists. Substance abusing and chemically dependent psychopaths engage in a plethora of destructive and risky behaviors that simply result in engagement in health service delivery systems. For example, these individuals are frequently arrested for DUI (driving under the influence) and subsequently are incarcerated or legally "forced" into various types of alcohol/drug treatment and educational programs. They are also mandatorily seen for treatment within mental health settings and correctional or probation settings. In sum, our American social system demands and dictates that these individuals will receive a broad spectrum of psychological/psychiatric treatments–regardless of the treatability of the individual patient or the efficacy of the treatments that are applied to large numbers of these persons!

Our social demand for the treatment of substance abusers with concurrent antisocial personality disorder can be expected to result eventually in the development of relatively new and more efficacious treatment modalities specific to this particular patient population. This is exactly what began to occur in the field of alcoholism and drug rehabilitation during the late 1960s and early 1970s. It has become increasingly apparent to behavioral scientists that the substance use disorders can be successfully treated. It is reasonable to expect that more effective treatment for substance abusers with concurrent ASPD will be developed during the next 10-20 years. Until therapists are able to develop more specific and more effective treatment modalities for this population, all of us who work with these patients will simply attempt to be effective change agents. The struggle to develop more efficacious treatments for substance abusing or chemically dependent antisocial patients will evolve from the therapeutic process. Until the time that we are able to provide highly effective treatment for these persons, the "treatability dilemma" will simply continue to be a dilemma! Therapists will continue to be forced to treat these patients with a regimen of therapies and treatments that have thus far not proven to be effective.

DURATION OF TREATMENT DILEMMA

The duration of treatment dilemma is closely associated with the other dilemmas that have been discussed in this chapter. In general, individuals who diagnostically manifest antisocial personality disorder in combination with a substance use disorder require more lengthy, intensive, and structured treatments than do substance abusers and chemically dependent persons who are not antisocial.

Although the dually diagnosed patient may need a more lengthy treatment involvement, these individuals tend to be less motivated to enter and remain committed to treatment than substance abusers who are not concurrently antisocial. In essence, these patients actively resist involvement in treatment models (Forrest and Gordon, 1990) that are most likely to help them change. Furthermore, the antisocial substance abuser's motivation and commitment to treatment is inversely related to his or her awareness of the need or requirement for long-term care. These patients may be highly motivated for involvement in treatment programs that last for a few days or a few weeks. They avoid and are unable to sustain working commitments to treatment models that involve several months or several years of active participation.

Therapists are confronted with the dilemma of engaging and then motivating these individuals to persist in long-term treatment programs. Brief therapies and short-term treatment programs (Forrest, 1978, 1984, 1985, 1991) are of little benefit in the rehabilitation of chemically dependent or substance abusing antisocial patients. The psychotherapist needs to utilize all available sources of therapeutic "leverage" in order to facilitate the patient's participation in extended therapy and rehabilitation programs. It is incumbent upon the therapist to creatively utilize appropriate legal, familial, work, health, and psychological strategies in order to foster patient participation in long-term treatment models.

Treatment personnel need to openly and honestly tell these individuals that their rehabilitation success or failure can be directly associated with such variables as length of time in treatment, motivation to change, and active commitment to the treatment process. Therapists also need to be firm, consistent, highly structured, and appropriately confrontive or direct in their therapeutic interactions with these patients. The antisocial substance abuser seeks treatments that are "easier, softer, and shorter." These types of therapy or rehabilitation simply do not "work" when used with this particular clinical population.

GENERAL TREATMENT MODEL FOR SUBSTANCE ABUSERS AND CHEMICALLY DEPENDENT PATIENTS WITH CONCURRENT ANTISOCIAL PERSONALITY DISORDER

The therapeutic difficulties and dilemmas that are associated with the psychotherapy and treatment of substance abusers with concurrent antisocial personality disorder can be overwhelmingly negative. Indeed, in view of these thorny issues, it is not surprising that most therapists choose not to work with antisocial addicts or substance abusers. Nonetheless, some of these persons can be successfully rehabilitated. The following general treatment model is based on the author's over 20 years of direct clinical experience with antisocial substance abusers and chemically dependent patients. This treatment approach or model can be utilized in both outpatient and inpatient rehabilitation settings.

Patient selection for inclusion in this treatment model is based primarily on the diagnosis of antisocial personality disorder. The reality that the patient is a substance abuser or is chemically dependent is of secondary clinical importance. This treatment model may not be well suited or appropriate for work with substance abusers and chemically dependent persons who manifest a concurrent thought disturbance (schizophrenia), affective disturbance, or the "classic" psychoneurotic symptom structures that are associated with the substance use disorders.

Substance abusers and chemically dependent persons who are not concurrently antisocial need to be involved in treatment programs and therapies that adequately address their specific needs. These particular patients have needs which may differ significantly from those of the antisocial person with a concurrent substance use disorder. For example, the nonantisocial chronic alcoholic patient with a concurrent severe depressive disorder may need to be placed on an antidepressant medication for three to six months. Most of these patients will not be actively involved with the law, and they do not need to be incarcerated in order to be motivated to seek treatment or to develop some degree of motivation to enter and remain in a treatment program. Substance abusers and chemically dependent persons who manifest a thought disturbance or schizophrenia also need to be placed on an appropriate psychotropic medication and involved in a highly structured long-term treatment program. Brain-damaged alcoholics may not be appropriate candidates for involvement in Antabuse (Forrest, 1985) maintenance programs.

An effective treatment program for substance abusers and chemically dependent patients with concurrent antisocial personality disorder must include the following components: (1) detoxification; (2) long-term treatment; (3) commitment to total abstinence; (4) intensive cognitive-behaviorally oriented treatment; (5) structure; and (6) holistic as well as individualized care.

Detoxification

It is impossible to work effectively with patients who are under the influence of alcohol and other drugs. Psychotherapists and behavioral scientists are in agreement (Forrest, 1984) that it is also impossible to do psychotherapy or provide other rehabilitation services with intoxicated persons. Thus, substance abusers and chemically dependent patients with concurrent ASPD need to be medically detoxified prior to entering any form of comprehensive treatment program. These individuals need to be completely "drug free" throughout the treatment process.

Since the vast majority of patients who manifest a substance use disorder in combination with antisocial personality disorder are substance abusers rather than substance dependent, a three- to seven-day detoxification period is appropriate for most of these patients. Less than 5 percent of these clients can be expected to experience acute alcohol or other drug withdrawal symptomatology. Clinicians need to remember that marijuana and some other drugs remain in the brain for several weeks after the patient discontinues all use of the drug.

Thus, the patient may not be completely "detoxed" for a period of time ranging from several hours to several weeks.

Tissue dependent antisocial patients require (Zimberg, 1982) medical care and detoxification services that parallel those that are appropriate for nonantisocial patients. These individuals may need direct medical care and hospitalization. Some of these patients manifest chronic medical problems that require ongoing medical treatment and supervision. Obviously, alcohol and/or drug detoxification constitutes the initial phase of treatment for substance abusers and chemically dependent persons with concurrent ASPD.

The Extended Treatment Program Model

As indicated earlier in this chapter, the antisocial person with a concurrent substance use disorder needs long-term treatment. A major treatment dilemma that therapists face in working with these clients is the client's resistance to enter extended treatment. Furthermore, this problem is compounded by a number of social and systemic factors. Institutions, agencies, and even therapists in the United States are designed or conditioned to provide short-term treatments and services. Budgets, funding, financial profits, and treatment models per se are based upon brief and limited patient care.

Institutions and health care providers need to begin to develop long-term treatment programs for these patients. Some antisocial substance abusers and chemically dependent persons need to be in intensive extended care programs for as long as ten or more years. Very few of these individuals can be successfully treated in less than three to five years. Unfortunately, traditional mental health care systems are not designed to provide treatment for people with addictive disorders and severe character pathology (Kernberg, 1984) for several years. Thus, federal, state, and private facilities need to be developed to provide extended care programs for antisocial substance abusers and chemically dependent persons.

When antisocial substance abusers enter a traditional residential or outpatient substance abuse treatment program or become engaged in any other facility which provides psychotherapy and structured mental health services, every effort should be made to involve the patient in an extended care treatment model. Therapists need to openly and honestly confront (Forrest, 1982, 1984) these individuals about their: (1) "dual diagnosis"; (2) special treatment needs and requirements; and (3) improbability of recovery associated with short-term treatment. The therapist also needs to work creatively with the patient and the patient's family and parole officer to develop an extended treatment program if no such program is available in the patient's community.

Therapists must be able to work with the patient's spouse and family, judges and attorneys, parole and correction counselors, mental health and chemical dependency treatment counselors, and significant others who are involved with the patient. The therapeutic process becomes significantly easier and more effective when these individuals are "locked in" to systems that are designed to provide consistent and extended care.

Extended treatment models are not 21- to 60-day residential programs! Extended treatment programs may *begin* with a three-week placement in a residential chemical dependency treatment center. Following this stage of treatment, the patient may enter a highly structured and intensive phase of treatment within a halfway house setting for a period of 18 to 60 months.

Antisocial personalities and chemically dependent patients with concurrent ASPD find it easy to placate and "get over" on counselors and treatment program personnel in brief treatment settings. Extended treatment relationships and programs force these patients to actualize and maintain long-term patterns of cognitive, behavioral, affective, and interpersonal change. Therapists also become progressively more aware, sensitive, tactically skilled, and effective when they are able to work with these patients within the context of a long-term psychotherapeutic relationship.

Brief psychotherapy and short-term rehabilitation programs are not effective in the treatment of antisocial persons who are substance abusers or chemically dependent. It may be unethical for psychotherapists and agencies to use brief treatment models with this clinical population. Therapists and program administrators may also need to refuse treatment services for patients, families, and systems that are not willing to make commitments to extended treatment models.

Lifelong Commitment to Total Abstinence

All chemically dependent and substance abusing antisocial persons need to be committed to a lifestyle of total abstinence. Recovery and responsible living are impossibilities for these persons when they remain ambivalent about substance use. Periodic episodes of drug use and intoxication consistently lead to acting-out and a plethora of destructive or self-defeating behaviors. The intoxicated antisocial personality is dangerous and has no internal system of control.

Therapists and rehabilitation programs that provide treatment services for these patients need to redundantly stress the importance of making a *daily* commitment to total abstinence. The patient cannot realistically be expected to make a commitment to "never drink again." However, these patients can actualize the behaviors and cognitions that are required to maintain abstinence on a daily basis. The "one day at a time" approach of Alcoholics Anonymous and other self-help groups can be a very therapeutic method for developing the goal of long-term drug abstinence. The conceptualization of "never again" ingesting alcohol or other mood-altering drugs can seem almost overwhelming to the 20- or 30-year-old chemically dependent antisocial patient. The goal of total abstinence today and in the immediate future is a concrete and realistically achievable goal for such patients. With extended abstinence, the patient becomes progressively more capable of realistically actualizing the goal of lifelong abstinence.

Why is it so important to instill in antisocial drug abusers and chemically dependent persons the requirement of a lifelong commitment to drug-free living? The answer to this question is really quite simple. Drug-taking relapses (Gorski and Miller, 1986; Gorski, 1991) result in the outcropping of antisocial behavior. Assault, homicide, incest and rape, vehicular homicide, and virtually all other forms of violent behavior (Forrest and Gordon, 1990) are precipitated by substance abuse and intoxication. Antisocial substance abusers consistently act-out destructive behaviors when they are under the influence of mood-altering drugs. Conversely, these individuals are better controlled and less likely to act-out when abstinent. Protracted periods of drug-free living and adequate behavioral control are the essentials of recovery for these persons.

Periodic or infrequent substance abuse is potentially lethal for the antisocial person as well as for society!

It is paradoxically unrealistic for the psychotherapist to expect or believe that the antisocial substance abuser will *never* relapse while in treatment. To the contrary, a relapse is not tantamount to therapeutic failure or even therapeutic impasse when the patient is committed to the treatment process or "locked in" to a structured and long-term rehabilitation program. Under these circumstances, a relapse can actually be constructively therapeutic. A relapse (Forrest, 1984) concretely shows the patient and therapist that the patient is addictive, self-destructive, and reveals the "power" or obsessive-compulsive control that drugs exert upon the patient. Furthermore, a relapse is always a dynamic reflection of the therapeutic relationship. Relapses reveal to the therapist/patient areas of therapeutic scotomization that require further work, progress and resistance in treatment, and futuristic as well as present barriers to recovery.

Active therapeutic interventions need to be utilized by the therapist and treatment program staff whenever antisocial substance abusers experience a relapse. The patient should never be permitted to continue drinking or taking other drugs for a period of several days or weeks. While the problem of extended relapse does not usually occur with patients who are involved in inpatient treatment programs, therapists who work with these persons on an outpatient basis may need to utilize family interventions, psychiatric, mental health, or alcohol/drug commitments, and other direct intervention techniques in order to curtail a relapse. Brief psychiatric hospitalizations, legal incarcerations for a few days, or short-term legal commitments to a "detox" facility or mental health facility can be very effective deterrents to relapse.

These therapeutic techniques and strategies help the highly recidivistic client, as well as the first-time patient, develop an awareness of the importance of a long-term commitment to total drug abstinence. The antisocial patient is no longer able to blame his or her present manipulative, impulsive, self-centered, destructive, and criminal behaviors on "alcohol and drugs" after several months of total drug abstinence and involvement in intensive treatment.

Intensive Cognitive-Behaviorally Oriented Treatment

Antisocial substance abusers require intensive treatment. These individuals also need to be involved in cognitive and behaviorally oriented treatment programs and therapies. It is rather widely recognized (Forrest, 1978; Gitlow and Peyser, 1980; Zimberg, 1982; Brown, 1985; Bratter and Forrest, 1985; Matuschka, 1988) that psychoanalytic, dynamic, and client-centered forms of psychotherapy or treatment are not efficacious with chemically dependent patients and substance abusers. These treatment approaches also do not work when used with psychopaths, criminals, and juvenile delinquents (Yochelson and Samenow, 1976, 1986; Ross and Lightfoot, 1985; Doren, 1987). Cognitive-behavioral treatment models are the treatments of choice for work with substance abusers and antisocial personalities (Ross and Lightfoot, 1985; Forrest, 1985, 1990; Yochelson and Samenow, 1986; Reid et al., 1986; Forrest and Gordon, 1990).

The antisocial substance abuser or chemically dependent patient needs to be seen in weekly individual, group, and possibly family and/or cojoint therapies, as well as involved in two or more self-help (AA, CA, NA, ACOA) meetings per week. These patients should also be working out and involved in a structured exercise program several (three to five) hours each week. This intensive treatment format encompasses a period of two to ten or more years. Most of the patients who enter a program like this will also develop a spiritually-oriented recovery. These individuals usually become more aware of the nutritional dimensions of recovery. Clearly, this treatment model is holistic in scope.

Intensive inpatient care may be a central component of this treatment model. Many antisocial substance abusers and chemically dependent patients need to be involved in a halfway or three-quarter-way house (Forrest, 1978) one or more times during their course of rehabilitation. The patient may stay in such a facility for three months to over one year at a time or reenter the facility on several occasions. Virtually all of these patients need to spend a minimum of 30 days in a residential alcohol/drug treatment program at the point of treatment engagement. It is also clinically appropriate to require *all* antisocial chemically dependent patients and substance abusers who are leaving a correctional facility to complete an extended residential alcohol/drug treatment program prior to release. These individuals must also be required to participate in long-term and intensive outpatient rehabilitation programs as a condition of release from a correctional facility.

It must be emphasized that the successful treatment of antisocial substance abusers is not simply contingent on the duration and intensity of care that these individuals receive. The "kind" or types of treatment and therapy that these patients receive while they are engaged in rehabilitation programs is a key variable that eventually determines treatment outcome status. It has been stressed throughout this book that psychoanalysis and psychoanalytically-oriented psychotherapies consistently do not produce successful treatment outcomes with these specific patient populations.

The cognitive-behavioral therapies (Lazarus, 1981; Goldberg, 1989) are perhaps best suited for clinical work with antisocial substance abusers and chemically dependent persons. Reality therapy (Glasser, 1965), rational emotive therapy (Ellis and Harper, 1961, 1990), multimodal therapy (Lazarus, 1981), behavioral therapy (Yost and Mines, 1985), and cognitive therapy (Beck, 1976; Ross and Lightfoot, 1985) are relatively specific "schools" of psychotherapy or approaches to treatment that can be used efficaciously with antisocial persons who manifest a concurrent substance use disorder. Yochelson and Samenow (1976, 1977, 1986) have developed an extensive cognitive-behavioral treatment model for work with criminals and antisocial substance abusers.

These treatment approaches focus upon the here and now rather than the patient's past or future. They also emphasize the importance of rational thinking, reality, effective choice-making and decision-making, expressing and recognizing different feeling states, developing alternative courses of action, behaving responsibly, accepting responsibility for one's behaviors and actions, and effective problem-solving techniques. The cognitive style of the antisocial substance abuser must be changed substantially in order for effective treatment and rehabilitation to occur. Yochelson and Samenow (1986) report, "In working with criminals, both drug users and nonusers, the core problem is criminal thinking patterns" (p. 13). These authors go on to explain how antisocial persons use drugs to "cut off" cognitive awareness of fear, enhance cutoff of deterrents to crime and acting-out, and thus enable the user to do what he or she otherwise is afraid to do.

Drugs per se do not make a man or woman a criminal. Rather, drugs facilitate criminal thinking and criminal behaviors. The intoxicated antisocial personality perceives himself or herself as omnipotent, invincible, and all-powerful. Interestingly, Yochelson and Samenow (1986) state that "without drugs the drug user, no matter how competent in the eyes of others, considers himself 'half a man'" (p. 10). Intensive and long-term involvement in cognitive-behavioral therapy or a CB-oriented rehabilitation program can significantly modify the faulty and maladaptive patterns of thinking, behaving, and emoting which maintain the antisocial personality disorder and chemical dependency. The action-oriented teaching nature of the cognitive-behavior therapies is also well suited to the personality style of antisocial substance abusers.

Structural Dimensions of the Treatment Process

The roles of structure in the treatment of antisocial substance abusers will be discussed at length in a later chapter in this text. Structure is an integral component of all psychotherapies and rehabilitation programs that involve individuals with impulse control problems and alloplastic adjustments.

At the onset of the treatment relationship, a therapeutic framework or structure needs to be established by the therapist and patient. Therapists and patients need to work together to develop a treatment plan that specifically delineates such issues as: (1) treatment format (types of treatment interventions that will be undertaken); (2) need for treatment and reason for patient involvement in a treatment program; (3) therapist-patient responsibilities within the treatment relationship; (4) goals of treatment; (5) expected duration of treatment; (6) hospitalization, residential care, and/or halfway house alternatives; (7) use of psychotropic medications; (8) relapse (pertaining to antisocial behavior as well as substance use); (9) motivation to change and commitment to the treatment process; and (10) termination of the treatment relationship. It is imperative that all persons and agencies who are involved in the treatment process clearly understand these structural dimensions of the treatment process.

Therapists sometimes fail to understand the ambivalent feelings that substance abusers and antisocial persons have that are associated with structure in their lives. These individuals generally dislike structure or the perception of being required or compelled to do anything. They generally behave, emote, and think in an impulsive, poorly controlled, spur of the moment manner. At the same time, these persons preconsciously and unconsciously realize that many of their living problems are related to their impulsiveness and inability to deal with structure. The antisocial substance abuser is unable to consistently behave in accordance with the social standards and structures which regulate behavior. These individuals also have an inadequately developed internal sense of self-structure.

The chemically dependent antisocial personality may need to be hospitalized or even incarcerated for a protracted period of time in order to develop the capacities for maintaining drug abstinence, developing a working therapeutic alliance, and establishing a basic sense of self-structure. The structure and control that a hospital or correctional environment can provide for the patient essentially amounts to a holding environment that deters acting-out and the perpetuation of self-defeating behavior. External structure vis à vis a therapeutic holding environment can facilitate the development of internal controls and an internalized self-structure. Self-regulation and a responsible style of living evolve from the process of establishing an adequately internalized sense of self or identity (Forrest, 1983a). Unstructured therapeutic approaches and models systematically do not work in the treatment of antisocial substance abusers and chemically dependent patients.

A Holistic and Individualized Treatment Model

The chemically dependent or substance abusing antisocial patient is diffusely conflicted and pathologic. These persons manifest concurrent pathologic impulse control problems, cognitive disturbance, affect regulation problems, substance use disorder, behavioral pathology, and interpersonal deficits. Chemically dependent antisocial patients also experience significant medical and neuropsychological (Matuschka, 1985; Sena, 1989, 1991) complications. These factors contribute to the treatability problem that psychotherapists and clinicians face whenever they attempt to work with antisocial substance abusers.

Effective treatment programs and models for antisocial substance abusers provide holistic interventions. These individuals need to change their basic styles of thinking, behaving, emoting, and interacting. Global lifestyle change is a basic ingredient in the recovery process of all addictive and impulsive persons. Chemically dependent antisocial patients are spiritually, morally, interpersonally, intrapersonally, vocationally, and even physically, bankrupt.

Holistic psychotherapy (Forrest, 1984) and holistically-oriented treatment programs address the needs of the whole person. Thus, a holistically-oriented psychotherapist is concerned about the psychological, social, physical, and spiritual needs of his or her clients. All too frequently, chemical dependency counselors and treatment programs focus only on the addictive aspects of their patients. Chemically dependent or abusing antisocial patients must accomplish more in treatment than simply establishing and/or maintaining a drug-free lifestyle. These persons also need to learn how to live responsibly, think rationally, behave appropriately, and develop the internal controls that are essential to regulating their affective lives. Antisocial substance abusers require effective holistic treatments for their addictive psychopathology as well as their psychopathy. Failure to help the patient effect radical change in both of these areas of functioning is tantamount to therapeutic failure.

Holistic care of the antisocial substance abuser involves the use of: (1) traditional psychotherapies (individual, group, family, and cojoint); (2) nutritional management; (3) medical assessment, care, and possibly medications; (4) active and long-term self-help programs (AA, Al-Anon, NA, CA, OA, ACOA, etc.); (5) rigorous physical exercise; (6) didactic education; (7) self-help sponsorship; (8) vocational education/training and employment; (9) religious and spiritual growth alternatives; and (10) residential treatment and/or incarceration. The families of these individuals also need to be involved in ongoing holistic treatment programs. A holistically-oriented program of recovery (Forrest, 1984) benefits both the antisocial substance abuser and his or her family.

Univariant treatment models simply do not work with these patients. Psychotherapy alone does not change the antisocial personality (Cleckley, [1941] 1976; Doren, 1987). Many alcoholics and substance abusers require more than AA involvement or self-help treatment in order to maintain drug abstinence and recover. Most chemically dependent patients are unable to recover by simply attending weekly individual, group, or family therapy. These recalcitrant patients need to be involved in holistic, long-term, highly structured treatment programs.

It is important that holistically-oriented treatment programs provide individualized care. The individual needs of each antisocial substance abuser or chemically dependent patient must be recognized and addressed in psychotherapy. Therapists and treatment programs often fail to appreciate the importance of individual differences among chemically dependent antisocial patients and other clinical populations. These patients are not "all the same." Some respond favorably to the use of Antabuse, while others may need to complete residential treatment more than once. Patients who have diabetes or some other form of health problem require special medical and dietary care. Highly aggressive and unsocialized patients usually need to be involved in more structured treatment environments.

In short, the individual needs of each antisocial substance abuser encompass psychological, social, familial, physical, cognitive, and spiritual factors. Psychotherapists are more effective in their therapeutic relationships with these individuals when they are sensitive to the various internal dynamics and needs of the patient. In general, it is important for the therapist to be open, honest, direct, supportive, empathic, and confrontive in his or her interactions with these persons. However, some of these clients respond more favorably to a spiritually-oriented type of counseling relationship while others respond better to a confrontation-oriented or strict behavior modification treatment format. Individual differences must be recognized, and individualized treatment strategies must be implemented if we are to be successful in our treatment efforts with antisocial substance abusers and chemically dependent patients.

SUMMARY

The dually-diagnosed antisocial substance abuser or chemically dependent patient presents clinicians and treatment facilities with a diversity of treatment-oriented dilemmas and problems. These patients generally reject involvement in any type of psychiatric/psychological treatment program, and they specifically tend to reject the types of treatment interventions that are most likely to help them change and recover. They are not motivated to enter and remain in treatment. Most reject the notion of complete abstinence, and the concept of long-term treatment is ego-alien. These individuals are also not capable of sustaining protracted involvement in self-help programs such as Alcoholics Anonymous or Narcotics Anonymous.

In spite of these many thorny dilemmas and problems that are associated with treating antisocial substance abusers, a general treatment model for successfully "working" with these individuals has been delineated in this chapter. This model includes: (1) detoxification; (2) long-term treatment; (3) patient commitment to total drug abstinence for life; (4) intensive cognitive-behavioral treatment; (5) structure; and (6) holistic as well as individualized care. The conceptual schematic shown in Table II outlines the treatment model that has been presented in this chapter.

The assessment phase of this treatment model is initiated and completed during Stages I, II, and III of the treatment process. Patients continue to be evaluated throughout the course of this treatment model. Treatment is initiated during the assessment and detoxification stages of the model and continues throughout the course of the patient's life.

The treatment model that has been outlined in this chapter is intensive, long-term, highly structured, cognitive-behavioral, holistic, and based on the individual needs of each patient. These particular patients need to be involved in psychotherapies and treatment programs that are specifically designed to modify their antisocial adjustment styles *and* their substance use disorder. The individual treatment needs of each client are addressed during all three stages of this treatment model.

Chemically dependent antisocial personalities have the potential for establishing and maintaining long-term drug abstinence. These persons are also capable of developing the internal controls that are essential to responsible living when they are actively involved in the treatment model that has been delineated in this chapter. Multimodal treatment interventions (Lazarus, 1981) can be utilized to

Table II: General Treatment Model for Antisocial Substance
Abusers and Chemically Dependent Patients

Stage I	Stage II	Stage III
Detoxification Three to 10 days; *Primarily for chemically dependent antisocial patients.	Residential Treatment 21 days; Several years for legally incarcerated patients; may be repeated by many patients; most patients will reside in halfway house setting for six to 36 months after completion of residential care or following prison release. *For all patients.	Lifelong Aftercare Program Lifelong involvement in various outpatient self-help treatment modalities. *For all patients.

modify the patient's cognitive, behavioral, physical, affective, vocational, familial, and spiritual adjustments. The quid pro quo and univariant treatment approaches do not work with these difficult patients. Recovery can only occur when the chemically dependent or substance abusing antisocial patient successfully changes his or her modus vivendi *for life*.

The case study that was presented in this chapter demonstrates the difficulties that therapists face when they attempt to treat chemically dependent antisocial personalities on an outpatient basis. Indeed, many of these individuals are constitutionally incapable of change and recovery in the absence of protracted involvements in programs such as the one that was delineated in this chapter. The treatment outcome prognosis is very poor for chemically dependent antisocial persons who receive traditional therapy and limited rehabilitation services (Forrest and Gordon, 1990; Forrest, 1991; Gorski, 1991).

Chapter IX

Uses of Structure in the Treatment of Chemically Dependent Patients with Impulse Control Problems

INTRODUCTION

Virtually all chemically dependent persons and most substance abusers (Forrest, 1983a, 1989; Mumey, 1986; Nace, 1990) manifest impulse control problems. These individuals have a low frustration tolerance, and they tend to be floridly impulsive in all areas of living. The alcoholic demands that his or her needs be met *now*–immediately! Chemically dependent persons find it difficult to "think through" problem situations. These individuals tend to use impulsive, all-or-none, poorly planned problem-solving techniques in order to deal with the conflicts of daily living. Indeed, substance abusers very often impulsively act out their various feelings, thoughts, and urges.

Chemically dependent persons are poorly controlled. The chemically dependent patient has insufficient internal controls. The internal, cognitive, affective, and behavioral mechanisms that regulate and govern adjustment are inadequate or underdeveloped in substance abusers. Chemical dependency and substance abuse per se are impulse control disorders. Likewise, the addictions (Forrest, 1983a) are acting-out disorders. Substance use evolves into substance abuse and eventually dependence as the drug user experiences a progressive loss of impulse control over his or her use of an addictive substance.

Chemically dependent patients act out impulsively (Forrest, 1983a) against themselves, significant others, and society. Verbal abuse, fights and physical assaults, suicide and homicide, physical illness, automobile accidents, accidents in the home, child abuse, and sexual assault are but a few of the realities that clearly demonstrate how chemically dependent persons engage in a plethora of destructive acting-out behaviors.

The impulse control problems and acting-out pathology of the chemically dependent person are precursors to the onset of addictive illness. Chemically dependent persons describe themselves as being "hyper," impulsive, and anxious during childhood and early adolescence. Yet, substance use per se generally reinforces and exacerbates the impulsiveness and acting-out behaviors of both adolescent and adult addicts or substance abusers. Thus, chemical dependency synergizes the impulse control pathology of the chemically dependent person.

Structure and external sources of control have been used for several decades in the United States and Western society as methods to help impulsive, poorly controlled persons develop more adequate self-regulation and an improved capacity for internal control. Structure can be utilized to help people who are literally out of control in one or several aspects of daily living reestablish a better sense of internalized self-control and self-regulation. External sources of control and structure may include the therapeutic alliance, hospitalization, residential treatment programs, and correctional or penal institutions.

Structure is an essential ingredient in the treatment of chemically dependent antisocial personalities and substance abusers with impulse control problems. This chapter includes a discussion of the: (1) structural components of therapeutic relationships involving chemically dependent patients who manifest severe impulse control problems; (2) uses of external structure other than the therapeutic alliance in the clinical management and treatment of chemically dependent antisocial patients; and (3) general psychotherapeutic considerations.

STRUCTURAL COMPONENTS
OF THE THERAPEUTIC ALLIANCE

Successful psychotherapeutic work with substance abusers takes place within the specific context and structure of a working and

productive therapeutic alliance (Forrest, 1984). All therapy relationships and all systems of counseling and psychotherapy involve
some degree of structure. Chemically dependent or substance abusing patients do not generally respond favorably to unstructured and
nondirective therapies and therapists. The impulsive, poorly controlled, antisocial substance abuser is also an unsuitable candidate
for unstructured and nondirective treatments. Many of these persons find it very difficult to commit themselves to the process of
developing a productive therapeutic alliance.

The therapeutic alliance provides a structural framework from
which the patient and therapist can begin to mutually comprehend
the patient's symptom structure, cognitive style, deficient areas, and
strengths. The therapy relationship structure also helps the therapist
and client establish strategies for facilitating constructive behavioral growth and change on the part of the client. Thus, an initial
therapeutic task for counselors and therapists who work with antisocial substance abusers is simply that of establishing the structure
of a working therapeutic alliance with the patient!

It is impossible, or at least very difficult, to develop a therapeutic
alliance with patients who are not motivated to enter a treatment
relationship. It is appropriate for therapists to choose not to treat
substance abusers who rigidly reject the need for therapy and treatment. However, many of these individuals can be successfully
treated if they are initially forced into a therapeutic relationship via
the courts, employers, spouses, or family members. Therapists need
to be able to assess patient readiness and motivation for therapeutic
engagement during the initial two or three contact sessions. It is
appropriate for the therapist to spend several treatment sessions
(three to ten) with an unmotivated client in an effort to develop and
foster the client's readiness and motivation for treatment. Counselors need to be wary of antisocial substance abusers who "play the
game" of getting ready for therapy or in other ways use the therapeutic relationship in a manipulative and self-serving manner. Clients who are unmotivated or unable to become committed to the
structure of a working and productive therapeutic alliance should
not be engaged in psychotherapy and treatment-oriented rehabilitation programs. Many of these individuals are appropriate candidates
for residential or correctional facilities where real motivation for

engagement in the treatment process can be developed. Unfortunately, some of these persons are not capable of developing a workable degree of readiness and motivation for treatment.

The structure of a working and productive therapeutic alliance provides the therapist and patient with an interpersonal and communicative relationship that fosters the development of several therapeutic substructures. These therapeutic substructures act to deter and modify the impulse control problems of the antisocial substance abuser. They also reinforce and strengthen the basic structure of the therapeutic relationship or alliance. These therapeutic substructures include: (1) regular involvement (three or more times per week) in self-help treatment groups (Alcoholics Anonymous, Cocaine Anonymous, Narcotics Anonymous, ACOA, etc.); (2) regular involvement (two or more times per week) in self-help treatment by spouse and/or other family members; (3) active sponsorship in self-help programs for self and significant others; (4) consistent involvement in a vigorous exercise program (four or more 30-minutes-plus exercise sessions per week); (5) appropriate nutrition and basic health habits (three well-balanced meals per day, adequate sleep, avoidance of the ingestion of other addictive substances such as sugar, nicotine, and caffeine, and appropriate weight control); (6) psychotropic maintenance when indicated; and (7) establishment of a spiritual or religious affiliation.

These therapeutic substructures are developed by the therapist and patient. They can be viewed as the structural components of intensive chemical dependency psychotherapy and rehabilitation (Forrest, 1984). The structural components of therapy and rehabilitation are always based on the relatively unique treatment needs of each individual patient. These facets of the treatment process constitute the basis for holistic health care and rehabilitation.

It is important to note that some patients need to be involved in additional therapeutic substructures. For example, patients who are unemployed or unskilled need to be involved in very structured vocational/educational or job training programs. It is very difficult for unemployed or unskilled antisocial substance abusers to maintain abstinence and a program of recovery in the absence of career growth and suitable employment.

All of the structural components of the therapeutic relationship as well as the therapeutic substructures need to be clearly defined by the therapist and patient. Moreover, these dimensions of the treatment process should be delineated in the initial three to five therapy sessions. All of the structural vicissitudes of treatment will be subject to change or modification as the treatment process evolves. Early in the treatment relationship, the therapist and patient need to develop a specific contractual agreement (Forrest, 1985) relative to: (1) when, where, how often, and how long the psychotherapy relationship will take place; (2) kind or types of therapy the patient and his or her family members need; (3) consequences of successful versus unsuccessful treatment; and (5) when, where, how often, and how long the patient (and possibly other family members) will be involved in various specified therapeutic substructures.

SOURCES OF THERAPEUTIC GAIN ASSOCIATED WITH THE STRUCTURAL DIMENSIONS OF THE TREATMENT RELATIONSHIP

How do the structural aspects of the therapeutic alliance and the therapeutic substructures facilitate adaptive growth and behavioral change in chemically dependent persons with impulse control problems? Actually, the structural components of the treatment process operate to facilitate positive change in several ways.

The therapeutic relationship becomes a "holding environment" in which the patient can learn to regulate and control his or her destructive impulses, affects, behaviors, and thoughts. A therapeutic environment is a place where impulsive persons learn to "act-in," rather than act-out, their impulses. The therapist can teach many of these patients to use cognitive-behavioral self-regulation techniques in order to deter impulsive acting-out. These patients also need to develop more effective patterns of problem-solving. Their coping techniques and abilities to deal with stress are inadequate or faulty. Thus, counselors can utilize relaxation training, self-hypnosis, and stress management training as deterrents or alternatives to impulsive living. Thought-stopping, time-out techniques, and cognitive-restructuring techniques are efficacious treatment strategies that can be used with people who manifest various impulse control problems.

Within the confines of the therapeutic alliance, an impulse control disordered individual can develop a sense of trust and relatedness. This basic sense of trust and relatedness eventually fosters the development of a capacity to work through problems and feelings within the explicit context of the therapeutic alliance. The ability to delay gratification and "think through" problem situations then generalizes to include various nontherapeutic situational contexts. Therapists and counselors can provide their impulsive clients with information, feedback, rehearsal exercises, support, and homework exercises that are deterrents to acting-out.

Therapists also serve as potent role models for their impulsive patients. The therapist models nonimpulsive problem-solving techniques and behaviors within the context of the therapeutic relationship. By remaining "cool," considering alternative behaviors and courses of action, and evaluating the probable consequences that can be expected to be associated with selecting alternative choices, the therapist models rational and responsible patterns of adjustment. It is healthy and adaptive for patients to emulate the nonimpulsive adjustment styles of their therapists. The psychotherapist should also model a plethora of prosocial behaviors to his or her patients.

It is very important for therapists to be able to provide positive as well as negative confrontational feedback (Forrest, 1982; Matuschka, 1988) to their clients within the context of the therapeutic alliance. Therapists need to be activists in their relationships with these persons. Thus, the psychotherapist consistently points out the positive behavioral changes that the patient is making throughout the course of therapy as well as the impulsive, irresponsible, or self-defeating patterns of behavior that are in need of change. The impulse control disordered patient develops the capacities to "stand still and hurt" and "stop and think" as he or she begins to change and recover in treatment.

These individuals have also developed pathologic patterns of confronting other people. The therapist needs to be able to use direct confrontation and feedback techniques with these persons in order to help them to begin to understand and change their aggressive, abrasive style of interpersonal behavior. Passive-reflective, analytic, and supportive therapist styles may actually reinforce the impulsive acting-out behaviors of many of these persons.

Many impulse control disordered patients are detached, cold, and globally insensitive in their interpersonal relations. They are deficient in their abilities to love and empathize. The warm, empathic, sensitive, genuine (Truax and Carkhuff, 1967) therapist who is simultaneously able to be concrete, confrontive, direct, and responsibility-focused in his or her therapeutic interactions is indeed an enigmatically therapeutic role model for these persons. The therapeutic relationship is a delicate human encounter that provides both the patient and therapist with an opportunity to learn how to express feelings, develop intimacy skills, and love. Basic human attachment and relatedness occur within the context of the therapeutic relationship.

A healthy therapeutic alliance provides the therapist and patient with a relationship structure which fosters a diversity of limit-setting behaviors. Antisocial persons and substance abusers reject the advice and guidance of significant others. These individuals become angry and resentful when others attempt to "tell them what to do." They sometimes become enraged at the limit-setting transactions and behaviors of others. Yet, the psychotherapist becomes an agent of internal control and is able to actively help the patient establish effective patterns of internal limit-setting within the context of the therapeutic relationship.

The following therapy vignette demonstrates some of the sources of therapeutic gain that are related to the structural dimensions of the psychotherapy relationship. This patient had recently been paroled from a state correctional facility. He had been incarcerated for 16 years and had been convicted of several armed robberies. This vignette was taken from the eighth therapy session between the author and patient.

> Fred C.: You know, it kinda pissed me off when you told me we were going to have to meet every week for a year or two. Uh, I mean when we first talked about that kind of stuff a month or two ago . . .
>
> Doctor F.: A year seems like a long time to be in therapy?
>
> Fred C.: No. Hell, a year ain't long . . . I've spent half my life locked up, damn near 17 years, so believe me, I can do a year

standing on my head . . . ha, ha . . . but the idea of coming in here every week for a year or two is different. We sure must have a lot to talk about . . . ha, ha.

Doctor F.: It's different making a commitment to a relationship for a year or two. Uh, more difficult, too . . . and we'll need to do a lot more work. It helps to think in terms of "one day at a time." So how'd you do this week with the meetings and taking care of the parole requirements?

Fred C.: Doc, I'm doin' what they told me I need to do, but I don't like all the meetings . . . er, I'm taking the Antabuse, and I still need to get a sponsor . . . but I don't even think about drinkin' or the other shit . . . not drinking is easy for me, and I sure don't crave a drink like some of the other people at AA. I know the drugs got me in a lot of trouble, but that's in the past . . . and I sure as hell don't want to be drinkin' or takin' the other shit if it's going to put me back in the slammer.

Doctor F.: You feel like there are a lot of demands being placed on you and you're not as bad as a lot of the others who are in treatment or at AA . . . but the . . .

Fred C.: Yeah, a lot of people in the meetings are a lot worse than me . . . Hell, I never drank a quart of vodka every day for 10 or 20 years!

Doctor F.: But you sure as hell did get in trouble when you were drinking and using drugs . . . Didn't you tell me last week that drugs and alcohol were part of most—or all—of the robberies you did?

Fred C.: Yeah, that's why they caught me twenty minutes after the job . . . shit, I didn't even know what I was doin' . . . pretty damned stupid. It was embarrassing, too. I sure didn't tell any of my buddies that part of it . . . ha, ha. It's still hard to admit a lot of what I did in the past, and I know I should be honest with you, too . . . if this is going to help.

Doctor F.: That goes back to where we were a few minutes ago . . . I guess it would get more difficult lying to me or playing games in here for an hour every week for a year or two?

Fred C.: I was such a liar and con artist for so long that I didn't know what the hell the truth was. That's still a part of me, too . . . like they say in AA, you only end up fooling yourself . . . conning yourself. I've got to be honest with you, though. I sure as hell don't want to go back! Guess the therapy, AA, and the other shit really ain't all that bad . . . ha, ha . . . better than jail! It's nice just being able to go shopping or walk around . . . free.

Doctor F.: We need to be honest with each other. I'm sure not going to con you . . . or hassle anything from you, but I do expect you to be completely honest with me.

Fred C.: Yeah, but you need to understand that I really don't trust anyone . . . ha, ha, ha . . . not even myself sometimes! Well, maybe that's why I'm a bit nervous about coming in here to see you . . . I don't like to get too close to people, and a lot of people have fucked me over in the past, even a couple of shrinks!

Doctor F.: People can be hurtful . . . uh, trust . . .

Fred C.: Yeah, I don't want to have to depend on anyone, not even you. I mean, I trust you, and I'm not saying you're going to let me down . . . but I know what I've got to do, and nobody's going to do it for me . . . er, staying straight . . . workin' hard and all that . . . and, uh, you have helped me to see that already.

Doctor F.: It takes time to build trust or a relationship . . . It's good that we can work on these things in here, and I guess that's part of building the relationship, too. Does that make sense?

The structure of the psychotherapeutic relationship becomes an interpersonal framework for resolving problems and helping the client develop more rational and internalized coping skills. Impulse control disordered persons can learn to work out their problems, express affects appropriately, communicate more effectively, change thinking patterns, and thus develop more adaptive internal controls within the explicit context of the therapeutic alliance.

This therapy vignette reveals the tenuous and fragile nature of the early stages of the psychotherapeutic process. The structural vicissitudes of the therapy relationship help patients establish alcohol/drug abstinence, build trust, and develop better living skills. It is apparent that Fred C. has never been able to work through his impulse control difficulties and other living problems within the context of a healthy human relationship. The parataxic aspects of the patient's impulse control disorder became consciously and behaviorally manifest, as well as amenable to change, within the context of a working and productive therapeutic alliance.

Therapists need to realize that most antisocial substance abusers initially perceive themselves as "weak" and inadequate when they "work" in therapy and actually follow the therapist's guidance and suggestions. These individuals need to develop methods for modifying their chronic style of rejecting help and healthy guidance.

SOURCES OF THERAPEUTIC GAIN ASSOCIATED WITH THE SUBSTRUCTURAL DIMENSIONS OF THE TREATMENT RELATIONSHIP

The substructural components of the therapeutic relationship are extensions of the patient-therapist holding environment. They are essential to the holistic treatment and recovery of substance abusers who manifest concurrent impulse control problems.

Active involvements in AA (or other self-help programs), sponsorship, rigorous exercise, and the other therapeutic substructures that were listed earlier in the chapter provide these patients with time-structuring activities that help bind or control their anxiety and impulsiveness. These therapeutic substructures also provide environments in which the patient can learn new social skills and behaviors as well as new or more rational patterns of thinking. For example, the Alcoholics Anonymous community (AA, Al-Anon, Ala-Teen, and Ala-Tot) is extremely (Forrest, 1978; Mumey, 1986;

McFadden and McFadden, 1989; McFadden, 1991) supportive, nurturant, and loving. The AA "way of life" also encourages an open and honest examination of one's behavior as well as thought process. AA members attempt to live life on a "day at a time" basis. *Rigorous* honesty is a key to recovery. It is important for AA members to continually work on changing their patterns of "stinkin' thinkin'" and their character defects.

Active sponsorship is the cornerstone of effective self-help treatment alternatives. The AA or NA sponsor can be an integral substructural component of the psychotherapeutic relationship. Most sponsors are willing to spend several hours each week with the persons they are sponsoring. These relationships can be intense, supportive, and therapeutic. Sponsors attempt to teach, communicate, and behaviorally show (via their personal "stories" and recovery) their "pigeons" how to remain drug abstinent and recover. A good sponsor is an extension of the psychotherapist. Sponsors also provide a therapeutic holding environment for the impulsive substance abuser. They actually take people to self-help meetings. They are available for advice or "sharing" 24 hours a day, and they actively confront their "pigeons" about irresponsible and/or irrational patterns of behavior and thinking. The AA sponsor and the AA community exude an "easy does it" attitudinal set.

In short, the basic 12-step program of recovery that is central to virtually all self-help treatment programs (AA, Al-Anon, NA, CA, OA, etc.) is antithetical to an impulse control disordered adjustment style. This is exactly why these recovery programs work so well for chemically dependent persons, substance abusers, and antisocial persons. Chemical dependency and substance use disorders are impulse control disorders. Antisocial personality disorder is also a type of impulse control disorder.

The structurally oriented treatment gains of self-help treatment programs also benefit the spouses and families of chemically dependent and antisocial persons. It is the author's observation that the children and families of impulse control disordered persons are often themselves impulsive and poorly controlled (Forrest, 1978, [1980] 1986, 1985, 1991). Family members of the impulsive patient can derive essentially the same gains from an active involvement in self-help treatment. As the spouse and family of the impulsive patient learn to behave less impulsively, they no longer synergize and reinforce the acting-out behaviors of the primary patient. Sponsorship, support, didactic education, social learning and reinforcement, and cognitive restructuring are but a few of the curative factors that the spouses and family members of impulsive patients experience within the context of Al-Anon, ACOA, or other self-help treatment programs. Living with a person who has an impulse control problem can be very stressful. Thus, anyone who lives with a chemically dependent or impulse control disordered person needs to be actively involved in a self-help recovery program.

Involvement in an ongoing, rigorous exercise program is essential to the recovery and effective treatment of chemically dependent patients with impulse control problems. There are several sources of therapeutic gain that are associated with this substructural component of the psychotherapeutic relationship.

Rigorous and consistent physical exercise results in healthy biophysiological and systemic change. Brain chemistry (Wallace, 1985, 1989, 1991) can be modified by physical exercise. Indeed, the organismic self-system changes as a result of active physical exercise. Physical exercise can help ameliorate depression, anxiety and stress, weight problems, and sleep disturbance. Impulsiveness can be reduced via involvement in a rigorous and consistent exercise program. The impulsive patient finds that he or she feels less "driven," or less impulsive, and more in control after jogging several miles or after exercising for 30 to 45 minutes.

A physical exercise program also helps the patient structure time more productively. Working out five or six times each week for 30 minutes to an hour at a time is a healthy alternative to structuring one's life around 20 to over 100 hours of weekly impulsive drug-related behavioral transactions.

The impulse control disordered person derives physical, psychological, and even social gains as a function of being involved in an ongoing exercise program. The psychological benefits of an active exercise program include improved body image, increased self-esteem, and identity consolidation. A capacity for "stick-to-itiveness" and a more healthy and modulated narcissism can be associated with an exercise program. New friendships and improved social skills can also accompany an involvement in a rigorous exercise program. The vast majority of people who are actively committed to jogging, bicycling, or body building are not drug addicts or substance abusers. The various gains that are associated with physical exercise synergistically interact to bind, control, and extinguish impulsiveness and acting-out.

A sound nutritional program and appropriate health maintenance behaviors also foster a reduction in impulsiveness. Impulse control disordered people seem to eat irregularly. They simultaneously ingest an inordinate number of foods and substances which actually contribute to their hyperactivity and impulsiveness. Many of these persons ingest several cups of coffee each day, or they consume a great deal of soda pop. They also eat too much sugar, tend to be chain smokers, and generally eat the wrong foodstuffs. Alcohol abuse and several other forms of substance abuse *per se* facilitate the outcropping of impulse control problems, agitation, and anxiety!

Therapists need to actively and consistently encourage their chemically dependent and impulsive patients to eat three well-balanced meals each day. Many of these patients have not eaten breakfast for 20 or 30 years! The chemically dependent patient may suffer from malnutrition and a diversity of medical conditions that are specifically caused by, or related to, poor nutrition. These patients also need basic guidance, information, and education about nutrition and health.

The basic and simple structure that is associated with regular and healthy eating habits, sleep, stress management, exercise, and general health maintenance behaviors serves as an important deterrent to acting-out. An enhanced sense of internal control and self-regulation evolves from an active involvement in a holistic health maintenance program.

It is important for the impulse control disordered patient to complete a medical/psychiatric examination at the time of treatment engagement. Impulse control problems (Sena, 1987, 1989, 1991) can be caused by brain tumors, lesions, and neurological complications. Indeed, a number of medical disorders and diseases can facilitate acting-out and behavior control problems. Proper medical care may reduce or eliminate the acting-out behaviors of some patients. Psychotropic medication helps some of these individuals control their impulses, emotions, and thoughts. However, therapists need to be very cautious in their use of psychotropics with all chemically dependent or substance abusing and impulse control disordered patients. The minor tranquilizers (Forrest, 1984, 1989) may initially reduce the impulse control problems of these patients, but abuse of tranquilizers by these patients quickly progresses to chemical dependency and further reinforces impulsive acting-out.

An active involvement in a church group, spiritual recovery program, or some other form of religious affiliation can serve as a deterrent to acting-out for some patients. This therapeutic substructure is an extremely helpful holding environment for some impulse control disordered persons. The growth-potentiating relationships as well as theological and philosophical dynamics of an involvement in a spiritual/religious program can be similar to those of a psychotherapy relationship or a self-help group. Love, support, modeling, learning and unlearning, conditioning and reinforcement, prosocial training, and the direct exposure to healthy social values, morals, and beliefs or attitudes are but a few of the ingredients of change that occur in most spiritual/religious recovery programs.

Some impulse control disordered substance abusers find that an active belief in God and a concerted effort to live according to the principles or doctrine of organized religion are deterrents to acting-out. Participation in a spiritually-oriented recovery program involves time structuring, cognitive restructuring, and controlling one's impulses and emotions. Even the AA slogan "Let go and let God" can be viewed as a cognitive-behavioral alternative to impulsive, driven, controlling forms of thinking and behaving.

In sum, there is a plethora of therapeutic sources of gain associated with the structural aspects of the psychotherapeutic relationship as well as the substructural dimensions of treatment. These sources of gain can be gleaned in psychotherapeutic work with impulse control disordered persons who are seen in both outpatient and inpatient treatment settings. The internal, cognitive, behavioral, relationship, environmental, and affective sources of impulse control modification that have been discussed in this section of the chapter are particularly relevant to the process of outpatient psychotherapy and treatment of antisocial substance abusers.

RESIDENTIAL TREATMENT
OF CHEMICALLY DEPENDENT PATIENTS
WITH IMPULSE CONTROL PROBLEMS

All forms of residential or inpatient care for impulse control disordered substance abusers are highly structured. Detoxification centers, residential alcohol and drug rehabilitation programs, psychiatric units, halfway houses, and day care programs can be viewed as structural approaches to the treatment of impulse control problems.

The hospital or residential treatment milieu imposes several sources of structure on patients. For example, patients are required to remain drug abstinent while in these environments, and various control measures are utilized to deter the use of alcohol/drugs in the treatment milieu. Locked doors, room searches, visitor restrictions, patient self-government, and urine testing are but a few of the mechanisms that are used to maintain a drug-free treatment environment.

Residential treatment settings are also environments where patients are required to get up each morning at a certain time, eat meals at a certain time and specific place, and go to bed at a specific hour. Furthermore, patients must participate in specific classes, groups, educational activities, recreational activities, and other social programs. A few of these programs still require that patients maintain a particular dress code!

A highly regimented treatment milieu imposes external structure and control on patients. Clinicians who work in these settings believe that externally imposed sources of control can be learned and internalized by the patient. Thus, the impulse control disordered person can learn to internalize and better control his or her acting-out behaviors within the confines of an environment which: (1) sets strict limits on acting-out behavior; and (2) consistently reinforces the use of control-oriented behaviors and living skills.

The structure of a detoxification unit has been literally lifesaving for millions of alcoholics and chemically dependent persons. The physiological and psychological craving for ethanol and other drugs is extinguished or controlled within the confines of a "detox" center. With the use of appropriate medical care in the detox unit or hospital, the drive or impulse to continue drinking is controlled or totally extinguished for a limited period of time. During this time interval, counselors and other staff members at the detoxification facility will attempt to get patients involved in a number of therapeutic activities that are also deterrents to substance use and acting-out. These deterrents to acting-out vis à vis intoxication and a wide range of alcohol/drug-related behaviors include the therapeutic substructures that were discussed earlier in the chapter.

Residential care for substance abusers, eating disordered persons, compulsive gamblers, sex offenders and sex addicts, and virtually all impulse control disordered people is based on the premise that many of these individuals can learn to modify or overcome their compulsions and impulse control problems. Residential treatment programs attempt to teach impulse control disordered patients how to use the therapeutic substructures as deterrents to acting-out.

Impulse control disordered persons seem to need different amounts and different types of "treatment" in order to significantly change their acting-out adjustment styles (Emrick, 1991). A few chronic alcoholics are able to stop drinking after completing a detox program or after one stay in a three- or four-week residential program. Many alcoholics are detoxified repeatedly but return to drinking shortly after leaving each inpatient program. It is reasonable (Forrest, 1984) to expect that over 70 percent of alcoholics and substance abusers can be successfully treated on an outpatient basis. Over 90 percent of obese patients (Mines, 1989, 1991) relapse and gain back the weight that they have lost while in a treatment program. Cleckley ([1941] 1976) reports that there are no effective treatments for antisocial patients.

In the clinical experience of the author, it is realistic to expect that many impulse control disordered clients will need to be actively involved in treatment and a program of recovery *for life* in order to recover from their impulse control problems. Involvement in a protracted outpatient self-help and/or professional treatment program is essential to the ongoing recoveries of most of these individuals. However, a sizable segment of impulse control disordered persons needs to be involved in halfway or three-quarter-way houses and residential treatment settings for several months, or perhaps a few years, in order to develop the living skills that are essential to recovery. Brief residential treatment, outpatient psycho-therapy, self-help, and detoxification are not potent vehicles of change for these individuals. They are in need of the long-term structure that a halfway house or similar long-term treatment setting is able to provide.

Chemically dependent persons and substance abusers are unable to curtail their global acting-out behaviors and impulse control problems in the absence of total drug abstinence. Impulse control disordered substance abusers resume their patterns of destructive and violent acting-out when they resume drinking and/or taking drugs (Forrest and Gordon, 1990). Thus, inpatient and residential treatment programs are generally most appropriate for chemically dependent patients who are poorly controlled in most areas of liv-ing. These individuals require progressively less treatment-oriented structure in their lives as they begin to recover and develop more effective internal sources of control.

It is essential that residential treatment programs address the various impulse control problems of chemically dependent patients and substance abusers. Many of these patients need psychotherapy and other treatments that transcend their chemical dependency or substance abuse problems. Residential treatment programs for chemically dependent or substance abusing impulse control disor-dered persons are most effective in their general treatment efforts when they actively engage these individuals in the therapeutic sub-structures that were outlined earlier in this chapter. Individualized and multimodal (Lazarus, 1981) treatment interventions are also essential to successful psychotherapy and rehabilitation work with these patients.

CORRECTIONAL FACILITIES AND PRISON ENVIRONMENTS

All prison environments are very structured. Correctional facili-ties that permit inmates to maintain jobs on the "outside" are far less structured than traditional prisons, but these programs and en-vironments are also highly structured.

Some chemically dependent inmates and substance abusers with impulse control problems require incarceration as an essential prerequisite to behavioral change. In fact, some of these individuals may need to be incarcerated several times in order to begin to work genuinely on their addictive illness and impulse control problems. It is important for mental health workers and correctional personnel to recognize that the incarcerated chemically dependent inmate with a concurrent antisocial personality disorder will *not* change significantly during any period of confinement or following any number of incarcerations in the absence of intensive long-term treatment. Therefore, the substance abusing impulse control disordered inmate needs to be involved in an intensive and structured treatment program while he or she is incarcerated and following prison release!

As all behavioral scientists and corrections counselors know, the vast majority of incarcerated impulse control disordered substance abusers do not receive rehabilitation and intensive treatment while they are in confinement or following release from a correctional facility (Ross and Lightfoot, 1985). Incarceration in a prison or correctional facility is not an ipso facto "cure" or treatment regimen for acting-out and chemical dependency. In fact, many prisoners (Yochelson and Samenow, 1986) become even more impulsive, angry, and aggressive as a result of the experience of being incarcerated. Drug abuse and chemical dependency are also widespread among prison populations. Thus, prison environments are not necessarily deterrents to acting-out or substance abuse!

A key to successful rehabilitation work with incarcerated impulse control disordered persons involves using the *structure* of the prison environment in a therapeutic fashion. Rather than simply "warehousing" these individuals in institutional facilities, a large scale and comprehensive effort needs to be directed at involving each impulse control disordered inmate in intensive long-term treatment. These patients should be required to participate in psychotherapy and *all* of the therapeutic substructures that have been discussed in this chapter. Furthermore, the patient needs to be actively involved in this treatment format throughout the course of his or her incarceration and for several months, or even years, after leaving the prison environment.

It is unrealistic to expect chemically dependent antisocial inmates and impulse control disordered inmates to benefit significantly from simply attending AA or NA on a weekly basis while in confinement. While "AA behind bars" has helped numerous substance abusers and chemically dependent offenders change their lives in a constructive manner, the vast majority of impulse control disordered inmates needs to be involved in far more intensive and multifaceted rehabilitation programs. Self-help programs alone simply do not meet the treatment needs of this clinical population (Hansen, 1991).

Under the right circumstances and with appropriate clients, incarceration can be a therapeutic process. Many impulsive chemically dependent inmates and substance abusers are not "ready" to enter psychotherapy and treatment. Clearly, some of these individuals are a very real danger to themselves and society. Incarceration can develop client readiness and motivation for treatment and result in a significant reduction in the threat to self and others. However, this can only occur when correctional and penal institutions provide real treatment and rehabilitation programs for substance abusing impulse control disordered inmates.

Clinicians, corrections workers, and the administrators of legal justice and the legal system also need to be cognizant of the fact that some impulse control disordered chemically dependent inmates and substance abusers cannot be successfully rehabilitated. It is very unrealistic to expect a 95 or 100 percent treatment outcome success rate with this population. Perhaps 15 percent of incarcerated antisocial personalities with concurrent chemical dependency are unsuitable candidates for involvement in long-term and intensive rehabilitation programs. These individuals consistently resist treatment involvement, they are chronic recidivists, and they frequently manifest neurologic or brain complications. Repeat violent offenders who fit this general profile may be considered appropriate candidates for institutional "warehousing." At present, we simply do not have the time, money, treatment modalities, or staff to be able to work effectively and productively with this small segment of impulse control disordered inmates.

The following brief case study demonstrates how repeated incarcerations and treatment can eventually facilitate change and recovery on the part of some impulse control disordered chemically dependent inmates.

Luther C. entered outpatient group therapy with the author shortly after his release from a state penitentiary. The patient had been placed on parole for a period of three years and was also required to meet with his parole officer on a monthly basis. He was required to attend Alcoholics Anonymous at least two times a week by his parole officer.

Luther was a 41-year-old divorced Caucasian. He was the father of two teenaged children by his first marriage. The patient was first incarcerated at the age of 16 for auto theft. He had been incarcerated five times between the ages of 16 and 41 and had actually spent over 15 years of his life in prisons or correctional facilities. Luther had been convicted of DUI (driving under the influence) nine times. He had multiple convictions for sale and distribution of drugs, auto theft, and assault. His last conviction was for attempted homicide.

The patient had been a polydrug abuser and chemically dependent since the age of 14. He was never involved in an intensive or long-term chemical dependency rehabilitation program while in prison. However, Luther did report that he had attended "10 or 20" AA meetings during the course of 15 years of confinement. He also indicated that he had completed a psychiatric evaluation while under the influence of a hallucinogenic drug (LSD). The patient attended "a few" marriage counseling sessions with his first wife.

This client was seen within the context of a weekly two-hour outpatient therapy group for two and one-half years. He attended AA regularly (two to five times each week) and functioned very well on the job. He also worked with an AA sponsor and attended a Baptist church on a weekly basis. The patient began living with a woman shortly after his release from prison. To date, he has been totally alcohol/drug abstinent for six years. He has not been arrested or involved in any form of legal difficulty since the time of his last prison release. The patient repeatedly verbalized throughout the course of therapy, "I was an alcoholic or drug addict before I ever got in trouble, whenever I got in trouble, and I still am . . . even though I don't touch the stuff anymore." He also told the author and his fellow group members that he denied his chemical dependency for years and that "it took all that pain and jail time for me to get to the program and turn my life around."

It is also of importance to note that Luther has played a major ongoing role in the AA and drug rehabilitation program of a state penitentiary that is located near his community. He spends between 15 and 20 hours a week working with chemically dependent inmates and parolees.

After several incarcerations and following 25 years of continual substance abuse and chemical dependency, this client entered an outpatient treatment program and recovered. His criminal activities had been drug related and drug facilitated for many years. Yet, the patient had received virtually no prior treatment for his chemical dependency and impulse control problems. This case clearly reveals the need for a comprehensive diagnostic assessment of all criminal offenders and subsequent engagement of these persons in an appropriate treatment/rehabilitation program.

GENERAL PSYCHOTHERAPEUTIC CONSIDERATIONS

As discussed earlier, psychotherapy takes place within the structural context of the patient-therapist relationship. Structure is an essential and basic component in all psychotherapy relationships and all models or "schools" of psychotherapy.

It is particularly difficult, if not impossible, to effectively treat impulse control disordered persons who also manifest a concurrent addictive disease without the use of several therapeutic substructures. In fact, it is impossible to establish the structure of a working and productive therapeutic alliance with many of these individuals when they refuse to be actively involved in the therapeutic substructures and a holistically-oriented program of recovery.

In view of these realities, it is of paramount importance that the psychotherapist make every effort to initially engage the patient in several therapeutic substructures very early in the treatment process. The therapist needs to actively confront and interpret the patient's resistance and parataxic maneuvers that are designed to avoid involvement in the structural components of the treatment process. It is equally important for the therapist to continually reinforce the patient's involvement in these treatment adjuncts through-out the course of psychotherapy and rehabilitation. The patient's internalized acceptance of the need to be actively involved in a long-term program of recovery is a major key to successful treatment.

It is strategically important for the therapist to repeatedly explain to the impulse control disordered patient that brief therapy and a lack of involvement in the therapeutic substructures will result in relapse and a poor treatment outcome. The therapist needs to consistently motivate (Anderson, 1989) the patient to both "work" in therapy and remain committed to a comprehensive recovery program. The successfully rehabilitated patient almost always persists in his or her ongoing commitment to the therapeutic substructures and recovery program *after* mandated treatment is completed. Chemical dependency does not simply go away or spontaneously remit after a few weeks or months of abstinence. Likewise, the character, behavioral, affective, cognitive, and interpersonal conflicts of these persons do not necessarily end following the initiation of abstinence.

Counselors and therapists must also avoid the pitfall of limiting the therapeutic process to a singular focus upon the patient's alcohol/drug abstinence (or use) in combination with a focus on his or her management of the therapeutic substructures. Approximately 15 minutes of each therapy hour can be devoted to these specific issues throughout the course of therapy. After the initial work of actively engaging the patient in the therapeutic substructures or program of recovery, the therapist needs to skillfully shift the focus of therapy to the genetic reconstruction (Forrest, 1984, 1991) and other phases of the treatment process.

Impulse control disordered persons manifest a plethora of problems and conflicts. All of these conflicts need to be explored and resolved in the process of therapy. These patients have social skill deficits, assertion problems, sexual and identity conflicts, and low self-esteem. They also find it difficult to establish and maintain intimate and loving relationships. Thus, the therapist must not allow the content of therapy to become fixated around the matters of substance use and acting-out. The maintenance of an addiction focus throughout the course of therapy is essential with these clients but not at the "expense" of failing to address other relevant clinical issues! The therapeutic substructures can be utilized by the patient and therapist to deal specifically with the patient's substance abuse and impulse control deficits, thereby "freeing up" the therapist to be more focused on other sources of patient conflict that need to be dealt with in therapy.

The therapeutic relationship and psychotherapy per se are rarely adequate vehicles for significant personality growth and change on the part of impulse control disordered chemically dependent patients or substance abusers. Therapists need to understand that their best therapeutic efforts are generally ineffective when these patients are not locked into a program of holistic recovery. Thus, it is clinically inappropriate and possibly even unethical to attempt to work with patients who refuse to participate in the therapeutic substructures and develop a program of recovery. Therapists may need to spend between three and ten sessions with some patients working on this specific issue.

Patients who reject therapy and refuse to participate in the therapeutic substructures may be: (1) referred to another psychotherapist or treatment center; or (2) simply told that they are not appropriate candidates for therapy and/or rehabilitation. These positions can be assumed by therapists in private practice as well as counselors and staff who are employed within the confines of state and federal mental health centers, chemical dependency rehabilitation programs, or psychiatric facilities. It is clinically unsound and self-defeating for mental health centers to spend hundreds of hours attempting to work with persons who actively and consistently reject treatment involvement. These persons also persistently maintain a complete lack of motivation to change. Such individuals need to be managed by the legal system or, if appropriate, by the nontherapeutic correctional community.

Therapists must remain supportive, nurturant, empathic, and genuine in their therapeutic encounters with these patients. It is strategically wise to avoid quid pro quo arrangements and interactions with the impulsive chemically dependent patient. The psychotherapist also needs to be patient and firm in his or her relationships with impulse control disordered clients. Acting-out pathology and active substance abuse problems in the therapist tend to exacerbate the symptom structure of these individuals. Reality therapy (Glasser, 1965), training, and cognitive-behavior therapy skills are essential components of the therapeutic armamentarium of clinicians who treat severely impulsive patients. A good sense of humor and the ability to not take oneself too seriously are qualities that help therapists maintain their own sanity and mental health as they work with this very difficult patient population.

Finally, it is often essential for the therapist to be able to work in concert with parole officers, judges, attorneys, and other members of the legal system when treating impulse control disordered substance abusers. Thus, the psychotherapist needs to be able to communicate openly, honestly, and fully with these persons and agencies as he or she works with the patient. The effective clinical management of homicide offenders and violent (Forrest and Gordon, 1990) persons who manifest a concurrent substance use disorder is dependent on therapist acumen and a working alliance with the legal or court system as well as the client.

SUMMARY

An impulse control disorder is defined as any repetitive pattern of behavior that is characterized by immediate gratification, low frustration tolerance, hedonism, impaired problem solving, inability to foresee or act in accordance with future consequences of an act, and loss of control of feelings, thoughts, or behavior.

Chemical dependency and substance abuse are impulse control disorders. Compulsive gambling, sexual addictions, eating disorders, and many forms of violent or destructive behavior can also be viewed as impulse control disorders. The general adjustment style of the impulse control disordered person is very self-defeating. The majority of impulse control disordered persons experiences global impulse control problems that affect virtually every aspect of their lives.

The psychotherapy relationship and the psychotherapeutic process can be viewed as structures which foster the development of internal control. The structure of the therapeutic alliance becomes a holding environment for the impulse control disordered client. Effective treatment facilitates the patient's capacity to act in rather than act out. Acting-in and developing internal problem-solving skills also becomes egosyntonic on the part of the patient.

Impulse control disordered persons with concurrent substance abuse problems need to be involved in several therapeutic substructures. These substructures and the various sources of therapeutic gain that are associated with the structural dimensions of treatment were discussed in this chapter. A therapy vignette and a clinical case study were included. Both demonstrate the therapeutic usefulness of structure in treating impulsive persons.

Residential treatment programs rely heavily on structure and external control as mechanisms of change and rehabilitation. The structural dynamics of constructive personality change that are associated with involvement in a detoxification center, residential chemical dependency rehabilitation program, psychiatric unit, halfway house, and day care program were explored in this chapter. These settings impose external and internal limits on the impulsive patient which serve as deterrents to acting-out. Patients also need to be involved in intensive psychotherapy and the therapeutic substructures while they participate in a residential treatment program.

Placement within a "highly structured environment" has been a standard historic treatment recommendation for antisocial and severely impulsive persons. Indeed, the prison milieu can accurately be viewed as a structural deterrent to acting-out. A key to the successful rehabilitation of incarcerated impulse control disordered persons involves using the structure of the prison environment in a therapeutic manner. Incarceration in combination with intensive and long-term treatment is essential to the successful rehabilitation of many impulse control disordered patients. It is also important for therapists and correctional workers to accept the reality that some of these persons simply cannot be successfully rehabilitated. Iron bar therapy is the ultimate treatment for these recalcitrant persons.

The roles of the psychotherapist in utilizing structure within the context of the psychotherapeutic process were also elucidated in this chapter. Psychotherapy can be an effective medium of change for these individuals when the therapist is able to: (1) actively engage the patient in the therapeutic substructures (comprehensive program of recovery); (2) maintain a consistent chemical dependency focus in therapy; (3) maintain a working and productive therapeutic alliance with the client; and (4) expand the content and focus of the therapeutic process to include virtually all aspects of the patient's psychopathology and adjustment style. Effective psychotherapeutic work with impulsive patients also frequently requires therapist acumen in the realm of dealing with various members of the legal system.

Chapter X

Treatment
of Chemically Dependent Offenders
in Correctional Settings

INTRODUCTION

Alcohol and drug abuse are associated with a wide range of criminal behaviors. As discussed throughout this text, alcoholism and substance abuse play major roles in most cases of criminal acting-out. Chemical dependency and substance abuse are also frequently cited as causative factors in most forms of violent behavior–among them rape, assault, vehicular homicide, and burglary. These realities have been recognized by some behavioral scientists and criminal justice system personnel for several decades.

Alcoholism and chemical dependency are crucial factors in many, if not most, cases of parole failure and recidivism (Ross and Lightfoot, 1985; Yochelson and Samenow, 1986; Forrest, 1990). Habitual offenders and "career criminals" are usually alcohol or polydrug abusers. Many are chemically dependent. The "revolving door" in the world of corrections is maintained vis à vis the unsuccessful treatment of thousands of chemically dependent offenders. It is the author's belief that successful treatment of chemically dependent offenders must begin by addressing their chemical dependency problems. Parole failures and the problems of recidivism are radically reduced when alcohol-dependent and/or substance abusing offenders terminate their use of mood-altering chemicals.

A good deal of the content of this chapter is taken from: Forrest, G. G., and Gordon, R. H., *Substance Abuse, Homicide, and Violent Behavior.* New York: Gardner Press, Inc., 1990.

Punishment is the criminal justice system's oldest and most frequently utilized method of dealing with all offenders. It is the author's belief that punishment rarely "works" as a deterrent to alcoholism and chemical dependency, and thus this model will *not* be effective in: (1) successfully rehabilitating chemically dependent substance abusing homicide offenders; (2) successfully rehabilitating other "types" of chemically dependent substance abusing offenders; or (3) reducing the rates of parole failure and recidivism for criminal homicide offenders as well as other offenders who manifest addictive symptomatology.

Research evidence does not support the efficacy of the punishment-deterrence model of rehabilitation in studies involving chemically dependent criminal offenders (Blumstein, Cohen, and Nagin, 1978; Hagan, 1982; Ross and Gendreau, 1983; Doren, 1987). As Ross and Lightfoot (1985) point out, "Very low correlations have been found between crime rate and the certainty of apprehension or the severity of punishment. Sometimes the correlations have been negative, i.e., the greater the chances of being caught and punished, the *higher* the crime rate! Deterrent effects are frequently unreliable and weak. Moreover, the strongest of these weak effects are for minor offenses. Deterrence effects, when they are achieved, are typically only temporary."

These authors go on to note astutely that prisons are already overcrowded and that using prison sentences more frequently and increasing their length does not affect crime rates. Furthermore, Ross and Lightfoot indicate that "the achievement of even a one percent reduction in crime might require an increase in costs [to the criminal justice system] of as much as three hundred percent to five hundred percent."

This chapter discusses: (1) traditionally utilized chemical dependency programs for criminal homicide offenders and other offenders; (2) traditional psychotherapy approaches; and (3) a structured model for treating chemically dependent criminal homicide offenders. It is absolutely imperative that the criminal justice system begin to provide comprehensive, long-term, highly structured, and effective chemical dependency treatment programs for all criminal homicide offenders with a prior history of chemical dependency problems. The dangerous and recidivistic nature of these offenders demands this type of treatment format.

TRADITIONAL CHEMICAL DEPENDENCY TREATMENT PROGRAMS FOR OFFENDERS

Historically, there have been no chemical dependency programs designed explicitly for criminal homicide offenders, although many correctional facilities have provided quasi-treatment programs for any or all inmates with self-admitted alcohol/drug problems. Therefore, the data and information provided in this section are derived from studies of traditional correctional chemical dependency treatment programs for *all* types of offenders. No doubt, most of the offenders involved in these programs and studies did have serious chemical dependency problems. Yet the many methodological flaws in most studies of alcohol and drug treatment programs in correctional settings must cause us to question the basic assumption that chemically dependent inmates are somehow selected for inclusion in these programs. For example, who chooses alcoholic or chemically dependent inmates for inclusion in a given correctional facility's treatment program? How are these inmates selected? What diagnostic criteria are used to identify "alcoholic" inmates? Numerous other design weaknesses contribute to the problem of evaluating the nature and effectiveness of traditional chemical dependency rehabilitation programs for offenders.

It was mentioned earlier in this chapter that the punishment-deterrence model of offender rehabilitation simply does not work. It must also be noted that many, if not most, workers in the criminal justice professions seem to believe that the "rehabilitation" of offenders per se does not work. Martinson (1974) published an extensive study of 231 investigations dealing with the effectiveness of correctional rehabilitation programs and concluded that most of these programs do not reduce crime. Furthermore, Martinson reported that correctional rehabilitation programs fail to reduce recidivism rates among both adult and juvenile offender populations. He stated, "In correctional rehabilitation, almost nothing works; correctional treatment is impotent." Other researchers (Bailey, 1966; Robinson and Smith, 1971; Fishman, 1977; Romig, 1978;

Yochelson and Samenow, 1986) have similarly concluded that correctional rehabilitation programs designed to facilitate inmate job placement, vocational training, behavior modification, and academic skills, and to enhance self-esteem, are grossly unsuccessful.

Many correctional facility administrators, behavioral scientists, and politicians interpreted these data as prima facie evidence that treatment and rehabilitation programs for offenders are inappropriate. The "nothing works" belief system resulted in confusion, "nonintervention," and a return to punitive methods of dealing with inmates. Szasz (1977) wrote, "The remedy is to reject the ethic of a fake psychiatric therapeutism masquerading as the rehabilitation of offenders, and to re-embrace the ethic of a truly dignified system of criminal sanctions consisting of minimal but fitting punishments meted out as inexorably and as fairly as possible." At best, rehabilitation programs and "forced" treatment were viewed as ineffective. At worst, they were believed to be dehumanizing, a waste of personnel and money, and psychonoxious. Lewis et al. (1985) stated that "to be 'cured' against one's will and cured of states which we may not regard as disease is to be put on the level of those who have not yet reached the age of reason or those who never will; to be classed with infants, imbeciles, and domestic animals. But to be punished . . . because we have deserved it, because 'we ought to know better,' is to be treated as a human person" (p. 171).

The finding that correctional rehabilitation programs are ineffective stimulated further investigations which subsequently refuted this position (Adams, 1976; Halleck and Witte, 1977; Ross and McKay, 1978; Gottfredson, 1980; Ross and Lightfoot, 1985). These researchers demonstrated that Martinson (1974) and other investigators had made numerous methodological errors in their work. For example, early investigators failed to assess programs according to duration, intensity, setting, offender characteristics, and staff training and experience. These studies evaluated only overall outcome effectiveness and failed to take into account the effectiveness of various intraprogram components. Even Martinson (1979) rejected his earlier position: "Contrary to my previous position, some treatment programs do have an appreciable effect on recidivism . . . The evidence in our survey is simply too overwhelming to ignore."

More recent research (Ross and Gendreau, 1983; Lee and Haynes,

1980; Blakely et al., 1980; Ross and Fabiano, 1985; Forrest and Gordon, 1990) indicates that correctional rehabilitation programs can reduce recidivism by as much as 30 to 60 percent. These results have been demonstrated to endure for 3 to 15 years after treatment. The research methodology employed in these studies (Gendreau and Ross, 1981) is also much improved. It should also be noted that these positive rehabilitation outcomes are reported for "hard-core" offenders as well as first-time offenders and delinquents.

Effective correctional rehabilitation programs: (1) are based upon a sound understanding and conceptualization of criminal behavior; (2) provide treatments that are based upon the principles of social learning theory or cognitive-behavioral theory rather than the disease/medical model; (3) are educational and training oriented rather than limited to one or two forms of "therapy"; (4) have concrete, realistic, attitudinal, and behavioral rehabilitation goals rather than goals centered in the realms of characterological and personality change; (5) are flexible and multifaceted; (6) involve program managers and treatment personnel who are skilled, competent, highly motivated people to be models of prosocial behavior; (7) are intensive; (8) are conducted in pleasant and favorable correctional environments; (9) maintain good program integrity and consistently provide services that are supposed to be provided; and (10) involve techniques for matching offenders and treatments.

Many treatment approaches or models can produce successful rehabilitation results. Reality therapy, social skills training, cognitive-behavioral therapy, family therapy, role playing, intensive alcoholism psychotherapy, and transactional analysis can be used effectively with offender populations. In their comprehensive study of effective correctional rehabilitation programs, Ross and Lightfoot (1985) reported that "not surprisingly, we found no panaceas and no magic elixir that could be thought of as the 'treatment of choice.'" Effective programs utilize different treatment models, but they consistently apply the program principles discussed earlier.

A major problem (Doren, 1987) that contributes to the lack of success of correctional rehabilitation programs is simply that most inmates never become involved in these programs. Kalish (1983) found in an investigation of state prisons in the United States that 70 percent of "habitually very heavy drinkers" had never been in a chemical dependency rehabilitation program. Thomas (1978) noted that treatment programs "have not yet been utilized to any appreciable degree in correctional facilities."

There are correctional rehabilitation alternatives that can "work" for many chemically dependent inmates. At worst, these programs benefit only some offenders. The following approaches or "programs" have been available to some offenders in some prisons and correctional facilities for many years.

ALCOHOLICS ANONYMOUS

Most prisons have had an Alcoholics Anonymous (AA) program for two decades or longer. Indeed, AA and/or AA-oriented programs are the most frequently offered rehabilitation models for incarcerated chemically dependent offenders. The AA program is essentially a self-help treatment model that is available to any offender who is willing to accept the first step of AA—"admitted we were powerless over alcohol; that our lives had become unmanageable." This treatment approach is based on the 12 steps of AA, the Big Book, and a great deal of AA literature, fellowship, sponsorship, and the support of other recovering alcoholics. The AA programs are very inexpensive and the easiest for prison administrators to implement. They do not require staff, consultants, or manpower hours. Very little institutional planning, supervision, or management are involved in maintaining a prison AA treatment program. Some prisoners are much more accepting of AA than of traditional psychological and/or psychiatric treatment. In many respects, it is probably far easier to admit and accept that one's criminal behavior is "caused by alcoholism" than by one's irresponsibility, antisocial personality makeup, or psychiatric/psychological disturbance (Doren, 1987; Forrest, 1990).

The basic issue that needs to be addressed with regard to AA-oriented correctional programs is again associated with the issue of program efficacy. Simply stated, do AA-oriented programs work? There are data available that indicate the AA model benefits alcoholic inmates as well as the correctional system. For example, Roth and Rosenberg (1971) found that inmate attendance at AA meetings resulted in improved institutional behavior. These investigators compared inmates with long histories of alcohol abuse who attended AA while incarcerated with similar inmates who did not attend AA, as well as with a control sample of inmates who did not have a history of alcohol abuse.

Ross and Lightfoot (1985) report data on the Mississippi State Penitentiary at Parchman indicating that only 4.6 percent of the rehabilitation program participants (parolees and discharges) are recidivists while 30 percent of the general inmate population are recidivists for parole violation alone. Unfortunately, this program is multifaceted in nature, and thus it was impossible to assess the direct effects of prisoner participation in the AA program upon recidivism rates.

Laundergan, Spicer, and Kammeier (1979) found that the Hazelden Rehabilitation Center's AA-based treatment program helped a significant percentage of court-ordered offenders to achieve total abstinence. Fifty percent of nearly 300 court-ordered offenders remained abstinent one year after treatment and involvement in this AA-oriented program.

A study (Wells, 1973) of multiple offenders who participated in several halfway house AA programs in Houston, Texas, reported radically reduced recidivism rates. Less than 5 percent of a sample of 561 highly recidivistic offenders involved in these AA/halfway house programs were returned to prison during the initial three and one-half years of operation. AA programs are included in many community correctional settings.

Similar positive outcome results are reported by Ball and Weiss (1976), Pallone and Tirman (1978), and Costello et al. (1976). Rates of success vary in these studies. It should also be noted that more recent research (Miller, 1980; Ogborne and Barnet, 1982; Ogborne and Glaser, 1985; Yochelson and Samenow, 1986) suggests that AA can be very helpful for select groups of alcoholics and alcohol abusers but ineffective, or perhaps even harmful, with other groups. Among alcoholics in general, AA appears to be most beneficial to individuals who: (1) are middle class or above; (2) are educated; (3) are not seriously disturbed; (4) have existential concerns; and (5) are over age forty. Other characteristics of AA members that are associated with successful AA affiliation include: (1) external locus of control; (2) cognitive simplicity; (3) dependency and field dependence; (4) high authoritarianism; and (5) low conceptual level (Ross and Fabiano, 1985; Ogborne and Glaser, 1985; Emrick, 1991).

TRADITIONAL PSYCHOTHERAPY APPROACHES

Reports of the effectiveness of traditional dynamically oriented psychotherapy on alcoholism and chemical dependency generally concluded that this form of treatment is ineffective (Hayman, 1956; Forrest, 1978; Armor, Polich, and Stambul, 1978; Bean and Zimberg, 1981; Forrest, 1983b, 1984a, 1984b, 1990; Bratter and Forrest, 1985). Analytically oriented treatment of the addictions is particularly ineffective (Pattison, 1987). It should be noted that there are at present no adequate outcome-effectiveness studies of analytic and/or psychodynamically oriented psychotherapy in the field of correctional alcohol/drug rehabilitation.

Individual and group counseling are basic components at many correctional chemical dependency treatment programs. Offenders usually receive behavioral, supportive, or confrontation-oriented (Forrest, 1982) varieties of individual and group therapy. The impact of therapeutic services provided by chemical dependency counselors in the corrections field has not been examined. The vast majority of counselors and providers of "psychotherapy" here do not have psychodynamically oriented training, experience, or supervision, and thus are unable to furnish this form of treatment.

Reality therapy (Glasser, 1965), rational emotive therapy (Ellis and Harper, 1961; Ellis, 1979, 1990), and rational behavior therapy (RBT) (Maultsby, 1974) are frequently acclaimed as the "most" or "only" effective therapeutic modalities for the treatment of criminal offenders. Unfortunately, there is a dearth of research data to support the global efficacy of any of these models of counseling and psychotherapy with offender populations.

Pallone and Tirman (1978) did find that two-thirds of a sample of 314 correctional clients were able to achieve total abstinence after receiving individual or group reality therapy. Nearly one-half of this sample was court-ordered into treatment. These authors also reported that 12 percent of the treated clients experienced partial success, and 20 percent evidenced "no significant change." Assessment of drinking behavior was conducted at the point of treatment termination, and no further followup data were collected in this study.

A study by Cox (1976) involving alcoholic inmates who were treated with RBT showed that treatment resulted in a radically reduced rate of institutional discipline infractions. These gains were maintained at six-month followup. RBT is a directive, step-by-step therapy that teaches more rational and effective reasoning or cognitive skills. Ziegler and Kohutek (1978) also report data on 79 inmates treated with RBT. The subjects were multiple offenders with histories of alcohol-related criminal offenses. It was found that treatment resulted in no disciplinary offenses, and 80 percent of this sample continued to adjust well within the community two years after treatment.

Family and marital therapy are frequently recommended for alcoholics and substance abusers (Forrest, 1978; Black, 1981; Wegscheider, 1981; Stanton, 1985). Unfortunately, it is almost impossible to utilize these modalities with offender populations. Most corrections counselors are not trained and experienced in the use of these treatments. Furthermore, correctional administrators are often reluctant to become involved in the basic logistics of providing such services. Thus, there are very few research investigations that explore the efficacy of family and marital therapy interventions and virtually no studies that deal with the effectiveness of these treatments with adult offender populations. A few investigators (Wade et al., 1977) have reported that family involvement in the treatment of adolescent offenders enhances rehabilitation outcome effectiveness.

Cognitive-behavioral strategies of treatment have been widely utilized in recent studies of offender populations (Miller, 1976; Marlatt, 1978; Kennedy, 1980; Ross and Fabiano, 1981; Ross and Lightfoot, 1985; Reid et al., 1986). Cognitive-behavioral treatments include assertiveness training, prosocial training, aversive conditioning, systematic desensitization, relaxation/self-hypnosis training, thought stopping, flooding, behavioral contracting, social skills training, role playing, and rational problem-solving skills. Most cognitive-behaviorally oriented chemical dependency treatment programs utilize multimodal (Lazarus, 1981) interventions. These programs attempt to change the offender's style of thinking, as well as his or her style of feeling and behaving. Different cognitive-behavioral interventions are used in order to facilitate positive changes in these different realms of human functioning. Cognitive strategies of intervention (Blane and Leonard, 1987; Forrest, 1991) may teach the offender to think more rationally, become aware of alternative solutions, and develop more effective problem-solving skills. Behavioral interventions may help the client relax, develop appropriate assertive behaviors or verbal skills, and develop alternatives to drinking and drug use. It is also very important to help offenders learn to control their emotions and to experience, express, and share their feelings in more appropriate ways.

Cognitive training and/or cognitive retraining (Ross and Fabiano, 1985) programs have been demonstrated to be effective in reducing recidivism rates among offender populations. Ross and Fabiano report that "such programs have led to reductions in recidivism ranging from thirty to sixty percent in followup studies for as long as three to fifteen years after treatment." The exhaustive investigations of Yochelson and Samenow (1976, 1977, 1986) into the inner structure and cognitive style of criminals clearly reveal that these individuals need to learn how to think more rationally. The cognitive style of the career criminal is pathologic and irrational and actively reinforces and maintains the criminal adjustment style (Yochelson and Samenow, 1976, 1986). Offender populations can be taught self-control techniques, rational thinking, and problem-solving skills that are not based upon irrational impulses or emotions.

Many correctional facilities provide some form of group psychotherapy for inmates who have chemical dependency problems. Group psychotherapy may be analytically oriented, cognitive-behavioral, supportive, or based upon the principles of reality therapy, RET, TA, or other systems and theories of counseling. Group treatment is almost always a major component of multifaceted correctional programs that attempt to provide treatment for chemically dependent offenders.

Several researchers and clinicians (Costello, Bechtel, and Giffen, 1973; Scott, 1976; Pallone and Tirman, 1978; Rachman and Raubolt, 1985) report that group psychotherapy is an effective treatment for addictive offenders. For example, Scott estimated that efforts with 55 percent of the convicts he treated with group therapy in an Oregon correctional institution were successful. Pallone and Tirman reported complete abstinence in 67 percent of 314 inmates at the time of termination of group treatment. Costello, Bechtel, and Giffen found that one-third of "chronic revolving-door alcoholics" from jails were abstinent and successful one year after completing group therapy.

Group psychotherapy was perceived as a virtual "cure-all" for substance use disorders within the correctional community during the late 1970s and early 1980s. Results of recent investigations in this field have been far less optimistic (Annis, 1979; Ross and Lightfoot, 1985). In a well-designed study involving 150 offenders with histories of alcohol abuse (Annis, 1979), it was found that group therapy produced no positive outcome effects in the specific areas of: (1) personality test results; (2) alcohol consumption levels; (3) arrests; (4) AA attendance; (5) one-year recidivism rates, and (6) postrelease employment status. Ross and Lightfoot point out that there is very little evidence supporting the efficacy of group therapy with alcohol-related offenders. These authors also point out that there are many design problems associated with the data and research findings regarding group therapy interventions with offenders. For example, they indicate that "in no studies of the outcome of multifaceted programs was the specific effect of group therapy studied, nor have the effects of group therapy been compared systematically with those of other treatment modalities." Group therapy has even been demonstrated to produce negative or psychonoxious outcome effects (Annis and Chan, 1983; Forrest, 1978) among some offender populations.

In spite of these inconsistent findings, it should be noted that several clinicians (Forrest, 1985, 1989; Bratter, 1980; Bratter, Pennacchia, and Gauya, 1985; Matuschka, 1985) have stressed the fact that effective chemical dependency treatment programs are group oriented or based upon the therapeutic community model. A number of studies and reports (Ends and Page, 1959; Hoff, 1968; Forrest, 1978) indicate that group psychotherapy is effective with non-offender alcoholics. It should also be noted that most correctional chemical dependency treatment programs rely heavily on the use of group discussion, group interaction and teaching, and group counseling techniques. The basic economics of the correctional system dictate that group treatment techniques will be an essential component of clinical work with chemically dependent offenders.

Cognitive-behavioral, reality, rational-emotive, transactional analysis, psychodynamically oriented, and other therapies may be utilized with individual offenders or groups of offenders. Many treatment programs for offenders attempt to provide both individual and group therapy services in addition to other treatments. Unfortunately, researchers are unable to discern clearly which of these various treatments are effective or ineffective for individual offenders as well as groups of offenders when two or more treatments are simultaneously applied to the individual or group.

Several other "traditional" forms of psychotherapy, education, and treatment have been used in attempts to rehabilitate substance abusing offenders. A diversity of psychotropic medications has also been used in treating alcoholism and the addictive disorders (Forrest, 1978, 1985; Zimberg, 1982, Blane and Leonard, 1987). Some addicts and substance abusers (Zimberg, 1982) manifest a major depression or affective disorder and thus are appropriate candidates for medications such as Prozac, Elavil, Desyrel, or lithium. Research (Wilsnack and Beckman, 1984) consistently indicates that women alcoholics are far more prone than are male alcoholics to serious affective disturbances in combination with their chemical dependency. A small percentage of secondary or reactive alcoholics (Knauert, 1980; Zimberg, 1982; Forrest, 1984) show thought disturbance, schizophrenia, or some other major psychiatric disorder. These individuals often clearly benefit from treatment with phenothiazine. The vast majority of alcoholics and substance abusers is clinically anxious and/or depressive. Thus, it is sometimes appropriate to treat them with a minor tranquilizer or an antidepressant on a short-term basis. However, it is very common for alcoholics and other substance abusers to "switch" addictions. Therefore, physicians need to be *very* cautious whenever they prescribe a mood-altering drug to these patients. Many, if not most, chemically dependent patients and substance abusers are in reality polydrug abusers or addicts (Pattison, 1987).

Antabuse (Schuckit, 1981; Forrest, 1985, 1989) is the most commonly prescribed medication for alcoholism and alcohol abuse. Antabuse (disulfiram) has been found to be an effective deterrent to drinking in approximately 50 percent of alcoholics (Milt, 1969; Mendelson and Mello, 1979; Forrest, 1985). This medication is an excellent adjunctive treatment that can be used on a short-term or long-term basis. While the global efficacy of Antabuse remains questionable, it is quite apparent that this treatment can be highly effective when used in combination with other treatment modalities. Fuller and Williford (1980) report that Antabuse resulted in a 77 percent abstinence rate. However, this short-term followup study employed a sample of nonoffender alcoholics.

Antabuse can be an effective treatment adjunct for alcoholics who are motivated to achieve and maintain abstinence. Many irrational beliefs are associated with its use in alcoholism treatment (Forrest, 1985). Alcoholics who have heart, respiratory, liver, brain, kidney, and other serious medical problems may not be appropriate candidates. Antabuse can be an adaptive "crutch" that helps the alcoholic recover. It can also facilitate the development of a working and productive therapist-patient alliance. Patient motivation and method or structure for Antabuse administration are the key variables that influence the effectiveness of this treatment.

It should be noted that Antabuse is commonly used in correctional settings. However, Ross and Lightfoot (1985) report that there are no controlled investigations of its effectiveness as a singular treatment modality for incarcerated offenders. Thus, there is little empirical evidence supporting the efficacy of Antabuse with offender populations.

Biofeedback and relaxation training (Yost and Mines, 1985) are sometimes utilized in the treatment of alcoholism and chemical dependency. These treatments attempt to reduce the stress and anxiety that often reinforce patterns of alcohol and drug abuse. Hypnosis and autogenic training have also been used to help alcoholics reduce feelings of stress, anxiety, and low self-esteem. Behavioral contracting (Forrest, 1985) is yet another treatment technique that is employed in alcoholism psychotherapy and chemical dependency rehabilitation programs. However, there are virtually no research data available that demonstrate the effectiveness of any of these treatments with incarcerated chemically dependent or substance abusing subjects.

OFFENDER PROGRAMS FOR DRINKING DRIVERS

A diversity of educationally oriented chemical dependency treatment programs has been developed in every state and major city of the United States during the past five to ten years. These programs are designed to educate and rehabilitate people who have been convicted of DUI (driving under the influence of alcohol) or DWI (driving while impaired). Most of these programs offer evaluation and assessment services, as well as individual and/or group counseling, lectures, discussion classes, and films. They provide clients with awareness of and education in the physical, social, behavioral, and legal consequences of drinking and alcohol abuse. Many, if not most, of the clients who participate are court-ordered into treatment. Such participation is also frequently offered to the client as an alternative to incarceration. Multiple DUI offenders may be required to take Antabuse and to attend an educational/treatment program for 12 to 18 months.

The data on DUI/DWI program effectiveness are inconsistent and inconclusive. Studies (Timkin, 1986) that deal with these issues are rather unsophisticated, methodologically weak, and limited to pre-post-designs that assess knowledge or attitudinal changes. Long-term followup data assessing drinking behavior are typically lacking in these investigations.

A number of studies indicates that the recidivism rate for DUI/DWI offenders who complete an alcohol education program is less than 5 percent (Walter, 1975; Hall, 1977). However, Holden's (1983) investigation of over 4,000 persons arrested for drunk driving in Memphis, Tennessee, reported that DUI/DWI programs are not effective with regard to DUI/DWI rearrests and subsequent misdemeanor and felony convictions. Holden pointed out that DWI programs are "too weak to have any effect on recidivism," "short-term and not very intensive," and "clearly inappropriate for a large proportion of the clients." The experimental design in this comprehensive investigation included random assignments to different treatments and a no-treatment control group.

Alcohol/drug education classes or programs that are similar to DUI/DWI programs are also offered in many correctional settings. These programs are designed to teach offenders the effects of alcohol/drug abuse. Many offenders learn that their basic beliefs about alcohol/drinking are distorted or irrational; some are helped to realize and accept the reality of being a problem drinker or chemically dependent. For these individuals, the decision to enter treatment may be directly associated with their participation in an alcohol/ drug education class or program. However, there are no evaluation research data available that support the effectiveness of such classes or programs as univariate treatments for offenders.

DETOXIFICATION FACILITIES

A final traditional treatment modality that has often been utilized with offenders is basic detoxification. Detoxification centers are found in some correctional facilities, and communities may have one or several centers that are affiliated with a hospital, community mental health center, or residential chemical dependency treatment program.

Detoxification centers were developed in cities and correctional facilities throughout the United States in the early 1970s. These community-based programs were felt to be an alternative to incarceration for public intoxication as well as a means of stopping the revolving-door incarceration of alcoholic offenders. Detoxification centers also reduce community costs for health care and help lessen problems associated with overcrowding of jails, courts, and the criminal justice system. A primary goal of the "detox" center is to ensure that patients or clients are involved in more intensive inpatient or outpatient chemical dependency treatment after leaving the detoxification center.

There is little doubt that detox centers generally provide very effective medically oriented interventions for acute and chronically intoxicated clients who need to be "dried out" or require other forms of immediate, short-term medical care. Detoxification centers in correctional settings can also be a deterrent to suicide and suicidal acting-out subsequent to the experience of incarceration (Forrest and Gordon, 1990). These programs have probably saved the lives of thousands of alcoholics and chemically dependent persons who have been jailed and then developed acute DTs, malnutrition, seizures, heart attacks, and various other life-threatening medical complications. Detoxification does result in alcohol/drug abstinence, which is the first step in treatment and recovery processes.

It has been difficult to demonstrate empirically that detox facilities have achieved their goals. Research (Hamilton, 1977) indicates that offenders who receive detoxification and referral services: (1) report longer periods of abstinence; (2) report improved quality of life; and (3) have better physical health at one year followup. The subjects in this study evidenced no gains in comparison with controls in the specific area of subsequent episodes of drinking/intoxication. Poor outcome data (Annis and Smart, 1978) have been reported in one six-month followup study. Nearly one-half of 522 detox clients were arrested once, one-fourth were arrested three or more times, and over half of the males in this sample were readmitted for subsequent detoxification. Twenty percent of the detox clients were readmitted three or more times for detoxification during the six-month followup interval.

Detoxification centers are frequently ineffective in their long-term treatment efforts because their clients do not actually enter ongoing rehabilitation programs. For example, Annis and Smart (1978) found that only 9.6 percent of 1,202 clients treated in a detoxification center ever made contact with the treatment agencies to which they were referred. In accordance with this finding, Smart, Finney, and Funston (1977) reported that nearly 40 percent of detoxified clients refused to enter postdetox treatment, and only 40 percent of those who agreed to enter subsequent treatment ever arrived at the treating agency. It is disappointing to note that Annis and Smart found that 80 percent of detox clients who entered followup treatment terminated or dropped out of treatment by the fifth appointment. These findings reveal several causal factors that explain how and why detoxification facilities often create and maintain their own revolving door. Brandsma and Maultsby (1977) also reported that 80 percent of chronic alcoholics drop out of treatment before one month, and one-third terminate after the initial evaluation for treatment. Burke (1977) studied individuals appearing in family court and found that less than 2 percent of alcohol abusers were willing to accept treatment. Their spouses also refused to enter any form of treatment program.

Many alcoholics refuse to enter detox centers as well as other treatment programs. Dropout and "no show" rates are very high even for alcoholics and chemically dependent persons who are court-ordered into treatment programs. As Ross and Lightfoot (1985) point out, "It appears that very often there is no adverse consequence to dropping out of enforced treatment." These authors also point out that there are no research data that assess the consequences of being brought back to court after dropping out of a court-ordered treatment program.

It should be noted that court-ordered or coercive treatments have been successful (McGrath, O'Brien, and Liftik, 1977; Laundergan, Spicer, and Kammeier, 1979). Employee assistance programs (EAPs) and alcohol and drug treatment programs for employees in industrial settings (Forrest, [1980] 1986; Cowen and Nittman, 1983; Harper, 1986; Wallace, 1989) commonly report 80 to 90 percent success rates. Many of the people who enter these programs are "pressured" or coerced into treatment but rarely are court-ordered to do so, and very few are offenders.

Many correctional facilities (Doren, 1987) have beds and personnel who are employed to provide detoxification services. However, hundreds of alcoholics die each year in jails and correctional facilities that are not equipped to treat the chemically dependent offender. A detox unit within the correctional facility can prevent alcohol/drug-related deaths and, in some cases, become the primary variable in an inmate's recovery and return to responsible living.

A MODEL FOR TREATING CHEMICALLY DEPENDENT CRIMINAL HOMICIDE/VIOLENT OFFENDERS

An effective treatment program for chemically dependent criminal homicide offenders and other violent offenders must be: (1) highly structured; (2) intensive; (3) long term; (4) multifaceted; and (5) legally mandated and thus highly coercive in nature. Violent or dangerous offenders who are alcohol and/or drug "abusers" also need to be involved in similar treatment programs.

Chemically dependent homicide offenders and other chemically dependent violent offenders do not constitute a homogeneous group. Yet their violent acting-out and lack of internal controls are reinforced and synergized through drinking and drug ingestion. Very few of these individuals will commit murder or other acts of violence in the absence of intoxication. Although alcohol and drug ingestion do not "make" or directly cause these individuals to commit acts of homicide and violence, the use/abuse of mood-altering chemicals is the *primary precipitating variable* in the vast majority of cases involving intoxicated homicide offenders. The vocational, familial, educational, socioeconomic, physical, legal, medical, racial, and personality-behavioral characteristics of any given group of homicide offenders are subject to a great deal of variability and homogeneity of variance. However, when such a group of offenders is limited to those with a history of clear-cut alcoholism/chemical dependency or abuse, this factor becomes the overriding clinical common denominator that predicts subsequent homicide and other violent acting-out behavior. Therefore, the successful treatment and rehabilitation of chemically dependent homicide offenders and other substance abusing violent offenders is first and foremost contingent upon effective and lifelong addiction recovery.

There are several stages of effective treatment for chemically dependent homicide offenders. Initially, they must be identified and complete a diagnostic evaluation. This process is designed to provide effective treatment and rehabilitation services for offenders who are chemically dependent or abusers of alcohol and other mood-altering chemicals. Therefore, the diagnostic or assessment phase of treatment is required to establish the appropriateness of an individual for entry into the rehabilitation program. All primary and most secondary alcoholics or chemically dependent inmates are appropriate candidates for this treatment program whereas schizophrenics, severe borderlines, severe psychopaths or sociopaths (Reid et al., 1986; Doren, 1987), and brain-injured individuals are not. These persons need to be referred for other types of psychiatric/psychological care.

Chemically dependent offenders and offenders with patterns of serious alcohol/drug abuse remain active in this treatment program for the duration of their incarceration. Upon release from the correctional facility, they are required to remain actively involved in the program for a minimum of five years. The program of active treatment in the facility may be followed by a ten-year followup stage of treatment within the community. Table III depicts the stages and time structure of this treatment model.

The actual components of this treatment program and their functional interactions are discussed in the following section.

STRUCTURAL COMPONENTS OF TREATMENT

Once an offender has been diagnosed as having alcoholism or chemical dependency, he or she is entered (or given the option of refusing treatment/program entry) into the treatment program. The tools and techniques needed to complete an accurate differential diagnosis on each offender were elucidated in Section One. Program participants are required to be actively involved in the following treatment regimen during their incarceration: (1) initial forty-hour alcohol/drug education class and program orientation; (2) weekly individual counseling; (3) weekly group psychotherapy; (4) three or more AA meetings each week with active sponsorship; (5) educational/career training; and (6) exercise program and holistic health maintenance. Participants are also encouraged to develop a spiritual life and a spiritually oriented program of recovery.

This treatment regimen is maintained throughout the offender's incarceration. Thus many offenders will be actively involved in Stage II of treatment for three to ten years, while a few might be in this stage for 20 years or longer. Some will need to be medically detoxified following arrest or before entering the diagnostic/assessment phase of the treatment model.

Stage III, or the phase of active community treatment, involves

Table III: Stages of Treatment Program

Stage I	Stage II	Stage III	Stage IV
Diagnosis & assessment	Active treatment for duration of incarceration	Active community treatment after incarceration (five-year minimum time structure)	Inactive community treatment & followup (five-year minimum followup)

the same treatment components. Upon being released from prison or a correctional facility, the offender must actively and consistently participate in: (1) weekly individual psychotherapy; (2) weekly group psychotherapy; (3) AA; and (4) an exercise and health maintenance program. Additionally, all program participants must: (1) maintain a full-time job or be enrolled in college/vocational training on a full-time basis; and (2) be active in a highly structured and monitored Antabuse maintenance program. The offender remains in this treatment regimen for no less than five years after being released from prison. Participants are also encouraged to attend church or otherwise develop a personally meaningful spiritually oriented lifestyle and value system.

This stage of treatment is critically important to the offender's well-being and society's sense of security. Relapse and recidivism (Gorski and Miller, 1986; Gorski, 1991) can be extinguished during this stage. This phase of treatment must be highly structured and the progress and behavioral responses of each offender monitored very closely. Antabuse should be dispensed three times per week at a specific time and place designated by the offender's counselor or parole officer. The client is given 750 mg of Antabuse each time. Program participants need to document AA attendance (at least two meetings per week while in this phase of treatment), as well as employment and involvement in an exercise program.

Each offender's progress is evaluated on a monthly basis by the parole officer and the offender's therapist. The offender is expected to attend *all* scheduled therapy sessions as well as *all* other components of the treatment program. Missed therapy sessions are not tolerated. Indeed, if the offender chooses to terminate his or her active involvement in the program, every effort is made to return the individual to a correctional facility for six months to one year. This procedure is explained in detail to the offender at the time of program entry and discussed throughout the treatment process.

It is imperative that the offender understand the consequences of missing treatment sessions, failing to take Antabuse, or skipping AA meetings. It is generally recommended that any offender who misses more than three scheduled treatments (a *total* of three individual and/or group therapy sessions, AA meetings, or Antabuse administrations) within a period of 12 months be returned to a correctional facility for no less than six months of incarceration. There is very little flexibility in this procedure. Following a third failure to participate in a scheduled treatment activity, the offender is automatically picked up and returned to prison or a correctional facility for the duration of his or her original/full sentence. There are very few, if any, acceptable excuses for missing a scheduled treatment activity in this program.

Entry into Stage IV of this treatment program occurs when the offender has successfully completed a minimum of five years in Stage III. Stage IV, or the inactive phase of community treatment and followup, encompasses another five years or more of program participation. Clients attend a minimum of one AA meeting per week, monthly individual psychotherapy, and quarterly contact with their parole officers during this stage of treatment. Some clients may choose to remain involved in an ongoing Antabuse maintenance program. They are expected to be employed and are encouraged to remain in a holistic health/exercise program, as well as some form of spiritually oriented program of recovery.

Drinking or drug-taking relapses (Gorski and Miller, 1986; Gorski, 1991) during Stages III or IV may result in the offender's being placed in a 21- to 30-day comprehensive chemical dependency rehabilitation center. However, the decision to reenter an offender into residential treatment is a clinical one that is determined by such factors as: (1) prior progress in treatment; (2) parole office/board input; (3) nature of relapse; and (4) legal factors that may or may not be associated with the relapse. Offenders who relapse during Stage III of this program should be returned to the correctional facility immediately and then entered into residential treatment 30 to 40 days before their release from the facility. Some will need to be detoxified for three to ten days before reentering the correctional facility.

Relapses during Stage IV of this program may also result in reentry into a residential treatment facility. It will generally be more difficult to monitor the behavior of offenders who have successfully completed several years (six to ten) in this program or who have actually completed the program. However, it is quite likely that these people would be much more apt to self-initiate residential or more intensive treatment following relapse. Offenders who relapse during the initial months or first two years of Stage IV might need to be reentered into Stage III and receive other appropriate intensive interventions.

This global treatment model for chemically dependent criminal homicide/violent offenders is structured, rather rigid, long-term, coercion-oriented, intensive, and multifaceted. It may be possible for some institutions and clinical staffs to successfully modify this program in the areas of providing differential treatments and matching offenders with relatively more precise or specific treatments. However, it is the author's clinical opinion that we do not possess the basic clinical skill and expertise that are prerequisite to effectively selecting and matching treatments for chemically dependent homicide offenders. The model that I have delineated can deter further acts of homicide and violence and result in continued chemical dependency recovery for an estimated 70 to 80 percent of chemically dependent criminal homicide offenders. Nonetheless, this program is not a panacea for chemically dependent offenders or correctional facilities. No treatment model is maximally effective for all chemically dependent offenders.

This treatment model will be most effective for offenders who manifest primary or secondary chemical dependency. The program will also be highly effective for incipient or early-stage alcohol abusers as well as polydrug dependent offenders. Research suggests that approximately 90 percent of young male alcohol abusers also abuse other mood-altering chemicals (O'Donnell, Lydgate, and Fo, 1980; Forrest, 1984; Yochelson and Samenow, 1986). It is reasonable to expect a 60 percent success rate when using this model to treat offenders who are polydrug dependent or are alcohol abusers.

A plethora of practical factors dictates that this treatment model will include polydrug dependent and substance abusing criminal homicide/violent offenders. In spite of the widespread belief that combined alcohol/drug treatment programs are less effective than separate programs, the funding, support, and adequately trained and experienced clinical/administrative personnel are not available to establish separate treatment programs for alcoholics and other "types" of substance abusers or chemically dependent persons. Likewise, we do not possess the research data or clinical acumen (Pattison, 1987; Emrick, 1986, 1991) that would enable correctional treatment personnel to select or match chemically dependent criminal homicide offenders and specific treatments and treatment modalities.

A final note of caution is in order. This program, or any similar treatment model for chemically dependent violent offenders, will not work or prove effective in the absence of a legal system that will actively, supportively, and expediently maintain it. For example, if an offender in Stage III of the proposed treatment model misses scheduled treatment sessions for two or three weeks, he or she must be picked up by the police immediately and quickly reincarcerated. In sum, such a treatment model needs to have a great deal of legal support and legal "teeth" in it in order to produce successful results.

SUMMARY

This chapter has included a review of the traditional approaches and models that are used to treat chemically dependent and drug abusing criminal offenders. The majority of these traditional treatment approaches are minimally effective. The punishment-deterrence model of offender rehabilitation is generally ineffective. The components of effective correctional rehabilitation programs are discussed and contrasted with the "nothing works" belief system. The vast majority of chemically dependent homicide/violent offenders never becomes involved in a treatment program before or during their incarceration.

The AA and AA-oriented treatment programs are the most frequently utilized approaches provided for incarcerated chemically dependent violent offenders. Self-help programs do not require staff or consultants, and they are cheaply and easily managed by correctional administrative personnel. Research suggests that self-help programs benefit many offenders.

Psychotherapy and rehabilitation programs for chemically dependent homicide/violent offenders are inadequate or lacking. Most correctional facilities do not provide comprehensive treatment services for incarcerated chemically dependent inmates. In fact, many corrections workers do not believe that rehabilitation and treatment services "work." The "nothing works" mentality or belief system has done a great deal to impede the development of effective treatment services for chemically dependent violent offenders. A number of recent investigations utilizing group therapy, reality therapy, RET, RBT, and cognitive-behavioral treatments for chemically dependent offenders were reviewed. Many of these studies report that "treatment" reduces recidivism and fosters abstinence, as well as other gains. Educational programs, DUI programs, detoxification services, and Antabuse maintenance programs benefit some drug abusing offenders. Unfortunately, research evidence does not overwhelmingly support the superiority of one of these various treatment modalities over the others. A great deal of methodologically sound research needs to be conducted in this realm of the corrections field.

The final section of this chapter included a basic model for treating chemically dependent and substance abusing violent offenders. This program is: (1) highly structured and involves multiple stages; (2) intensive; (3) long-term; (4) multifaceted; and (5) legally mandated, supported, and thus highly coercive in nature. It involves several years of structured treatment and supervision. There is very little flexibility in the program procedures that regulate participation in treatment modalities and relapse. The success or failure of this basic treatment model is largely contingent upon the power or control of the legal system that is responsible for its maintenance.

Behavioral scientists, corrections workers, the legal system, and the American collective are beginning to recognize and understand the causative roles of alcohol and other drug use in homicide and a diversity of violent behaviors. Violent offenders, victims, families of both offenders and victims, and every segment of society will benefit through the effective treatment of chemically dependent criminal homicide/violent offenders. Perhaps in the near future, we will be able to identify and successfully rehabilitate more of these persons earlier in their careers of crime, violence, and chemical dependency—before they kill!

Chapter XI

Therapist-Patient Relationship Dynamics

INTRODUCTION

As touched upon in Section One, and in Chapters IX and X of Section Two, substance abusers and chemically dependent antisocial patients have historically been perceived (Bean and Zimberg, 1981; Zimberg, 1982; Forrest, 1984; Bratter and Forrest, 1985; Brown, 1985, 1988; Nace, 1990) as poor candidates for psychotherapeutic treatment. Many psychiatrists, psychologists, and other psychotherapists actually refuse to work with these clinical populations (Lawson, Ellis, and Rivers, 1984; Bratter, 1985; Forrest, 1991). It is only in recent years that the behavioral science professions have actively initiated treatment and rehabilitation efforts with substance abusers and chemically dependent antisocial patients.

It is in many ways significant that psychotherapists and health professionals have avoided working with these patients. Certainly, all health care facilities have been inundated with chemically dependent or substance abusing patients for several decades. Prisons, correctional facilities, psychiatric hospitals, mental health centers, state hospitals, and Veterans Administration medical centers provide various clinical services for hundreds of thousands of antisocial and/or chemically dependent/abusing patients each year. Yet, these patients continue to receive very little psychotherapy per se. Less than 10 percent of incarcerated substance abusers have received rehabilitation services or psychotherapy prior to being institutionalized (Ross and Lightfoot, 1985).

In spite of our growing national awareness and concerns about substance abuse, chemical dependency, and crime, the fact remains that very, very few substance abusers receive psychotherapy and comprehensive treatment. Even fewer antisocial persons who manifest a concurrent substance use disorder are seen for psychotherapy or comprehensive rehabilitation services. Why is it that therapists and health service providers have not been active in the psychotherapy and rehabilitation of these patients? In fact, there are several realistic and cogent answers to this question. Many of these answers have been discussed in earlier chapters: collective, individual, and familial denial; financial and economic factors; education and training issues; and beliefs and attitudes associated with treatability or treatment outcome effectiveness.

This chapter focuses on the most salient single factor associated with health service provider avoidance of professional involvements with substance abusers and chemically dependent antisocial patients: the treatment *relationship*. It is the author's opinion that clinical relationships with chemically dependent impulse control disordered clients generally prove to be extremely thorny and conflictual for therapists and health care providers. Thus, a pragmatic solution to these conflictual situations for the therapist or physician is simply not to provide professional services for such patients.

The nature of the therapeutic alliance, transference dynamics, countertransference dynamics, sexual issues, and other sources of dissonance between the psychotherapist and these "difficult" patients is examined in this chapter. The reader will discover, or perhaps rediscover, the very real sources of conflict that develop and evolve between therapists and their chemically dependent, acting-out patients. Solutions and strategies for resolving these deterrents to more productive therapeutic relationships between therapists and impulse control disordered persons are also presented in this chapter.

THE THERAPEUTIC ALLIANCE

The therapeutic relationship, or alliance, begins to form during the initial patient-therapist interactions. Relationship building between the therapist and patient takes place during the assessment and diagnostic phase of treatment (see Chapters II and III, Section One). The process of relationship building continues throughout the course of therapy.

A working and productive therapeutic alliance is essential to the effective psychotherapy of all substance abusers and chemically dependent antisocial persons. The therapeutic alliance can be defined as a basic professional and human relationship involving two (or more) persons who are mutually committed to the process of facilitating personality growth and behavioral change upon the part of the person in the relationship who is conflicted. The person who is defined as a "psychotherapist" in such a relationship manifests the essential training, education, experience, internal strengths, and other skills that are essential to the process of helping the person who is identified as a "client" or "patient" initiate constructive personality growth and behavioral change. The interactions of the therapist and patient facilitate the development of a therapeutic relationship that eventually becomes a therapeutic *alliance*–a union of interests, a union by relationship, and a connection for mutual advantage between persons or groups.

The therapeutic alliance is *working* and *productive* when both parties, therapist and patient, are actively committed to the process of fostering patient change. A working and productive psychotherapy relationship is not a perfunctory interpersonal exchange whereby a therapist attempts to somehow induce a patient to change. Both parties in the therapeutic encounter are willing to work for change. The patient is actually an ally of the therapist or co-agent of growth and recovery. The therapeutic dyad becomes the essential agent of patient change, and the experience of psychotherapy is consistently a productive and very meaningful experience for the therapist as well as the patient.

As I have indicated (Forrest, 1984), "facilitative psychotherapy relationships evolve as a process. They do not simply occur as a function of several hours of therapist-patient contact. The therapist and patient need to be especially committed to creating a therapy relationship that is a potent and meaningful vehicle of change. Mutual trust, respect, and concern are essential ingredients of the therapeutic alliance. The basic humanness and relatedness of the therapeutic alliance are curative" (p. 56).

There are a number of essential therapist and patient characteristics that contribute to the development of a working and productive therapeutic alliance. Key therapist ingredients (Forrest, 1984, 1991) in the development and maintenance of a working and productive therapeutic alliance include nonpossessive warmth, empathy, concreteness, and genuineness. These therapeutic characteristics pertain to the therapist's ability to: "(1) accept the patient unconditionally; (2) be affectively and cognitively attuned to the patient's feelings, experiences, and behaviors; (3) communicate to the patient an understanding of this awareness; and (4) be open to his or her own experience within the therapeutic encounter. Furthermore, the therapist is able to honestly and genuinely express his or her feelings and experience with the patient. The psychotherapist is a 'real person' within the therapeutic encounter. Effective therapists are able to consistently provide high levels of nonpossessive warmth, empathy, genuineness, and concreteness *throughout* the course of their psychotherapy relationships with primary alcoholics" (Forrest, 1984, pp. 56-57). Truax and Carkhuff (1967) repeatedly demonstrated the positive impact of high levels of these therapist characteristics on psychotherapy outcome with a diversity of treatment populations.

Psychotherapists who work with substance abusers and chemically dependent antisocial persons also must expect their patients to change as a function of the treatment relationship. Indeed, a basic belief in the ability of the patient to change in a constructive fashion is one essential prerequisite to the therapist's decision to initiate the process of psychotherapy with these difficult persons. Therapists also need to be personally comfortable with these persons in order to be able to establish a working and productive therapeutic alliance. The constructive therapeutic alliance evolves as a function of the counselor's sensitive and in-depth understanding of the patient's personality structure and psychopathology.

The therapeutic alliance is nurtured and strengthened vis à vis the therapist's consistent communication of respect and dignity for the patient. Therapy involves actively teaching these persons to respect themselves and like themselves. A consistent and healthy sense of self-worth is essential for recovery. The constructive therapeutic alliance is not steeped in patient or therapist narcissism. It is essential for the therapist and patient to be able to simply like one another for effective long-term psychotherapy to take place.

A plethora of additional therapist skills contributes to the development of productive psychotherapy relationships with chemically dependent and impulse control disordered persons. Therapists who work with these patients need to be active, focused, and assertive in their therapeutic relationships. They also must be able to set limits with patients and avoid being engaged in "patsy" oriented transactions by the patient. Effective confrontation skills (Forrest, 1982, 1985) are an essential component in the therapist's armamentarium. Passive-dependent and avoidant therapist styles do not work effectively with these patients. Therapists who manifest substance use disorders, impulse control problems, or narcissistic personality disorders are also ineffective in their clinical work with chemically dependent antisocial persons. The productive therapeutic alliance is comprised of an amalgam of therapist-patient factors.

It is important for psychotherapists to clearly recognize their own personal limitations. Therapist limitations are determined via training, education and supervision, personal life experiences, and the "personal equation." Many therapists consciously choose not to treat substance abusers and/or antisocial persons. Many counselors simply do not like these patients. It is imperative for therapists and change agents not to become scotomatous in their personal feelings, beliefs, and attitudes about the persons they attempt to treat in psychotherapy. Thus, a good therapeutic "fit" is essential to effective psychotherapy with all "kinds" of clients. Psychotherapists need to assess all of these factors before they attempt to work with the types of clients who are the focus of this text. A good therapeutic fit is determined by *both* therapist and patient characteristics and the interaction effect that *both* parties generate within the therapeutic relationship.

What are the essential *patient* characteristics that contribute to the development of a working and productive therapeutic alliance? This general question has been addressed at length as it pertains to the process of psychotherapy relationships with a diversity of treatment populations other than chemically dependent persons, substance abusers, and antisocials (Fromm-Reichmann, 1949; Rogers, 1952; Glasser, 1965; Kernberg, 1975, 1984). Recently (Armor, Polich, and Stambul, 1978; Zimberg, 1982; Bratter and Forrest, 1985; Brown, 1985, 1988; O'Connell, 1990), clinicians have begun to present cursory information and data that describe chemically dependent/substance abusing patient characteristics that are correlated with or related to successful treatment outcome. There are presently no clear-cut predictive variables related to the successful psycho-therapy and treatment of ASPD (Reid et al., 1986; Yochelson and Samenow, 1986; Doren, 1987; Forrest, 1990).

Alcoholics and substance abusers generally have a more favor-able treatment prognosis if they are employed, socially stable, nonpsychotic, married, and motivated to seek help (Armor, Polich, and Stambul, 1978). Unfortunately, there are virtually no treatment outcome data available that pertain to chemically dependent antiso-cials. Several authors (Paolino and McCrady, 1977; Wilsnack and Beckman, 1984; Nace, 1990) note that the chemically dependent or substance abusing antisocial person is difficult to treat and has a poor treatment prognosis. Ross and Lightfoot (1985) review several studies which indicate that incarcerated alcoholics and substance abusers who receive "treatment" while incarcerated are far less recidivistic following institutional release than incarcerated alco-holics and substance abusers who do *not* receive treatment while incarcerated.

In spite of the dearth of prognostic data and research evidence pertaining to the characteristics of antisocial substance abusers or chemically dependent patients who can be successfully treated in psychotherapy and rehabilitation programs versus those who cannot be successfully treated, it is my observation that there are clinical variables which grossly differentiate between the relative treatabil-ity of these clinical subgroups. In general, psychotherapy is most efficacious with substance abusers and chemically dependent anti-social patients who: (1) have stable work histories; (2) have at least a rudimentary capacity to empathize with the psychotherapist and significant others; (3) have some capacity to internalize feelings and conflict; (4) have maintained family and/or marital relationships; (5) manifest a primitive or archaic superego structure; and (6) are, for *whatever reasons,* motivated to be involved in psychotherapy and/or a comprehensive treatment program.

Many substance abusers manifest these favorable prognostic characteristics. These individuals can be expected to do well in psychotherapy and chemical dependency rehabilitation programs. To the contrary, many *antisocial* substance abusers do not manifest these positive prognostic traits. This reality poses a number of on-going treatment-oriented problems for the psychotherapist. Is it clinically appropriate or even ethical to attempt to treat individuals who do not have these basic characteristics? Is it rational to expect these patients to need several months of psychotherapy in order to develop the degree of "readiness" that is required for effective treatment to take place? How should the psychotherapist handle clients who are forced into therapy even when these individuals manifest some of these favorable prognostic characteristics? These are but a few of the practical and ethical problems with which therapists are confronted when they work with substance abusing and/or chemically dependent antisocial persons.

Perhaps the most salient point that can be made in this realm is simply that patients play a major role in determining the outcome of psychotherapy. Therapist skills and styles affect the process and outcome of psychotherapy with these patients, but patient-oriented factors also orchestrate and impact the process and outcome of treatment. It has been my consistent observation in working with antisocial substance abusers that the patient's capacity for experiencing empathy is crucially important to the development of the therapeutic alliance. It is impossible to develop a working and productive therapeutic alliance with persons who are basically unable to empathize with the psychotherapist. These patients are almost always incapable of empathizing with significant others as well. The impulse control disordered substance abuser who is genuinely able to "feel with" the therapist and significant others is a far better candidate for psychotherapeutic treatment than the cold, affectless substance abuser.

Therapists need to spend between 5 and 15 hours with their patients assessing patient readiness for treatment. If it becomes apparent during this time that the patient has no motivation to participate in therapy, is unable to experience empathy, has no superego or conscience, cannot work, and is not ready to accept the reality of his or her substance use disorder, it is clinically inappropriate for the therapist to attempt to develop a therapeutic alliance with the patient. Such persons are not appropriate candidates for psychotherapy or intensive rehabilitation programs. Again, therapists must accept the reality that they alone do not shape the therapeutic alliance. A psychotherapy relationship requires at least two participants!

The following therapy vignette was taken from the third treatment session with a recalcitrant and highly resistant chemically dependent antisocial client. It is apparent that the client was not motivated to participate in the psychotherapeutic process. This client was not capable of developing an emotional attachment to the therapist. Hence, it would not have been possible to develop a therapeutic alliance between the therapist and client.

Keith R.: It was my fourth DUI, but I've had it with those bastards . . . I'll be damned if I'll take those classes again, and they can put me back in the slammer again, er . . . like I told you when I first walked in here.

Doctor F.: Sounds like you haven't changed your mind on that one . . . I mean, you feel the same about therapy or rehab?

Keith R.: You got that one right, Doc . . . It was my lawyer's idea to see you, but I can tell you I don't like shrinks. Uh, nothing personal, but you can't make me stop drinking and nobody can. I've been seein' shrinks and put in treatment programs since I was 14 years old, and as far as I'm concerned, none of 'em ever helped me . . . just a waste of time and money . . . ha, ha.

Doctor F.: So you've been in treatment a number of times, and it really hasn't been helpful for you?

Keith R.: Yeah . . . only it helped me get smarter . . . I mean, I sure learned that I didn't want to get caught . . . not for anything, and the only real bad thing I did was pull an armed robbery . . . and I'll admit, I was dumber and higher than shit when I did it . . . real dumb, but I did my time and . . . I'll be damned if anybody is going to lock me up again, especially not for drunk drivin' . . .

Doctor F.: It's going to be hard for me, or any other therapist, to help you if you don't want to be helped . . . the drinking seems to have caused a lot of problems for you . . . drinking and problems with the law . . . or society.

Keith R.: That's true, but that's before I got smart . . . like I told you last week, I stopped drinking the hard stuff the last time I got out of jail, and I'm stayin' away from the speed . . . I'm okay as long as I stick with the beer . . . uh, I don't get as crazy . . . ha, ha.

Doctor F.: It's easier to stay out of trouble as long as you only drink beer and aren't using the uppers?

Keith R.: That's damned straight! At least I know what I'm doin' and I don't get as fucked up . . . ha, ha. You wouldn't believe some of the shit I pulled a few years ago, but I'm smarter now . . . no damned counselor helped me with that either . . . They all said I had to stop drinking . . . I mean, no booze, and that's a bunch of shit . . . and I'll be damned if I'm going to another center, uh . . . I'd tell the judge to kiss my ass on that one . . . ha, ha. My lawyer's got that one straight, too!

Doctor F.: You know, I agree with *part* of what you're saying . . . it's clear that you sure don't want to be in therapy, but you and I disagree about your needing to be in treatment . . . even though you don't want to be in therapy, I think you do need to be in therapy . . . plus, my other concern is that you'll keep on screwing up until you really make a commitment to change.

Keith R.: That's where you and I disagree, Doc . . . I've made a few mistakes, but a lot of people . . . and, uh . . . the system fucked me over a few times, too . . . you're a nice guy . . . uh, like I said, nothing personal . . . but I've had about all the damned rehab I'll ever need!

Doctor F.: I hear you loud and clear . . . you don't want to be in therapy or a rehabilitation program . . . and, at this point, it would be very difficult to attempt to work with you in therapy . . . we need to discuss this with your attorney.

It is exceedingly difficult, if not impossible, to establish a working and productive therapeutic alliance with some substance abusers and many chemically dependent or substance abusing antisocial patients. The client in this therapy vignette had repeatedly been unable to establish a productive psychotherapy relationship. He had seen over 15 different therapists during a period of some nine years! The sum total of therapist characteristics plus patient characteristics and the global interactive effect of the therapist-patient dyad determines the nature of the therapeutic alliance as well as treatment outcome.

TRANSFERENCE DYNAMICS

Transference is a concept that was originally developed by Freud (1924). The transference concept continues to be widely used among psychoanalysts and psychoanalytically-oriented psychotherapists (Fromm-Reichmann, 1949; Kernberg, 1975, 1984). Basically, transference refers to the feelings, cognitions, and emotional attitudes that the patient displays toward the analyst or therapist during the course of psychoanalysis. Freud observed in his early psychoanalytic work that his patients began to manifest a variety of personal feelings toward him. He referred to this phenomenon as "transference" since the patient's feelings and reactions had little or nothing to do with the actual situation or with the behavior and personality of the physician. The patient's feelings and responses to the analyst were transferred from the past. Freud (1924) reported that he was being made the object of the patient's feelings that were being repeated or carried over (transferred) from earlier relationships. The affectionate and positive feelings of the patient toward the analyst were referred to as "positive transference" while the hostile, fearful, and negative feelings of the patient toward the analyst were referred to as "negative transference."

Freud (1924) and other orthodox psychoanalysts (Fenichel, 1945; Reik, 1948) purport that the essence of "cure" occurs in psychoanalysis or psychoanalytic psychotherapy vis à vis the therapeutic resolution of the "transference neurosis." The transference neurosis (White, 1964) refers to "an acute development that occurs fairly regularly in full-length psychoanalysis and that is considered essential for a complete cure. The relation to the analyst is intensified to a point where it becomes more important to the patient than does his own recovery. He seems to be engaged in a struggle with the analyst, trying to win various kinds of emotional satisfaction from him. In this struggle it becomes abundantly clear that the patient's attitudes have little relation to the actual situation; they are transferred from earlier ones, especially from childhood conflicts with the parents" (p. 301). The major unresolved and unconscious problems of the patient that are associated with childhood become manifest in the transference neurosis. The patient is unconsciously striving for what he or she failed to gain or had to do without in actual childhood.

Psychoanalysts and the nature of the analytic situation foster the development of a transference reaction in the patient. The length of treatment, analyst aloofness, use of the couch, and other factors facilitate this response. The patient is cured or experiences significant personality change as a result of "working through" the transference neurosis. The analyst uses interpretation, free association, and insight in order to help the analysand (patient) modify and resolve his or her inappropriate emotions that constitute the transference neurosis.

Transference dynamics continue to play a significant role in most systems of counseling and psychotherapy. Indeed, transference dynamics (Forrest, 1984, 1989, 1991; Brown, 1988; Yalisove, 1989) are particularly relevant to the process of psychotherapy and counseling with alcoholics, adult children of alcoholics, and impulse control disordered persons who manifest a concurrent substance use disorder. Transference relations occur in virtually all psychotherapy relationships. The emotional reactions of the client to the therapist and the psychotherapeutic process are transference phenomena. Substance abusers and chemically dependent patients tend to manifest intense emotional reactions to therapists and the therapeutic process. Therapists also seem to be generally very sensitive and emotionally reactive to substance abusers and antisocial clients.

The transference reactions of the substance abuser or chemically dependent patient are often negative. These patients tend to be iconoclastic, angry, manipulative, passive-aggressive, impulsive and poorly controlled, self-centered, and even dishonest (Forrest, 1978, [1980] 1986, 1985, 1990). They act-out while in therapy and experience considerable difficulty establishing and maintaining intimate human relationships. These patients respond to the therapist as an authority figure, and their historic relationships with authority figures have almost always been very conflictual and disturbed.

The negative transference set of the chemically dependent patient often begins before the actual psychotherapy relationship is developed. Many of these patients are "forced" into treatment by family members or the legal system. Such individuals may resent and consciously resist the reality of being forced into treatment before they have even had an opportunity to meet the therapist or begin the therapeutic relationship. In such situations, the patient perceives the therapist as an extension of the legal system, spouse, employer, or family system. Thus, the patient initially projects his or her feelings of anger and resentment for family members or significant others onto the therapist. This form of negative transference can usually be extinguished via the therapist's objectivity and active support for the patient during the initial one or two treatment sessions. The psychotherapist needs to reassure the patient that he or she will: (1) objectively assess the patient's pattern of substance use; (2) honestly discuss the results of the assessment process with the patient; and (3) establish a treatment regimen *with* the patient if treatment is indicated.

When substance abusers and chemically dependent persons become involved in psychotherapy relationships, it is rational for the therapist to be alert to the development of transference conflicts in the following areas: (1) therapeutic relatedness and intimacy; (2) therapeutic limit setting; (3) substance abuse and/or chemical dependency; (4) trust; (5) all matters pertaining to impulse control; and (6) personal responsibility. These sources of transference dissonance become more intense as the intensity and depth of the therapeutic relationship evolve.

The most primitive and conflictual source of transference for these patients is early-life narcissistic injury (Forrest, 1983a, 1984, 1985, 1989, 1991). Primary alcoholics and chemically dependent persons, as well as most substance abusers, have experienced profound early-life narcissistic need and entitlement deprivation. These persons have experienced consistent psychological and/or physical abuse by significant others throughout the course of infancy, early childhood, and into adolescence. Thus, the patient prototaxically fears annihilation, rejection, abuse, and abandonment by significant others. The patient has also learned to fear closeness and intimacy in all human encounters.

These issues are germane to the patient's fear of therapy and the therapist, anxiety in the therapeutic encounter, sabotaging transactions within the therapeutic alliance, authority conflicts with the therapist, rage and affective problems in relation to the therapist, difficulties trusting the psychotherapist, and control issues between the therapist and patient. Early in therapy, the chemically dependent patient unconsciously identifies with the psychotherapist as a bad parental ego introject. Thus, the patient consciously and unconsciously rejects the therapist's communications which validate the reality of the patient's substance abuse or chemical dependency and the need for treatment. Some of these individuals are unconsciously committed to failing in therapy and thus defeating the psychotherapist. Katagogically (Stekel, 1929), the patient is unconsciously determined to remain chemically dependent and demonstrate to the therapist that he or she deserves to be punished.

These patients tend to act-out against the therapist and thus challenge the therapeutic limit-setting transactions of the clinician. Alcoholic and chemically dependent patients are notorious for their ability to tell physicians to "go to hell," refuse medications and medical advice, or even verbally abuse health providers. These patients can be extremely difficult to manage in hospital emergency rooms, outpatient clinics, and psychotherapy settings!

The negative transference reactions of chemically dependent or substance abusing antisocial patients are more intense and problematic for the psychotherapist than those of nonantisocial chemically dependent patients and substance abusers. The chemically dependent antisocial patient is volatile, explosive, and may pose a physical and psychological danger to the therapist. These persons are the victims of early-life narcissistic injury in combination with severe physical abuse. They react to the therapist as an authority figure and are unable to empathize with the supportive, limit-setting, rapport-building behaviors of the therapist. Many of these patients are able to repress and mask their transference reactions for a few treatment sessions, but they very quickly begin to react to the counselor with intense feelings of anger and subsequently reject the treatment process. The chemically dependent antisocial patient may attempt to placate the therapist and manipulate the therapist for narcissistic gains early in treatment. However, these manipulative patient maneuvers prove unsustainable after several hours of psychotherapy. Ocular blocking in therapy is common among these patients (Baker, 1967). Murderous impulses and fantasies are also common in the transference of the chemically dependent antisocial patient.

The next therapy vignette reveals some of the transference dynamics that occur between therapists and nonantisocial chemically dependent patients. This vignette was taken from the fifth therapy session between the author and a 36-year-old alcohol dependent dentist.

> Robert C.: Like we were discussing last week, I've never liked to be told what to do. I've been able to think for myself, and I've always done well in life . . . but my father and mother were always great at giving directions . . . ha, ha . . . kinda like my wife!

> Doctor F.: So it's been difficult for you to listen to others, uh, or accept advice from others . . .

> Robert C.: No, not to accept advice . . . if you try to tell me how to do something or make me do something, that's when we'll have problems. An example of it is my wife . . . she really made me angry when she told me I was an "alcoholic" or that I needed treatment, and uh . . . it really pissed me off when she said it was going to be a divorce if I didn't get into treatment . . . that kind of stuff.

> Doctor F.: I see what you're saying . . . it's one thing for me to tell you that I think you have alcoholism and that you need to stop drinking . . . er, and another thing to tell you that you *must* stop drinking!

> Robert C.: That's right! But it's not just you, it's my wife or anybody else . . . and believe me, I appreciated the way you went over my test results and were up front about my diagnosis . . . the way you handled it was okay and I accepted the bad

news . . . ha, ha . . . but, like we discussed last week, I've known that I was an alcoholic for two or three years . . . I just couldn't accept it, but your style somehow made it easier and I don't feel like I have to fight you about my diagnosis . . . you were right and I don't feel so damned defensive and sensitive about it now.

Doctor F.: It's sure easier to see yourself and the alcoholism when you're sober . . . ha . . . easier.

Robert C.: But you didn't hit me over the head with it like Sally [wife] or my father . . . my father has been on me about the drinking for a long time . . . like everything else . . . he's always been real clear about my inability to do anything right. Maybe that's a general's perspective on everything and everybody!

Doctor F.: In spite of the fact that you've been super-successful in nearly everything you've tried . . . college to athletics to finances to your family . . . except for the alcoholism.

Robert C.: That's it . . . exactly . . . and I feel bad enough about the drinking, but when I'm really objective about the "big picture," I feel positive about my accomplishments . . . and believe me, I'm just getting started but I'm committed to recovery . . . getting sober and staying sober, and Dad will never really understand that . . . probably never accept it either and, hey, that's okay, too.

Doctor F.: The important part of your recovery is your acceptance of being addicted and then you doing something about it . . . That's what you seem to be doing to me, and that's a key to recovery. Battling with your wife, dad, or even me over the issue of being forced into treatment will involve a lot of wasted energy and bad feelings . . . you and I need to be working on the struggle you've had with authority figures . . . I think that's an area for us to be focused on in therapy and really important for your growth and recovery.

Transference dynamics are in part related to the gender of the therapist and the patient. The transference reactions that have been discussed thus far in the chapter generally apply to psychotherapy relationships with chemically dependent or substance abusing persons regardless of the gender of the patient or therapist. Treatment relationships are affected and somewhat skewed as a result of gender and different therapist-patient gender combinations. For example, opposite sex therapist-patient relationships tend to involve more intense sexually-oriented transference reactions. Chemically dependent males tend to be seductive in their relationships with female therapists, and some chemically dependent females are very sexually seductive in their treatment relationships with male therapists. These dynamics can be viewed as indicative of: (1) the patient's long-term sexual/relationship/intimacy pathology; and (2) resistance to the development of the therapeutic alliance and the real work of psychotherapy. Chemically dependent males and females (Wilsnack, 1973; Forrest, 1983b; Wilsnack and Beckman, 1984; O'Connell, 1990) manifest significant identity and sexual conflicts. The psychotherapy relationship per se and the specific gender-oriented realities associated with the therapeutic dyad exacerbate these sources of conflict.

The overt sexually-oriented transference reactions of chemically dependent males and females are often a defense against feelings of anger and rage against the opposite sex. At least one-third (Wilsnack and Beckman, 1984) of chemically dependent women are the victims of incest or some other form of sexual abuse. A surprising percentage of chemically dependent men have also been sexually victimized. Therapists need to be particularly sensitive to these transference dynamics. It is absolutely imperative that the therapist not become sexually involved with his or her clients. Sex is the neurotic medium of interpersonal and intrapersonal relatedness for many of these patients. The psychotherapeutic relationship can be a potent vehicle for modifying the chemically dependent client's long-term sexual and identity pathology. Therapists must be able to openly address the patient's sexual experiences, feelings, and struggles in the therapeutic encounter. It is also essential for the therapist to be able to focus openly on sexually-oriented transference issues with the patient.

Transference dynamics are always globally operational in the psychotherapeutic encounter. The therapeutic resolution of these feelings contributes to a corrective emotional experience for the patient. The therapist's active and felicitous examination of the transference is a sine qua non of effective dynamically-oriented therapeutic work with chemically dependent persons.

COUNTERTRANSFERENCE DYNAMICS

In 1910, Freud introduced the term "countertransference" to refer to the emotional involvement of the analyst in the process of psychoanalysis. Interestingly, it was not until 30 years later that the analyst's reactions and their significance to the treatment process were explored. Countertransference has been defined (Patterson, 1966) as "those reactions of the therapist which are inappropriate to the patient-therapist relationship, being determined by the therapist's own characteristic preformed reaction pattern" (p. 318). Countertransference is an unavoidable byproduct of the therapeutic relationship.

Psychoanalysts were taught to eschew their personal feelings and emotions within the psychoanalytic relationship. Indeed, a major objective of the analyst's personal analysis is to help the analyst better understand and control personal reactions to the patient. For several decades, analysts have attempted to be a "blank screen" onto which the patient can reflect his or her own feelings and reactions. This therapeutic approach encourages the development of a transference reaction in the patient.

Modern psychoanalysts (Kernberg, 1975, 1980, 1984) realize that it is impossible for the analyst to always maintain a position of technical neutrality. The analyst is ultimately a real person who feels, thinks, reacts, and communicates within the context of the treatment relationship. However, the analyst may also experience personal feelings, thoughts, and emotional reactions in the treatment relationship that are nonfelicitous, which cannot be concealed or repressed, which become grist for the therapeutic process, and which may actually interfere with the patient's progress in therapy. This is countertransference!

Kernberg (1976) points out that the therapist tends to experience (in treatment relationships with borderline or severely regressed patients) very intensive early emotional reactions to the patient.

Thus, countertransference becomes an important diagnostic tool for the psychotherapist. The therapist's diagnosis and awareness of his or her personal reactions to the patient is a key to the assessment of the patient's primitive object relations in the transference.

The countertransference reactions of the therapist must be understood and controlled. Spontaneous countertransference reactions may be more difficult for the psychotherapist to manage. Alexander (1956) suggested that the therapist "should attempt to replace his spontaneous countertransference reactions with attitudes which are consciously planned and adopted according to the dynamic exigencies of the therapeutic situation" (p. 93). Knowledge about the patient enables the psychotherapist to understand the patient's transference reactions as well as the therapist's own countertransference reactions. Personal analysis, clinical experience, and supervision are tools that help the therapist understand and control countertransference reactions.

Elsewhere (Forrest, 1982, 1984), I have written about the recondite aspects of countertransference in the psychotherapy of alcoholism and substance abuse. Many therapists wisely avoid working with chemically dependent persons due to a keen awareness of their personal negative feelings and reactions to these individuals. Indeed, it is clinically and ethically important for therapists to be aware of countertransference dynamics that: (1) impede the therapist's ability to function in an optimally therapeutic fashion; (2) contribute to the therapist's inability to initiate or sustain a productive psychotherapy relationship with a particular patient or subgroup; or (3) impact the process of therapy in a parataxic fashion. Therapists need to be firm in their refusal to initiate treatment relationships with persons who fall into the second category. Personal analysis and active supervision make it possible for the psychotherapist to work effectively with some patients who provoke countertransference reactions that fall within the scope of categories (1) and (3).

Substance abusers and chemically dependent patients tend to elicit countertransference reactions in the psychotherapist that are associated with matters pertaining to control, rescuing, persecution, victimizing, narcissism, competency and self-worth, impotence, rage, sexuality, and intimacy (Forrest, 1982, 1984, 1991). These patients are frequently depressed, dysfunctional, and involved in "victim" roles within the family system and community when they are initially seen for treatment. It is all too easy for the psychotherapist to respond to such persons in an overdetermined, zealous, rescuing-oriented fashion. Recovering counselors and therapists are especially prone to experiencing this type of countertransference reaction. Overdetermined rescuing transactions on the part of the therapist may eventually provoke a role-reversal situation whereby the therapist actually becomes angry or enraged at the patient and assumes a persecutory therapeutic stance. These countertransference reactions are extremely psychonoxious and can result (Forrest, 1979) in relapse and suicidal acting-out by the patient. When the therapist's rescuing efforts fail, it is possible to feel frustrated and angry at the patient and then unconsciously move against the patient in a victimizing and persecuting manner. The therapist neurotically attempts to control the patient in these situations.

Many substance abusers and chemically dependent patients have an uncanny ability to feed the psychotherapist's inadequately met narcissistic needs early in the therapeutic process. During the "honeymoon" phase of therapy, the patient becomes drug abstinent, may be a "model" patient, and continually extols the many virtues of the psychotherapist. In sum, the patient reinforces the therapist for the therapist's rescuing activities. The emotional demands of the middle stages of therapy and/or relapses while in treatment often result in a rupture of the therapeutic alliance. The omnipotent status of the psychotherapist is reduced to meaninglessness by the patient. In these situations, it is absolutely imperative that the therapist avoid countertransference reactions that involve directing feelings of anger, rage, and retaliation against the patient.

The therapist is not able to control his or her chemically dependent patients, and it is the patient who must assume the lion's share of responsibility for remaining drug abstinent and maintaining a recovery program. It may be necessary for the therapist to exert control over a patient vis à vis hospitalization or intervention, but it is impossible and countertransference-oriented for the clinician to attempt to control the patient. Furthermore, these patients are extremely rebellious and act-out against the controlling tactics of all people whom they perceive as authority figures. Thus, it is important for the therapist to verbally and behaviorally communicate to the patient that the patient is responsible for becoming self-regulated and self-controlled within and beyond the context of the therapeutic relationship.

The chemically dependent patient and his or her family sometimes blame the psychotherapist or treatment center for relapses or continued pathologic behaviors. These stressful situations may result in a sense of failure, guilt, and lowered sense of professional competency in the therapist. The extremely recalcitrant patient can exacerbate feelings of incompetence and impotence in the counselor. These countertransference responses are damaging to the therapist and the therapeutic alliance. Indeed, the chemically dependent patient is capable of challenging the healthy narcissism and basic sense of self-worth of the psychotherapist! These persons also anger the therapist by failing to keep appointments, resisting the treatment process, not taking medications, continuing to ingest alcohol and/or other drugs while in treatment, and acting-out. Rage-oriented retaliations against the patient by the therapist are an example of extremely iatrogenic countertransference. Angry, hostile thoughts and fantasies about the patient are often precursors to countertransference situations that involve the therapist acting-out against the patient.

Chemically dependent patients often stir countertransference reactions in the therapist that are sexually-oriented or associated with intimacy or dependency issues. Chemically dependent patients and substance abusers sometimes consciously attempt to seduce the psychotherapist. It is not uncommon for these patients to dress seductively, interact with the therapist in an overtly seductive manner, or even verbally suggest to the therapist that he or she would like to engage in sexual intercourse or some other form of sexual activity with the therapist. Some of these individuals (Forrest, 1983b) have led very promiscuous lifestyles. The heterosexual and interpersonal modus operandi of many substance abusers is pathologically sexualized.

The sexually-oriented countertransference dynamics that evolve in the process of psychotherapy with chemically dependent and substance abusing persons vary from client to client and are generally multifaceted. Most of these persons manifest sexual problems, and many fear or avoid sexual intimacy (Forrest, 1983a; Wilsnack and Beckman, 1984; Wilsnack and Klassen, 1988; Stuckey, 1991). Identity disturbance is central to the psychopathology of addictive diseases. Thus, some of these patients are uncomfortable with same-sex therapists while others are conflicted in the context of an opposite-sex therapist-patient relationship. The psychotherapist needs to be sensitive to these realities and cannot permit himself or herself to become enmeshed in sexual and/or gender-oriented countertransference reactions.

Therapists sometimes become frustrated and confused about their personal feelings or reactions to the chemically dependent patient's intimacy conflicts within the explicit context of the therapeutic alliance. These individuals are very ambivalent about all close or intense human relationships. Consciously, the patient wants and needs to feel loved, close, and dependent in his or her relationship with the therapist and significant others. At preconscious and unconscious levels of awareness, the chemically dependent patient is extremely anxious and terrified by human contact and interpersonal intimacy. Early-life narcissistic need and entitlement deprivation (Forrest, 1983a, 1985, 1991) experiences have prototaxically conditioned the patient to expect to be profoundly hurt within the context of all intimate human encounters. Thus, the patient vacillates in his or her interpersonal movements toward, against, and away from the therapist and the therapeutic relationship. Chemically dependent patients fear a loss of self or psychosis within the context of all intimate human relationships. Identity defusion and self-system fragmentation (Forrest, 1983a, 1989) are long-term experiential realities with which these individuals struggle and which they reexperience whenever they become involved in an intimate encounter.

These patients can also be extremely demanding, dependent, and parasitic in their relationships with therapists. The psychotherapist may experience countertransference reactions in treatment relationships with such persons that involve feelings of engulfment, being trapped, and being "sucked dry." It is essential that the therapist not allow the extremely passive-dependent patient to establish a parasitic/dependency-oriented therapeutic relationship through which the psychotherapist becomes a fixated mother-object. A neurotic or false sense of intense intimacy tends to develop in psychotherapeutic relationships involving passive-dependent addicts and therapists who are either extremely dependent or allow themselves to become a fixated mother-object to the patient. The therapist can minimize this form of countertransference reaction by consistently helping the patient to be responsible for himself or herself, maintaining appropriate therapeutic boundaries, and sustaining and reinforcing limit-setting behaviors.

The severely passive-dependent substance abuser may wish to be seen in treatment several times a week, call the therapist on the telephone in the evenings or whenever he or she experiences some minimal level of dissonance, and develop an inability to make any decision without first consulting the therapist. The psychotherapist's needs for privacy, autonomy, and a private life can facilitate the outcropping of various countertransference dynamics.

Therapists also experience countertransference conflicts with these persons that are associated with the patient's inability to develop a basic sense of closeness, intimacy, and relatedness with the therapist. It is relatively easy for neophyte therapists to: (1) blame themselves for a lack of in-depth relatedness and intimacy in the psychotherapeutic relationship; (2) fail to appreciate the impact of the patient's intimacy disturbance on self and the development of the therapeutic alliance; and (3) respond to the patient's intimacy disturbance in a fashion that is essentially unhealthy and countertransference determined. Therapists need to be able to accept the fact that they cannot magically resolve or undo the chemically dependent patient's intimacy disturbance in a few therapy sessions. The patient's intimacy conflicts evolve and become real within the context of the therapeutic relationship, and this particular nexus of pathology is only subject to resolution via the process of an extended and productive therapeutic experience.

Chemically dependent or substance abusing antisocial patients are sometimes quick to blame their therapists when they relapse or persist in pathologic patterns of behavior. It is a simple but real fact that these individuals are difficult to treat, and a few seem to be constitutionally incapable of changing or recovering. The parents and/or spouse of the patient may also blame the therapist for relapses or therapeutic failure. Attorneys and even the legal system

(Forrest and Gordon, 1990) can become a source of dissonance for the clinician who works with these patients. All of these realities impact the psychotherapist. Indeed, countertransference reactions that involve therapist self-doubting, therapist feelings of failure, inadequacy, and impotence, and basic questions about professional incompetence do occur in clinical work with chemically dependent and substance abusing persons. Some of these patients are consciously determined to defeat (Stekel, 1929; Forrest, 1984) the psychotherapist. The unconscious katagogic strivings of the patient encompass a symbolic castration of the therapist.

Multiple relapses (Gorski and Miller, 1986; Gorski, 1990, 1991) by the same patient or simultaneous massive regressions on the parts of several patients at the same time can facilitate therapist feelings of self-doubt. In these situations, the therapist may become depressive and act-out a variety of countertransference reactions. Therapist reactions and transactions that are in any way governed by the talion principle are clearly destructive and therapeutically malignant. Lex talionis represents the most regressive and pathologic form of countertransference reaction that is associated with patient relapse/massive regression within the context of the intensive psychotherapy relationship (Forrest, 1991). The basis self-worth of the psychotherapist as well as the patient is severely damaged when this form of countertransference reaction becomes fully manifest.

The following case study demonstrates several areas of countertransference-oriented acting-out and unethical therapist behavior.

Susan W. entered psychotherapy with the author shortly after ending a four-month "live-in" relationship with one of her former clients. Susan was a 33-old, twice-divorced mother. Her son was 11 years old, and her daughter was nearly six. The patient reported a long history of dysfunctional relationships with males. She was mildly depressive at the point of treatment engagement. Susan was a recovering alcoholic. She had been totally abstinent from alcohol and all other mood-altering drugs for over seven years. The patient had completed a Master's degree in counseling several years earlier and had been employed in the alcoholism/drug rehabilitation field for six years.

The patient revealed in the initial therapy session that her former boyfriend had completed residential treatment for alcoholism and then moved in with her some five months later. Susan was actually the program director of the rehabilitation program where her former boyfriend had completed treatment. Susan went on to explain to the therapist that her second husband had also been one of her clients from the treatment center. In fact, she had lived with several of her male clients after they completed alcohol/drug treatment! These relationships would typically last for two to six months, and then the various "boyfriends" would either resume drinking/drug use or simply terminate their relationships with Susan.

Susan stated that she felt very used, exploited, and manipulated in her relationships with men. She was depressive, angry, and confused about the termination of her most recent relationship. She told the therapist in an early therapy session that she realized how she needed to "mother" her clients and how her own projections contributed to her establishment of destructive relationships with men. She felt "sorry" for her chemically dependent clients and believed for several years that her love, support, and personal involvements with these men would facilitate their recoveries. Shortly before entering therapy, she had begun to realize some of the irrational, inappropriate, and unethical aspects of her relationships with male clients. Susan had also attended a training seminar a few months before entering therapy that fostered her conscious awareness of the unethical dimensions of sexual involvements and social relationships with former clients.

In therapy, the patient began to examine her relationship with her alcoholic father. As a child, Susan had felt very close to her father. She also remembered feeling very sorry for her father when she was a child and young adolescent. Her mother was described as cold, manipulative, and detached: "Mom was always right, always complaining, and a real bitch." Susan recalled that her mother constantly found fault with her father. "My dad could never do anything right in my mother's eyes; she was always on his case." Susan's mother was continually angry or enraged at her father because of his alcoholism. In fact, Susan was able to recall vividly that her mother verbally as well as physically abused her father. On one occasion, her mother knocked her father unconscious after he came home intoxicated. Susan was repeatedly told by her mother, "Your father is a no-good, drunk, son-of-a-bitch."

The patient's father died from alcoholic liver disease when she was 16 years old. Her father was only 45 years old at the time of his death. Susan's therapy accounts of her father and her paternal relationship revealed that her father was a very passive-dependent type of person. However, in spite of his alcoholism and other problems, he was supportive and loving in his relationship with the patient. He had "sided" with Susan in hundreds of familial conflicts, and she perceived him as a "protector" within the context of her relationship with her mother. Susan actually feared her mother until she was 30 years old.

Susan had blamed her mother for her father's alcoholism since she was a teenager. She also felt that her mother was responsible for her father's death. She told the therapist, "If my mother had loved my father and treated him like a decent human being, he would have probably not been an alcoholic . . . he sure wouldn't have needed to drink himself to death!" The patient began to consciously realize in therapy that she had repeatedly attempted to rescue and treat her father vis à vis her relationship with chemically dependent clients. This interpersonal and intrapersonal repetition compulsion also included the unconscious dynamic of differentiating herself from her mother. It was very important for Susan to be able to love and experience intimacy with men. She did not want to be "like" her mother! Susan had attempted to be a good mother-object in these relationships, and yet she was unable to love her male companions into recovery just as she had been unable to rescue her father from alcoholism. She was able to modify her own alcoholism and thus build upon the healthy components of her maternalized relationship with her father.

Susan remained in weekly psychotherapy for over one year. She remained alcohol/drug abstinent and discontinued her pattern of establishing relationships with clients and newly recovering alcoholics. In fact, Susan terminated her position with the alcohol/drug rehabilitation center, moved to a large metropolitan area, and developed a new career as an EAP (Employee Assistance Program) manager for a large corporation. At present, she has been married for three years, and this relationship appears to be healthy and functional. Her husband is a nonrecovering Lutheran pastor.

This case is a very clear example of how countertransference dynamics can psychonoxiously impact the therapeutic relationship and even the professional demeanor of the psychotherapist. The patient's unresolved psychopathology clearly resulted in personally, therapeutically, and professionally inappropriate and unethical behaviors.

Chemically dependent antisocial patients experience and manifest many of the same transference reactions in psychotherapy. However, the transference reactions of the chemically dependent antisocial patient are generally more intense and pathologic than those of substance abusers. Chemically dependent antisocial persons resist treatment engagement, deny their chemical dependency, react to the psychotherapist as a persecutory authority figure, act-out in therapy, "con" the therapist, and exploit the therapeutic relationship for selfish purposes. These individuals can also become very angry and enraged at the therapist. Chemically dependent antisocial patients will sometimes act out physically, as well as verbally, against the psychotherapist. Indeed, the transference reactions of the chemically dependent antisocial patient are essentially negative.

Therapists who work with chemically dependent antisocial patients need to remember (see Chapters IV and V, Section One) that these individuals are unable to empathize with other human beings. Furthermore, these persons are unable to develop close, emotionally meaningful human attachments. They are unable to be concerned about the health and emotional well-being of the therapist or significant others. These intrapersonal and interpersonal realities affect the nature of the therapeutic alliance as well as the course of the therapeutic process. These factors, in part, explain why Rogerian, analytic, humanistic, and interpersonal styles of therapy are ineffective in clinical work with chemically dependent antisocial patients. The patient is unable to or incapable of establishing an attachment to the psychotherapist. Therapist-patient attachment, intimacy, and human relatedness are the essential prerequisites to therapeutic change within the theory and practice of all relationship-oriented models of psychotherapy.

Positive transference dynamics facilitate the development of constructive personality and behavior change in therapeutic work with substance abusers and chemically dependent persons who are not concurrently antisocial. The substance abuser or chemically dependent patient who is not antisocial is capable of developing a working and productive therapeutic alliance and experiences positive transference reactions within the context of the therapeutic relationship. Chemically dependent or substance abusing antisocial patients are not usually capable of actualizing either of these tasks. As indicated earlier in the chapter, these factors are clearly related to the differential diagnosis of chemical dependency and chemically dependent antisocial persons as well as treatability and treatment prognosis of these clinical subgroups. The chemically dependent patient is simply able to experience a transference neurosis while most chemically dependent or substance abusing antisocial patients are not.

The positive transference reactions of the chemically dependent or substance abusing patient include: liking and respecting the therapist, emulating and modeling therapist behaviors, attitudes, and feelings, developing a basic sense of concern about the therapist's physical and psychological well-being, deeply valuing the therapeutic relationship, empathizing with the therapist, and developing a healthy capacity for love within the confines of the therapeutic relationship. These positive transference dynamics occur in combination with ambivalent and negative transference reactions. Thus, the transference is never purely positive or negative but, rather, an amalgamation of the patient's ambivalent responses to the therapist and the psychotherapeutic process.

Likewise, the countertransference reactions of the psychotherapist may range from negative to positive. Earlier (Kernberg, 1975,

1976) conceptualizations of the countertransference phenomenon were always negative. It is now recognized (Kernberg, 1975, 1984; Brown, 1988; Forrest, 1991) that the countertransference reactions of the psychotherapist can positively impact the therapeutic relationship and process. The therapist's total response set to the patient and the therapeutic process can be utilized to foster various sources of treatment gain or constructive change.

The chemically dependent antisocial patient usually elicits far more destructive or potentially katagogic (Stekel, 1929) countertransference reactions in the therapist than does the chemically dependent or substance abusing nonantisocial patient. Indeed, the more antisocial the patient is, the greater the risk or probability that the psychotherapist will act-out and experience negative countertransference reactions in the treatment relationship. Lex talionis-oriented countertransference relationships are far more common within the context of treatment relationships involving chemically dependent or substance abusing antisocial persons. Most therapists find it very difficult to simply "like" the chemically dependent antisocial patient. To the contrary, it is generally far easier to like and interact productively with substance abusers and chemically dependent patients who are not concurrently antisocial.

THE PSYCHOTHERAPEUTIC PROCESS

A plethora of positive, negative, neutral, and ambivalent therapist-patient relationship dynamics affects the process and outcome of psychotherapy relationships involving substance abusers and chemically dependent antisocial patients. In general, these interactive realities can be examined and explained vis à vis the transference-countertransference rubric.

The psychotherapeutic process is difficult and often conflictual for both the therapist and the patient. This is especially true when the patient is chemically dependent and/or antisocial. Therapists who work with these persons are confronted with a multiplicity of tasks. In a very real sense, the therapist must first of all attempt to treat the patient's psychopathology while also treating the patient's addictive illness or disease. Paradoxically, this herculean therapeutic task usually cannot be successfully accomplished without the patient first becoming drug abstinent. Thus, the therapist must help the patient become drug-free and committed to the process of resolving his or her chemical dependency before it is reasonable to expect growth and healthy change to occur in other major areas of the patient's life. Chemically dependent patients continue to act-out and remain dysfunctional in the absence of an extended commitment to abstinence and recovery.

As discussed throughout this chapter and section, substance abusers and substance abusing or chemically dependent antisocial patients reject their addictive disorders. They also reject the need for treatment and are frequently unable to accept that they are chemically dependent, and thus pain or a severe trauma may be needed to simply motivate them to enter therapy or a treatment program.

The resistive patient's transference conflicts can reinforce or synergize the therapist's countertransference distortions vis à vis the therapeutic process. It is absolutely essential that the therapist fully understand the psychodynamics and psychopathology of chemical dependency (Forrest, 1983b, 1984, 1991) as well as his or her personal pathology in order to minimize countertransference reactions. Self-awareness, personal therapy, and continuous and active professional supervision are deterrents to the outcropping of countertransference problems in therapy. These processes also help the therapist understand and better manage the patient's transference reactions in therapy.

Effective psychotherapy can take place when the psychotherapist and patient are able to maintain a commitment to the therapeutic relationship. It takes a great deal of therapeutic skill, experience, and emotional strength to be able to be *with* these persons for an extended period of time. These ingredients are also essential to the task of facilitating constructive personality change on the part of the patient. The therapist needs to be able to recognize and use the patient's transference reactions as instruments of change within the context of the therapeutic relationship. By the same token, the therapist must also be able to use his or her personal feelings, thoughts, experiences, and reactions as constructive vehicles of change within the treatment relationship. The unfolding of transference and countertransference dynamics and interactions in therapy constitutes the "stuff" of therapeutic change.

The therapeutic process is an ongoing and unending mosaic of transference and countertransference dynamics. It is important for the therapist to realize that the therapeutic relationship is initiated and maintained by these dynamics. Transference and countertransference reactions are not ipso facto negative or positive. These processes contribute to the living, changing, human nature of the therapeutic relationship. The therapeutic alliance is, first and foremost, a human relationship. The patient and therapist bring their basic human feelings, experiences, cognitions, and "being" to the therapeutic encounter. Psychotherapy is an art and a science that is shaped by the relatively unique interplay of the basic humanness of the therapist and the patient. Therapists need to be able to skillfully, artfully, and creatively direct or orchestrate the therapeutic relationship and the therapeutic process in a manner which fosters adaptive personality change and growth on the part of the patient. The therapeutic process should also be a generally positive and growth-enhancing experience for the psychotherapist.

It will be helpful for psychotherapists to remember that transference and countertransference reactions are generally more problematic or conflictual with antisocial and severely disturbed patients. The more antisocial the chemically dependent or substance abusing patient is, the greater the probability that transference and countertransference problems will develop in the course of therapy. Furthermore, the degree and depth of patient psychopathology is directly related to the global malignancy of the transference reaction. Severely antisocial chemically dependent persons and substance abusers also tend to elicit more conflictual and pathologic countertransference reactions in the psychotherapist. Antisocial patients tend to foster the outcropping of feelings of anger, frustration, despondency, impotence, and helplessness in many therapists. These patients may synergize the impulsive, acting-out conflicts of the therapist.

It is absolutely imperative for psychotherapists who work with these persons to be consistently focused on *their personal needs* and psychological well-being. Therapist self-survival skills (Wellman, 1988) are essential to the maintenance of the therapist's emotional and physical health. Thus, therapists need to be actively involved in a support system, exercise program, supervision relationship, and holistic health maintenance regimen. In juxtaposition to this regimen, it may be wise for the psychotherapist to be involved in personal therapy, take frequent vacations, and see only four or five of these patients on a daily basis. Therapist well-being is an averred essential prerequisite to effective psychotherapy with all types of patients. This is especially true in clinical work with alloplastic persons.

SUMMARY

Most substance abusers and chemically dependent antisocial persons are not seen in psychotherapy. These persons are infrequently treated in comprehensive rehabilitation programs.

A working and productive therapeutic alliance is essential to the effective psychotherapy of all substance abusers and chemically dependent antisocial patients. A definition of "working and productive therapeutic alliance" has been included in this chapter. Therapist and patient characteristics that contribute to the development of an effective psychotherapy relationship were also delineated. A therapy vignette with a resistant antisocial alcoholic also has been included.

Transference dynamics affect and shape the process and outcome of virtually all psychotherapy relationships. Transference refers to the feelings, cognitions, and emotional reactions that the patient experiences in the therapeutic situation. Freudian analysts believe that a "cure" occurs in psychoanalysis vis à vis a therapeutic resolution of the "transference neurosis." The patient's transference reactions can be negative or positive. The mendacious nature of the chemically dependent patient contributes to the development of transference as well as countertransference problems in the psychotherapy relationship. The origin, types, and course of transference problems that develop in the treatment of substance abusers and chemically dependent antisocial persons have been discussed. The capacity of the patient to experience positive transference reactions in the therapeutic context may be related to effective treatment outcome. Sexual and gender-oriented transference dynamics have also been discussed.

Countertransference refers to the emotional, cognitive, and interactional responses of the therapist to the patient and the therapeutic situation. Countertransference dynamics affect and shape the process and outcome of the psychotherapy relationship. It is important for the psychotherapist to be aware of his or her personal reactions to the patient. The therapist's reactions to the patient and the therapeutic situation also need to be controlled. Personal analysis or therapy and supervision may help the therapist recognize and control his or her countertransference reactions.

Countertransference dynamics can adversely impact the course of psychotherapy with substance abusers and chemically dependent antisocial patients. These patients consistently evoke parataxic countertransference reactions in the psychotherapist that are associated with issues of control, transactional roles, narcissism, rage, self-worth, intimacy, impotence, and power. Chemically dependent patients have an uncanny ability to foster therapist feelings of anger, frustration, impotence, helplessness, and inadequacy. These patients often blame their therapists for relapses and continued acting-out. The intimacy and relationship-oriented pathology of these persons may also be emotionally conflictual for the therapist.

A case study included in this chapter demonstrated several areas of countertransference-oriented acting-out and unethical therapist behavior. It is axiomatic that the more antisocial the patient is, the more conflictual and disturbed the transference and countertransference reactions will be. The talion makeup of the antisocial personality is especially disturbing for many therapists. Many therapists find it difficult to simply "like" the chemically dependent or substance abusing antisocial person.

A number of facets of the therapeutic process have been explored. The psychotherapeutic process is an ongoing and unending mosaic of transference and countertransference dynamics. It is important for the therapist to realize that the therapeutic relationship is initiated and maintained vis à vis these dynamics. Intensive psychotherapeutic work with chemically dependent and antisocial substance abusers can be extremely stressful for the psychotherapist (Forrest, 1984; 1990). It is essential for therapists who work with these patients to be consistently focused on personal needs and well-being. Therapist self-survival skills are needed to maintain the sanity and physical well-being of clinicians who work with these persons.

Chapter XII

Psychotherapy and Assessment of the Dangerous Patient

INTRODUCTION

Most psychotherapists do not perceive their work and profession as dangerous. Therapists rarely think of their patients as being dangerous unless they are involved in correctional work or clinical work with people who have somehow been identified as being violent, poorly controlled, or potentially dangerous. The independent practitioner is rarely confronted with the task of analyzing or treating dangerous patients. Yet, perhaps most psychotherapy patients can be considered to be potentially dangerous at some juncture in the treatment process?

Therapists are shocked, angered, emotionally distressed, and hurt when a colleague is physically assaulted by a patient or former client. Physical assault of a therapist by a patient also precipitates feelings of anxiety and fear within the mental health community. These transactions facilitate a more conscious awareness of the physical and emotional health hazards that may be associated with practicing psychotherapy or working in the mental health field. In a corollary fashion, therapists are especially distressed when their patients and former patients assault, or perhaps murder, a family member or some other person. Indeed, the dangerous patient may be considered a physical and/or psychological danger to: (1) self; or (2) others, including the therapist. It is also important to note that there are gradients of dangerousness.

Several months ago, a patient who was being seen in psychotherapy at a community health center in Pueblo, Colorado, shot his psychiatrist 16 times before killing himself. The therapist in this case miraculously survived and was eventually able to resume his clinical practice. The patient in this case was tragically dangerous to himself and his therapist! No doubt, he was also a potential danger to himself and significant others as well as people with whom he may have only had superficial contact. Transactions such as these are very difficult to explain and predict. Why would a patient become so enraged at his or her therapist? Do therapists possibly provoke or potentiate the homicidal impulses of their patients? Are certain patients more likely to physically and/or psychologically attack their therapists? What patient characteristics are predictably related to violent acting-out against therapists and significant others? Are there specific therapist characteristics that contribute to these situations? Finally, how can therapists and patients work together to minimize and manage the patient's dangerousness?

Each of these questions and problematic situations is addressed in this chapter. The vicissitudes of patient dangerousness are also discussed. Research evidence pertaining to patient dangerousness, assessment of dangerousness, clinical and practical assessment of dangerousness, and management and treatment of potentially dangerous patients are also topics that are elucidated in this chapter. There are no easy solutions or quick answers to these questions.

Therapists (Truax and Carkhuff, 1967) as well as the general public began to understand two decades ago that psychotherapy and psychologically-oriented treatments are potentially *hazardous* to the mental health and well-being of the *patient*. More recently, clinicians (Freudenberger, 1979, 1981, 1984) are beginning to realize the potential dangers and risks that are associated with being a psychotherapist or mental health worker. The psychotherapy profession can be hazardous to the mental health and well-being of the *therapist*! Therapist burnout, depression, substance abuse, stress, divorce and family problems, and even psychosis may in part be precipitated by the arduous work of counseling and psychotherapy.

THE "DANGEROUS" PATIENT

As indicated earlier, the dangerous patient poses a direct physical and/or psychological threat to self and/or others, including the psychotherapist. This basic definition of the "dangerous patient" is broader than models or definitions that are limited to the physical parameters of dangerousness. Patients who inflict physical injury upon themselves or others are obviously dangerous and present a very real threat to self and/or possibly others. Patients who are verbally, transactionally and behaviorally, cognitively, and/or affectively a threat to self and/or others may also be considered "dangerous" or potentially dangerous. There are gradients of physical and psychological threat to self and others. Thus, the various physical and psychological dimensions of patient dangerousness exist on a continuum.

Persons who have physically assaulted a spouse, family member, physician, or significant other are identified and easily recognized as dangerous. Patients who have repeatedly attempted suicide are also usually recognized as being a danger to themselves. Acts of physical assault may range from murder to shoving, scuffling, rape, or perhaps even kissing! In all of these situations, the dangerous patient or person inflicts direct *physical* harm/injury upon self or another human being.

It is generally far more difficult to identify and recognize when the behaviors or acts of a patient pose a direct psychological threat to self and/or others. Repeated verbal attacks and confrontations that are directed against self and/or others can pose a direct psychological or even physical threat to self and/or others. More subtle patterns of communicative undercutting and scapegoating may or may not be "dangerous" in the sense of posing a direct psychological or physical threat to the well-being of a person. Psychologists and behavioral scientists have been far more concerned about the "physically dangerous" patient than they have about the "psychologically dangerous" patient. Yet, far more people present a psychological danger or risk to self and/or others. Comparatively few people pose a direct physical danger to self and/or others.

It may be psychologically dangerous for the psychotherapist to become therapeutically engaged with any person. However, it is especially dangerous or risky, in a psychological sense, when the psychotherapist chooses to therapeutically involve himself or herself with select clinical populations. Therapeutic work with antisocial, chemically dependent, and acute or chronically psychotic persons can be especially threatening or potentially damaging to the health and emotional well-being of the psychotherapist. Therapists risk their own emotional health, and perhaps even their physical health, every time they decide to enter a psychotherapy relationship with a severely disturbed person.

Therapists (Rogers, 1952; Szasz, 1961, Truax and Carkhuff, 1967; Forrest, 1978, 1984, 1989, 1991) have long recognized that counseling and psychotherapy can be potentially destructive or psychonoxious for the patient. Iatrogenic treatment has long been a nemesis in the helping professions! Therapists have been less willing to systematically examine the effects of psychotherapy on themselves. In this sense, some and/or all patients may indeed be psychologically "dangerous" to the mental health of psychotherapists and other mental health workers. Young clinicians sometimes joke about the social behaviors, cognitive slippage, or "burned out" appearance of their older colleagues. "She's (he's) been in the trenches too damned long . . . you get to the point where you can't tell if it's the doctor or the patient." Indeed, it can be hypothesized that, the longer a therapist practices psychotherapy with a specific patient population, the greater the risk that he or she will begin to take on the basic personality, behavioral, social, cognitive, and even affective characteristics of the people with whom he or she works.

The "dangerous patient" may, in fact, be any patient! In recent years, mental health workers have become increasingly cognizant of the various legal issues that can be associated with treating dangerous patients. The parameters of legality that are associated with treating "dangerous patients" can be exceedingly diffuse and nebulous. In general, the psychotherapist is responsible for: (1) protecting himself or herself from the potentially dangerous acts and/or behaviors of patients; (2) protecting patients from potentially dangerous acts and/or behaviors that might be directed against themselves; and (3) protecting significant others and society from the potentially dangerous acts and/or behaviors of patients. The recent *Tarasoff* (1976) ruling makes it clear that therapists are responsible for the protection of society. The therapist has a legal duty and/or ethical obligation to warn any person(s) when he or she learns that a patient intends to physically harm that person. Thus, therapists must protect society from the destructive and potentially dangerous behaviors of their clients.

There is a plethora of recondite clinical and legal issues associated with the treatment of dangerous persons. Is it realistic to expect the clinician to be able to protect others from the destructive acts of his or her patients? Is the therapist responsible for the behaviors of patients who have terminated the treatment relationship? Can therapists realistically be expected to protect patients from themselves? Should therapists be held responsible for protecting themselves from the potentially dangerous acts and/or behaviors of their patients? Finally, should a violent or psychotic person be held responsible for assaulting his or her therapist? The general legal and clinical answer to all of these questions is "yes." Yet, experienced psychotherapists (Matuschka, 1989; Wellman, 1988; Williams, 1991) are in agreement that it can be very difficult, if not unrealistic, to expect the clinician to protect self, patients, significant others, and society from the acts of every emotionally disturbed person who enters a professional psychotherapy relationship. The multiple layers of responsibility that the therapist is expected to assume in these situations are diffuse and interactive!

Another tacit dimension of patient dangerousness involves the matter of legal actions initiated by the patient or the patient's family against the therapist. Lawsuits and malpractice actions (Stromberg, 1989) against mental health workers are becoming increasingly common. While these transactions may be appropriate in some cases, many are clearly inappropriate and/or frivolous. It is important for clinicians to be able to accept the reality of being sued for some form of malpractice by *any* patient. In this sense, any person who chooses to enter a psychotherapy relationship potentially poses a legal threat to the treating therapist. Thus, all patients may be considered to be potentially "dangerous" to the therapist from a legal perspective.

The experience of being sued for malpractice can be very traumatic for the therapist. The "dangers" of being sued range from loss of income to loss of professional identity. Physical illness, or even death, may be associated with legal actions that are directed against the psychotherapist. Depression, grief, marital and family problems, anxiety and stress, lowered self-esteem, suicide, professional alienation, and financial difficulties can be related to the therapist's experience of being sued. Clearly, the practice of psychotherapy is fraught with a diversity of legal dangers for even the most competent, ethical, and experienced clinicians and therapists.

ASSESSMENT OF PATIENT DANGEROUSNESS: THE RESEARCH EVIDENCE

The identification of patients who pose a direct or covert physical danger to self and/or others (including the psychotherapist) is generally difficult. Indeed, the assessment of patient dangerousness is certainly less than an exact science! It is impossible for the physician or mental health worker to know if or when a patient will attempt suicide, commit suicide or homicide, or act-out in a dangerous manner.

The ability of mental health professionals to predict violent acting-out has been widely questioned. Ennis and Emery (1978) suggest that mental health workers have *no* ability to predict violent acting-out. These authors also indicate that, under the best circumstances for prediction, the mental health professional is likely to be wrong in at least two out of three predictions of violence.

Research evidence (Litwack and Schlesinger, 1987) supports the position that it is very difficult for behavioral scientists to predict intra-institutional violence as well as violence in the community. These authors state, "Even when an individual has a known history of recent violence, predictions of that individual's behavior in environments very different from that in which his or her violence occurred in the past are likely to be highly subject to error . . . Little, if anything, can legitimately be concluded from most studies of predictions of violence" (p. 207).

The Kozol, Boucher, and Garafolo (1972) study has been widely cited (*Barefoot vs. Estelle,* 1983) to support the position that predictions of violence are likely to be wrong in two out of three cases. Kozol, Boucher, and Garafolo (1972) conducted extensive clinical examinations, life histories, and psychological tests on a sample of 592 males who were convicted of assault (many cases involved sexual assault offenses). A team of mental health professionals eventually evaluated 386 of these offenders as *not* dangerous. These subjects were eventually released from the special treatment facility where they were being held. Forty-nine men who were evaluated as being still dangerous were released from the facility by judicial or parole authorities *against* the recommendations of the professional evaluation team. As these individuals were followed up in the community after release, it was found that 8 percent of the patients who were evaluated as nondangerous and 34.7 percent of the patients who were viewed as still dangerous by the treatment staff committed a serious assault or crime after leaving the treatment facility. Although Kozol, Boucher, and Garafolo (1972) indicate that their investigation demonstrates that "dangerousness *can* be reliably diagnosed," several methodological errors (65 percent false-positive rate, small number predicted to be violent, etc.) limit the actual usefulness of the study.

Wenk, Robinson, and Smith (1972) developed a violence prediction scale based on offense, number of prior commitments, opiate use, age, and length of imprisonment. This scale was used in an attempt to predict which parolees would violate parole by a "violent or potentially violent" act. Only 14 percent of parolees predicted to be violent by this instrument were discovered to have violated their parole, compared with 5 percent of parolees in general. These same authors conducted two other studies that attempted to assess parolee dangerousness. Both efforts proved futile.

Monahan (1984) maintains that these studies and the Baxstrom and Dixon studies demonstrate that "clinical predictions of violent behavior among institutionalized mentally disordered people are accurate at least one third of the time" (p. 13). The Baxstrom and Dixon studies involved hundreds of patients who had been confined, often for many years, in hospitals for the criminally insane because they were considered too dangerous to be released to civil mental hospitals or community mental health centers.

Mulvey and Lidz (1984) point out that it is extraordinarily difficult to predict violent behavior: "Two issues arise regularly in the theoretical literature related to the prediction and management of violent or dangerous behavior. First, it is a relative, context-bound behavior with multiple definitions. Second, it is attributable to a complex interaction of individual predispositional and situational factors. Given these two pervasive themes, the clinician, searching for a grasp of the current state of the art regarding these issues, is faced with a formidable task" (pp. 379-380).

It is also very difficult to predict intra-institutional violence or dangerousness. Cocozza and Steadman (1978) evaluated the accuracy of assessments of dangerousness made by psychiatrists. This study involved institutionalized defendants who were found incompetent to stand trial. The authors found that 42 percent of patients who were evaluated as dangerous did commit an assaultive act shortly after being hospitalized. However, Cocozza and Steadman report that "the patients evaluated as dangerous by the psychiatrists were not more dangerous than those evaluated as not dangerous" (p. 272). It is also significant that 73 percent of the patients in this study who were charged with a violent crime were determined to be dangerous. Cocozza and Steadman (1978) conclude by stating that the findings of this investigation "clearly indicate that no [psychiatric] expertise [to predict dangerous behavior] exists and that the attempt to apply this supposed knowledge to predict who will be dangerous results in complete failure" (p. 274).

Werner, Rose, and Yesavage (1983) and Werner et al. (1984) report similar findings pertaining to the intra-institutional prediction of dangerousness. In this study, 15 psychiatrists and 15 psychologists attempted to predict whether or not 40 psychiatric inpatients would commit an assaultive act within one week after admission. The prediction of violence was based on Brief Psychiatric Rating Scale (BPRS) scores and whether or not patient assaultive behavior was associated with hospitalization. Litwack and Schlesinger (1987) summarize the findings of this study: "Although evidence of hostility, excitement, uncooperativeness, grandiosity, conceptual disorganization, tension, suspiciousness, and mannerisms and posturing [on the BPRS]–and a recent assaultive act prior to admission–were significantly correlated with predicted violence, none of those BPRS variables significantly correlated with actual violence on the ward . . . Thus, in this study, the correlation between actual violence and psychiatrists' and psychologists' predictions of violence was not significant" (p. 215). These authors go on to point out astutely that this study attempted to predict the occurrence of future violent behavior in a context that was very different from that in which prior violence had occurred.

Recent investigations by Rofman, Askinazi, and Fant (1980), Webster et al. (1984), and Hooper and Evans (1984) suggest that intra-institutional violence or dangerousness can be predicted. The Rofman, Askinazi, and Fant (1980) study investigated the in-hospital assaultiveness of 59 patients who were psychiatrically committed for mental illness and dangerousness. Over 40 percent of these patients engaged in an assaultive act or threat following hospitalization, while only 8 percent of voluntary patients engaged in these behaviors. Rofman, Askinazi, and Fant conclude that their research "supports the hypothesis that predictions of dangerous behavior have validity when the time of prediction and the time of validation are relatively close together" (p. 1063).

The Webster et al. (1984) study evaluated the "dangerousness to others in the future" of over 200 hospitalized patients. Psychiatrists and a team of mental health professionals evaluated each patient with a 7-point scale, and patients were subsequently examined at a two-year followup examination on an 11-point scale for "discovered dangerousness." Predictions correlated with outcomes at the level of 0.19. The prediction-outcome correlations in studies of this type are found to vary between 0 and 0.50.

Litwack and Schlesinger (1987) summarize the findings of Hooper and Evans (1984) and others as follows: "When applied to juvenile offenders with a base rate of previous violence in the community, variable combinations of subtest scores from the Psychological Screening Inventory and the Shipley-Hartford Scale could predict as high as 91 percent of the offenders who acted out aggressively in a residential treatment facility, while correctly classifying 80 percent of those who did not. Similarly, in a postdictive study (Jones, Beidleman, and Fowler, 1981), it was found that a discriminant function equation based on a discriminant analysis derived from twenty-two MMPI scales and four demographic variables (age, race, IQ, and a reading achievement test score) correctly classified 73 percent of violent prison inmates and 80 percent of nonviolent inmates" (p. 217). These findings do suggest that clinical examinations and psychological test data can be useful in identifying violent or dangerous inmates. It is also important to note that these investigations utilized multiple predictors of violence rather than a single variable (tests, interviews, etc.)

Studies by Levinson and Ramsay (1979) and Mullen and Reinehr (1982) suggest that caseworkers and paraprofessionals are also generally unable to predict dangerous behavior and violent acting-out among mentally disturbed or forensic patients.

Research indicates (MacDonald, 1963, 1967; Beck, 1982; Williams, 1991) that it is difficult to predict dangerousness vis à vis verbalized threats of violence. For example, MacDonald (1963, 1967) investigated the postrelease behaviors of a group of 100 patients who were hospitalized because they had threatened to kill. Followup data were available on only 77 percent of these patients. Three of the patients who were followed actually did kill someone after release, and four committed suicide. Litwack and Schlesinger (1987) interpret this finding as follows: "Predictions of violence based on threat of violence have little validity" (p. 219). Beck (1982) studied 39 cases in which professional mental health workers feared violence, based on patients' *fantasies* of committing violence. Two of these patients acted-out violently later, but none acted-out violently in the immediate situation. Again, Litwack and Schlesinger (1987) indicate, "There is no research [to our knowledge] that indicates how well, if at all, violence can be predicted regarding individuals who are clearly threatening or stating intentions to commit violence" (p. 219). Furthermore, Monahan (1981) points out that the ethical problems of conducting randomized experiments with dangerous persons make it "doubtful whether definitive tests of predictive accuracy in many situations will ever be done" (p. 37).

Mental health professionals seem to utilize a diversity of tools, techniques, methods, and sources of information in assessing dangerousness. Pfhol (1978) cited the following common sources of diagnostic and predictive error in assessing dangerousness: "1. Preconceptions derived from the patient's [possibly inaccurate] record that biased subsequent interviews and, thus, evaluations; 2. Selective questioning during interviews; 3. Assuming explanations of patient's behavior and assessing the patient's insight by his or her agreement with preconceived evaluations; 4. Selectively hearing the patient's answers to questions—or mishearing answers—according to prior expectations; 5. Focusing on facts that support preconceptions and conclusions and de-emphasizing or ignoring those that do not; 6. Discounting cultural, class, and political realities in favor of a focus on the individual roots of violence; and 7. Denying individual and collective doubts and presenting theories and hunches as findings" . . . (Litwack and Schlesinger, 1987, p. 220). Thus, a plethora of contextual, personal, and practical factors contributes to the problem of assessing dangerousness.

Aside from the various difficulties of predictive assessment that have already been discussed, the statistical problem of predicting acts of violence via the establishment of base rates of violent behavior is even more difficult! Livermore, Malmquist, and Meehl (1968) provide an excellent practical example of the statistical problem of base rates in the prediction of violence and dangerousness:

> Assume that one person out of a thousand will kill. Assume that an exceptionally accurate test is created which differentiates with 95 percent effectiveness those who will kill from those who will not. If 100,000 people were tested, out of the 100 who would kill, 95 would be isolated. Unfortunately, out of the 99,900 who would not kill, 4,995 people would also be isolated as potential killers. In these circumstances, it is clear that we could not justify incarcerating all 5,000 people. If, in the criminal law, it is better that ten guilty men go free than one innocent man suffer, how can we say in the civil commitment area that it is better that 54 harmless people be incarcerated lest one dangerous man be free? (p. 84)

The problem of base rates also includes the reality that actual base rates of violent behavior may not be available for select individuals or even groups of individuals.

In sum, research evidence pertaining to the assessment of patient dangerousness clearly indicates that it is generally very difficult to predict violent/dangerous acting-out. It is difficult for the behavioral scientist to predict intrainstitutional violence, violence in the community, or dangerous acting-out on the part of private psychiatric patients. It is important to note that most researchers and clinicians are not optimistic about future attempts to identify violent and dangerous persons. Megargee (1981) states: "The identification of the violent individual with any degree of precision appears to be an impossible task . . . The identification of the potentially violent individual with sufficient accuracy to warrant preventative detention is an impossible quest" (p. 181). Nonetheless, therapists and mental health workers are increasingly being called upon to identify and treat dangerous persons. The mental health worker is frequently expected to actively deter violent acting-out on the part of his or her patients and may, in fact, be severely punished if he or she fails in this endeavor.

ASSESSMENT OF PATIENT DANGEROUSNESS IN CLINICAL PRACTICE

In spite of the fact that research evidence rather clearly demonstrates that it is very difficult to accurately predict dangerousness and violent acting-out, clinicians are frequently called upon to evaluate these exact parameters of patient behavior. The spouse, family, or employer of a patient who is being seen by a psychotherapist in private practice may call the therapist and inquire about the patient: Is he (or she) suicidal, or is there any chance he (or she) might hurt me or try to kill me? These significant others are in effect asking the therapist to assess and communicate about the matter of patient dangerousness. Mental health workers are often asked, paid, or required to provide clinical assessments of dangerousness for attorneys, judges, families, parole officers or parole boards, and institutions.

In any of these situations, it may be globally appropriate and even imperative for the clinician to provide an assessment of patient dangerousness. Yet, the essential problem of predicting violence or dangerousness in these situations remains the same–how can the psychotherapist predict dangerousness? What criteria or set of assessment data can the clinician employ in his or her efforts to accurately and reliably predict patient dangerousness? While there are no "exact" or absolute criteria or set of criteria that can be used by the clinician to predict violent acting-out and dangerousness in any and/or all situational contexts, it is essential that mental health professionals recognize and accept: (1) the need to predict or attempt to predict patient dangerousness; and (2) the current flaws and limitations inherent in the process of attempting to predict dangerousness.

Simply put, mental health workers can expect to be involved in situations where they will be called upon to assess and/or predict patient dangerousness. The clinician will need to utilize his or her experience, training, education, and supervision to the fullest in order to provide the most accurate and professional prediction available in each situation that involves a potentially dangerous person. It is absolutely imperative that the clinician fully comprehend the limitations of his or her predictive ability in all of these difficult situations. The clinician also needs to be open and honest about the parameters of predictions of dangerousness with all parties involved in such cases. When the clinician is called upon to render a prediction of violence and/or dangerousness, the issue is not whether such predictions can be made with perfect accuracy but, rather, if a prediction is sufficiently accurate to justify specific preventive actions on the part of the mental health worker, police, corrections personnel, or significant others. The fact is that mental health professionals can predict violence and dangerousness with reasonable accuracy in many situations!

A number of models have been developed to help the clinician assess, classify, and predict patient dangerousness in clinical practice. Revitch and Schlesinger (1978, 1981) developed a motivational spectrum system for classifying antisocial behavior. According to this system, five factors are utilized to predict and classify dangerousness (antisocial behavior): (1) environmental or sociogenic; (2) situational; (3) impulsive; (4) catathymic; and (5) compulsive. The *environmental offender* commits acts of violence because of his or her identification and involvement with a social group that involves violence. *Situational offenders* react violently as a result of situational stress. Perhaps 70 percent of all homicides are situational and related to alcohol and/or substance abuse (Forrest and Gordon, 1990). *Impulsive offenders* usually have a long history of impulse control problems, and their violent acting-out is both predictable and egosyntonic. The *catathymic offender* (Wertham, 1973) acts out violently in an unprovoked manner. These individuals are not brain injured. Acute or chronic catathymia is usually accompanied by personality disorganization and characterized by an accumulation of intrapsychic tension which is released through the violent act. Violent acting-out is usually followed by a sense of relief. Depression, schizoid ideation and/or borderline personality style, and obsessive rumination for a period of weeks or months prior to the violent acting-out is characteristic of chronic catathymia. Victims of the catathymic offender are often family members, spouses, lovers, or self. *Compulsive offenders* are driven by internal psychogenic pathology, and these individuals may act out violently in a ritualistic or repetitious manner. Schlesinger and Revitch (1983) indicate that most compulsive acts of violence involve underlying sexual pathology. When the compulsive offender begins to act out violently, the violence may be repeated frequently and at close intervals.

Kozol, Boucher, and Garafalo (1972) suggest that the clinician should always evaluate the offender's motivational stimuli for violent acting-out vis à vis the: (1) context of the offender's ego organization; (2) ethical standards of the offender; and (3) offender's capacity for empathy.

The recidivism prognosis seems to be worst for compulsive offenders. Situational offenders have the best treatment prognosis, and these individuals are least likely to persist in violent acting-out. Environmentally stimulated offenders have an excellent prognosis when they can establish stable social relationships with significant others who are *not* prone to violence and aggressive acting-out. Impulsive offenders tend to have engaged in a variety of antisocial acts. These individuals manifest an inadequate degree of personality integration, and it is generally very difficult to predict how they will do in treatment. Blackman, Weiss, and Lamberti (1963) report that acute catathymic acts of violence are "typically one-shot incidents." Chronic catathymic acts of violence are sometimes repeated even after years of incarceration.

Litwack and Schlesinger (1987) provide the following common sense principle for predicting dangerousness in persons who have acted violently in the nonrecent past but who have been incarcerated for lengthy periods of time without subsequent acting-out: "If it can be demonstrated that the individual retains the same complex of attitudes and psychodynamics and, if released, is likely to confront the same set of circumstances that led to violence in the past, it should strongly be suspected that, if released, the individual will act violently again" (p. 241). Kozol, Boucher, and Garafalo (1972) state: "The essence of dangerousness appears to be a paucity of feeling—concern for others . . . the potential for injuring another is compounded when this lack of concern is compiled with anger" (p. 379). These authors also advocate the use of projective testing, group therapy, evaluation of offender insight pertaining to the genesis and dynamics of his or her prior violent acting-out, and evaluation of the self-esteem of the offender as methods for assessing patient dangerousness in clinical practice.

Clinicians also need to be aware of the fact that paranoid pathology and paranoid psychoses are frequently associated with violent acting-out. For example, Lanzkron (1963) investigated 150 mental patients who had been charged with murder. Nearly 40 percent of this sample reported paranoid delusions, and 20 percent cited jealousy as the trigger for the murder.

Brain impairment, organic conditions, and the use of intoxicants may be causative factors in violent acting-out (Sena, 1991). Ethanol (Forrest and Gordon, 1990) is the most commonly used psychoactive substance connected with violent and aggressive behavior. Fifty to 80 percent of homicide offenders and 40 to 60 percent of victims in homicide cases involve alcohol intoxication. Litwack and Schlesinger (1987) indicate that phencyclidine (PCP or "angel dust") is the most likely of all abused psychoactive substances to cause extreme violence. Acute PCP intoxication induces "feelings of estrangement, expansion of time, poor muscular coordination, increased sense of strength, auditory and visual hallucinations, and anxiety with a sense of impending doom. PCP may cause an acute florid psychosis, which may not remit for several months. Patients are a danger to others because of paranoia and strong tendencies towards violence" (p. 245). Cocaine and amphetamine abuse or addiction also results in agitation, anxiety, paranoid ideation, or even paranoid psychosis. These drugs are associated with homicide and other acts of extreme violence (Knauert, 1989).

It is important to recognize that the ingestion of alcohol and other mood-altering drugs always alters an individual's judgment, perceptions, motor skills, impulse control, cognitive abilities, and affective expression. In general, the more intoxicated an individual becomes, the less controlled and potentially more dangerous he or she becomes. Drugs such as alcohol, amphetamines, "crack" cocaine, and PCP are most likely to facilitate violent acting-out. These substances cause mental confusion, agitation, impaired judgment, and paranoid thinking.

Clinicians need to be able to utilize the information and data that can be derived from all of these models in their efforts to assess the dangerousness of a particular patient. In the author's experience, the dangerousness of each individual patient needs to be evaluated from a multivariant perspective (Forrest, 1983, 1984, 1989a). Thus, several factors or variables interactively cause acts of violence and the outcropping of dangerous behaviors. Perhaps the most dangerous patients are those who: (1) manifest a long history of repeated violent acting-out; (2) are substance abusers or chemically dependent; (3) are involved in an interpersonal network that actively encourages both acting-out and substance abuse; and (4) are experiencing acute situational stress. Individuals who manifest this particular set of traits or characteristics are especially prone to acting-out.

The psychotherapist who works with potentially violent and dangerous patients should attempt to evaluate these persons from a multifaceted perspective. The following case study demonstrates how mental health professionals can utilize multivariantly-oriented clinical models to assess and predict patient dangerousness.

Bennie S. was a 36-year-old, single (divorced), Caucasian male who was treated within the context of group therapy by the author. The patient was referred for treatment by his parole officer following a series of minor parole violations and hospitalization for drug (amphetamine) detoxification.

This patient was initially incarcerated at the age of 16 following a series of arrests for breaking and entering into homes, assault, and possession of illegal drugs. He subsequently served time in state correctional facilities in California, Colorado, and Utah for armed robbery, vehicular theft, forgery, and sales and distribution of dangerous drugs. The patient had also been arrested over 20 times in Colorado for DUI, DWI, and driving without a license. He had been chemically dependent since the age of 14. He also sustained a serious head injury at the age of 19 after being involved in a serious automobile accident. The patient was driving while acutely intoxicated when the head injury and automobile accident occurred.

After attending weekly group therapy on an outpatient basis for three months, the patient began smoking marijuana and drinking beer. He explained to the therapist and other group members that he could "handle" beer and that his prior alcohol-related problems were associated with drinking "the hard stuff." Bennie told the group that "pot" helped him relax—"It really mellows me out." Three weeks after Bennie began drinking and smoking marijuana, he also began to take "speed." He actually attended one therapy group after drinking and ingesting amphetamines. The patient was agitated, angry, and "strung out" in this session. It was also very apparent to the therapist and other group members that Bennie's prior style of criminal thinking and impulse control problems were synergized by the use of alcohol, amphetamines, and other chemical drugs. In short, the patient very quickly relapsed into florid dependency and criminality—he had become a danger to himself and others within a period of one month!

The author contacted the patient's parole officer shortly after learning of the patient's alcohol/drug relapse and again immediately after the patient left group therapy under the influence of speed and ethanol. Bennie was apprehended by the police two days later and placed in a 30-day residential chemical dependency treatment facility at the state hospital. The patient successfully completed this program and was released back into the community. He was again ordered to attend an outpatient therapy program and was placed in active parole status.

Unfortunately, Bennie was fired from his job shortly after relapsing. He also developed an involved relationship with another felon and parolee in the treatment center. These factors, in combination with the exacerbation of his criminal thinking and intensely projected anger at the "system" for forcing him back into rehabilitation, led to Bennie's immediate reinitiation of drinking and drug use following release from the state hospital facility. Thus, the patient was not seen in any form of treatment or parole capacity after leaving the treatment center.

Bennie's parole officer learned of his continued drug use

and failure to reengage in therapy within a matter of days after Bennie was released from the state hospital. The author was subsequently contacted by Bennie's parole officer and informed of Bennie's disappearance. Both the parole officer and I agreed that the patient was potentially a danger to himself and others, and thus a police "pickup" and warrant for arrest were issued for Bennie.

Nearly two weeks later, the patient was involved in a fatal shooting and was himself shot five times. He and an alcoholic companion had stolen a car and left the state of Colorado. Following a ten-day "binge" of alcohol, amphetamines, and cocaine, both were involved in a shootout with the state patrol. Bennie's companion was killed in the shootout, and Bennie was nearly killed. Presently, the patient is serving a 40-year prison sentence in a state correctional facility. He has recently been described as a "model prisoner" and has never previously reacted to incarceration in a violent or dangerous manner. In fact, this patient has apparently never been violent or acted-out in a dangerous fashion in the absence of alcohol/drug intoxication.

The author felt that this patient reached the point of being a bona fide danger to self and others as a result of: (1) prior history of dangerousness associated specifically with chemical dependency; (2) relapse in the immediate situation; and (3) environmental-situational factors involving his new companion, recent response to hospitalization and treatment, disappearance, and job loss following reinitiation of drug use.

In sum, the assessment of patient dangerousness in clinical practice is most accurately and appropriately accomplished via the clinician's utilization of multiple predictors of violence and/or dangerous behavior. Predictions of violence that are based on a single or univariant predictor are generally far less accurate than predictions that are multivariantly determined. The psychotherapist or mental health professional needs to focus on the patient's *recent* as well as *past* history of violence, environmental-situational stressors in the immediate situation, adjustment style, psychodynamics and personality makeup, chemical dependency pattern, and medical-neurolog-

ic factors. A prediction of dangerousness, or even degree of dangerousness, is made by individually and collectively evaluating each of
these variables as they pertain to a patient. An antisocial or acutely
psychotic person who is acutely intoxicated, has a protracted history of violent acting-out, is unemployed, and is in the process of
being divorced by his or her spouse would be easily evaluated as
"dangerous." To the contrary, it may be far more difficult for the
clinician to evaluate the dangerousness of a person who has threatened to kill his spouse after learning of her unfaithfulness, if this
person has: (1) no prior history of violent acting-out; (2) no history
of substance abuse or chemical dependency; and (3) led a generally
well-adjusted lifestyle and is experiencing no other major life
stress.

Most psychologists and many other behavioral scientists utilize
psychological tests in their efforts to assess dangerousness. The
Minnesota Multiphasic Personality Inventory, or MMPI (Dahlstrom
and Welsh, 1960; Gilberstadt and Duker, 1965), and various other
psychological tests have been used to evaluate dangerous or violent
persons. A psychological test profile should always be used in
combination with the previously discussed factors in the clinician's
attempt to assess patient dangerousness. The results of a personality
test (or tests) should never be used as the sole criterion predictor of
dangerousness. However, psychological test data can definitely improve the clinician's level of accuracy in predicting violence and
dangerousness. Psychological testing is one important component
of the mental health worker's armamentarium that can aid in the
assessment and prediction of violence.

It has been the author's experience that psychological testing is
most efficaciously used in predicting dangerousness when the
psychologist: (1) is clinically experienced in this specific realm; and
(2) has utilized a *particular* psychological *test* or *battery of tests* to
assess dangerousness with literally hundreds of patients in a diversity of professional settings and/or contexts. For example, I have
found that alcohol dependent and substance abusing patients who
have 4 - 6 - 9 - 8 MMPI profile configurations (t-scores above 85,
with L, F, and K t-scores below 70) are especially prone to violent
acting-out against others. Alcoholic persons with concurrent brain
impairment and an antisocial personality structure are especially at

risk for violent acting-out (Sena, 1988, 1991; Gust, 1989, 1992). Individuals who are severely depressive are more at risk for dangerous acting-out against the self. Indeed, t-score elevations on the MMPI Depression subscale that are above 90 should alert the clinician to the possibility of a patient's being a danger to self. Acute and/or chronic psychosis that is reflected via psychological testing may be a valid measure of patient dangerousness. Psychotic and schizophrenic persons can sometimes present a very real danger to self and/or others.

In short, mental health workers can utilize psychological test data to improve or enhance the prediction of dangerousness in clinical practice. Objective personality tests, projective tests, neuropsychological assessment batteries, perceptual motor tests, and comprehensive intelligence/abilities tests have been utilized with varying gradients of success to assess dangerousness. Comprehensive medical and neurological examinations (to include CT scans and EEGs) may also be used to help the mental health worker assess dangerousness. Whenever possible, it is appropriate and clinically astute for the mental health worker to employ any and/or all of these assessment tools in his or her efforts to identify and deter dangerous patients.

PSYCHOTHERAPEUTIC CONSIDERATIONS

Psychotherapists are agents of constructive change and growth. We are also sometimes engaged in roles and relationships that serve the explicit or implicit purpose of deterring violence and dangerous acting-out. Indeed, therapists are advocates and even teachers of nonviolent problem solving strategies. As discussed thus far in the chapter, therapists and mental health workers are frequently called upon to evaluate violent persons and/or assess the dangerousness of a patient. Mental health workers also provide direct psychotherapy and rehabilitation services to violent persons and/or potentially dangerous patients.

The actual psychotherapy and treatment of a dangerous person begins when it is established that a person or patient is dangerous or presents a potential danger to self and/or others and subsequently begins treatment. The clinical process for establishing the reality that a person is dangerous has been delineated earlier in this chapter. Psychotherapy relationships with violent and/or dangerous persons are complex, multifaceted, and highly individual in nature. Dangerous patients do not constitute a highly homogeneous clinical subgroup. Indeed, persons who have been diagnosed as dangerous or potentially dangerous vary significantly in the areas of intelligence, verbal skills, education, psychopathology, neuropsychological functioning, race, socioeconomic class, ethnic background, vocation, and religious background. There is no one particular demographic "set" or singular clinical profile that encompasses 70 to 95 percent of all violent and dangerous persons. The most essential and basic shared clinical characteristic of this group of people is simply their propensity for violent and/or dangerous acting-out. Furthermore, it is difficult to know precisely when or under what circumstances many of these persons will behave in a violent or uncontrolled manner.

The clinical management of *all identified* dangerous patients requires that the therapist initiate special and/or different treatment interventions specific to the individual characteristics and needs of each patient. Therapists and mental health workers must realize that it is impossible to identify (or recognize) some dangerous persons. These individuals may pose a direct danger to self, others, or self and a particular significant other.

Some persons become acutely depressed, acutely psychotic, or for some other reason are a very real danger to self. These individuals are determined to kill themselves. Clinicians are able to evaluate a patient's potential for suicide and suicidal acting-out vis à vis the utilization of multivariant predictors of self-destructive behavior: prior history of suicide attempts and self-destructive behavior, acute and/or chronic depression (affective disorder), acute psychosis (thought disturbance), job loss and/or object loss, psychological test data, and verbal statements to the therapist and/or significant others about intent and/or an actual plan to harm self. Thus, the clinician relies on situational, historic, environmental, affective, psychodynamic and interpersonal, psychometric, and communicative factors in his or her assessment of suicidal and self-destructive persons.

The psychotherapy and clinical management of suicidal persons differs significantly from the treatment of persons who are violent and represent a danger to others and society. Suicidal persons who are not concomitantly homicidal and violent toward others may need to be hospitalized or placed in a safe environment. These persons are generally easier to work with than are violent persons or persons who are both suicidal and present a danger to others or society. Most acutely depressed and suicidal patients are not homicidal. These persons do not pose a direct physical danger to others. In fact, the involvement of significant others is often a key to the successful treatment of these persons. The spouse, family, or even employer of the suicidal patient can be therapeutically supportive and an integral component of the treatment process. These persons can administer medications, observe the patient, provide an important source of feedback to the therapist, and in a multiplicity of ways foster the rehabilitation and recovery of the severely depressed and self-destructive client. It is frequently therapeutically efficacious to involve significant others in conjoint and/or family therapy with the acutely self-destructive patient.

As touched upon earlier, the psychotherapist may need to hospitalize these persons for a few days or weeks. In some cases, it is essential that the patient return to the family environment or enter some other form of supportive "holding environment" for a limited period of time. The clinician may even need to initiate a mental health commitment in a few cases. In these situations, the patient is legally committed to a hospital milieu for comprehensive treatment and observation until such time as it is determined by the professional staff that he or she is no longer a danger to self. It is almost axiomatic that persons who need to be hospitalized as a result of severe depression, acute psychosis, and self-destructiveness require psychotropic medications and direct medical care. Thus, the psychotherapist will need to provide these treatment services directly to the patient or make arrangements for other health providers to provide and manage such services. Nonmedically trained therapists will need to be able to work with physicians, nurses, and hospital administrators relative to such matters as: (1) hospitalization; (2) medications; (3) inpatient treatment services; (4) billing and insurance; and (5) discharge and aftercare planning.

It is important for clinicians to realize that hospitalization and/or a mental health commitment usually constitutes only one phase of the treatment process with self-destructive persons. Many of these patients have been in psychotherapy for weeks or months prior to the actual onset of their acute self-dangerousness. Most will follow up in some form of therapy after seeking help or leaving an inpatient treatment program. It is essential that the psychotherapist supportively reinforce the patient's commitment to therapy during and following an acute self-destructive or suicidal episode.

The processes of effective psychotherapy and the therapeutic alliance are long-term deterrents to self-dangerousness. The psychotherapy relationship is an extension of the therapeutic holding environment that is provided by the hospital staff and hospital milieu. A few patients become acutely self-destructive and/or depressive after entering therapy. Situational factors may precipitate suicidal acting-out at any point in the treatment process. The therapist-patient relationship can be a powerful deterrent to patient self-dangerousness at any juncture in the psychotherapeutic process. This is particularly true during the middle and later stages of treatment (Forrest, 1984). Therapist support, nurturance, warmth, authenticity, and love are crucial relationship ingredients that become potent deterrents to suicidal acting-out. The patient's emotional attachment to the psychotherapist also serves as a paradoxical boundary to self-destructiveness. Therapists need to teach the self-destructive person direct problem-solving skills, coping skills, and a diversity of cognitive-behavioral coping techniques in these situations. These tools or techniques for rational (Ellis, 1990) and more effective living continue to form the transactional, educational, communicative, and change-producing content of effective psychotherapy when the patient is no longer acutely self-destructive.

Many persons become a far greater risk to others as they become increasingly self-destructive and self-dangerous. Perhaps there is, in general, a highly correlated and linear relationship between dangerousness to self and to others? In situations where this is true, the therapeutic amelioration of self-destructiveness would predictably result in a concomitant reduction in dangerousness toward others. Therapists and mental health workers protect the emotional and even physical well-being of countless numbers of people every time they effectively treat and/or manage an acutely disturbed person. I suspect that most mental health workers overlook and/or are unaware of the global prophylactic effects of their work with acutely depressed and acutely disturbed patients.

A recent newspaper article (*Denver Post,* February 1990) described a young man in Denver, Colorado, who went berserk and killed several people, including a 67-year-old woman and her 47-year-old daughter, took hostages, and eventually killed himself. He had been involved in a drug treatment program shortly before this episode occurred and was apparently under the influence of cocaine when the killings took place (based on the presence of cocaine in his body on autopsy). A machine gun was used in this case. Apparently, this young man had been chemically dependent for several years and had been repeatedly in trouble with the police as a result of acting-out and impulse control problems. Why did this tragedy take place? Why do hundreds of similar cases occur in the United States each year? Can mental health workers and psychotherapists be expected to intervene effectively in cases such as this? Perhaps psychotherapy is a deterrent to suicidal and homicidal acting-out?

There are no simple answers to questions such as these. The fact is that numbers of multiple homicides, ruthless murders, and suicides (Forrest and Gordon, 1990) are on the rise in the U.S. and Western society. It is also becoming increasingly clear that alcohol and/or drug intoxication play a crucial role in at least 50 to 75 percent of homicides and suicides (Banks, 1985; Forrest and Gordon, 1990). Thus, psychotherapists and all mental health workers need to realize that the probability of homicidal and/or suicidal acting-out on the part of any patient is significantly reduced when that person is alcohol/drug abstinent. This means that the therapist is at least partially responsible for the effective treatment, or attempted treatment, of all substance abusing clients who are concurrently dangerous and violent. Clinicians must, first of all, recognize and diagnose the substance use problem of their dangerous clients. Secondly, clinicians must be able to either effectively treat these persons for chemical dependency/substance abuse or refer them to an appropriate treatment facility or health service provider for chemical dependency treatment.

The psychotherapist needs to be able to communicate openly and honestly with the dangerous patient about the matters of dangerousness and violence. These communicative transactions also need to encompass the various realities that are associated with dangerousness and substance abuse. Thus, the therapist needs to didactically explain to these individuals how alcohol and drug use impairs judgment, fosters acting-out, and escalates dangerousness. Alcohol and most other psychoactive substances are pharmacologic as well as psychological disinhibitors of behavior, affect, and cognition. Alcohol and drugs can be powerful central nervous system depressants that cause and/or synergize a depressive disorder. Psychoactive substance use also results in confused thinking, paranoia, violence, and even mental illness. In essence, the patient needs to clearly understand that continued alcohol and/or drug abuse will actively contribute to his or her feelings of depression, anger, rage, and loss of control.

It is essential that the therapist not avoid dealing with the patient's feelings of rage and violence. The violent, destructive, and dangerous fantasies, thoughts, cognitions, and impulses of these patients need to be grist for continued discussion and exploration within the context of the therapeutic encounter. The therapist must not fear the patient or the dangerous and violent vicissitudes of the patient's behavior to the extent of avoiding, denying, and repressing these realities. A therapeutic resolution of the patient's dangerousness is impossible in the absence of an open, honest, and persistent examination of the patient's dangerous or violent feelings, impulses, behaviors, and cognitions.

It has been the author's consistent clinical observation (Forrest, 1978, 1983a, 1984, 1985, 1989b, 1991) that the violent and sadomasochistic behaviors of alcoholic and chemically dependent patients can be linked to the experience of early-life narcissistic injury. Infantile and childhood narcissistic need and entitlement deprivation experiences that also involve intermittent physical abuse may constitute the essential psychological precursor to generalized violent acting-out during late adolescence and throughout adulthood. For these reasons, the effective psychotherapy of chemically dependent chronically dangerous or violent persons must involve genetic reconstruction work (Forrest, 1984, 1989b, 1991) and a therapeutic resolution of early-life narcissistic injuries. Brief therapy will not accomplish these therapeutic tasks. Antisocial and thought-disordered dangerous persons have also been the victims of severe narcissistic injury and need similar intensive psychotherapeutic treatment. The dangerous behaviors of the antisocial person can sometimes be linked to the experience of repeated physical abuse during the development epochs of infancy, childhood, and adolescence (McCord and McCord, 1964).

The acutely or situationally dangerous patient may need to be hospitalized. In situations where the patient has been in therapy prior to becoming acutely dangerous, it may be possible for the psychotherapist to rationally persuade the patient to enter a psychiatric unit for brief hospitalization and intensive care. In other situations, the mental health worker will need to do a formal involuntary psychiatric commitment. If a patient intends to harm a specific person in either of these situations, it is essential for the mental health worker to notify the endangered person. Therapists need to make every effort to keep these individuals actively engaged in treatment once they are released from the hospital. Many of these patients will also need to be maintained on an appropriate psychotropic medication following hospital discharge and during followup treatment.

There are a number of practical considerations of which therapists need to be cognizant in the ongoing outpatient psychotherapy of potentially dangerous persons. First of all, it is wise to see these patients while colleagues and/or secretarial staff are also in the office. The presence of others can serve as a general deterrent to acting-out and, in the unlikely event of violence actually taking place in the therapist's office, these individuals could notify the police or initiate other appropriate actions. Second, it is almost always clinically inappropriate to see these individuals for therapy in their homes or outside of the therapist's office. Third, it is imperative that the therapist require these patients to be totally alcohol/drug abstinent for all therapy sessions. It is also unwise to attempt to do therapy with these patients by telephone when they have been drinking and/or are under the influence of other mood-altering drugs. Indeed, the psychotherapist needs to consistently emphasize the importance of total and ongoing alcohol/drug abstinence in his therapeutic encounters with these persons. Fourth, clinicians should actively discourage these patients from carrying and possessing guns and other potentially dangerous weapons. Fifth, it is strategically psychonoxious for the therapist to:

(1) "side" with the patient against his or her spouse; and/or (2) "side" against the patient with the patient's spouse, family, or significant others. A therapeutic stance of technical neutrality and support is required in these various transactional situations. Finally, it is important for therapists who work with this patient population to maintain copious clinical notes and take a careful history on each patient. A complete social, medical, legal, and behavioral history can alert the therapist to the possibility of patient dangerousness. Detailed clinical notes are an excellent source of evidence corroborating the therapist's hard work, professionalism, and therapeutic demeanor. More importantly, the therapist's notes provide verification that dangerousness was or was not predictable and reflect the direct clinical actions of the therapist in these situations.

The psychotherapist must also teach these patients a number of specific and practical cognitive-behavioral techniques for stress management and anger control. Therapists are routinely successful in their efforts to "defuse" the angry feelings and violent or poorly controlled impulses of their patients. Therapy per se (Williams, 1991) can be an effective treatment for dangerousness. The therapeutic relationship and communicative interacting between the therapist and patient cathartically modify the patient's feelings of rage and anger. Psychotherapists who work with dangerous persons need to didactically teach these individuals thought-stopping techniques, time-out exercises, relaxation training, stress management, and feeling reduction/expression skills. Therapy teaches these patients to "talk out" and "talk through" violent or dangerous feelings, impulses, and cognitions. Self-hypnosis training, yoga or meditation, proper nutrition, religious or spiritual programs, and rigorous physical exercise are useful therapeutic adjuncts with these individuals.

On very rare occasions, the therapist may personally become an object of the angry, violent, and dangerous acting-out behaviors of a patient. As discussed at the beginning of this chapter, psychotherapy is always a potentially dangerous profession for the *psychotherapist*, and certain patients may pose a direct physical and/or psychological danger to the therapist. How can therapists effectively manage these difficult clinical situations? What actions should the therapist take in situations where the patient becomes personally threatening? What can the therapist do if the patient actually threatens to physically harm the therapist? Are there measures the therapist can initiate whenever he or she feels fearful within the context of a therapeutic relationship–even when the patient has not verbally or behaviorally threatened the psychotherapist?

Unfortunately, there are no simple or easy answers to questions such as these. Yet, there are a number of helpful guidelines the therapist can follow in these difficult situations. These guidelines can significantly reduce the probability of patient acting-out against the psychotherapist and/or others. Therapists who follow these guidelines also are better able to maintain their own emotional well-being, sanity, and sense of professional competence in treatment relationships with violent and potentially dangerous persons.

The following actions need to be initiated by the psychotherapist whenever he or she feels *personally* threatened, at risk, or in any way potentially endangered by a patient: (1) discuss your feelings and thoughts about potential endangerment openly, honestly, and directly with the patient; (2) discuss these issues with your clinical supervisor or seek out a professional colleague for consultation; and (3) if you are unable to significantly resolve your feelings of fear and threat using these alternatives, refer the patient to an appropriate colleague or initiate the process of treatment termination. It is unwise to persist in a treatment relationship beyond a period of two or three months if you are unable to work through and/or resolve feelings of threat, anxiety, and fear associated with patient dangerousness directed at the therapist.

At some point, it becomes impossible for the psychotherapist to conduct effective treatment with a person whom he or she fears. The therapist must feel basically secure, nonthreatened, and valued within the context of the therapeutic relationship. Effective therapy cannot take place when the psychotherapist consistently feels vulnerable, insecure, threatened, anxious, and fearful in his or her relationship with the patient. These realities may need to be explained to the patient who poses a direct risk to the therapist. Productive and effective therapeutic alliances develop when both the therapist and patient experience a sense of trust, respect, dignity, and security within the context of the helping relationship (Forrest, 1984, 1991).

A final psychotherapeutic consideration for therapists who work with dangerous persons involves a basic understanding of the legal parameters of dangerousness and the legal duty to warn. When should a therapist know that a patient is dangerous? The American Psychological Association (Stromberg, 1989) has proposed that a legal duty to warn be recognized when "the patient has communicated to the therapist an actual threat of physical violence against a clearly identified or reasonably identifiable victim or victims" (p. 14). Furthermore, the courts have generally concluded that "professional inaccuracy in predicting violence cannot negate the therapist's duty to protect the threatened victim," and that the "risk that unnecessary warnings may be given is a reasonable price to pay for the lives of possible victims that may be saved" (pp. 15-16). Therapists are held legally liable in these situations when it can be demonstrated that their skill or judgment falls below the "ordinary standard of care of the profession." Thus, a therapist is required to predict violence "at least as well" as is customary among his or her colleagues.

Psychologists who see a potentially dangerous patient should take certain initial steps during the assessment stage of treatment: "(1) exploring with the patient the full extent of his violent feelings; (2) inquire about prior violent acts; (3) seek to elicit the identities of potential victims; (4) explore the nature of likely precipitating events; and (5) consider how to deflect or defuse the patient's violent impulses" (Stromberg, 1989, p. 15). Stromberg (1989) points out that these legal-clinical transactions may be conflictual as the clinician's pointed focus on the violent patient's rage and violent impulses may actually reinforce further violent acting-out!

The problem of knowing when potential victims are identifiable enough to be warned is equally difficult and thorny. Recently, the courts (Stromberg, 1989) have concluded that the duty to warn or protect exists only where "the therapist receives a credible threat against victims who are *reasonably foreseeable* or *readily identifiable*" (p. 15). Thus, the therapist is required to warn specifically targeted victims. The American Psychological Association has recommended legislation that provides legal immunity for psychologists who fail to "predict, warn, or take precautions against patient violence" *unless* "the patient has expressed to the therapist an actual threat of physical violence against a clearly identifiable or reasonably identifiable victim or victims" (Stromberg, 1989, p. 15). It is interesting that the court dismissed a suit against John Hinckley's psychiatrist despite testimony that Hinckley kept "talking about shooting people and blowing things up" and that he had written actress Jodie Foster stating that, "If you don't love me, I'm going to kill the President." The court found that "Hinckley had no history of violence and had made no prior specific threats against individuals. It regarded the universe of possible victims as too numerous to require the therapist to warn them" (Stromberg, 1989, p. 15).

It is apparent that the psychotherapy of dangerous and/or potentially dangerous persons is clinically difficult and fraught with numerous legal as well as clinical sources of trepidation for the psychotherapist. The therapist must be experienced and well versed in strategies of treatment and clinical management techniques that are relatively specific to this clinical population. Therapists also need to clearly understand the various legal-ethical parameters (Williams, 1991) that are associated with treating this particular clinical population.

Finally, psychotherapists need to remind themselves periodically that antisocial patients are globally dangerous, intoxicated and chemically dependent antisocial patients are at least doubly dangerous, and all patients become potentially more dangerous when they use, abuse, or become addicted to mood-altering drugs. The therapist must make every effort to establish and maintain patient alcohol/drug abstinence in his or her treatment relationships with all potentially dangerous persons.

SUMMARY

This chapter has addressed the many issues that are associated with assessing and treating dangerous or potentially dangerous patients. In fact, most psychotherapy patients pose some form of danger to the psychotherapist, self, and/or others.

The "dangerous patient" poses a direct physical and/or psychological threat to self and/or others, including the therapist. Various parameters of patient dangerousness have been elucidated in this chapter, as are the dangers that the psychotherapist risks within the context of his or her treatment relationships with dangerous persons.

Research evidence (Ennis and Emery, 1978; Litwack and Schlesinger, 1987) consistently indicates that it is very difficult for behavioral scientists to accurately predict dangerousness and violent acting-out. Indeed, some investigations (Kozol, Boucher, and Garafalo, 1972) report that predictions of violence are likely to be wrong in two out of three cases. Several research studies pertaining to the prediction of violence and dangerousness were reviewed in this chapter. A number of common sources of diagnostic and predictive error in assessing dangerousness were also examined.

In spite of the fact that research evidence clearly demonstrates that it is very difficult to accurately predict dangerousness, clinicians and mental health workers are frequently required to evaluate this facet of patient behavior. Mental health workers can expect to be involved in situations where they will be called upon to predict violence and dangerousness. This reality need not be obfuscated by the clinician's realization and acceptance of the limits of his or her skill in this particular realm. Several models that have been used in the assessment and prediction of dangerousness in clinical practice were discussed in this chapter: environmental or sociogenic, situational, impulsive, catathymic, and compulsive. Litwack and Schlesinger (1987) state: "If it can be demonstrated that the individual retains the same complex of attitudes and psychodynamics and, if released, is likely to confront the same sort of circumstances that led to violence in the past, it should be strongly suspected that, if released, the individual will act violently again" (p. 241).

Paranoids, acute psychotics, and brain-injured persons may be more at risk for violent acting-out. Juxtaposed to these at-risk populations are chemically dependent individuals who manifest a concurrent psychiatric illness (Forrest and Gordon, 1990). Simple intoxication increases the probability of violent acting-out in most people. A case study included in this chapter demonstrated how mental health professionals can utilize multivariantly-oriented clinical models to assess and predict patient dangerousness. The assessment of patient dangerousness in clinical practice is most accurately and appropriately accomplished vis à vis the therapist's utilization of multiple predictors of violence and/or dangerousness. Psychological test data can also be useful in this regard.

The psychotherapist is a teacher and advocate of nonviolent problem-solving strategies. Psychotherapy does help some individuals become less violent. Psychotherapy relationships with violent and/or dangerous persons are complex, multifaceted, and individual in nature. The clinical management of potentially suicidal and homicidal persons has been elucidated in this chapter. The uses of the therapeutic relationship, hospitalization, medication, and adjunctive treatment interventions in the management of dangerous persons were discussed. The psychotherapy relationship is a "holding environment" that can be utilized as a deterrent to violent acting-out. Therapists need to be able to communicate openly and honestly with dangerous persons about their violent thoughts, feelings, and impulses. Several practical considerations or guidelines for therapists who treat violent persons were explored. Therapists need to be able to didactically teach these persons specific cognitive-behavioral-affective control techniques. Actions that the psychotherapist can initiate whenever he or she feels *personally* threatened, or in any way potentially endangered, by a patient were also discussed.

Finally, the legal parameters of dangerousness and the duty to warn were elucidated. The American Psychological Association (Stromberg, 1989) has proposed that psychologists have a duty to warn when "the patient has communicated to the therapist an actual threat of physical violence against a clearly identified or reasonably identifiable victim or victims" (p. 14).

The psychotherapy and assessment of dangerous or potentially dangerous persons is difficult and fraught with numerous legal as well as clinical sources of trepidation for the therapist. Therapists need to periodically remind themselves of the fact that antisocial persons are globally dangerous, intoxicated and chemically dependent antisocial patients are at least doubly as dangerous, and all patients become potentially more dangerous when they use, abuse, or become addicted to mood-altering drugs.

Chapter XIII

Treatment Outcome Effectiveness, Relapse, and Recovery

INTRODUCTION

As several researchers and clinicians have indicated (Blane, 1968; Emrick, 1974, 1991; Forrest, 1978, 1991; Zimberg, 1982; Wilsnack and Beckman, 1984; Bratter and Forrest, 1985; Brown, 1988, 1990; Wallace, 1989, 1991; Forrest and Gordon, 1990), the health service professions have historically believed that chemically dependent patients are poor candidates for psychotherapy and reha- bilitation. This particular patient population was felt to be generally unsuited for most, if not all, standard forms of psychiatric and psychological treatment. Behavioral scientists have long believed that chemically dependent persons cannot be effectively treated. Furthermore, many clinicians (Bratter, 1985) avoid treatment rela- tionships with chemically dependent patients because they have been unsuccessful in their therapeutic attempts to help these persons change.

It is generally accepted that substance abusers and chemically dependent persons are very difficult to treat (Forrest, 1984, 1991; Brown, 1985; Blane and Leonard, 1987). Chemically dependent clients frequently miss scheduled therapy or treatment sessions, lie to the therapist, fail to pay for professional services, and continue to drink or ingest mood-altering substances while engaged in therapy. Gorski and Miller (1986) indicate that relapse is a basic dynamic that must be effectively managed in the treatment of all persons who manifest an addictive disease or illness.

Over the past decade, it has become increasingly clear that many chemically dependent persons are able to become drug-abstinent and evidence a diversity of other gains as a direct result of being involved in psychotherapy and other professional treatment modalities (Wegscheider, 1981; Wallace, 1985, 1991; Miller, 1988; Gorski, 1990, 1991). Indeed, it is becoming increasingly apparent that many different types or "kinds" of chemically dependent persons can benefit or recover from their addictive disorders as a result of being involved in various treatment regimens. Some chemically dependent persons and substance abusers become drug-abstinent and recover in the absence of receiving treatment.

Behavioral scientists have also historically questioned the treatment efficacy of psychotherapy and various other rehabilitation modalities used to treat antisocial persons and other personality disordered persons (McCord and McCord, 1964; Cleckley, [1941] 1976; Brantley and Sutker, 1984; Doren, 1987). Can the antisocial personality change or benefit as a function of being involved in intensive psychotherapy or other models of treatment and rehabilitation? Are criminals and antisocial persons capable of changing? Clinicians have utilized a variety of treatment approaches (Yochelson and Samenow, 1986; Reid et al., 1986; Nace, 1990) in their efforts to help antisocial persons change. What treatment strategies or models are most effective in clinical work with these persons? Do treatment outcome effectiveness rates differ between chemically dependent/substance abusing antisocial persons and antisocial persons who are not chemically dependent and are not substance abusers?

The persistent acting-out and destructive behaviors of the ASPD have not been viewed from the perspective of the relapse model. Yet, the behaviors and thought processes of the antisocial patient are often obsessive-compulsive, progressive, interpersonally damaging and conflictual, and potentially fatal. Is antisocial personality disorder a disease? Most antisocial persons periodically and situationally terminate their antisocial activities and behaviors. Perhaps these individuals have experienced a "relapse" when they again begin to act-out and return to former patterns of antisocial thinking and antisocial behaving? Drug use fosters the antisocial acting-out and antisocial relapses of many, if not most, antisocial personalities.

Finally, is it possible for the bona fide antisocial personality to recover? We know that many alcoholics and chemically dependent persons recover from their addictions–they have been alcohol and drug-abstinent for perhaps 10 to 40 years and have concurrently modified various other patterns of maladaptive behavior. How do we define and measure the "recovery" of antisocial persons? What are the recovery rates among antisocial patients who receive various treatments versus antisocial persons who receive no treatment?

This chapter addresses the thorny problems of treatment outcome effectiveness, relapse and relapse prevention, and recovery specific to: (1) chemical dependency and the substance use disorders; (2) antisocial personality disordered persons with concurrent chemical dependency and/or substance use disorder; and (3) antisocial personality disorder.

TREATMENT OUTCOME EFFECTIVENESS FOR CHEMICAL DEPENDENCY AND THE SUBSTANCE USE DISORDERS

Researchers and clinicians generally agree (Emrick, 1974, 1991; Emrick and Hansen, 1983; Forrest, 1984b; Miller and Hester, 1986; Longabaugh, 1988) that the treatment outcome effectiveness assessment of chemical dependency and the substance use disorders needs to be multidimensional. The sole criterion of substance abstinence versus continued use or frequency and amount of substance use was employed as the principal measure of treatment outcome effectiveness several years ago. Recent investigations of treatment outcome effectiveness (Armor, Polich, and Stambul, 1978; Forrest, 1984b; Miller, 1988; Longabaugh, 1988) either call for the use of multiple criteria assessment of treatment outcome effectiveness or actually utilize multiple criteria in the evaluation of treatment outcomes. Job performance and job stability, marital and family relations, physical health, legal status, psychological test data, and abstinence versus use or quantitative measures of substance use have recently been employed as measures of treatment outcome effectiveness.

Behavioral scientists also tend to agree that there are several inherent difficulties associated with assessing treatment outcome effectiveness (Hill and Blane, 1967; Emrick, 1974, 1991; Crawford and Chalupsky, 1977). These methodological inadequacies include operational definitions (different researchers utilize different operational definitions of "alcoholic," "substance abuser," etc.), sample size and sampling techniques, instrumentation, control groups, statistical tools, and followup measures. It is important to note that many of these methodological flaws were modified during the 1980s, and thus a greater percentage of recent research publications report differential treatment effectiveness. Nonetheless, the reader needs to bear in mind as he or she reads this volume that many investigations of treatment outcome effectiveness among alcoholics and other chemically dependent patients have probably included subjects who were substance abusers rather than bona fide chemically dependent subjects. Investigations of substance abusers also have probably included chemically dependent subjects (Emrick, 1990, 1991). Thus, all investigations of treatment outcome effectiveness need to be viewed as *imperfect* estimates and measures.

Alcoholism and alcohol abuse treatment outcome effectiveness have been investigated for several decades (Voegtlin and Lemere, 1942; Hill and Blane, 1967; Emrick, 1974, 1991; Armor, Polich, and Stambul, 1978; Sobell and Sobell, 1982; Miller and Hester, 1986; Stout, 1988). O'Connor (1978) reports on the historical effect of Father Mathew of Cork, Ireland, one of the most famous temperance reformers of Irish drunkenness in the 1830s and 1840s: "The transformation of Ireland during the Father Mathew years was by any test remarkable . . . By the end of 1841 it was claimed that there were at least five million on the teetotal roll in a population of eight million. Brewers and distilleries went out of business and publicans deserted their trade" (p. 114). It is estimated that, during his public tours of Ireland, Father Mathew administered 2 million "pledges" of abstinence to nearly a quarter of the population (O'Connor, 1978). Orford (1985) states: "In comparison with the influence of Father Mathew, the present-day effect of individual practitioners who painstakingly 'treat' the 'disease' of 'alcoholism' seems ludicrously insignificant" (p. 295).

McPeek (1972) reports on the effectiveness of the Washington Temperance Society in 1841 (McPeek cites a prohibitionist senator who, 50 years later, could view the Washingtonians' success with greater objectivity): "In a few years 600,000 drunkards have been reformed of whom, however, all but 150,000 returned to their cups.

The moral of this movement is that we must save the boy if we would be sure of the man . . . To be sure, 150,000 reformed men had adhered to their pledges and were saved; but what are 150,000 among so many?" (p. 411). The senator estimated the followup success rate to be approximately 25 percent. McPeek (1972) also refers to a historical account of the temperance movement entitled "Battling with the Demon" which estimates that seven out of ten of those who received temperance medals from Father Mathew in his campaigns relapsed into drinking.

Recent research evidence suggests that diverse treatments for alcoholism and alcohol abuse can be expected to produce positive outcome effects in 30 to 75 percent of cases. Hill and Blane (1967) concluded that alcoholism treatment effectiveness was generally less than 50 percent. Emrick (1974, 1975, 1979, 1991) has conducted extensive reviews of the alcoholism treatment outcome effectiveness research data and concludes that most treatments result in some improvement of patient functioning. In his classic investigation of 265 evaluation-outcome studies of psychologically-oriented alcoholism treatments, Emrick (1974) reported a nearly 70 percent improvement rate. One-half of the alcoholics who improved as a result of treatment achieved varying periods of abstinence.

Psychoanalysis and psychoanalytically-oriented psychotherapy are perhaps the least effective treatments for alcoholism and chemical dependency. Moore and Ramseur (1960) indicated a 30 percent improvement rate for alcoholics who were treated in psychoanalysis for three and one-half years. Hayman (1956) studied the success of psychiatrists who treated alcoholics in psychoanalytically oriented individual therapy and found that over one-half of these psychiatrists reported no treatment successes. In a related investigation of 385 studies published between 1952 and 1973 reporting on the results of mostly dynamically-oriented psychotherapy with alcoholics, Emrick (1975) concluded that "alcoholics are, in a practical sense, as likely to stop drinking completely for six months or longer when they have no or minimal treatment as when they have more than minimal treatment" (pp. 97-98).

The controversial Rand Report (Armor, Polich, and Stambul, 1976) evaluated the outcomes of treatment of 15,000 alcoholics who received treatment at 44 federally funded alcoholism rehabilitation centers. This study revealed that substantial numbers of treated alcoholics resumed or maintained nonproblem drinking patterns following treatment. Nearly 70 percent of the alcoholics in this study benefited from even minimal levels of treatment. Nathan and Hay (1984) conclude that the latest Rand Report data indicate: (1) that roughly one in five patients followed through four years who was alive and could be interviewed at the four-year mark was judged to be drinking without problems; (2) that nonproblem drinkers were not more likely than abstainers to relapse into problem drinking; and (3) that nonproblem drinkers were not more likely than abstainers to be psychiatrically disturbed. Thus, the Rand Reports have raised significant questions pertaining to the goals of alcoholism treatment.

Orford (1985) indicates that "there is in fact a remarkable consistency in the conclusions reached by those who have reviewed studies of the effectiveness of treatment for different forms of excessive appetitive behavior" (p. 249). In reviewing the effectiveness of treatments for obesity, smoking, alcohol problems, and other forms of substance abuse and chemical dependency, Orford (1985) concludes: "(1) Followup success rates at 6-12 months after treatment mostly lie within the range of 20-45 percent, averaging around one-third; and (2) when those receiving treatment have been randomly assigned to different forms of treatment, or when groups receiving different treatments have been carefully matched, the large majority of findings have been uniform, i.e., different treatments tend to produce very similar results" (p. 249).

The alcohol treatment outcome effectiveness literature also suggests that little difference results when "long-term inpatient treatment is compared with short-term inpatient treatment, when inpatient treatment is compared with outpatient treatment, when long-term outpatient treatment is compared with short-term outpatient treatment, or when relatively costly treatments such as 'self-control' training are compared with relatively inexpensive therapies such as 'bibliotherapy'" (Orford, 1985, p. 251). Several investigators (Edwards and Guthrie, 1967; Williams, Letemendia, and Arroyave, 1973; Armor, Polich, and Stambul, 1978; Miller and Taylor, 1980; Miller, 1988) report evidence in support of the Orford (1985) conclusions about alcohol treatment outcome effectiveness.

Antabuse or disulfiram maintenance has been used in the treatment of alcoholics for nearly 40 years. It is generally believed (Forrest, 1984, 1985, 1991) that Antabuse treatment is most efficacious when used in combination with other treatment modalities. While the global efficacy of Antabuse treatment remains questionable (Schuckit, 1981; Forrest, 1985; Forrest and Gordon, 1990), short-term followup studies (Fuller and Williford, 1980) indicate that Antabuse results in a 77 percent abstinence rate. Milt (1969) suggests that Antabuse treatment has a success rate of approximately 50 percent over a prolonged period of time. Forrest (1985) states: "Less .han twenty percent of alcoholics who simply take Antabuse can be expected to remain totally abstinent for twelve to eighteen months. When used in combination with individual therapy, group therapy, family therapy, and Alcoholics Anonymous, Antabuse can help to facilitate recovery rates of sixty to eighty percent" (p. 457). It is important for clinicians to identify alcoholics who are particularly well-suited for an Antabuse maintenance program if recovery rates are to be enhanced via the use of this treatment modality (Mendelson and Mello, 1979).

Industrial alcohol and drug treatment programs (Wallace, 1985) report treatment outcome effectiveness rates in the range of 70 to 90 percent. A very high percentage of the people who become involved in these treatment programs stop drinking or become totally abstinent from alcohol and/or other drugs. Treatment outcome effectiveness is also very high for EAP program participants in the area of job performance, health and accidents, absenteeism, employee-supervisor-management relations, and litigation.

Bratter, Pennacchia, and Gauya (1985) examine the history of heroin addiction treatment in the United States and report that many hospitals discontinued chemical dependency treatment programs during the 1940s and 1950s because these programs were "economically unwarranted because longitudinal studies documented recidivism rates to exceed ninety percent" (p. 259). Dumont (1972) indicates that the medical-psychiatric establishment believes "heroin addicts are not in control of their own behavior and are not curable by any known treatment. Until one is found, the best we can hope for is to block the addict's craving, monitor his social behavior, and reduce the profit of an illegal market in heroin" (p. 43).

Methadone maintenance programs have been used to treat heroin addicts with minimal positive treatment outcome effectiveness for approximately 25 years.

The treatment outcome effectiveness for a diversity of eating disorders is not particularly promising. Obesity, bulimia, anorexia nervosa, and other forms of compulsive eating disorders are difficult to treat. Foreyt and Frohwirth (1977) quote Stunkard about the pervasive therapeutic pessimism regarding the treatment of obesity: "Most obese persons will not stay in treatment for obesity. Of those who stay in treatment, most will not lose weight, and of those who do lose weight, most will regain it" (p. 79). Elliott (1977) also concluded in her review of treatments for "excessive eating" that no studies involving more than a few subjects demonstrated "clinically significant losses in a significant proportion of the sample" (p. 2).

Recent cognitive-behavioral treatments for compulsive overeating (Mines, 1989, 1991) report significantly more favorable treatment outcomes. The surgical treatment of obesity, involving the jejunoileal bypass with retention of 14 inches of jejunum and four inches of ileum (James, 1976; Ley, 1980) produces very favorable results. Patients experience large weight losses when compared with patients receiving more traditional treatments for obesity and weight loss for 18 months or more has been reported (Ley, 1980). This treatment modality (Quaade, 1978) also frequently helps patients feel less irritable, less depressed, less insecure and lonely, and improves sexual functioning. However, there is a 2 to 7 percent operative mortality rate and postoperative complications include problematic diarrhea, a high frequency of complaints of abdominal pain, and flatulence with the treatment (James, 1976). Other treatments for obesity and compulsive overeating include "jaw wiring," medications such as amphetamines, diet suppressants, and thyroid hormone, starvation and fasting, acupuncture and hypnosis, exercise, a plethora of behavioral modification techniques, and self-help groups such as Weight Watchers, OA (Overeaters Anonymous), and TOPS (Take Off Pounds Sensibly). There has been a widespread proliferation of commercial weight-reduction programs throughout the United States over the past decade. Indeed, the treatment of obesity and other eating disorders (Valette, 1990) has become "big business" in the U.S. Virtually all of these treatments can be initially effective and beneficial. Yet the problem of maintaining weight loss, weight gain, or weight satisfaction after treatment, or for an extended period of time after treatment, renders most of these models ineffective (Orford, 1985; Goldberg, 1989).

Compulsive gambling has been viewed as an addiction for several decades (Stekel, 1924). Perhaps the Russian novelist Dostoevsky is the most famous of all "compulsive gamblers." Minihan (1967) reports: "Dostoevsky lost everything, and at night in despair he ran in search of a Russian priest . . . At midnight he wrote to his wife, 'Now this fantasy has ended forever . . . Moreover, I have, as it were, been wholly reborn morally . . . A great thing has happened to me. The hideous fantasy that tormented me for almost ten years has vanished . . . ' Actually, he underwent some sort of mystical experience. The 'fantasy' had disappeared instantly and for good" (p. 385). Perhaps the essence of gambling consists of an abandonment of reason.

Compulsive gambling has been referred to as an "addictive disease" (Hunter, 1988), and treatment centers for pathologic gamblers are being developed throughout the United States and other countries. American society reinforces gambling and betting forms of behavior vis à vis state lotteries, horse racing, sporting events, and even church-sponsored bingo games. Tragically, thousands of people are willing to gamble their paychecks away each week in hopes of winning a lottery "jackpot." The probability of being a winner in these situations may range from 1 in 10 million to 1 in 100 million!

Addicted gamblers may participate in a diversity of treatments for their illness. Gamblers Anonymous (GA) was successfully started in America in 1957. This treatment program is modeled after Alcoholics Anonymous and is based on the self-help principles of AA. Behavioral modification techniques, group therapy, and psychotropic medications can be used in the treatment of compulsive gambling. Hunter (1988) reports that at least 25 percent of compulsive gamblers who enter residential treatment programs recover or are significantly improved following treatment.

Behavioral scientists and the general public have recently recognized that tobacco is one of the most ubiquitous and socially significant drugs known to mankind. Tobacco and nicotine dependence are associated with cardiovascular disease, chronic bronchitis, emphysema, lung cancer, and other diseases (Bernstein and McAllister, 1976; Koop, 1989). Bernstein (1970) notes that many people who wish to stop smoking are unable to do so. He also indicates that only 24 percent of smokers have ever tried to quit and that only one-third of those who attempt to quit are successful. Russell (1971) describes nicotine or smokers' withdrawal symptoms and points out that intermittent or occasional use of tobacco is a rarity–most people who smoke go on to become regular smokers.

In general, smoking reduction studies (Orford, 1985) report that most treatments reduce smoking rates approximately 20 to 30 percent at the end of treatment, being restored to 45 to 75 percent at six-week followup, and increasing to between 70 and 80 percent at six-month followup. Hypnosis and relaxation training (Matuschka, 1989), aversion therapy, group treatment, psychotropic medications, self-help, and nicotine gum are but a few of the treatment modalities that have been utilized to extinguish or modify smoking behavior.

Sexual addictions (Carnes, 1985; Forrest, 1989) and obsessive-compulsive sexual behaviors (Forrest, 1983) have recently been identified and referred to as "diseases" and bona fide "addictions." Perhaps it was Richard von Krafft-Ebbing (1886) who first identified this pattern of sexual behavior. He referred to this abnormal increase in sexual desire as "hyperaesthesia" and "an impulsive insatiable succession of sexual enjoyment." Krafft-Ebbing also cited case reports of "nymphomania" and "satyriasis." Interestingly, Daniel Defoe (Stone, 1979) purported that sexual excess leads to "palsies and epilepsies, falling sickness, trembling of the joints, pale dejected aspects, leanness, and at least notennes and other filthy and loathsome distempers" (p. 313).

Kinsey, Pomeroy, and Martin (1948) provided research data that demonstrated differences between high frequency and low frequency sexual behavior among American males. While sexologists and sex researchers (Klassen, Williams, and Levitt, 1989) have long recognized that there are significant differences in sexual responding, desire, and arousal patterns between and among men and women, it is only recently that the concept of sexual addiction has been used to define and describe the pathologic sexual adjustments of a select population of people. These individuals establish an obsessive-compulsive and uncontrollable pattern of sexual responding.

The treatment of sex addicts is a very new and emerging discipline within the behavioral science field (Eisenstadt, 1989). Self-help groups such as Sexaholics Anonymous were formed in the United States during the early 1980s. Residential treatment programs and psychological/psychiatric outpatient treatment strategies for sex addicts are currently being developed (Carnes, 1985). Unfortunately, the efficacy of these treatments and treatment outcome effectiveness data pertaining to sex addicts remains unknown. Recovering sex addicts (Eisenstadt, 1989) give personal testimonies and anecdotal reports of their addictions and recoveries, but large-scale scientific investigations and treatment outcome data germane to this population have yet to be reported.

The treatment outcome effectiveness for marijuana dependence, cocaine dependence, polydrug dependence, prescription drug dependence or abuse, and other chemical dependencies seems to vary. Polydrug use and/or polydrug dependence (Forrest, 1989) is a trend in recent years among drug users within the United States and Western culture. More and more people who ingest illicit and/or legal mood-altering substances tend to abuse or become dependent on more and more drugs! For example, most cocaine addicts (Knauert, 1989) also abuse and/or are dependent on ethanol, marijuana, amphetamines, and tranquilizers.

Variables such as age, sex, socioeconomic class, race, education, and job status also may influence treatment outcome effectiveness rates. Treatment specific variables (types of treatment, patient motivation for treatment, legal status, duration of treatment, and criteria for successful versus unsuccessful treatment can also influence treatment outcome effectiveness rates (Miller, 1988; Emrick, 1990, 1991).

While there are no longitudinal data available pertaining to the treatment outcome effectiveness of different treatments for cocaine or "crack" addiction, it is generally believed by chemical dependency treatment specialists (Knauert, 1989, 1992) that these addictions are very difficult to treat, and recovery rates are significantly lower for this population than for alcohol and other chemically dependent populations. The major goal of treatments for cocaine and polydrug dependence is principally drug abstinence, and these forms of chemical dependency are so "new" that we know comparatively little about treatment outcome effectiveness in this realm. In the author's experience, most treatments for substance abuse and chemical dependency other than alcohol abuse and alcoholism are effective in 20 to 30 percent of cases.

Psychotherapy and treatment programs for alcohol abuse and alcoholism are significantly more effective than treatments for cocaine dependence, marijuana dependence, heroin addiction, and polydrug dependence. As Pattison (1987) indicates, the treatment of polydrug dependent or "dually-addicted" patients usually involves a lengthy succession of treatments for each addiction. Heroin addicts very frequently become alcoholics after being treated "successfully" for their heroin dependence. These individuals later need to be involved in treatment for their alcoholism or drinking disorder.

In sum, the research evidence pertaining to the effectiveness of a diversity of treatments for a diversity of addictive disorders suggests that many addictive individuals derive some degree of positive gain from most treatments. Indeed, it is reasonable to expect that between 25 and 75 percent of chemically dependent persons and substance abusers will, in some way, benefit from involvement in one or several forms of treatment. It is also clear that there is not one specific treatment modality or panacea that works best, or is most effective, with *all* alcoholics, bulimics, compulsive gamblers, or some other specific subpopulation of chemically dependent persons.

It is important for chemical dependency treatment personnel to realize that sound methodological investigations of treatment outcome effectiveness are currently being conducted. Unfortunately, such studies were not conducted 30, 40, or 100 years ago. Researchers and clinicians know a great deal more about treatment outcome effectiveness than they did ten or more years ago, but in actuality we are only now beginning to understand the precise relationships among different treatments, different patient populations, and outcomes. It is also wise to bear in mind that the treatment of many addictive illnesses by professionally trained health care workers is a relatively new undertaking. Even the self-help treatment alternatives for addicts and substance abusers are "new." The prototype of all self-help treatment programs is Alcoholics Anonymous which was developed in the mid-1930s and early 1940s. We are collectively emerging from the "dark ages" of chemical dependency treatment and rehabilitation. Significantly, the essential problem and criterion of treatment outcome effectiveness seems to be the matter of living drug-addiction-free. As W. C. Fields said several decades ago, "Stopping drinking is no problem . . . I've done it thousands of times." The essential problem or task of treatment for all chemically dependent patients and therapists remains the same–"staying stopped" or sustaining various adaptive behavioral, cognitive, and affective changes over a protracted period of time.

TREATMENT OUTCOME EFFECTIVENESS FOR CHEMICALLY DEPENDENT AND SUBSTANCE ABUSING ANTISOCIAL PATIENTS AND NONADDICTIVE ANTISOCIAL PERSONALITIES

There is a marked dearth of comparative treatment outcome effectiveness studies that involve chemically dependent and/or substance abusing antisocial personalities, nonaddictive antisocial personalities, and nonantisocial chemically dependent patients and substance abusers. No doubt, significant numbers of antisocial substance abusers and chemically dependent subjects were randomly included in the outcome effectiveness studies that have just been reviewed. The vast majority of chemical dependency outcome effectiveness studies has not examined the effects of diverse treatments on specific subpopulations of chemically dependent and substance abusing subjects.

Several investigators (Gilbert and Lombardi, 1967; Sutker, 1971; Cloninger, Bohman, and Siguardsson, 1981; Nathan and Hay, 1984; Forrest, 1989b) report that male and female drug addicts, alcoholics, and criminals manifest a very similar personality makeup. Gilberstadt and Duker (1965) characterize the basic MMPI 4-9 personality descriptors of these populations as immaturity, hostility, rebelliousness, impulsivity, low frustration tolerance, poor work and marital adjustment, poor socialization, and heavy drinking. Perverse sexual behavior and acting-out are related to this profile, and alcoholism is one of the most frequent causes for hospital admission within MMPI 4-9 groups.

While some addictionologists and many psychiatrists and psychologists who have worked extensively with chemically de-pendent and substance abusing patients have long realized that a very significant percentage of these individuals are antisocial, it is only in recent years that most counselors and treatment personnel who work with chemically dependent persons have truly come to understand the various diagnostic and treatment manifestations that are associated with the "dually-diagnosed" chemically dependent or substance abusing antisocial personality. In a strict clinical sense (Forrest, 1978, 1983a, 1984, 1991), the vast majority of chemically dependent and substance abusing patients manifests several clusters of diagnostic symptoms and syndromes and, thus, should be "dual-ly-diagnosed." Many alcoholics and chemically dependent persons manifest concurrent antisocial or passive-aggressive personality disorder, affective disturbance, psychoneurosis, thought distur-bance, or brain dysfunction (Forrest, 1979, 1984, 1991, 1992).

It is reasonable to expect that behavioral scientists will increas-ingly address the problem of treatment outcome effectiveness among "dually-diagnosed" antisocial chemically dependent and substance abusing patients. The effectiveness of different treatment modalities on chemically dependent and substance abusing prison-ers and incarcerated offenders *may* provide a reasonably accurate treatment outcome effectiveness database rate for antisocial addicts and substance abusers. Prisoners and incarcerated offenders are by definition "antisocial." These individuals have broken laws, and they behave in a grossly antisocial manner. Most incarcerated of-fenders have not completed extensive psychiatric and psychological examinations, testing, and diagnostic interviewing. Nonetheless, the antisocial behaviors and acts of the incarcerated individual are, in fact, the basis for his or her imprisonment. It is also significant that over 70 percent of inmates in the United States are incarcerated for crimes that they commit while under the influence of alcohol and/or other mood-altering drugs (Forrest and Gordon, 1990).

While incarcerated addicts and drug abusers are *individuals*, rather than a homogeneous group of antisocial people with concurrent drug abuse problems, we do know that several treatments produce positive outcomes when utilized with chemically dependent inmates. Clinicians and researchers need to bear in mind that prison populations are comprised of individuals who manifest considerable variance with regard to antisocial personality disorder and generalized psychopathology. Penal populations also differ significantly from other clinical subgroups as well as the general population with respect to the incidence of ASPD and psychopathology. For example, Polich, Armor, and Braiker (1981) found that alcoholic felons manifest *fewer* serious social and personal problems than clinic-treated alcoholics.

A major problem in assessing treatment outcome effectiveness among incarcerated antisocial chemically dependent inmates is simply the reality that most of these persons receive no treatment. Kalish (1983) conducted a survey of prisons in the U.S. and found that 70 percent of "habitually very heavy drinkers" had never been involved in an alcohol or drug rehabilitation program! In a related investigation of U.S. federal prisons (Thomas, 1978), it was concluded that "while promising treatment approaches have emerged in recent years, they have not yet been utilized to any appreciable degree in correctional facilities" (p. 4).

Ross and Lightfoot (1985) reviewed the 1970-1980 literature pertaining to alcohol treatment programs in correctional settings and concluded that "given the many rather negative assessments of reviews of the efficacy of treatment of alcoholism in the general population, and the prevalent 'nothing works' view of correctional treatment in general, one might be less than optimistic for treatment programs for alcohol/drug related offenders. However, there is some evidence that *some* programs may benefit *some* offenders" (p. 57).

Alcoholics Anonymous (Hansen, 1990) and similar self-help programs (Narcotics Anonymous, Cocaine Anonymous, etc.) are the most common treatment modalities that are available for chemically dependent/substance abusing antisocial inmates. Virtually all prisons now have an AA program. Roth and Rosenberg (1971) compared inmates who attended AA with those who did not attend AA and a control group and found that alcohol abusers attending

AA manifested significantly better institutional behavior than the other groups. Research evidence suggests that AA programs in prisons reduce recidivism rates. For example, Ross and Lightfoot (1985) report: "In 10 of the 18 camps which comprise the Mississippi State Penitentiary at Parchman, inmates are provided with group and individual therapy when they participate in AA. Contingent on their participation for at least six months they also receive postrelease job placements and are provided with a volunteer sponsor or 'big brother' to assist them in the community. The results of this program have been very encouraging: over a three-year period only 4.6% of program participants (parolees and dischargees) have returned for any reason, whereas 30% of the inmate population as a whole have been returned for parole violations alone" (p. 58).

AA and treatment programs in community correctional settings also report significant treatment outcome effectiveness rates. Less than 5 percent of 561 multirecidivistic offenders who were involved in the AA programs in four halfway houses in Houston, Texas, had to be returned to prison during the initial three and one-half years of program operation (Wells, 1973). Ball and Weiss (1976) indicate that New York State's PACT program has a 40 percent success rate with 6,000 offenders. The offenders in this study who were "success" cases maintained total alcohol/drug abstinence one year after treatment. Laundergan, Spicer, and Kammeier (1979) reported that 50 percent of a group of 288 court-ordered offenders were abstinent for 12 months after treatment. This study was conducted at the Hazelden Rehabilitation Center in Minnesota. Pallone and Tirman (1978) report similar findings in an investigation of 469 clients with drinking problems. Forty-three percent of this sample were court-referred for treatment. Those subjects who attended AA and the regular therapy program had significantly higher remission rates than those who did not attend AA.

Recently, Hansen (1991) reported followup data pertaining to the treatment outcome effectiveness of Alcoholics Anonymous for alcoholic and chemically dependent inmates at the State Penitentiary in Canon City, Colorado. The success rate of this program is 75 percent. Conversely, the success rate of the prison, as a whole, is only 25 percent. Seventy-five percent of inmates who are not involved in the Canon City AA program are again incarcerated or in legal trouble within four years. Less than 8 percent of returnees have been involved in the AA program. Furthermore, the more AA meetings and treatment an inmate receives while he is incarcerated, the less likely he is to become a repeat offender. It should be noted that the Rand study (Armor, Polich, and Stambul, 1978) found that AA attendance is almost as effective (56 percent remission) as a variety of agency treatment programs (63 to 72 percent remission).

Several treatment programs for alcoholic and/or chemically dependent inmates report significant improvement rates and high levels of treatment outcome effectiveness. Group therapy has been reported to be effective in the treatment of 55 to 67 percent of incarcerated alcoholics (Scott, 1976; Pallone and Tirman, 1978). Reality therapy, rational behavior therapy, cognitive training, behavioral counseling, and multimodal treatment programs report successful outcomes with this patient population (Marlatt, 1978; Pomerleau and Adkins, 1980; Ross and Fabiano, 1985). For example, a two-year followup investigation by Ziegler and Kohutek (1978) reports that 80 percent of inmates returned to the community were doing well and were not returned to custody. The subjects in this study were incarcerated alcoholics who participated in a treatment program that involved transactional analysis, rational self-counseling, biofeedback training, confrontation, and encounter groups.

The consistent and historic viewpoint about treatment outcome effectiveness for ASPD has been pessimistic. Several decades ago, McCann (1948) stated: "As a probation or parole risk the psychopath's chances of failure are 100 percent . . . There is no evidence to my knowledge that any psychopath has ever been cured by imprisonment–or by anything else" (p. 551). Darling (1945) observed, "The disease is of lifelong duration in almost every case." Indeed, many behavioral scientists have concluded that ASPD may not be treatable. For example, Chornyak (1941) concluded, "We must learn to face the fact . . . Psychopathy is untreatable." Perhaps the one psychiatrist who treated more psychopaths than any other behavioral scientist in the world during the past century is Harvey Cleckley. Cleckley (1959) commented on the failure of psychoanalysis in the treatment of psychopathy: "All other methods available today have been similarly disappointing in well-defined adult cases of this disorder with which I am directly acquainted" (p. 586). Cleckley remained very pessimistic about the treatment prognosis of psychopaths following some 35 years of direct clinical experience with this clinical subgroup.

Clinicians and researchers who work extensively with antisocial personalities in contemporary America (Yochelson and Samenow, 1976, 1986; Brantley and Sutker, 1984; Reid et al., 1986; Doren, 1987) continue to be pessimistic about the possibility of successful treatments and effective treatment outcomes with nonchemically dependent antisocial personalities. It is significant that Brantley and Sutker (1984) do not even formally address the issue of treatment in their extensive examination of the various facets of "Antisocial Behavior Disorders." These authors do note that the "treatment" that these persons frequently receive is *prison*! They also state, "Pessimism reigns as to the potential for constructive change among sociopaths" (p. 470).

Suedfeld and Landon (1978) report that the results of various treatment approaches to the problem of ASPD are "not much to show for the amount of money, time, and effort spent" (p. 369). A study of sociopathic narcotic addicts (Burt, Brown, and DuPont, 1980) found that few, if any, behavioral changes could be attributed to the effects of treatment.

Brantley and Sutker (1984) note: "Most commentaries share a penchant for describing negative personality features among sociopaths and for detailing dismal prospects for their treatment success . . . [yet] it must be acknowledged that sociopaths as a group seem to be robust, socially facile, and ingenious in many situations. Among their ranks, however, are daring, adventuresome, resourceful persons who may be able to outperform so-called normals when the going gets rough. Possibly, it is time for us to turn our research efforts to understanding some of the personal strengths of sociopaths" (pp. 470-471). These authors also describe "successful sociopaths." The adaptive strengths of the psychopath or ASPD include adroit social manipulation, persistent goal-seeking, capable intellectual resources and special strengths in observation skills for both the social and tangible environment, and social survival skills in modern society (Brantley and Sutker, 1984).

Historical investigations (McCord and McCord, 1964) of the

effectiveness of individual therapy, institutional treatment, punishment and incarceration, group therapy, shock treatment (ECT), lobotomy, military rehabilitation centers, and isolation on psychopaths report 13 to 40 percent success rates. Interestingly, McCord and McCord (1964) state, "The prospect for successful treatment, while gloomy, is not altogether discouraging. Although inadequately assessed, psychotherapy seems to hold the most promise" (p. 117). These authors also indicate that the "therapeutic community" treatment approach may be promising and that "our best hope lies in the successful treatment of child psychopathy; in changing youths before they mature into hardened psychopaths" (p. 119).

Recent textbooks that address the issues of diagnosing and treating ASPD (Reid et al., 1986; Yochelson and Samenow, 1986; Doren, 1987) provide a wealth of information and techniques for working with this population. Unfortunately, there are no new treatment outcome effectiveness data in these volumes. Doren (1987) does state, "This book has been designed to offer an understanding and method of treating a client population most often considered untreatable. In writing this book, I have tried to convey that the situation is not hopeless, just difficult . . . I believe that therapy is extremely useful in making these people less destructive citizens than they would be without therapy . . . I have seen substantial changes in psychopathic clients using the above techniques" (pp. 245-246). The author does provide considerable information and strategies for treating antisocial persons. The statements of one of his incarcerated psychopathic drug smugglers is significant: "They can do what they want with me, but they'll never break me. I'll never surrender to the system" (p. 246). Doren's comment on his client's statement is also significant: "I expect he never will."

In sum, the treatment outcome effectiveness data pertaining to antisocial substance abusers and chemically dependent persons and nonaddictive antisocial persons is limited and methodologically very weak. It is erroneous to assume that all prison inmates are bona fide psychopaths, and obviously inmate recidivism rates are not an accurate measure of treatment outcome effectiveness if incarceration per se is "treatment." Furthermore, prison samples of antisocial personalities, substance abusers, and chemically dependent inmates are generally poorly defined. Self-help treatments are currently available in most correctional facilities, but other forms of "treatment" are limited in prisons. The longitudinal investigations and even short-term followup studies of treatment outcome effectiveness with chemically dependent or substance abusing antisocial inmates are not available. While numerous investigations (Sutker, 1971; Paolino and McCrady, 1977; Brantley and Sutker, 1984; Forrest, 1989b) report that a sizable segment of alcoholics, narcotic addicts, and substance abusers are antisocial, the long-term effects of standard chemical dependency treatment models upon these persons have not been adequately investigated. Large sample investigations of the effects of various treatment regimens upon non-chemically dependent antisocial personalities are also lacking. Several clinicians have suggested (McCord and McCord, 1964; Brantley and Sutker, 1984) that psychopaths may "burn out" in their 50s and 60s, but this concept has never been systematically examined.

RELAPSE AND RELAPSE PREVENTION

Chemically dependent persons frequently experience "slips," "massive regressions," and "relapses." The chemical dependency literature of the 1960s and 1970s referred to the patient's return to substance dependence as a "slip" or "falling off the wagon" (Milt, 1969; Forrest, 1975). The chemical dependency treatment literature of the 1980s refers to the reinitiation of alcohol/drug use by chemically dependent persons as a "relapse" (Gorski and Miller, 1986; Gorski, 1991).

Many clinicians who treat chemically dependent substance abusing patients (Gitlow and Peyser, 1980) have identified the relapse phenomenon as a primary diagnostic criterion of an addictive disease. Indeed, the disease model of alcoholism and chemical dependency is based on the progressive and recurrent nature of an addiction. Continued chemical dependency and relapses also eventually result in the deaths of countless numbers of chemically dependent persons. For these reasons, most chemical dependency treatment models and programs attempt to help addicts maintain long-term drug abstinence. Total and lifelong drug abstinence is a theoretical treatment goal for the chemically dependent patient (Della-Giustina and Forrest, 1979; Bean et al., 1981).

Comprehensive relapse prevention models (Gorski and Miller, 1986; Gorski, 1989, 1990, 1991) identify the essential characteristics of the relapse syndrome. Gorski and Miller (1986) indicate: "Once you abandon a recovery program it is only a matter of time until the symptoms of post acute withdrawal appear, and if nothing is done to manage them, you will experience a period of out-of-control behavior that we call the *relapse syndrome*. Loss of control of post acute withdrawal symptoms results in the relapse syndrome" (p. 129). The relapse syndrome involves internal dysfunction (cognitive impairment, affective impairment, memory problems, high stress, sleep problems, and coordination problems), external dysfunction (denial returns, avoidance and defensiveness, crisis building, immobilization, and confusion and overreaction), and loss of control (depression, loss of behavioral control, recognition of loss of control, option reduction, and the actual *relapse episode*). These authors also provide an elaborate cognitive-behavioral plan for preventing relapse. Many warning signs precede a relapse, and certainly relapse does not occur suddenly and spontaneously. A relapse can often be prevented by a knowledge of these early warning signs and the initiation of a specific course of action designed to interrupt the relapse progression.

Relapse is an essential characteristic of all addictive diseases and obsessive-compulsive disorders. Thus, eating disordered persons may relapse into patterns of compulsive overeating or "binging." Cocaine and heroin addicts experience relapses as they attempt to become drug abstinent. Compulsive gamblers may "break down" and return to their pattern of destructive and compulsive gambling. Sex addicts find it difficult to abstain from compulsive sexual acting-out.

A plethora of interrelated factors can precipitate a relapse. Treatment programs attempt to provide addictive patients with new skills and alternatives to relapse. Substance abusers and chemically dependent persons can be taught stress management techniques (Yost and Mines, 1985), relaxation training, self-esteem enhancement, assertion skills, health maintenance, exercise, social/interpersonal skills, and cognitive retraining. All of these skills are deterrents to relapse. Thus, smokers or alcoholics can learn to use self-hypnosis (Matuschka, 1989) and relaxation training to reduce feelings of anxiety and stress that are associated with the drive or compulsion to return to substance use. Twelve-step self-help recovery programs (Alcoholics Anonymous, Narcotics Anonymous, Overeaters Anonymous, Cocaine Anonymous, etc.) and other comprehensive recovery programs (Forrest, 1984, 1991) provide cognitive, social and interpersonal, spiritual (Booth, 1989) and emotional alternatives to relapse. These programs have helped countless numbers of addicts and substance abusers overcome the relapse syndrome.

Chemically dependent and/or substance abusing antisocial personalities experience relapses. Obviously, these persons are especially prone to continued chemical abuse. As noted in earlier chapters, it is very difficult for antisocial substance abusers to sustain a long-term commitment to total alcohol/drug abstinence. These persons may also be *addicted* to their psychopathy! There is a diversity of addictive dimensions to the antisocial adjustment style. Thus, antisocial substance abusers are prone to experiencing relapses that involve both substance use and antisocial acting-out. Chemically dependent and/or substance abusing antisocial personalities can be expected to become more antisocial whenever they ingest more mood-altering substances (Forrest and Gordon, 1990). In juxtaposition to this, these individuals can also be expected to relapse into substance abuse and/or chemical dependency when their antisocial acting-out escalates.

The criminal acting-out of the antisocial person who has been in intensive psychotherapy and/or a comprehensive rehabilitation program can be conceptualized as a "relapse." The return to antisocial acting-out by a previously incarcerated person can likewise be viewed as a relapse. Any return to antisocial acting-out by antisocial patients constitutes a relapse. Bank robbers or rapists who are incarcerated for ten years and return to robbing banks or raping after being released from a correctional facility have experienced relapses *if* they received comprehensive and intensive treatment while incarcerated. Antisocial inmates who have not received proper treatment while incarcerated cannot be viewed as having experienced "relapses" when they return to patterns of robbing banks, raping, or other antisocial activities after being released from a correctional institution. Like the untreated alcoholic or chemically dependent patient, the untreated antisocial patient does not possess the internal strength and coping mechanisms that are prerequisite to remaining alcohol/drug abstinent or living and behaving within the parameters of a "normal" social structure.

The cognitive style of the antisocial personality or criminal (Yochelson and Samenow, 1986) plays a major role in the relapse process. A return to criminal thinking results in the outcropping of criminal and antisocial behavior problems. Just as alcoholic or addictive thinking constitutes one important precursor to a drinking relapse, criminal thinking invariably leads to a relapse into antisocial behavior. Therapists who work with substance abusing or chemically dependent psychopaths need to understand that any substance use by these persons usually precipitates a return to both criminal thinking and criminal behaving. Alcohol and drug use also helps to block or "freeze" the feelings and emotions of the antisocial personality, thus making it easier for these individuals to engage in a plethora of antisocial activities. Antisocial thought processes, behaviors, and emotions (anger, impulsiveness, excitement, etc.) also facilitate the alcohol/drug use dimension of the relapse process (Nace, Saxton, and Shore, 1986; Nace, 1990).

While it is simplistic and, perhaps, naive to conceptualize the psychopath's return to antisocial acting-out as a "relapse," it is important to recognize that many of these individuals do attempt to modify their various patterns of destructive behavior. They may be successful in this endeavor for a few hours, days, or even months. Yet, it is generally believed that the antisocial personality can be expected to eventually "relapse" into prior patterns of destructive and ineffective behavior. Many criminals report (Ross and Lightfoot, 1985; Yochelson and Samenow, 1986) that they are able to abstain from their criminal activities for extended periods of time before they "weaken" and resume an antisocial or criminal lifestyle.

Relapse prevention programs for antisocial substance abusers need to be multifaceted. Several relatively specific stressors (Gorski, 1990, 1991) precipitate the relapse syndrome. Thus, it is imperative that clinicians develop relapse prevention programs that will adaptively modify and ameliorate the stressors which facilitate the relapse syndrome in chemically dependent and substance abusing antisocial patients. A specific relapse prevention model for these patients was developed in Chapters VIII and IX. A relapse prevention model for chemically dependent and/or substance abusing homicide offenders and violent persons is also delineated in the text *Substance Abuse, Homicide, and Violent Behavior*, (Forrest and Gordon, 1990).

RECOVERY

In recent years (Forrest, 1984; Mumey, 1984; Brown, 1988; Emrick, 1990, 1991), it has become increasingly clear that thousands of chemically dependent and substance abusing persons are able to terminate or significantly modify their destructive patterns of drug use. Chemically dependent persons can achieve abstinence via their utilization of a diversity of psychological and self-help treatment alternatives (Forrest, 1978, 1984, 1989, 1991). In fact, a significant number of substance abusers (Zimberg, 1982; Orford, 1985; Emrick, 1990, 1991) modify or terminate their addictive behaviors without professional or self-help treatment. The current vernacular for successfully terminating one's addiction is "recovering." Thus, alcoholics and chemically dependent persons who have been completely drug abstinent for several days or, perhaps, several years commonly refer to themselves as "recovering" alcoholics or "recovering" addicts.

Two or three decades ago, alcoholics and chemically dependent persons were generally perceived to be "hopeless" by most clinicians and behavioral scientists. There were a few inpatient settings where these individuals could receive treatment and psychotherapy. Alcoholics and chemically dependent persons entered such treatment settings in order to be "cured" or to "take the cure." At this juncture in the development of treatment programs and rehabilitation alternatives for chemically dependent persons, "recovery" simply meant drug/alcohol abstinence. Alcoholics and chemically dependent persons were felt to be "cured" or "recovered" when they were able to remain drug-free.

Total drug abstinence is the essential precursor to recovery for alcoholics and chemically dependent persons. However, as I stated a number of years ago (Forrest, 1978): "Sobriety alone is never enough." Recovery begins with abstinence, but a holistic recovery can never occur in the absence of an ongoing commitment to a program of recovery (Forrest, 1984, 1991). Chemically dependent persons recover via the growth and change that takes place only within the context of an involvement in a structured program of recovery. The chemically dependent patient learns to change maladaptive patterns of thinking, behaving, emoting, communicating, and interacting by involving himself or herself in intensive psychotherapy, family counseling, self-help with active sponsorship, rigorous exercise, healthy nutrition, and some form of spiritual (Booth, 1989) growth program. Marital therapy, psychotropic medication, medical care, and other specific treatment adjuncts may be essential to the full recovery of some substance abusers and chemically dependent persons.

Chemically dependent persons are ultimately unable to change and recover by themselves or in the absence of an extended intimate involvement in a healthy human relationship. The active alcoholic's belief that "I can do it on my own" or without intervention is irrational and fallacious.

Impulse control disordered or antisocial substance abusers begin to recover when they become drug-abstinent and actualize a commitment to a responsible lifestyle. These persons face the doubly difficult task of recovering from their chemical dependency as well as their severe personality disorder. The multiplicity of parataxic problems that the substance abusing antisocial patient manifests are refractory to significant modification in the absence of total drug abstinence and a long-term commitment to a multimodal recovery program. All "dually-diagnosed" substance abusers and chemically dependent patients are confronted with the difficult task of remaining alcohol/drug free while simultaneously attempting to change or modify maladaptive patterns of thinking, interacting, behaving, and emoting.

As I have indicated earlier (Forrest, 1984), there are different stages of recovery. Recovery from alcoholism and chemical dependency is a process. There are different stages of recovery, and chemically dependent or substance abusing persons vary in their capacities for recovery. These individuals also differ significantly with regard to the time and emotional work that must take place in order to achieve recovery. A primary alcoholic who is actively committed to a holistic recovery program may be able to progress successfully through the various stages of recovery in 18 to 24 months. While this person will need to continue "working" a recovery program for life, he or she has been able to accomplish the major tasks in a matter of months. The chemically dependent antisocial personality or thought-disordered patient may never reach this level of growth and recovery. Chemically dependent and substance abusing antisocial patients who are able to remain actively engaged in holistic treatment programs seem to need between five and ten years of care in order to manifest the various gains that are associated with the later stages of the recovery process.

In brief, the early stages of the recovery process involve: (1) achieving total alcohol/drug abstinence and/or significantly reducing substance use; (2) developing and implementing a personal program of recovery; (3) establishing a recovery-oriented identity; (4) learning to live and focus in the here-and-now (one day at a time); (5) coping with the various interpersonal and intrapersonal issues that are associated with relapse; and (6) improving basic living skills. The first six months of recovery encompass the "early stages" of the recovery process. The middle stages of the recovery process encompass the sixth month through the first year and a half to two years of treatment. This stage of recovery focally involves: (1) self-discovery; (2) dealing with feelings; (3) overcoming developmental deficiencies; (4) changing conflicted patterns of marital and family interaction; (5) building self-esteem; (6) learning how to trust and love; and (7) working on a continued and expanded personal program of recovery. The later stages of recovery usually begin during the eighteenth month of treatment and encompass the remainder of the individual's life. This stage of recovery involves: (1) identity consolidation and integration; (2) resolution of work/career difficulties; (3) resolution of intimacy and sexual conflicts; (4) establishment of a healthy and balanced narcissism; (5) actualized commitment to abstinence and the ongoing processes of change and growth; and (6) a heightened spiritual sense of being.

Recovering chemically dependent persons become more fully functioning. They are: (1) more open to their own experience;

(2) able to live fully each moment of each day; and (3) better able to trust their own judgment and choices. Thus, the recovering person has a more internalized locus of control and is less dependent upon external sources of approval and/or disapproval.

Recovery fosters the chemically dependent patient's abilities to think more rationally and behave more responsibly. The cognitive abilities of the actively addicted person are impaired. Irrational thinking is a sine qua non of the chemically dependent person. Alcoholism and chemical dependency create delusional thinking. The thought process and cognitive style of the chemically dependent person are disturbed. Addicts project blame, distort and deny reality, and manifest confused patterns of thinking. The behavioral style of the chemically dependent person is irresponsible. The patients commonly fail to pay bills, miss appointments, lie, fail to follow through on promises and commitments, and are generally unreliable. Indeed, drug use facilitates irrational thinking and irresponsible behavior.

Drug abstinence and involvement in a treatment program help the chemically dependent person develop the capacity to modify faulty patterns of thinking and behaving. Chemically dependent persons become progressively more rational and responsible human beings as they begin the recovery process. The alcoholic or substance abuser becomes more fully "humanized" as he or she recovers. Recovery enables the chemically dependent person to better cope with and accept reality. Recovering addicts are responsible persons. They tell the truth, work more productively, pay bills, follow through on commitments, and deal more responsibly with the myriad obligations of modern living.

Recovery from chronic alcoholism or chemical dependency entails a restoration of the self (Forrest, 1984b, 1991, 1992) and the establishment of an adequately consolidated nuclear sense of self (Forrest, 1983a). The self-system is also restored and/or consolidated in individuals who recover from schizophrenia and other forms of severe mental illness or severe personality disorders (Kernberg, 1984). Many chemically dependent persons have experienced chronic identity conflicts, self-system fragmentation, and "blurred" ego boundaries. The consistency, consensual validation, support and love, and healthy nurturing that occurs within the context of an intensive psychotherapy relationship in combination with a holistic recovery program helps the chemically dependent patient consolidate a basic self. In the sense of selfhood, recovery is a rebirth.

Substance abusers and chemically dependent persons develop the capacities for intimacy, relationship, and love via the recovery process. Drug impaired persons are unable to be genuinely intimate and loving. These individuals are also unable to establish and maintain healthy relationships with significant others, the community, or a higher power. Tragically, alcoholics and chemically dependent persons are unable to love themselves in a healthy fashion. Their self-relationship is disturbed, and they lack the capacity for intimacy with self or others.

Intimate and loving human relationships involve emotional depth, openness, self-disclosure (Hountras and Forrest, 1970) and a sharing of the real self. Intimacy and love begin with the capacity to communicate openly with another human being. Expressing feelings, sharing experiences, empathy, honesty, and authenticity are some of the other important ingredients in intimate and loving human relationships. Intoxicated and chemically dependent persons are incapable of being genuinely intimate. These individuals develop the capacity for intimate human relating once they have become abstinent and are committed to a program of recovery.

Recovery also fosters the capacity for healthy sexual intimacy. Active alcoholics and chemically dependent persons are unable to be intimate and loving within the context of their sexual relationships. Relationship, self, and spiritual intimacy are precursors to healthy sexual intimacy and sexual loving. Chemically dependent individuals most commonly avoid sex (Forrest, 1983a, 1989), but even the most sexually promiscuous and sexually active addict is not intimate and loving in his or her sexual encounters. The sexuality of the drinking alcoholic or chemically dependent person is self-centered or narcissistic, exploitive, lacking or distorted, and pathologic in myriad ways. Abstinence, psychotherapy, and involvement in a recovery program help addicts develop the capacity for a healthier and fuller sex life. Many alcoholics recover the physical and psychological abilities to respond sexually. Irrational beliefs and attitudes about sex can be changed with recovery. Sexual dysfunctions, desire and arousal difficulties, and aberrant forms of sexual responding (Forrest, 1983a, 1989) can often be modified by treatment and the recovery process. In sum, the establishment of healthy sexual intimacy is but one important "symptom" of the recovery process for many chemically dependent persons.

Father Joseph C. Martin has stressed that drinking alcoholics are incapable of loving. He is tragically correct! Yet, with recovery, many of these individuals develop the capacity to love. They begin to experience and express feelings of affection, caring, and attachment for other human beings. Love is giving of self, placing loved ones above or on an equal level with self . . . love is caring, experiencing compassion and empathy, and being fully committed to the well-being, development, and growth of another. With time and a great deal of personal *work*, many recovering persons either recover or develop for the first time in their lives the ability to love. The angry, self-centered, manipulative, insensitive, and resentful self can become a loving and caring self in recovery! Love is contagious and, thus, the families of chemically dependent persons also develop and share the improved capacities for open, intimate, and loving interaction as they become involved in the recovery process.

All chemically dependent persons manifest the potential for some form or degree of self-actualization. Self-actualization represents the ultimate level of effective human functioning. Self-actualization is the fullest, most complete differentiation and harmonious blending of all aspects of a person's total being. This concept also includes the creative drive in every human being. Self-actualized people continually strive to become more fully developed, complete, and integrated. Many chemically dependent persons in the later stages of the recovery process manifest some of the 15 characteristics of self-actualized people that Abraham Maslow (1954) described: (1) being reality-oriented; (2) acceptance of self, others, and the material world; (3) spontaneity; (4) problem-centeredness rather than self-centeredness; (5) detachment and a need for privacy; (6) autonomy and independence; (7) appreciation of people and things in a fresh, rather than stereotyped, manner; (8) history of profound mystical or spiritual experiences, although not necessarily religious in nature; (9) identification with mankind; (10) intimate relationships with a few specially loved people that tend to be

profound and deeply emotional rather than superficial; (11) democratic values and attitudes; (12) ability to distinguish means from
ends; (13) sense of humor that is philosophical rather than hostile;
(14) manifestation of a wealth of creativeness; and (15) resistance
to conformity to the culture.

Recovery from chemical dependency and serious mental health
problems always encompasses becoming more reality-oriented, becoming more accepting of self and others, changing self-centeredness, initiating new relationships, becoming more democratic, and
even resisting cultural imperatives to conform. Many recovering
chemically dependent persons report that a profound spiritual and/
or mystical experience fosters and maintains their recovery.

Optimal recovery includes the development of social awareness
and social concern. Recovering people help themselves in a variety
of healthy ways, but they also help others and actively contribute to
the well-being of the human community. These growth- and health-
oriented processes involve death and rebirth. The recovering person
is reborn vis à vis the death or termination of dysfunctional behaviors, beliefs, attitudes, relationships, and emotions. Recovery can
encompass the symbolic death and rebirth, or perhaps birth, of the
addict as well as every member of the addict's family (Forrest,
1991).

Finally, it is important to realize that recovery is always an individual matter. Recovery is as much an individual matter as chemical
dependency. Every substance abuser is different and uniquely human. The recovery process is just as unique and different for each
addict. Some chemically dependent persons are able to move
through the later stages of the recovery process in two or three
years, while others require five or six more years to accomplish the
task. There are chemically dependent persons who never recover or
begin the journey into growth and wellness. Perhaps these unfortunate few are "constitutionally" incapable of recovery? Chemically
dependent persons who manifest concurrent ASPD, schizophrenia,
brain injury, identity and/or sexual disturbance, or other severe
personality disorders generally need a great deal more time and
personal work in order to actualize the various gains of recovery
that are discussed in this section of the chapter. It is also wise for
clinicians and chemically dependent individuals to remember that

the recovery process is ultimately a one-day-at-a-time, lifelong process!

The following case study illustrates the reality of recovery. This woman was polydrug dependent and extremely passive-aggressive at the point of treatment engagement.

Martha S. initially entered outpatient psychotherapy after her husband told her that he would file for a divorce if she did not stop drinking and taking drugs and enter treatment. The patient was 32 years old when she entered therapy. She had been married over ten years and had no children. Martha was a counselor in a state correctional facility, and she had completed her Master's degree in psychology. Her husband was a psychiatrist.

The patient indicated in the initial therapy session that she had known she was "drinking too much and in trouble with drugs" since her junior or senior year of undergraduate studies. She revealed that her biological father had died from chronic alcoholism several years after her parents divorced. Her parents divorced when she was eight years old, and she had rarely seen her father prior to the time of his death when she was 17. The patient had one older sister. She reported that she had "never" gotten along well with her mother and described her mother as critical, demanding, and "obsessed" with money. The patient was a "student activist" in college. She began to smoke marijuana, drank heavily, used psychedelic drugs, and acted-out sexually while in college. Her political and drug-taking activities involved her husband, whom she married shortly after college graduation. Mr. S. entered medical school that fall, and Mrs. S. began taking graduate courses in psychology the following spring. Both continued to abuse alcohol and a variety of other drugs until the patient entered therapy.

At the point of treatment engagement, Mrs. S. was very "motivated" to terminate her polydrug dependence. She consciously realized that she was chemically dependent and that many of her relationships and living problems were drug facilitated. She also did not want to be divorced and told the therapist, "I'll do anything it takes to keep my marriage together." During the initial few months of treatment, Dr. and Mrs. S. were seen together in several conjoint therapy sessions. Both agreed that Dr. S. was able to "control" his drug use and that "recreational" cocaine and marijuana use on his part would not create further relationship difficulties. Mrs. S. terminated all alcohol/drug use during the initial four months of therapy. She also attended AA three or four times but concluded that her therapy was so successful that she did not need to be involved in a self-help program.

During her fifth month of recovery, Dr. and Mrs. S. went on a vacation to Aruba and other islands in the West Indies. While on vacation, the patient decided to resume drinking one evening. This decision was made after she and her husband had "tooted a few lines" of cocaine. She proceeded to consume several drinks, the couple went dancing at an elegant night club, and later, while dancing, Mrs. S. completely disrobed on the dance room floor! Although Dr. S. was not particularly upset about this course of events, Mrs. S. felt very embarrassed and ashamed of her behaviors when Dr. S. told her what she had done the following morning. The patient had been in a "blackout" and did not remember taking her clothes off on the dance floor! She continued to drink and abuse cocaine and marijuana for the duration of the vacation and discontinued therapy upon return from vacation. She did call the therapist's receptionist and indicated that she was doing very well and would call for an appointment if she needed one in the future.

Eight months later, Mrs. S. called and scheduled a therapy session for herself. She indicated that her drinking and drug use had escalated and that she felt "out of control." The patient was agitated, depressive, and somewhat suicidal. She reported that her husband had moved out of the house. Mrs. S. indicated that she was consuming a half-gallon of wine nightly, smoking marijuana each night, and "doing coke" on the weekends. She was also experiencing significant conflict with her immediate job supervisor and had missed several days of work. The patient referred to herself as a "real psychopath" in this session and realistically noted, "I'm more out of control than most of the people I work with." She revealed that she habitually lied to her husband, job supervisor, and others, and that she had recently become involved in selling and distributing marijuana. Mrs. S. also discussed her sexual promiscuity and unhappiness with her role in an "open marriage" agreement with her husband. She again pointed out that she did not want a divorce and that she was willing to terminate her alcohol/drug abuse in order to resolve her marital problems.

Mrs. S. agreed to enter a residential chemical dependency rehabilitation program after this session. She completed 28 days of inpatient care and was subsequently seen in weekly outpatient psychotherapy for over six months. The patient remained totally alcohol/drug-abstinent and participated in a weekly recovery support group as well as several AA and CA meetings each week. She began an AA sponsorship program, terminated her job, and started exercising several times each week. Dr. S. developed an intense relationship with a work colleague at this time and subsequently filed for divorce. This divorce was actually final when Martha had established nearly one year of recovery.

At present, the patient has been totally alcohol/drug-abstinent for over five years. She remarried two years ago, and this relationship is quite functional and healthy. Martha also returned to the world of work several months after completing residential treatment. However, she did return to college and completed further training before actualizing a significant career change. She has been employed as a therapist in a large residential chemical dependency treatment center for nearly two years. In sum, Martha has evidenced very significant growth and change in many areas of her life. Her recovery encompasses major changes in the areas of marriage and interpersonal relationships, internal self-structure, substance dependence, impulse control and acting-out, career and the world of work, cognitive functioning, and spiritual awareness.

Martha's holistically-oriented recovery began when she entered psychotherapy and established a commitment to alcohol/drug abstinence and the recovery process. Her damaged self-esteem, conflicted relationship with a narcissistic mother, father's alcoholism, drug dependent and co-dependent marital relationship, early-life narcissistic injuries, and impulse control disordered lifestyle were ongoing areas of therapeutic focus and work vis à vis the process of several months of intensive addiction psychotherapy (Forrest, 1984, 1991).

The patient has been able to establish and maintain several healthy relationships as a result of treatment. She is a more nurturant person who is better able to love, work, and experience and share intimacy. Martha is far less impulsive, narcissistic, and manipulative. She continues to grow and recover on a daily basis.

This patient's recovery encompasses many areas of her life. She not only terminated her addictive illness but continues to grow and change in her relationship with self, significant others, and the phenomenal world. Martha is a "living example" of the reality of recovery!

SUMMARY

Historical and current research evidence pertaining to the effectiveness of a diversity of treatments for a diversity of addictions and substance use disorders indicates that many addictive persons benefit from involvement in a variety of "treatments." Orford (1985) reports that the success rate of treatments for obesity, alcohol problems, smoking, and other forms of substance abuse ranges between 20 and 45 percent 6-12 months after treatment. As noted in this chapter, it is also clear that there is no specific treatment modality that is most effective with all alcoholics, bulimics, or other subpopulations of chemically dependent persons.

Treatment outcome effectiveness data pertaining to compulsive gamblers, sex addicts, cocaine or "crack" addicts, and marijuana addicts are generally lacking. It is estimated (Knauert, 1989) that treatment proves efficacious in at least 25 percent of cases involving cocaine and polydrug dependence. Most clinicians believe (Forrest, 1990, 1992) that polydrug and "crack" addicted persons are more difficult to treat than "pure" alcoholics and other persons who manifest one addiction. However, it is also becoming increasingly apparent (Forrest, 1983; Lasater, 1988) that most chemically dependent patients and/or substance abusers have multiple addictions.

There are virtually no comparative treatment outcome effectiveness studies available that involve substantial numbers of chemically dependent and/or substance abusing antisocial patients, nonchemically dependent antisocial patients, and nonantisocial chemically dependent patients and substance abusers. Several studies (Ross and Lightfoot, 1985) were reviewed which indicate that treatment is generally beneficial for incarcerated alcoholics and chemically dependent persons.

The historical treatment prognosis for ASPD has been very poor. Chornyak (1941) concluded that "psychopathy is untreatable." More recently, Suedfeld and Landon (1978) report that the results of different treatments for the problem of psychopathy are "not much to show for the amount of money, time, and effort spent." Contemporary clinicians (Yochelson and Samenow, 1986; Reid et al., 1986; Doren, 1987; Forrest, 1989b) are not optimistic about the treatment prognosis of antisocial personalities.

The relapse syndrome and a relapse prevention model were delineated in this chapter. Relapse is an essential characteristic of all addictive diseases and obsessive-compulsive disorders. The antisocial acting-out of the psychopath who has been involved in a comprehensive treatment program was conceptualized as a "relapse" in this chapter.

Behavioral scientists (Mumey, 1984; Brown, 1988, 1990) are becoming increasingly cognizant of the realities of recovery from alcoholism and chemical dependency. Total drug abstinence is the basic precursor or gateway to recovery for alcoholics and chemically dependent persons. Three stages of the recovery process were outlined in the chapter. Recovering addicts become more fully functioning. These people also learn to think more rationally, and they behave more responsibly. Recovery fosters the development of a better integrated identity. Indeed, the self is restored, or actually develops, vis à vis the recovery process. Recovery also fosters the capacity for intimacy, relationship, and love. Many chemically dependent persons are able to establish a healthy sexual adjustment style as they enter the middle and later stages of the recovery process. Many chemically dependent patients become more self-actualizing in recovery. The characteristics of self-actualized persons (Maslow, 1954) were listed in the chapter. Finally, it was emphasized that recovery is always an individual matter, and a case study was presented to demonstrate this reality.

It is important for therapists, as well as chemically dependent persons, to remember that treatment and recovery are one-day-at-a-time, lifelong processes!

Chapter XIV

Conclusion to Section Two

Section One addressed the assessment and diagnosis, differential diagnoses, and concurrent diagnosis of substance use disorder and antisocial personality disorder. Section Two addressed the treatment of substance use disorder with concurrent antisocial personality disorder.

Clinicians and mental health workers have a long history of avoiding the treatment of chemically dependent and antisocial patients. However, this historical mental health stance changed rather radically in the late 1970s and early 1980s when the behavioral science professions became actively involved in the treatment of chemical dependency and the substance use disorders. During the decade of the 1990s, the behavioral science professions will become significantly more involved in the treatment of antisocial patients as well as antisocial persons who manifest concurrent substance use disorder.

Counselors and therapists who work in correctional and prison settings have long known that offender populations include a high percentage of antisocial individuals who manifest a concurrent substance use disorder. The author indicates that between 70 and 85 percent of incarcerated offenders are chemically dependent and/or manifest a substance use disorder in combination with antisocial personality disorder. Recently, many correctional facilities have initiated some form of chemical dependency treatment program for inmates who have a history of alcohol and/or other drug-related problems.

This text examines many of the most difficult and clinically problematic issues that are associated with the psychotherapy and rehabilitation of chemically dependent and/or substance abusing antisocial patients: resistance, structure, transference and counter-transference, treatment models within the correctional setting, the therapeutic alliance, clinical management and assessment of dangerouness, abstinence, cognitive-behavioral treatment strategies, treatment format and duration, relapse, treatment outcome effectiveness, recovery, and self-help alternatives. Chapter VIII addressed the various difficulties and dilemmas associated with the psychotherapy and treatment of chemically dependent patients with concurrent antisocial personality disorders. Chapter IX evaluated the uses of structure in the treatment of chemically dependent persons with impulse control problems. Chapter X examined all facets of the treatment of chemically dependent or substance abusing inmates within correctional settings. The therapist-patient relationship was examined in depth in Chapter XI, and Chapter XII addressed the assessment and treatment of dangerous patients. Treatment outcome effectiveness, relapse, and recovery were discussed in the final chapter of the text.

The chemically dependent patient with concurrent antisocial personality disorder is more difficult to treat than patients who are simply substance abusers or chemically dependent (Nace, 1990; Forrest, 1991, 1992). These "dually-diagnosed" patients present myriad problems for corrections counselors, residential chemical dependency counselors, mental health clinicians, and even private therapists. This patient population is poorly understood, misdiagnosed, and undertreated or treated inappropriately. The in-depth treatment strategies and information in this text will greatly enhance the treatment effectiveness of all clinicians who work with this difficult population.

Chemically dependent or substance abusing antisocial personalities need to be involved in highly structured, long-term, multifaceted treatment programs that address the patient's substance use disorder as well as his or her severe personality disorder. Among incarcerated populations chemically dependent inmates remain highly recidivistic in the absence of drug/alcohol abstinence and effective chemical dependency treatment. Substance abuse and chemical dependency synergize the acting-out and antisocial behaviors of *all* persons. Thus, early diagnosis and effective chemical dependency treatment are essential deterrents to antisocial acting-out upon the part of countless number of substance abusing persons.

This book represents a major contribution to the chemical dependency treatment field. However, it is only a beginning point in the evolution of the development of more effective treatment programs for chemically dependent and substance abusing antisocial personalities. A great deal of further research is needed in every area of chemical dependency and antisocial personality disorder. Effective treatment programs for substance abusers and chemically dependent persons are only now beginning to be utilized with significant numbers of concurrently antisocial persons. Longitudinal research, studies of differential treatments and programs, genetic and biophysiologic studies, interactive investigations of criminal behavior and substance abuse, studies of duration and intensity of treatment, and hundreds of other areas of investigation need to be conducted.

Incarceration is a very ineffective form of treatment or rehabilitation for the vast majority of substance abusing persons with concurrent antisocial personality disorder. Yet, effective treatment programs for incarcerated chemically dependent and substance abusing offenders can result in a significant reduction in all forms of future antisocial acting-out upon the inmates who are involved in these treatment programs. Psychotherapy and treatment can also be effective deterrents to incarceration for thousands of substance abusers who may or may not manifest a concurrent antisocial personality disorder.

This section has shown the reader how and why treatment can be effective with substance abusers and chemically dependent persons who manifest concurrent antisocial personality disorder.

Bibliography

Abrams, D. B. and R. S. Nianura. "Social Learning Theory." In: *Psychological Theories of Drinking and Alcoholism*, edited by H. T. Blane and K. E. Leonard. The Guilford Press: New York, 1987.

Adams, S. "A Way Out of the Rhetoric." *Rehabilitation Recidivism and Research*, National Council on Crime and Delinquency, 1976.

Alcoholics Anonymous. Alcoholics Anonymous World Service, Inc.: New York, 1939.

Alexander, F. M. *Psychoanalysis and Psychotherapy*. W. W. Norton: New York, New York, 1956.

American Psychiatric Association (APA). Diagnostic and Statistical Manual of Mental Disorders (DSM III). Washington, DC, 1980.

American Psychiatric Association (APA). Diagnostic and Statistical Manual of Mental Disorders (DSM III-R). Washington, DC, 1987.

Anderson, J. "Developing Patient Motivation and Readiness for Treatment," presented at Psychotherapy Associates, P.C., 15th Annual Advanced International Winter Symposium on the Treatment of Addictive Disorders, Colorado Springs, Colorado. February 7, 1989.

Annis, H. and R. G. Smart. "Arrests, Readmissions and Treatment Following Release from Detoxification Centers." *Journal of Studies on Alcohol* 39, pp. 1276-1283. 1978.

Annis, M. "Group Treatment and Incarcerated Offenders with Alcohol and Drug Problems: A Controlled Evaluation." *Canadian Journal of Criminology 21*, pp. 3-15. 1979.

Annis, N. M. and D. Chan. "Differential Treatment Assignment: Empirical Evidence from a Typology of Adult Offenders." *Criminal Justice and Behavior 10*, pp. 159-173. 1983.

Armor, D. J., J. M. Polich and H. B. Stambul. *Alcohol and Treatment*. Rand Corporation, Santa Monica, California, 1976.

Armor, D. J., J. M. Polich, and H. B. Stambul. *Alcoholism and Treatment: A Rand Corporation Research Study*. Wiley: New York, 1978.

Bailey, W. C. "Correctional Outcome: An Evaluation of 100 Reports." *Journal of Criminology and Police Science 57*, pp. 153-160. 1966.

Baker, E. F. *Man in the Trap*. The Macmillan Co.: New York, 1967.

Ball, J. H. and C. W. Weis. "Police Officers as Community Organizers." *Police Chief 18*, pp. 46-47. 1976.

Bandura, A. *Principles of Behavior Modification*. Holt, Rinehart, and Winston: New York, 1969.

Banks, R. E. "Alcoholism and Violent Behavior," presented at Psychotherapy Associates, P. C., 11th Annual Advanced International Winter Symposium on the Treatment of Addictive Disorders, Colorado Springs, February 1, 1985.

Barefoot vs. Estelle (1983). 77L. Ed. 2d. 1090.

Bean, M. H. and N. E. Zinberg. *Dynamic Approaches to the Understanding and Treatment of Alcoholism.* Free Press: New York, 1981.

Beck, A. T. *Cognitive Therapy and the Emotional Disorders.* International Universities Press: New York, 1976.

Beck, J. C. "When the Patient Threatens Violence: An Empirical Study of Clinical Practice after *Tarasoff.*" *Bulletin of the American Academy of Psychiatry and the Law 10,* pp. 189-201. 1982.

Bell, T. "Treatment of Adolescent Alcoholism and Substance Abuse," presented at Psychotherapy Associates, P.C., 17th Annual Advanced International Winter Symposium on the Treatment of Addictive Disorders, Colorado Springs, February 3, 1991.

Bender, L. "Psychopathic Behavior Disorders in Children." In *Handbook of Correctional Psychology,* edited by R. Lindler and R. Seliger. Philosophical Library: New York, 1947.

Bender, L. "Drug Addiction in Adolescence," *Comprehensive Psychiatry 4,* pp. 181-194. 1963.

Berglas, S. "Self-Handicapping Model." In *Psychological Theories of Drinking and Alcoholism,* edited by H. T. Blane and K. E. Leonard. The Guilford Press: New York, 1987.

Bernstein, D. "The Modification of Smoking Behavior: An Evaluative Report." In *Learning Mechanisms in Smoking,* edited by W. Hunt. Aldine: Chicago, 1970.

Bernstein, D. and A. McAllister. "The Modification of Smoking Behavior: Progress and Problems." *Addictive Behaviors 1,* pp. 89-102, 1976.

Black, C. *It Will Never Happen to Me.* M.A.C.: Denver, 1981.

Blackman, N., J. M. A. Weiss, and J. W. Lamberti. "The Sudden Murder." *Arch. General Psychiatry 8,* pp. 289-294. 1963.

Blakely, C. H., W. S. Davidson, C. A. Saylor, and M. J. Robinson. "Kentfield's Rehabilitation Program: Ten Years Later." In *Effective Correctional Treatment,* edited by R. R. Ross and P. Gendreau. Butterworth: Toronto, 1980.

Blane, H. T. *The Personality of the Alcoholic: Guises of Dependency.* Harper and Row: New York, 1968.

Blane, H. T. and K. E. Leonard, eds. *Psychological Theories of Drinking and Alcoholism.* The Guilford Press: New York, 1987.

Blum, E. and R. Blum. *Alcoholism: Modern Psychological Approaches to Treatment.* Jossey-Bass: San Francisco, 1969.

Blumstein, A., J. Cohen, and E. Nagin, eds. *Deterrence and Incapacitation: Estimating the Effects of Criminal Sanctions on Crime Rates.* National Academy of Sciences: Washington, DC, 1978.

Bohman, M. "Alcoholism and Crime: Studies of Adoptees." *Substance Alcohol Actions Misuse 4,* pp. 137-147. 1983.

Booth, L. "Say Yes to Life: Positive Attitudes in Recovery," presented at Psychotherapy Associates, P. C., 15th Annual Advanced International Winter Symposium on the Treatment of Addictive Disorders, Colorado Springs, February 8, 1989.

Booth, L. "Discovering our Potential for Living and Loving in Recovery," presented at Psychotherapy Associates, P. C., 16th Annual Advanced International Winter Symposium on the Treatment of Addictive Disorders, Colorado Springs, February 7, 1990.

Bourne, P. G. and E. Light. "Alcohol Problems in Blacks and Women." In *The Diagnosis and Treatment of Alcoholism*, edited by J. H. Mendelson and N. K. Mello. McGraw-Hill: New York, 1979.

Bowen, M. *Family Therapy in Clinical Practice*. Jason Aronson: New York, 1978.

Brandsma, J. M. and M. C. Maultsby. "The Court-Probated Alcoholic and Outpatient Treatment Attrition." *British Journal of Addiction 72*, pp. 23-30. 1977.

Brantley, P. J. and P. B. Sutker. "Antisocial Behavior Disorders." In *Comprehensive Handbook of Psychopathology*, edited by H. E. Adams and P. B. Sutker. Plenum Press: New York, 1984.

Bratter, T. E. "Advanced Reality Therapy Techniques in the Treatment of Alcoholism and Substance Abuse," presented at Psychotherapy Associates, P. C., 6th Annual Advanced International Winter Workshop, "Treatment and Rehabilitation of the Alcoholic," Colorado Springs, February 5, 1980.

Bratter, T. E. "The Psychotherapist as a Twelve-Step Worker in the Treatment of Alcoholism." In *Alcoholism and Health*, edited by S. V. Davidson. Aspen: Germantown, Maryland, 1980.

Bratter, T. E. "Special Clinical Psychotherapeutic Concerns for Alcoholic and Drug-Addicted Individuals." In *Alcoholism and Substance Abuse: Strategies for Clinical Intervention*, edited by T. E. Bratter and G. G. Forrest. Free Press: New York, 1985.

Bratter, T.E. and G.G. Forrest, eds. *Alcoholism and Substance Abuse: Strategies for Clinical Intervention*. Free Press: New York. 1985.

Bratter, T. E., M. C. Pennacchia and D. C. Gauya. "From Methadone Maintenance to Abstinence: The Myth of the Metabolic Disorder Theory." In *Alcoholism and Substance Abuse: Strategies for Clinical Intervention*, edited by T. E. Bratter and G. G. Forrest. Free Press: New York, 1985.

Brecher, E. M., and the editors of Consumer Reports. *Licit and Illicit Drugs*. Little, Brown: Boston, 1972.

Brown, S. *Treating the Alcoholic: A Developmental Model of Recovery*. John Wiley and Sons: New York, 1985.

Brown, S. *Treating Adult Children of Alcoholics: A Developmental Perspective*. John Wiley and Sons: New York, 1988.

Brown, S. "Assessment and Treatment of Adult Children of Alcoholics," presented at Psychotherapy Associates, P. C., 16th Annual Advanced International Winter Symposium on the Treatment of Addictive Disorders, Colorado Springs, February 5, 1990.

Brown, S. "Psychotherapy and ACAs: An Integrated Model for Assessment and Treatment," presented at Psychotherapy Associates, P. C., 16th Annual Advanced International Winter Symposium on the Treatment of Addictive Disorders, Colorado Springs, February 5, 1990.

Burke, S. *Alcohol Use and Its Relationship to Involvement with the Provincial Court (Family Diversion), Judicial District of York (Etobicoke)*. Etobicoke Family Court Committee: Islington, Ontario, 1977.

Burns, T. "Working With Parents of Adolescent Abusers," presented at Psychotherapy Associates, P. C., 13th Annual Advanced International Winter Symposium on the Treatment of Addictive Disorders, Colorado Springs, February 3, 1987.

Burt, M. R., B. S. Brown, and R. L. DuPont. "Follow-Up of Former Clients of a Large Multi-Modality Drug Treatment Program." *International Journal of the Addictions 15*, pp. 391-408. 1980.

Buss, A. H. *Psychopathology*. Wiley: New York, 1966.

Cadoret, R. J. "Genes, Environment and Their Interaction in The Development of Psychopathology. In *Genetic Aspects of Human Behavior*, edited by J. Sakai and T. Tsuboi. Aino Hospital Foundation: Toyko and New York, 1985.

Cadoret, R. J. "Epidemiology of Antisocial Personality." *Unmasking The Psychopath: Antisocial Personality and Related Syndromes*, edited by W. H. Reid, D. Dorr, J.I. Walker, and J.W. Bonner. W. W. Norton and Co.: New York, 1986.

Cadoret, R. J. and C. Cain. "Environmental and Genetic Factors in Predicting Adolescent Antisocial Behavior in Adoptees." *Psychiatric Journal of University of Ottawa 6*, pp. 220-225. 1981.

Cadoret, R. J., C. A. Cain and W. M. Grove. "Development of Alcoholism in Adoptees Raised Apart from Alcoholic Biologic Parents." *Arch. General Psychiatry 37*, pp. 561-563. 1980.

Cadoret, R. J., T. O'Gorman, E. Troughton, and E. Haywood, "Alcoholism and Antisocial Personality: Interrelationships, Genetic and Environmental Factors." *Arch. General Psychiatry 42*, pp. 161-167, 1985.

Cahalan, D. "Subcultural Differences in Drinking Behavior in U. S. National Surveys and Selected European Studies." In *Alcoholism: New Directions in Behavioral Research and Treatment*, edited by P. E. Nathan and G. A. Marlatt. Plenum Press: New York, 1978.

Cappell, H. and J. Greeley. "Alcohol and Tension Reduction: An Update on Research." In *Psychological Theories of Drinking and Alcoholism*, edited by H. T. Blane and K. E. Leonard. The Guilford Press: New York, 1987.

Cappell, H. and C. P. Herman. "Alcohol and Tension Reduction: A Review." *Journal of Studies on Alcoholism 33*, pp. 33-64. 1972.

Carnes, P. *Out of the Shadows*. Comp. Care: Minneapolis, 1985.

Caster, D. U. and O. A. Parsons. "Relationship of Depression, Sociopathy, and Locus of Control to Treatment Outcome in Alcoholics." *Journal of Consult. and Clinical Psych. 45*, pp. 751-756. 1977.

Chavez, R. "Hispanic Alcoholism and Substance Abuse," presented at Psychotherapy Associates, P. C., 17th Annual Advanced International Winter Symposium on the Treatment of Addictive Disorders, Colorado Springs, February 6, 1991.

Chornyak, J. "Some Remarks on the Diagnosis of the Psychopathic Delinquent." *American Journal of Psychiatry 97*, pp. 1327-1331. 1941.

Christie, R. and F. Geis. "Some Consequences of Taking Machiavelli Seriously." In *Current Perspectives in Social Psychology*, edited by E. P. Hollander and R. G. Hunt. Oxford University Press: New York, 1976.

Cleckley, H. "Psychopathic States." In *American Handbook of Psychiatry*. Basic Books: New York, 1959.

Cleckley, H. *The Mask of Sanity*. C. V. Mosby: St. Louis, 1941 (1st printing), 1976 (5th printing).

Cloninger, C. R. "Genetic and Environmental Factors in the Development of Alcoholism." *Journal of Psychiatric Treatment and Evaluation 5*, pp. 487-496. 1983.

Cloninger, C. R., M. Bohman, and S. Siguardsson. "Inheritance of Alcohol Abuse: Cross-Fostering Analysis of Adopted Men." *Arch. General Psychiatry 38,* pp. 861-868, 1981.

Cloninger, C. R., T. Reich, and S. B. Guze. "Genetic-Environmental Interactions and Antisocial Behavior." In *Psychopathic Behavior: Approaches to Research*, edited by R. D. Hare and D. Schalling. Wiley: Chichester, England, 1978.

Cocozza, J. J. and H. J. Steadman. "Prediction in Psychiatry: An Example of Misplaced Confidence in Experts." *Social Problems 25*, pp. 265-276, 1978.

Costello, R. M., J. E. Bechtel, and M. B. Giffen. "A Community's Efforts to Attack the Problem of Alcoholism." *International Journal of Addiction 8*(6), pp. 875-888. 1973.

Costello, R. M., M. B. Giffen, S. L. Schneider, P. W. Edington, and K. R. Mandees. "Comprehensive Alcohol Treatment Planning, Implementation and Evaluation." *International Journal of Addictions 11*, pp. 553-570. 1976.

Cowen, R. J. and M. Nittman. "Treatment Outcome Effectiveness of EAP Programs." Paper, Mountain Bell: Colorado Springs, 1983.

Cox, S. G. "Rational Behavior Training as a Rehabilitative Program for Alcoholic Offenders." *Offender Rehabilitation 3*(3), pp. 245-256. 1976.

Cox, W. M. "Personality Theory and Research." In *Psychological Theories of Drinking and Alcoholism*, edited by H. T. Blane and K. E. Leonard. The Guilford Press: New York, 1987.

Crawford, J. J. and A. B. Chalupsky. "The Reported Evaluation of Alcoholism Treatment, 1968-71: A Methodological Review." *Addictive Behaviors 2*, pp. 63-74. 1977.

Crothers, T. D. "Some New Studies of The Opium Disease." *Journal of American Medical Association 18*, pp. 227-230. 1891.

Crowe, R. "An Adoption Study of Antisocial Personality." *Arch. General Psychiatry 31*, pp. 785-791. 1974.

Dahlstrom, W. G. and G. S. Welsh. *An MMPI Handbook*. University of Minnesota Press: Minneapolis, 1960.

Darling, H. F. "Definition of Psychopathic Personality." *Journal of Nervous and Mental Disease 101*, pp. 121-126. 1945.

Della-Giustina, V. E. and G. G. Forrest. "Depression and The Dentist." *Georgia Journal of Dentistry*, pp. 15-17, August 1979.

Doren, D. M. *Understanding and Treating the Psychopath*. John Wiley and Sons: New York, 1987.

Dornbush, D. and P. J. Fink. "Recent Trends in Substance Abuse." *International Journal of the Addictions 2*, pp. 143-151. 1977.

Drake, R. E. and G. E. Vaillant. "A Validity Study of Axis II of DSM III." *American Journal of Psychiatry 142(5)*, May 1985, pp. 553-558.

DuBois, C. *The People of Alor*. University of Minnesota Press: Minneapolis, 1944.

Dumont, M. D. "Methadone Maintenance? It's More Than a Clinical Question." *Medical Insight 4*, p. 43. 1972.

Edwards, G. and S. Guthrie. "A Controlled Trial of In-Patient and Out-Patient Treatment of Alcohol Dependence." *Lancet I*, pp. 555-559. 1967.

Eisenstadt, P. "Treatment of Addicted Sex Offenders," presented at Psychotherapy Associates, P. C., 15th Annual Advanced International Winter Symposium on the Treatment of Addictive Disorders, Colorado Springs, February 7, 1989.

Eisenstadt, P. "Treatment of Chronically Dependent Sex Offenders," presented at Psychotherapy Associates, P. C., 18th Annual Advanced International Winter Symposium on the Treatment of Addictive Disorders, Colorado Springs, February 5, 1992.

Elliott, S. "The Implications of Follow-up Data for Current Conceptions of Obesity and its Treatment," presented at the Annual Conference of the British Psychological Society, Exeter, England, April 1977.

Ellis, A. "Rational-Emotive Therapy Training," presented at Psychotherapy Associates, P. C., 5th Annual Advanced International Winter Workshop, "Treatment and Rehabilitation of the Alcoholic," Colorado Springs, February 1, 1979.

Ellis, A. "Rational Emotive Therapy Training," presented at Psychotherapy Associates, P. C., 16th Annual Advanced International Winter Symposium on the Treatment of Addictive Disorders, Colorado Springs, February 8, 1990.

Ellis, A. and R. Harper. *A Guide to Rational Living*. Prentice-Hall, Inc.: Englewood Cliffs, New Jersey, 1961.

Emrick, C. D. "A Review of Psychologically-Oriented Treatment of Alcoholism: I. The Use and Interrelationships of Outcome Criteria and Drinking Behavior Following Treatment." *Quarterly Journal of Studies on Alcoholism 35*, pp. 523-549. 1974.

Emrick, C. D. "A Review of Psychologically-Oriented Treatment of Alcoholism: II. Effectiveness of Treatment Versus No Treatment." *Journal of Studies on Alcoholism 36*, pp. 88-108. 1975.

Emrick, C. D. "Perspectives in Clinical Research: Relative Effectiveness of Alcohol Abuse Treatment." *Family and Community Health 2(2)*, pp. 71-88. 1979.

Emrick, C. D. "Alcoholism Treatment Effectiveness: What Works Best for

Whom?" presented at Psychotherapy Associates, P. C., 12th Annual Advanced International Winter Symposium, "Treatment of Addictive Disorders," Colorado Springs, February 3, 1986.

Emrick, C. D. "Contemporary Issues in the Evaluation and Treatment of Alcohol Problems," presented at Psychotherapy Associates, P. C., 16th Annual Advanced International Winter Symposium on the Treatment of Addictive Disorders, Colorado Springs, February 8, 1990.

Emrick, C. D. "The Assessment and Treatment of Alcohol and Drug Problems: Special Emphasis on Community-Based and Self-Help Resources," presented at Psychotherapy Associates, P. C., 17th Annual Advanced International Winter Symposium on the Treatment of Addictive Disorders, Colorado Springs, February 5, 1991.

Emrick, C. D. and J. Hansen. "Assertions Regarding Effectiveness of Treatment for Alcoholism: Fact or Fantasy?" *American Psychologist*, pp. 1078-1088, October 1983.

Ends, E. J. and C. W. Page. "Group Psychotherapy and Concomitant Psychological Change." *Psychological Monographs 73*(480), 1959.

Ennis, B. J. and R. Emery. *The Rights of Mental Patients*. Avon: New York, 1978.

Evans, J. and L. E. Wellman. "Applied Social Learning Theory." In *The Diagnosis and Treatment of Alcoholism (Rev. 2nd Edition)*, edited by G. G. Forrest. Charles C Thomas: Springfield, Illinois, 1978.

Eysenck, H. J. *Crime and Personality*. Methuen: London, 1964.

Eysenck, H. J. and S. B. G. Eysenck. "Psychopathy, Personality, and Genetics." In *Psychopathic Behavior: Approaches to Research*, edited by R. D. Hare and D. Schalling. Wiley: Chichester, England, 1978.

Fenichel, O. *The Psychoanalytic Theory of Neurosis*. W. W. Norton: New York, 1945.

Field, M. "Maternal Attitudes Found in 23 Cases of Children With Primary Behavior Disorder." *American Journal of Ortho-Psychiatry 10*, pp. 293-311. 1940.

Fishman, R. *Criminal Recidivism in New York City*. Praeger: New York, 1977.

Foreyt, J. and R. Frohwirth. "Introduction." In *Behavioral Treatments of Obesity*, edited by J. Foreyt. Pergamon: Oxford, 1977.

Forrest, G. G. *The Diagnosis and Treatment of Alcoholism*. Charles C Thomas: Springfield, Illinois, 1975.

Forrest, G. G. *The Diagnosis and Treatment of Alcoholism*. Rev. 2nd ed., Charles C Thomas: Springfield, Illinois, 1978.

Forrest, G. G. "Setting Alcoholics Up for Therapeutic Failure." *Family and Community Health 2*(2), pp. 59-64. 1979.

Forrest, G. G. *How to Live With a Problem Drinker and Survive*. Atheneum: New York, 1980, 1986 (pbk).

Forrest, G. G. *Confrontation in Psychotherapy with Alcoholics*. Learning Publications, Inc.: Holmes Beach, Florida, 1982.

Forrest, G. G. *Alcoholism, Narcissism and Psychopathology*. Charles C Thomas: Springfield, Illinois, 1983(a).

Forrest, G. G. *Alcoholism and Human Sexuality.* Charles C Thomas: Springfield, Illinois, 1983(b).

Forrest, G. G. *Intensive Psychotherapy of Alcoholism.* Charles C Thomas: Springfield, Illinois, 1984(a).

Forrest, G. G. *How to Cope with a Teenage Drinker: New Alternatives and Hope for Parents and Families.* Fawcett-Crest: New York, 1984(b).

Forrest, G. G. "Psychotherapy of Alcoholism and Substance Abuse: Outcome Assessment Revisited." *Family and Community Health: The Journal of Health Promotion and Maintenance,* p. 40, August 1984(c).

Forrest, G. G. "Psychodynamically Oriented Treatment of Alcoholism and Substance Abuse." In *Alcoholism and Substance Abuse: Strategies for Clinical Intervention,* edited by T. E. Bratter and G. G. Forrest. Free Press: New York, 1985(a).

Forrest, G. G. "Behavioral Contracting in Psychotherapy with Alcoholics." In *Alcoholism and Substance Abuse: Strategies for Clinical Intervention,* edited by T. E. Bratter and G. G. Forrest. Free Press: New York, 1985(b).

Forrest, G. G. "Antabuse Treatment." In *Alcoholism and Substance Abuse: Strategies for Clinical Intervention,* edited by T. E. Bratter and G. G. Forrest. Free Press: New York, 1985(c).

Forrest, G. G. "Intimacy, Sex, and Love Dynamics in Addictions Psychotherapy," presented at Psychotherapy Associates, P. C., 13th Annual Advanced International Winter Symposium on the Treatment of Addictive Disorders, Colorado Springs, February 4, 1987.

Forrest, G. G. *Guidelines for Responsible Drinking.* Charles C Thomas: Springfield, Illinois, 1989(a).

Forrest, G. G. "Therapist-Patient Relationship Dynamics in the Psychotherapy of Substance Abusers and Addicted Psychopaths," presented at Psychotherapy Associates, P. C., 15th Annual Advanced International Winter Symposium on the Treatment of Addictive Disorders, Colorado Springs, February 8, 1989(b)

Forrest, G. G. "Common Sexual Problems in Chemically Dependent Clients," presented at 31st International Summer School of Alcohol Studies, University of North Dakota, Grand Forks, July 19, 1989(c).

Forrest, G. G. "Clinical Management of Substance Abusing Psychopaths," presented at Psychotherapy Associates, P. C., 16th Annual Advanced International Winter Symposium on the Treatment of Addictive Disorders, Colorado Springs, February 8, 1990.

Forrest, G. G. "Intensive Psychotherapy of Alcoholism," presented at Psychotherapy Associates, P. C., 17th Annual Advanced International Winter Symposium on the Treatment of Addictive Disorders, Colorado Springs, February 6, 1991.

Forrest, G. G. "Role Slippage and Adaptation in the Alcoholic Family System." *Family Dynamics of Addiction Quarterly, I*(3), pp. 31-39. 1991.

Forrest, G. G. "Managing the Dual-Diagnosis Patient: Chemical Dependency and Persistent and Chronic Severe Mental Illness," presented at Prairie View, Inc. Psychiatric Hospital, Newton, Kansas, March 26, 1992.

Forrest, G. G. and R. Gordon. *Substance Abuse, Homicide, and Violent Behavior.* Gardner Press: New York, 1990.

Frances, R. J., S. Timm, and S. Bucky. "Studies of Familial and Nonfamilial Alcoholism." *Arch. General Psychiatry 37*, pp. 564-566. 1980.

Freud, S. *Collected Papers*, Vol. I. Translated by J. Riviere. International Psychoanalytic Press: London, 1924.

Freudenberger, H. J. *The Hazards of Being a Psychoanalyst. Psychoanalytic Review 66*, (22), 1979.

Freudenberger, H. J. *Burnout: How to Beat the High Lust of Success.* Bantam Books: New York, 1981.

Freudenberger, H. J. "Burnout and Job Dissatisfaction: Impact on the Family." *Perspectives on Work and the Family*, edited by J. C. Hansen. Aspen Publications: Rockville, Maryland, 1984.

Friedman, A. S., E. Pomerance, R. Sanders, Y. Santo, and A. Utada, "The Structure and Problems of the Families of Adolescent Drug Abusers." *Contemporary Drug Problems 9*, pp. 327-356. 1980.

Fromm-Reichmann, F. *Principles of Intensive Psychotherapy.* University of Chicago Press: Chicago, 1949.

Fuller, R. K. and W. D. Williford. "Life-Table Analysis of Abstinence in a Study Evaluating the Efficacy of Disulfiram." *Alcoholism: Clinical and Experimental Research 4*, pp. 298-301. 1980.

Gendreau, P., and R. R. Ross. "Correctional Potency: Treatment and Deterrence on Trial." In *Evaluation and Criminal Justice Policy*, edited by R. Roesch and R. R. Corrado. Sage: Beverly Hills, 1981.

Gilberstadt, H. and J. Duker. *A Handbook for Clinical and Actuarial MMPI Interpretation.* Saunders: Philadelphia, 1965.

Gilbert, J. G. and D. N. Lombardi. "Personality Characteristics of Young Male Narcotic Addicts." *Journal of Consult. Psych. 31*, pp. 536-538. 1967.

Gitlow, S. E. and H. S. Peyser. *Alcoholism: A Practical Treatment Guide.* Grune and Stratton: New York, 1980.

Glasser, W. *Reality Therapy: A New Approach to Psychiatry.* Harper and Row: New York, 1965.

Glueck, B. "A Study of 608 Admissions to Sing Sing Prison." *Mental Hygiene II*, pp. 85-151. 1918.

Glueck, B., and E. Glueck. *Physique and Delinquency.* Harpers: New York, 1956.

Gold, M. S. and A. C. Pottash. "Neurobiological Aspects of Opiate Addiction and Withdrawal." In *Etiological Aspects of Alcohol and Drug Abuse*, edited by E. Gottheil, K. A. Druley, T. E. Skoloda, and H. M. Waxman. Charles C Thomas: Springfield, Illinois, 1983.

Goldberg, C. "Cognitive-Behavioral Therapy of Eating Disorders," presented at Psychotherapy Associates, P. C., 15th Annual Advanced International Winter Symposium on the Treatment of Addictive Disorders, Colorado Springs, February 8, 1989.

Goldman, M. S., S. A. Brown, and B. A. Christensen. "Expectancy Theory: Thinking About Drinking." In *Psychological Theories of Drinking and Alco-*

holism, edited by H. T. Blane and K. E. Leonard. The Guilford Press: New York, 1987.

Goodwin, D. W. "The Genetics of Alcoholism." In *Etiological Aspects of Alcohol and Drug Abuse* edited by E. Gottheil, K. A. Druley, T. E. Skoloda, and H. M. Waxman. Charles C Thomas: Springfield, Illinois, 1983.

Goodwin, D. W., F. Schulsinger, and N. Molster. "Drinking Problems in Adopted and Nonadopted Sons of Alcoholics." *Arch. General Psychiatry 31*, pp. 164-169. 1974.

Goodwin, D. W., F. Schulsinger, J. Knop, S. Mednick and S. B. Guze. "Psychopathology in Adopted and Nonadopted Daughters of Alcoholics." *Arch. General Psychiatry 34*, pp. 1005-1009. 1977.

Gorski, T. T. "Relapse Prevention Training," presented at Psychotherapy Associates, P. C., 16th Annual Advanced International Winter Symposium on the Treatment of Addictive Disorders, Colorado Springs, February 7, 1990.

Gorski, T. T. "Cocaine Craving and Relapse Prevention," presented at Psychotherapy Associates, P. C., 17th Annual Advanced International Winter Symposium on the Treatment of Addictive Disorders, Colorado Springs, February 6, 1991.

Gorski, T. T. "Relapse Prevention Training," presented at Psychotherapy Associates, P. C., 17th Annual Advanced International Winter Symposium on the Treatment of Addictive Disorders, Colorado Springs, February 6, 1991.

Gorski, T. T. and M. Miller. *Staying Sober: A Guide for Relapse Prevention.* Independence Press: Independence, Missouri, 1986.

Gottfredson, M. R. "Treatment Destruction Techniques," In *Effective Correctional Treatment*, edited by R. R. Ross and P. Gendreau (Eds.). Butterworth: Toronto, Canada, 1980.

Gottheil, E., K. A. Druley, T. E. Skoloda, and H. M. Waxman. *Etiologic Aspects of Alcohol and Drug Abuse.* Charles C Thomas: Springfield, Illinois, 1983.

Gottlieb, J. S., M. C. Ashley, and J. R. Knott. "Primary Behavior Disorders and the Psychopathic Personality." *Arch. of Neurology and Psychiatry 56*, pp. 381-400. 1946.

Gough, H. G. "A Sociological Theory of Psychopathy." *American Journal of Sociology 53*, pp. 359-366. 1948.

Gust, T. "Substance Abuse and Traumatic Brain Injury," presented at Psychotherapy Associates, P. C., 15th Annual Advanced International Winter Symposium on the Treatment of Addictive Disorders, Colorado Springs, February 7, 1989.

Gust, T. "Neuropsychological Factors in the Assessment of Treatment of Substance Abusers," presented at Psychotherapy Associates, P. C., 18th Annual Advanced International Winter Symposium on the Treatment of Addictive Disorders, Colorado Springs, February 3, 1992.

Guze, S. B., D. W. Goodwin, and J. B. Crane. "A Psychiatric Study of the Wives of Convicted Felons: An Example of Assortative Mating." *American Journal of Psychiatry 126*, pp. 1773-1776. 1970.

Hagan, J. *Deterrence Reconsidered: Methodological Innovations.* Sage: Beverly Hills, 1982.

Haggard, H. W. "Critique of the Allergic Nature of Alcohol Addiction." *Quarterly Journal of Studies on Alcoholism 4*, pp. 233-241. 1944.

Hall, R. W. "Alternative to the Criminality of Driving While Intoxicated." *Journal of Police Science and Administration 5*(2), pp. 138-144. 1977.

Halleck, S. L. and A. D. Witte. "Is Rehabilitation Dead?" *Crime and Delinquency 23*, pp. 371-381. 1977.

Hamilton, J. R. "Evaluation of a Detoxification Service for Habitual Drunken Offenders." *British Journal of Psychiatry 135*, pp. 28-34. 1977.

Hansen, A. A. "Effectiveness of Alcoholics Anonymous in the Treatment of Incarcerated Offenders," personal communication, Colorado Springs, February 10, 1990.

Hansen, A. A. "Addiction Recovery in Prison," presented at Psychotherapy Associates, P. C., 17th Annual Advanced International Winter Symposium on the Treatment of Addictive Disorders, Colorado Springs, February 7, 1991.

Hare, R. D. *Psychopathy: Theory and Research.* Wiley: New York, 1970.

Harper, R. A. "Use of Stories and Metaphors in Psychotherapy," presented at Psychotherapy Associates, P. C., 12th Annual Advanced Winter Symposium, "Treatment of Addictive Disorders," Colorado Springs, February 7, 1986.

Harris, T. *I'm OK/You're OK: A Practical Guide to Transactional Analysis.* Harper and Row: New York, 1969.

Hayman, M. "Current Attitudes to Alcoholism of Psychiatrists in Southern California." *American Journal of Psychiatry 112,* pp. 484-493. 1956.

Hedlund, J. L. "MMPI Clinical Scale Correlates," *Journal of Consulting and Clinical Psych. 45*, pp. 739-750. 1977.

Helfrisch, A. A. "Treatment of Cocaine Dependency," presented at Psychotherapy Associates, P. C., 12th Annual Advanced International Winter Symposium on the Treatment of Addictive Disorders, Colorado Springs, February 4, 1986.

Helzer, J. E. and T. R. Pryzbeck. "The Co-Occurrence of Alcoholism with Other Psychiatric Disorders in the General Population and its Impact on Treatment." *Journal of Studies on Alcoholism 49*(E), pp. 219-224. 1988.

Hesselbrock, M. N. and Przybeck, J. R. "The Co-occurrence of Alcoholism with Other Psychiatric Disorders in the General Population and Its Impact on Treatment." *Journal of Studies on Alcoholism,* 49(3), 219-224, 1988.

Hesselbrock, M. N., R. E. Meyer, and J. J. Kenner. "Psychopathology in Hospitalized Alcoholics." *Arch. General Psychiatry 42*, pp. 1050-1055. 1985.

Hetherington, G. M., R. J. Stouwie and E. H. Ridberg. "Patterns of Family Interaction and Child-Rearing Attitudes Related to Three Dimensions of Juvenile Delinquency." *Journal of Abnormal Psychology 78*, pp. 160-176. 1971.

Hill, M. I and H. T. Blane. "Evaluation of Psychotherapy with Alcoholics: A Critical Review." *Quarterly Journal of Studies on Alcoholism 28*, pp. 76-104. 1967.

Hill, S. Y., C. R. Cloninger and F. R. Ayre. "Independent Familial Transmission of Alcoholism and Opiate Abuse," *Arch. General Psychiatry 35*, pp. 941-951. 1977.

Hoff, E. L. "Group Therapy with Alcoholics." *Psychiatry Residency Report 24*, pp. 61-70. 1968.

Hofmann, F. G. *A Handbook on Drug and Alcohol Abuse: The Biomedical Aspects*. 2nd Ed. Oxford University Press: New York, 1983.

Holden, R. T. "Rehabilitative Sanctions for Drunk Driving: An Experimental Evaluation." *Journal of Research in Crime and Delinquency 20*(1), pp. 55-72. 1983.

Hooper, F. A. and R. G. Evans. "Screening for Disruptive Behavior of Institutionalized Juvenile Offenders." *Journal of Per. Assess. 48*, pp. 159-161. 1984.

Horn, J. L, K. Wanberg and F. M. Foster. *The Alcohol Use Inventory–AUI*. Center for Alcohol-Abuse Research and Evaluation: Denver, 1974.

Hountras, P. T. and G. G. Forrest. "Personality Characteristics and Self-Disclosure in a Psychiatric Outpatient Population." *Coll. of Education Record, 55*, pp. 206-213. University of North Dakota, 1970.

Hull, J. G. "Self-Awareness Model." In *Psychological Theories of Drinking and Alcoholism,* edited by H. T. Blane and K. E. Leonard. The Guilford Press: New York, 1987.

Hunter, R. E. "Treatment of Compulsive Gambling," presented at Psychotherapy Associates, P. C., 14th Annual Advanced International Winter Symposium on the Treatment of Addictive Disorders, Colorado Springs, February 2, 1988.

Jacobs, P. A., M. Brunton, J. R. Knott, and E. B. Platt. "Aggressive Behavior, Mental Sub-Normality and the XYY Male." *Nature 208*, pp. 1351-1352. 1965.

Jackson, J. "The Assessment and Treatment of Afro-American Alcoholism," presented at Psychotherapy Associates, P. C., 17th Annual Advanced International Winter Symposium on the Treatment of Addictive Disorders, Colorado Springs, February 2, 1991.

James, W. *Research on Obesity: A Report on the Department of Health and Social Security/Medical Research Council Group*. HMSO: London, 1976.

Jellinek, E. M. "Heredity and Alcohol, Science and Society." *Quarterly Journal of Studies on Alcoholism*, pp. 104-113. 1945.

Jellinek, E. M. *The Disease Concept of Alcoholism*. College and University Press: New Haven, 1960.

Jenkins, R. L. "The Psychopathic or Antisocial Personality." *Journal of Neurology and Mental Disease 131*, pp. 318-334. 1960.

Jessor, R. and S. L. Jessor. *Problem Behavior and Psycho-Social Development*. Academic Press: New York, 1977.

Jones, T., W. B. Beidleman, and R. Fowler. "Differentiating Violent and Nonviolent Prison Inmates by Use of Selected MMPI Scales." *Journal of Clinical Psychology 37*, pp. 673-678. 1981.

Kahn, E. *Psychopathic Personalities*. Yale University Press: New Haven, 1931.

Kalish, C. B. "Prisoners and Alcohol." *Bureau of Justice Statistics Bulletin*, January, 1983.

Kallman, F. J. *The Genetics of Schizophrenia*. J. J. Augustin: New York: 1939.

Kandel, D. "Adolescent Marijuana Use: Role of Parents and Peers." *Science 181*, pp. 1067-1070. 1973.

Karpman, B. "On the Need of Separating Psychopathy into Two Distinct Clinical Types: The Symptomatic and The Idiopathic." *Journal of Criminal Psychopathology 3*, pp. 137. 1941.

Kegan, R. G. "The Child Behind The Mask: Sociopathy as Developmental Delay." In *Unmasking the Psychopath: Antisocial Personality and Related Syndromes*, edited by W. H. Reid, K. A. Druley, T. E. Skoloda, and H. M. Waxman. W. W. Norton and Company: New York, 1986.

Kennedy, D. J. "The Rideau Alcohol Program: A Multidisciplinary Approach to Alcohol-Related Problems of Incarcerated Offenders." *Canadian Journal of Criminology 22*, pp. 428-442. 1980.

Kernberg, O. F. *Borderline Conditions and Pathological Narcissism*. Jason Aronson: New York, 1975.

Kernberg, O. F. *Object Relations Theory and Clinical Psychoanalysis*. Jason Aronson: New York, 1976.

Kernberg, O. F. *Internal World and External Reality*. Jason Aronson: New York, 1980.

Kernberg, O. F. *Severe Personality Disorders: Psychotherapeutic Strategies*. Yale University Press: New Haven and London, 1984.

Khantzian, E. J. and C. Treece. "DSM III Psychiatric Diagnosis of Narcotic Addicts." *Arch. General Psychiatry 42*, pp. 1067-1071. 1985.

Kinsey, A., W. Pomeroy and C. Martin. *Sexual Behavior in the Human Male*. Saunders: Philadelphia, 1948.

Klassen, A. D., C. J. Williams, and E. E. Levitt, eds. *Sex and Morality in the U.S.*, Wesleyan University Press: Middletown, Massachusetts, 1989.

Klee, T. E. "Treating Dual Disorders: A Model of Professional Education and Training." In *Managing the Dually Diagnosed Patient*, edited by P. F. O'Connell. The Haworth Press: New York, 1990.

Knauert, A. P. "The Treatment of Alcoholism in a Community Setting." *Family and Community Health 2*(1), pp. 91-102. 1979.

Knauert, A. P. "Differential Diagnosis in the Treatment of Alcoholism," presented at Psychotherapy Associates, P. C., 6th Annual Advanced International Winter Workshop, "Treatment and Rehabilitation of the Alcoholic," Colorado Springs, February 8, 1980.

Knauert, A. P. "Differential Diagnosis of Substance Use Disorders," presented at Psychotherapy Associates, P. C., 15th Annual Advanced International Winter Symposium on the Treatment of Addictive Disorders, Colorado Springs, February 4, 1989.

Knauert, A. P. "Treatment of Cocaine Dependency," presented at Psychotherapy Associates, P. C., 15th Annual Advanced International Winter Symposium on the Treatment of Addictive Disorders, Colorado Springs, February 7, 1989.

Knauert, A. P. "Advanced Differential Diagnosis of Substance Abuse Disorders," presented at Psychotherapy Associates, P. C., 18th Annual Advanced International Winter Symposium on the Treatment of Addictive Disorders, Colorado Springs, February 3, 1992.

Knight, R. P. "Psychodynamics of Chronic Alcoholism." *Journal of Nervous Mental Disorders 86*, pp. 538-548. 1937.

Koeningsberg, H. W., R. D. Kaplan, M. M. Gilmore, and A. M. Cooper. "The Relationship Between Syndrome and Personality Disorder in DSM III: Experience with 2,462 Patients." *American Journal of Psychiatry 142*(2), pp. 207-212. February 1985.

Koop, C. E. "Effects of Smoking on Health." Monograph, Office of the Surgeon General: Washington, DC, 1989.

Korsten, M. A. and C. S. Lieber. "Hepatic and Gastrointestinal Complications of Alcoholism." In *The Diagnosis and Treatment of Alcoholism*, edited by J. H. Mendelson and N. K. Mello. McGraw-Hill: New York, 1979.

Kozol, H. L., K. J. Boucher, and R. F. Garofalo. "The Diagnosis and Treatment of Dangerousness." *Crime and Delinquency 19*, pp. 371-392. 1972.

Krafft-Ebbing, R. von. *Psychopathia Sexualis*. Stein and Day: New York, 1886.

Lange, J. *Crime and Destiny*. C. Boni: New York, 1936.

Lanzkron, J. "Murder and Insanity." *American Journal of Psychiatry 119*, pp. 254-258. 1963.

Lasater, L. *Recovery from Compulsive Behavior*. Health Communications, Inc.: Deerfield Beach, Florida, 1988.

Laundergan, J. C., J. W. Spicer, and M. L. Kammeier. *Are Court Referrals Effective? Judicial Commitment for Chemical Dependency in Washington County, Minnesota*. Hazelden Research Foundation: Minneapolis, 1979.

Lawson, G. and A. Lawson, (Eds.). *Adolescent Substance Abuse: Etiology, Treatment and Prevention*. Gaithersburg: Aspen, 1992.

Lawson, G. W., D. C. Ellis, and P. C. Rivers. *Essentials of Chemical Dependency Counseling*. Aspen Systems Corporation: Rockville, Maryland, 1984.

Lazarus, A. A. *The Practice of Multi-Modal Therapy*. McGraw-Hill: New York, 1981.

Lee, R. and M. Haynes. "Project CREST and the Dual-Treatment Approach to Delinquency: Methods and Research Summarized." In *Effective Correctional Treatment*, edited by R. R. Ross and P. Gendreau. Butterworth: Toronto, 1980.

Leigh, G. "Psychosocial Factors in the Etiology of Substance Abuse." In *Alcoholism and Substance Abuse: Strategies for Clinical Intervention*, edited by T. E. Bratter and G. G. Forrest. Free Press: New York, 1985.

Levinson, R. M. and G. Ramsay. "Dangerousness, Stress and Mental Health Evaluations." *Journal of Health and Social Behavior 20*, pp. 178-187, 1979.

Lewis, C., L. Robins, and J. Rice. "Association of Alcoholism with Antisocial Personality in Urban Men." *Journal of Mental and Nervous Disorders 173*, pp. 166-174, 1985.

Ley, P. "The Psychology of Obesity: Its Causes, Consequences and Control." *Contributions to Medical Psychology*, edited by S. Rachman. Vol. 2. Pergamon, Oxford, England, 1980.

Lindbeck, V. L. "The Woman Alcoholic: A Review of the Literature." *International Journal of Addictions 7*, pp. 567-580. 1972.

Lindner, R. *Rebel Without A Cause–The Hypoanalysis of a Criminal Psychopath.* Grune and Stratton: New York, 1944.

Lindner, R. "Psychopathy as a Psychological Problem." In *Encyclopedia of Psychology.* Philosophical Library: New York, 1948.

Litwack, T. R. and L. B. Schlesinger. "Assessing and Predicting Violence: Research, Law and Applications." In *Handbook of Forensic Psychology,* edited by I. B. Weiner and A. K. Hess. John Wiley and Sons: New York, 1987.

Livermore, J., C. Malmquist, and P. Meehl. "On the Justification for Civil Commitment." *University of Pennsylvania Law Review 117*, pp. 75-96. 1968.

Longabaugh, R. "Recommended Research Priorities for the Assessment of Treatment Outcomes." *Psychology of Addictive Behavior 2*(3), pp. 131-141. 1988.

MacAndrew, C. "The Differentiation of Male Alcoholic Outpatients from Nonalcoholic Psychiatric Outpatients by Means of the MMPI." *Quarterly Journal of Studies on Alcoholism 26*, pp. 238-246, 1965.

MacDonald, I. "High Schoolers Show Decline in Cocaine/Marijuana Use." *Wings: A Brockhurst Ranch/Riegel Center Publication.* The Penrose Health System: Colorado Springs, 1986.

MacDonald, J. M. "The Threat to Kill." *American Journal of Psychiatry 120*, pp. 125-130. 1963.

MacDonald, J. M. "Homicidal Threats." *American Journal of Psychiatry 124,* pp. 475-482. 1967.

Manchester, D. "Genetics of Alcoholism," presented at Psychotherapy Associates, P. C., 18th Annual Advanced International Winter Symposium on the Treatment of Addictive Disorders, Colorado Springs, February 5, 1992.

Marlatt, G. A. "Craving for Alcohol, Loss of Control and Relapse: A Cognitive-Behavioral Analysis." In *Alcoholism: New Directions in Behavioral Research,* edited by P. E. Nathan, G. A. Marlatt, and T. Loberg. Plenum Press: New York, 1978.

Martinson, R. "What Works? Questions and Answers about Prison Reform." *The Public Interest 35*, pp. 22-54. 1974.

Martinson, R. "New Findings, New Views: A Note of Caution Regarding Sentencing Reform." *Hofstra Law Review 7*(2), pp. 243-258. 1979.

Maslow, A. H. *Motivation and Personality.* Harper and Row: New York, 1954.

Matuschka, E. "Treatment, Outcomes, and Clinical Evaluations." In *Alcoholism and Substance Abuse: Strategies for Clinical Intervention,* edited by T. E. Bratter and G. G. Forrest. Free Press: New York, 1985.

Matuschka, E. "Confrontation in Psychotherapy with Substance Abusers," presented at Psychotherapy Associates, P. C., 14th Annual Advanced International Winter Symposium on the Treatment of Addictive Disorders, Colorado Springs, February 3, 1988.

Matuschka, E. "Treatment of Nicotine/Smoking Addictions," presented at Psychotherapy Associates, P. C., 15th Annual Advanced International Winter Symposium on the Treatment of Addictive Disorders, Colorado Springs, February 9, 1989.

Maultsby, M. C. *More Personal Happiness Through Rational Self-Counseling.* Institute for Rational Living: New York, 1974.

Mawson, A. R. and D. C. Mawson. "Personality and Arousal: A New Interpretation of the Psychophysiological Literature." *Biological Psychiatry 12*, pp. 49-74. 1977.

May, R. "Psychotherapy and the Daimonic." In *Creative Developments in Psychotherapy*, edited by A. Mahrer and L. Pearson. Aronson: New York, 1973.

McCann, W. H. "The Psychopath and the Psychoneurotic in Relation to Crime and Delinquency." *Journal of Clinical and Experimental Psychopathology 9*, p. 551. 1948.

McClelland, D. C., W. N. Davis, R. Kalin, and E. Wanner. *The Drinking Man: A Theory of Human Motivation.* Free Press: New York, 1972.

McCord, W. and J. McCord. *The Psychopath: An Essay on the Criminal Mind.* D. Van Nostrand Co., Inc.: Princeton, New Jersey, 1964.

McFadden, H. "Alcohol and Drug Abuse Treatment: Past, Present, and Future," presented at Psychotherapy Associates, P. C., 17th Annual Advanced International Winter Symposium on the Treatment of Addictive Disorders Colorado Springs, February 6, 1991.

McFadden, H. and S. McFadden. "Alcoholics Anonymous and the Self-Help Community: How It Works," presented at Psychotherapy Associates, P. C., 15th Annual Advanced International Winter Symposium on the Treatment of Addictive Disorders, Colorado Springs, February 9, 1989.

McGarth, J., J. O'Brien, and J. Liftik. "Coercive Treatment for Alcoholic 'Driving Under the Influence of Liquor' Offenders." *British Journal of Addiction 72*(3), pp. 229-233. 1977.

McGuffin, P. and T. Reich. "Psychopathology and Genetics." In *Comprehensive Handbook of Psychopathology*, edited by H. E. Adams and P. B. Sutker. Plenum Press: New York, 1984.

McPeek, F. "The Role of Religious Bodies in the Treatment of Inebriety in the United States." *Alcohol, Science, and Society: 29 Lectures with Discussions as given at the Yale Summer School of Alcohol Studies.* Greenwood Press: Westport, Connecticut, 1972.

Megargee, E. I. "Methodological Problems in the Prediction of Violence." In *Violence and the Violent Individual*, edited by J. R. Hays, T. K. Roberts, and K. S. Solway. Spectrum: New York, 1981.

Mendelson, J. H. and N. K. Mello. *The Diagnosis and Treatment of Alcoholism.* McGraw-Hill: New York, 1979.

Miller, P. M. "Theoretical and Practical Issues in Substance Abuse Assessment and Treatment." In *The Addictive Behaviors*, edited by W. R. Miller. Pergamon: New York, pp. 265-291. 1980.

Miller, P. M. *Behavioral Treatment of Alcoholism.* Pergamon: New York, 1976.

Miller, W. E. and R. K. Hester, "Inpatient Alcoholism Treatment: Who Benefits?" *American Psychologist 15*, pp. 794-805. 1986.

Miller, W. R. "Alcoholism Treatment Alternatives: What Works, and For Whom?" presented at Psychotherapy Associates, P. C., 14th Annual Advanced

International Winter Symposium on the Treatment of Addictive Disorders, Colorado Springs, February 1, 1988(a).

Miller, W. R. "Treatment Modalities: Process and Outcome," panel on Opportunity for Research on the Treatment of Alcoholism and Related Problems, Institute of Medicine, National Academy of Sciences, 1988(b).

Miller, W. R. and C. Taylor. "Relative Effectiveness of Bibliography, Individual and Group Self-Control Training in the Treatment of Problem Drinkers." *Addictive Behaviors 5,* pp. 13-24. 1980.

Milt, H. *Basic Handbook on Alcoholism.* Scientific Aids Publications: New Jersey, 1969.

Mines, R. "Treatment of Compulsive Over-Eating," presented at Psychotherapy Associates, P. C., 15th Annual Advanced International Winter Symposium on the Treatment of Addictive Disorders, Colorado Springs, February 5, 1989.

Mines, R. "Treatment of Compulsive Eating and Obesity," presented at Psychotherapy Associates, P. C., 17th Annual Advanced International Winter Symposium on the Treatment of Addictive Disorders, Colorado Springs, February 7, 1991.

Minihan, M. *Dostoevsky: His Life and Work by Konstantin Mochalsky.* Princeton University Press: Princeton, New Jersey, 1967.

Monahan, J. *Predicting Violent Behavior: An Assessment of Clinical Techniques.* Sage: Beverly Hills, 1981.

Monahan, J. "The Prediction of Violent Behavior: Toward a Second Generation of Theory and Policy." *American Journal of Psychiatry 141*, pp. 10-15, 1984.

Moore, R. A. and R. Ramseur. "Effect on Psychotherapy in an Open-Ward Hospital in Patients with Alcoholism." *Quarterly Journal of Studies and Alcoholism 21*, pp. 233-252. 1960.

Morrison, J. "Adult Psychiatric Disorders in Parents of Hyperactive Children." *American Journal of Psychiatry 137*, pp. 825-827. 1980.

Morse, R. M. and W. M. Swenson. "Spouse Response to A Self-Administered Alcoholism Screening Test." *Journal of Studies on Alcoholism 36*, pp. 400-405. 1975.

Mullen, J. M. and R. C. Reinehr. "Predicting Dangerousness of Maximum Security Forensic Mental Patients." *Journal of Psychiatry and the Law 10*, pp. 223-231. 1982.

Mulvey, E. P. and C. W. Lidz. "Clinical Considerations in the Prediction of Dangerousness in Mental Patients." *Clinical Psychology Review 4*, pp. 379-401. 1984.

Mumey, J. *The Joy of Sobriety.* Contemporary Books, Inc.: Chicago, 1984.

Mumey, J. *Loving An Alcoholic: Help and Hope for Significant Others.* Contemporary Books, Inc.: Chicago, 1986.

Nace, E. P. "Substance Abuse and Personality Disorder." In *Managing the Dually-Diagnosed Patient: Current Issues and Clinical Approaches*, edited by P. F. O'Connell. The Haworth Press: New York, 1990.

Nace, E. P., J. J. Saxton, Jr. and N. Shore. "Borderline Personality Disorder and

Alcoholism Treatment: A One-Year Follow-Up Study," *Journal Study on Alcoholism*, 47(3), pp. 196-200. 1986.

Nathan, P. E. and W. H. Hay. *"Alcoholism: Psychopathology, Etiology, and Treatment."* In *Comprehensive Handbook of Psychopathology*, edited by H. E. Adams and P. B. Sutker. Plenum Press: New York, 1984.

Newkirk, P. R. "Psychopathic Traits are Inheritable." *Diseases of the Nervous System 18*, pp. 52-54. 1957.

Nichols, J. R. and S. Hsiao. "Addiction Liability of Albino Rats: Breeding for Quantitative Differences in Morphine Drinking." *Science 157,* pp. 561-581. 1967.

O'Connell, P. F., ed. *Managing the Dually-Diagnosed Patient: Current Issues and Clinical Approaches*. The Haworth Press: New York, 1990.

O'Connor, J. *The Young Drinkers: A Cross-National Study of Social and Cultural Influences*. Tavistock: London, 1978.

O'Donnell, C. R., R. Lydgate, and W. S. Fo. "The Buddy System: Review and Follow-Up." In *Effective Correctional Treatment*, edited by R. R. Ross and P. Gendreau. Butterworth: Toronto, 1980.

Ogborne, A. C. and A. Barnet. "A Brief Report: Abstinence and Abusive Drinking Among Affiliates of Alcoholics Anonymous: Are These the Only Alternatives?" *Addictive Behaviors,* pp. 1896-2002. 1982.

Ogborne, A. C. and F. B. Glaser. "Evaluating Alcoholics Anonymous." In *Alcoholism and Substance Abuse: Strategies for Clinical Intervention*, edited by T. E. Bratter and G. G. Forrest. Free Press: New York, 1985.

Olwens, P. "Antisocial Behavior in the School Setting." In *Psychopathic Behaviors: Approaches to Research*, edited by R. D. Hare and D. Schalling. Wiley: New York, 1978.

Orford, J. *Excessive Appetites: A Psychological View of Addictions*. John Wiley and Sons: New York, 1985.

Pallone, N. J. and R. J. Tirman. "Correlates of Substance Abuse Remission in Alcoholism Rehabilitation: Effective Treatment of Symptom Abandonment." *Offender Rehabilitation 3*(1), 1978.

Paolino, T. J. and B. S. McCrady. *The Alcoholic Marriage: Alternative Perspectives*. Grune and Stratton: New York, 1977.

Partridge, G. E. "A Study of 50 Cases of Psychopathic Personality." *American Journal of Psychiatry 7*, pp. 953-973. 1928.

Patterson, C. H. *Theories of Counseling and Psychotherapy*. Harper and Row: New York, 1966.

Pattison, E. M. "Borderline, Narcissistic, and Addictive Disorders: Differential Diagnosis and Treatment Considerations," presented at Psychotherapy Associates, P. C., 13th Annual Advanced International Winter Symposium on the Treatment of Addictive Disorders, Colorado Springs, February 2, 1987.

Pfhol, S. J. *Predicting Dangerousness*. Lexington Books/P. C. Heath: Lexington, Massachusetts, 1978.

Polich, J. M., D. J. Armor, and H. B. Braiker. *The Course of Alcoholism: Four Years After Treatment*. Wiley: New York, 1981.

Pomerleau, O. and D. Adkins. "Evaluating Behavioral and Traditional Treatment for Problem Drinkers." In *Evaluating Alcohol and Drug Treatment Effectiveness*, edited by L. L. Sobell, M. B. Sobell, and E. Ward. Pergamon: Toronto, 1980.

Porges, S. W. "Peripheral and Neurochemical Parallels of Psychopathology: A Psychophysiological Model Relating Autonomic Imbalance to Hyperactivity, Psychopathy, and Autism." In *Advances in Child Development and Behavior*, Vol. 2, edited by H. W. Reese. Academic Press: New York, 1976.

Pritchard, J. C. *A Treatise on Insanity.* Haswell, Barrington and Haswell: Philadelphia, 1835.

Quaade, F. "Intestinal Bypass for Severe Obesity: A Randomized Trial. A Report from the Danish Obesity Group." In *Recent Advances in Obesity Research, II*, edited by G. Bray. Proceedings of the Second International Congress on Obesity, Washington, DC, 1977. Newman: London, 1978.

Quay, H. C. "Psychopathic Personality As Pathological Stimulation Seeking." *American Journal of Psychiatry 122,* pp. 180-183. 1965.

Quay, H. C. "Psychopathic Behavior: Reflections on Its Nature, Origins, and Treatment." In *The Structuring of Experience*, edited by I. Uzgiris and F. Weizmann. Plenum: New York, 1977.

Rachal, J. V., et al. "Adolescent Drinking Behavior, Attitudes and Correlates: A National Study." (Final Report, RTI Project No. 23U-891). Research Triangle Institute: Research Triangle Park, North Carolina, 1975.

Rachman, A. W. and R. R. Raubolt. "The Clinical Practice of Group Psychotherapy with Adolescent Substance Abusers." In *Alcoholism and Substance Abuse: Strategies For Clinical Intervention*, edited by T. E. Bratter and G. G. Forrest. Free Press: New York, 1985.

Regier, D., J. Myers, M. Kramer, L. Robins, et al. "The NIMH Epidemiologic Catchment Area Program: Historical Context, Major Objectives, and Study Population Characteristics." *Arch. General Psychiatry 41*, pp. 934-941. 1984.

Reid, W. H., D. Dorr, J. I. Walker and J. W. Bonner, eds. *Unmasking the Psychopath: Antisocial Personality and Related Syndromes.* W. W. Norton and Co.: New York, 1986.

Reik, T. *Listening with the Third Ear.* Pyramid Books: New York, 1948.

Revitch, E. and L. B. Schlesinger. "Murder: Evaluation, Classification, and Prediction." In *Violence: Perspectives on Murder and Aggression*, edited by I. L. Kutash, S. B. Kutash, and L. B. Schlesinger. Jossey-Bass: San Francisco, 1978.

Revitch, E. and L. B. Schlesinger. *Psychopathology of Homicide.* Charles C Thomas: Springfield, Illinois, 1981.

Robins, L. W., J. E. Helzer and D. H. Davis. "Narcotic Use in Southeast Asia and Afterward." *Arch. General Psychiatry 32*, pp. 955-961. 1975.

Robinson, J. and G. Smith. "The Effectiveness of Correctional Programs." *Crime and Delinquency 17*, pp. 67-80. 1971.

Rofman, E. S., C. Askinazi and E. Fant. "The Prediction of Dangerous Behavior in Emergency Civil Commitment." *American Journal of Psychology 137*, pp. 1061-1064. 1980.

Rogers, C. R. *Client-Centered Therapy,* Houghton-Mifflin: Boston, 1952.

Romig, D. A. *Justice for Our Children.* D. C. Heath: Lexington, Massachusetts, 1978.

Rosenthal, D. *Genetic Theory and Abnormal Behavior.* McGraw-Hill: New York, 1970.

Ross, R. R. and E. Fabiano. *Thinking Straight: The Cognitive Model of Crime and Delinquency Prevention and Rehabilitation.* Institute of Social Sciences and Arts: Johnson City, Tennessee, 1981.

Ross, R. R. and P. Gendreau. *Offender Change: An Effective Alternative to Incarceration.* Solicitor General: Ottawa, 1983.

Ross, R. R. and L. O. Lightfoot. *Treatment of the Alcohol-Abusing Offender.* Charles C Thomas: Springfield, Illinois, 1985.

Ross, R. R. and H. B. McKay. "Behavioral Approaches to Treatment in Corrections: Requiem for a Panacea." *Canadian Journal of Criminology 20*(2), pp. 279-295. 1978.

Roth, L. H. and N. Rosenberg. "Prison Adjustment of Alcoholic Felons." *Quarterly Journal of Studies on Alcoholism 32*, pp. 382-392. 1971.

Rounsaville, B. J., S. L. Eyre, M. M. Weissman and H. D. Kleber. "The Antisocial Opiate Addict." *Advances in Alcohol and Substance Abuse* 1983, 2(4), pp. 29-42. 1983.

Russell, M. "Cigarette Smoking: Natural History of a Dependency Disorder." *British Journal of Medical Psychiatry 44*, pp. 1-16. 1971.

Sadava, S. W. "Other Drug Abuse and Dependence Disorders." In *Comprehensive Handbook of Psychopathology*, edited by H. E. Adams and P. B. Sutker. Plenum Press: New York, 1984.

Sarason, I. G. "A Cognitive Social-Learning Approach to Juvenile Delinquency." In *Psychopathic Behavior: Approaches to Research*, edited by R. D. Hare and D. Schalling. Wiley: New York, 1978.

Satterfield, J. H. "The Hyperactive Child Syndrome: A Pre-Cursor of Adult Psychopathy?" In *Psychopathic Behavior: Approaches to Research*, edited by R. D. Hare and D. Schalling. Wiley: Chichester, England, 1978.

Sauls, J. Urinalysis Testing in the Work Place. Unpublished Doctoral Dissertation. Columbia Pacific University, San Rafael, California, 1988.

Schlesinger, L. B. and E. Revitch. "Sexual Dynamics in Homicide and Assault." In *Sexual Dynamics of Anti-Social Behavior*, edited by L. B. Schlesinger and E. Revitch. Charles C Thomas: Springfield, Illinois, 1983.

Schuckit, M. A. "Disulfiram (Antabuse) and the Treatment of Alcoholic Men." *Raleigh Hill Foundation, Advances in Alcoholism II*(4), pp. 1-5. April 1981(a).

Schuckit, M. A. "Gamma Glutamyl Transferase and the Diagnosis of Alcoholism." *Raleigh Hill Foundation, Advances in Alcoholism II* (5), pp. 26-32, 1981(b).

Schulsinger, F. "Psychopathy: Heredity and Environment." *International Journal of Mental Health 1*, pp. 190-206. 1972.

Schulsinger, F. "Psychopathy: Heredity and Environment." In *Biosocial Bases of Criminal Behavior*, edited by A. Mednick and K. O. Christiansen. Gardner Press: New York, 1977.

Schwartz, R. H. "Marijuana Dependency," presented at Psychotherapy Associates, P. C., 12th Annual Advanced International Winter Symposium on the Treatment of Addictive Disorders, Colorado Springs, February 3, 1986.

Scott, E. M. "Group Therapy with Convicts on Work Release in Oregon." *International Journal of Offender Therapy and Comparative Criminology 20*(3), pp. 225-235. 1976.

Selman, R. D. "A Therapeutic Milieu for Treating the Antisocial, Substance-Abusing Adolescent." In *Unmasking the Psychopath: Antisocial Personality and Related Syndromes*, edited by W. H. Reid, D. Dorr, J. I. Walker, and J. W. Bonner. W. W. Norton and Co.: New York, 1986.

Selzer, M. L. "The Michigan Alcoholism Screening Test: The Quest For A New Diagnostic Instrument." *American Journal of Psychiatry 127*, pp. 89-94. 1971.

Sena, D. A. "Neuropsychological Considerations in Addictions Treatment," presented at Psychotherapy Associates, P. C., 13th Annual Advanced International Winter Symposium on the Treatment of Addictive Disorders, Colorado Springs, February 2, 1987.

Sena, D. A. "Neuropsychological Considerations in Addictions Treatment," presented at Psychotherapy Associates, P. C., 14th Annual Advanced International Winter Symposium on the Treatment of Addictive Disorders, Colorado Springs, February 3, 1988.

Sena, D. A. "Neuropsychological Assessment in the Psychotherapy and Rehabilitation of Substance Abusers," presented at Psychotherapy Associates, P. C., 15th Annual Advanced International Winter Symposium on the Treatment of Addictive Disorders, Colorado Springs, February 6, 1989.

Sena, D. A. "Neuropsychological Factors in the Assessment and Treatment of Substance Use Disorders," presented at Psychotherapy Associates, P. C., 17th Annual Advanced International Winter Symposium on the Treatment of Addictive Disorders, Colorado Springs, February 7, 1991.

Sher, K. J. "Stress Response Dampening." In *Psychological Theories of Drinking and Alcoholism*, edited by H. T. Blane and K. E. Leonard. The Guilford Press: New York, 1987.

Smart, R. G., J. W. Finney, and K. Funston. "The Effectiveness of Post-Detoxification Referrals: Effects on Later Detoxification Admissions, Drunkenness and Criminality." *Drug and Alcohol Dependence 2*(3), pp. 149-155. 1977.

Smith, J. J. "The Endocrine Basis of Hormonal Therapy of Alcoholism." *New York State Journal of Medicine 50*, pp. 1704-1706, 1711-1715. 1950.

Sobell, L. C. and M. B. Sobell. "Alcoholism Treatment Outcome Evaluation Methodology." *Prevention, Intervention, and Treatment*, pp. 293-321; *Alcohol and Health*, Monograph 3, NIAAA, 1982.

Stanton, M.D. "The Family and Drug Abuse: Concepts and Rationale." In *Alcoholism and Substance Abuse: Strategies For Clinical Intervention*, edited by T. E. Bratter and G. G. Forrest. Free Press: New York, 1985.

Stekel, W. *Peculiarities of Behavior: Wandering Mania, Dipsomania, Cleptomania, Pyromania, and Allied Impulsive Acts*. Bodley Head: London, 1924 (English publication, 1938).

Stekel, W. *Sadism and Masochism. Vol. I.* Liveright Publishing Company: London, 1929.

Stimmel, B. "The Socioeconomics of Heroin Dependency." *New England Journal of Medicine 287,* pp. 1275-1280. 1972.

Stone, L. *The Family, Sex and Marriage in England: 1500-1800.* Penguin and Harmondsworth, Middlesex, England, 1979.

Stout, R. L. "Analyzing Treatment Outcome Over Time." Center for Alcohol and Addiction Studies: Brown University, Providence, Rhode Island, 1988.

Stromberg, C. D. "The Duty to Warn and Protect." *Register Report: The Newsletter for Psychologist Health Service Providers 15*(2), pp. 11-17, 1989.

Stuckey, J. "Treatment of Sexual Compulsions/Dependency," presented at Psychotherapy Associates, P. C., 17th Annual Advanced International Winter Symposium on the Treatment of Addictive Disorders, Colorado Springs, February 5, 1991.

Sudduth, W. "The Psychology of Narcotism." *Journal of American Medical Association 27,* pp. 796-798. 1896.

Suedfeld, P. and P. B. Landon. "Approaches to Treatment." In *Psychopathic Behavior: Approaches to Treatment,* edited by R. D. Hare and D. Schalling. Wiley: New York, 1978.

Sutker, P. B. "Personality Differences and Sociopathy in Heroin Addicts and Nonaddict Prisoners." *Journal of Abnormal Psychology 78*(11), pp. 247-251. 1971.

Sutker, P. B. and A. N. Allain. "Behavior and Personality Assessment in Men Labelled Adaptive Sociopaths." *Journal of Behavioral Assessment 5,* pp. 65-79. 1983.

Sutker, P. B. and R. P. Archer. "Opiate Abuse and Dependence Disorders." In *Comprehensive Handbook of Psychopathology,* edited by H. E. Adams and P. B. Sutker. Plenum Press: New York, 1984.

Sutker, P. B., R. P. Archer and A. N. Allain. "Drug Abuse Patterns, Personality Characteristics, and Relationships with Sex, Race, and Sensation Seeking." *Journal of Counseling and Clinical Psychology 46,* pp. 1374-1378. 1978.

Szasz, T. S. *The Myth of Mental Illness.* Dell Publishing Company: New York, 1961.

Szasz, T. S. *Ceremonial Chemistry.* Doubleday: New York, 1974.

Szasz, T. S. *Schizophrenia: The Sacred Symbol of Psychiatry.* Basic Books: New York, 1976.

Szasz, T. S. "Psychiatric Diversion in the Criminal Justice System: A Critique." In *Assessing the Criminal: Restitution, Retribution, and the Legal Process,* edited by R. E. Barnett and J. Hagel. Ballinger: Cambridge, Massachusetts, 1977.

Szurek, S. A. "Notes on the Genesis of Psychopathic Personality." *Psychiatry 5,* pp. 1-6 1942.

Tarasoff vs. Regents of the University of California, 551, p. 2d, 334, 346 (Cal., 1976).

Teboe, R. "The Assessment and Treatment of Native American Alcoholism," presented at Psychotherapy Associates, P. C., 17th Annual Advanced International Winter Symposium on the Treatment of Addictive Disorders, Colorado Springs, February 4, 1991.

Tennant, F. S., M. R. Preble, C. J. Groesbeck, and W. I. Banks. "West Germany." *Military Medicine 137,* pp. 381-383. 1972.

Thomas, W. A. *Alcoholism Program Survey: Federal Prison System.* NIAAA, Washington, DC, July 1978.

Thompson, G. N. *The Psychopathic Delinquent.* Charles C Thomas: Springfield, Illinois, 1953.

Timkin, D. S. "Alcohol-Drug Program Evaluation: Testing the Null Hypothesis," presented at Psychotherapy Associates, P. C., 12th Annual Advanced International Winter Symposium, "Treatment of Addictive Disorders," Colorado Springs, February 5, 1986.

Timkin, D. S. "Assessment and Treatment of High Risk DUI Offenders," presented at Psychotherapy Associates, P. C., 13th Annual Advanced International Winter Symposium on the Treatment of Addictive Disorders, Colorado Springs, February 4, 1987.

Truax, C. B. and R. R. Carkhuff. *Toward Effective Counseling and Psychotherapy.* Aldine: Chicago, 1967.

Vaillant, G. *The Natural History of Alcoholism.* Harvard University Press: Cambridge, 1983.

Valette, B. *A Parent's Guide to Eating Disorders.* Walker: New York, 1990.

Voegtlin, W. L. and F. Lemere. "The Treatment of Alcohol Addiction: A Review of the Literature." *Quarterly Journal of Studies on Alcoholism 2,* pp. 717-803. 1942.

Vraa, C. "Compulsive Sex and Treatment of Sexual Compulsions," presented at Psychotherapy Associates, P. C., 14th Annual Advanced International Winter Symposium on the Treatment of Addictive Disorders, Colorado Springs, February 5, 1988.

Wade, T. C., T. Morton, J. Lind, and N. Ferris. "A Family Crisis Intervention Approach to Diversion from the Juvenile Justice System." *Juvenile Justice* 28(3), pp. 43-51. 1977.

Wallace, J. *Alcoholism: New Light on the Disease.* Edgehill Publications: Newport, Rhode Island, 1985.

Wallace, J. "Treatment of Addictive Disorders: Clinical Implications of Recent Research in Neurobiology," presented at Psychotherapy Associates, P. C., 15th Annual Advanced International Winter Symposium on the Treatment of Addictive Disorders, Colorado Springs, February 6, 1989.

Wallace, J. "Neurobiology of Addictions," presented at Psychotherapy Associates, P. C., 17th Annual Advanced International Winter Symposium on the Treatment of Addictive Disorders, Colorado Springs, February 4, 1991.

Walter, B. *Lafayette City Court Alcohol Rehabilitation Program: A Statistical Evaluation.* NJCRS: Rockville, Maryland, 1975.

Wayne, G. H. *Minority Alcoholism: Myths vs. Research.* Aspen Educational Consulting: Colorado Springs, 1984.

Webster, C. D., P. S. Sepejak, R. J. Menzies, D. J. Slomen, F. A. S. Jensen, and B. T. Butler. "The Reliability and Validity of Dangerous Behavior Predictions." *Bulletin of the American Academy of Psychiatry and the Law 12*, pp. 41-50. 1984.

Wegscheider, S. *Another Chance: Hope and Health for the Alcoholic Family.* Science and Behavior Books, Inc.: Palo Alto, California, 1981.

Weller, R. A. and J. A. Halikas. "Objective Criteria For the Diagnosis of Marijuana Abuse." *Journal of Nervous and Mental Diseases 168*, pp. 98-103, 1980.

Wellman, L. E. "Therapist Self-Survival Strategies," presented at Psychotherapy Associates, P. C., 14th Annual Advanced International Winter Symposium on the Treatment of Addictive Disorders, Colorado Springs, February 4, 1988.

Wells, A. *Alcoholism Detection, Treatment and Rehabilitation Within the Criminal Justice System.* NIAAA, Washington, DC, July 1973.

Wenk, E. A., J. O. Robinson, and G. W. Smith. "Can Violence Be Predicted?" *Crime and Delinquency 18,* pp. 393-402. 1972.

Werner, P. D., T. L. Rose and J. A. Yesavage. "Reliability, Accuracy, and Decision Making Strategy in Clinical Predictions of Imminent Dangerousness." *Journal of Consultation and Clinical Psychiatry 51,* pp. 815-825. 1983.

Werner, P. D., T. L. Rose, J. A. Yesavage and K. Seeman. "Psychiatrists' Judgements of Dangerousness in Patients on an Acute Care Unit." *American Journal of Psychiatry 141,* pp. 263-266. 1984.

Wertham, F. "The Catathymic Crisis: A Clinical Entity." *Arch. Neurology and Psychiatry 37,* pp. 974-977. 1973.

White, R. W. *The Abnormal Personality.* The Ronald Presi Co.: New York, 1964.

Williams, E. R. "Assessment and Prediction of Client Dangerousness," presented at Psychotherapy Associates, P. C., 17th Annual Advanced International Winter Symposium on the Treatment of Addictive Disorders, Colorado Springs, February 8, 1991.

Williams, P., F. Letemendia, and F. Arroyave. "A Two-Year Follow-Up Study Comparing Short with Long-Stay Inpatient Treatment of Alcoholics." *British Journal of Psychiatry 122,* pp. 637-648. 1973.

Wilsnack, S. C. "Femininity by the Bottle." *Psychology Today,* pp. 39-43, April, 1973.

Wilsnack, S. C. "Women and Alcohol: Recent Research and Treatment Implications," presented at Psychotherapy Associates, P. C., 16th Annual Advanced International Winter Symposium on the Treatment of Addictive Disorders, Colorado Springs, February 7, 1990.

Wilsnack, S. C. and L. J. Beckman. *Alcohol Problems in Women.* The Guilford Press: New York, 1984.

Wilsnack, S. G. and A. Klassen. "Sexuality, Sexual Dysfunction, and Women's Drinking," presented at Psychotherapy Associates, P. C., 14th Annual Advanced International Winter Symposium on the Treatment of Addictive Disorders, Colorado Springs, February 4, 1988.

Woodruff, R. A., S. B. Guze, and P. J. Clayton. "The Medical and Psychiatric

Implications of Antisocial Personality (Sociopathy)." *Diseases of The Nervous System 32,* pp. 712-714 1971.

Woolf-Reeve, B. S. "A Guide to the Assessment of Psychiatric Symptoms in the Addictions Treatment Setting." In *Managing the Dually Diagnosed Patient,* edited by P. F. O'Connell. The Haworth Press, New York, 1990.

World Health Organization (WHO). In *The Diagnosis and Treatment of Alcoholism,* 2nd Ed., edited by G. G. Forrest. Charles C Thomas: Springfield, Illinois, 1978.

Yalisove, D. L. "Psychoanalytic Approaches to Alcoholism and Addiction: Treatment and Research." *Psychology of Addictive Behaviors 3*(3), pp. 107-112. 1989.

Yochelson, S. and S. E. Samenow. *The Criminal Personality, Vol. I: A Profile for Change.* Jason Aronson: New York, 1976.

Yochelson, S. and S. E. Samenow. *The Criminal Personality Vol. II: The Change Process.* Jason Aronson, New York, 1977.

Yochelson, S. and S. E. Samenow. *The Criminal Personality Vol. III: The Drug User.* Jason Aronson: Northvale, New York, 1986.

Yorke, C. "A Critical Review of Some Psychoanalytic Literature on Drug Addiction." *British Journal of Medical Psychology 43,* pp. 141-159. 1970.

Yost, J. K. and R. A. Mines. "Stress and Alcoholism." In *Alcoholism and Substance Abuse: Strategies for Clinical Intervention,* edited by T. E. Bratter and G. G. Forrest. Free Press: New York, 1985.

Ziegler, R. and K. Kohutek. "A Multimodal Treatment Approach for Incarcerated Alcoholics." *Journal of Clinical Psychology 34*(4), pp. 1005-1009. 1978.

Zimberg, S. *The Clinical Management of Alcoholism.* Brunner/Mazel, Inc.: New York, 1982.

Index